W9-DIZ-801

DISCARD

WILLIAM F. KIRCHNER, Department Commander

ABSTRACT OF GENERAL ORDERS AND PROCEEDINGS

OF THE

Fifty-second Annual Encampment

DEPARTMENT OF NEW YORK, G. A. R.

HELD AT ITHACA, JUNE 25, 26 AND 27, 1918

TRANSMITTED TO THE LEGISLATURE APRIL 9, 1918

ALBANY
J. B. LYON COMPANY, PRINTERS
1918

STATE OF NEW YORK

No. 61

IN SENATE

APRIL 9, 1918.

Fifty-second Annual Encampment, Department of New York, Grand Army of the Republic

DEPARTMENT OF NEW YORK, G. A. R.

CAPITOL, ALBANY, *April* 9, 1918.

To the Legislature:

SIRS.— I have the honor to transmit herewith the abstract of General Orders and Proceedings of the Fifty-second Annual Encampment, Department of New York, Grand Army of the Republic, for the year 1918.

Very respectfully,

WILLIAM F. KIRCHNER,

Department Commander.

ALBANY, N. Y., *January* 1, 1919.

ROSTER OF OFFICERS
1917–1918

DEPARTMENT OFFICERS

WILLIAM F. KIRCHNER......Department Commander
HENRY S. REDMAN........... Senior Vice-Commander
FRANK JOHNSON .... Junior Vice-Commander
REV. REUBEN KLINE .... Chaplain
WILLIAM TAYLOR, M. D............. Medical Director

OFFICIAL STAFF

EDWARD J. ATKINSON.... { Asst. Adjutant-General
{ Asst. Quartermaster-General
SAMUEL McAULIFFE........... Department Inspector
JOSEPH E. EWELL....................Judge Advocate
JOHN McCLOSKEY............. Chief Mustering Officer
GEORGE L. HUGHSON..............Patriotic Instructor
ISIDORE ISAACS.................Senior Aide-de-Camp

COUNCIL OF ADMINISTRATION

ELIAS W. BEACH,   HENRY LILLY,
SAMUEL IRVINE,   WILLIAM H. KILFOILE,
     AUSTIN H. STAFFORD.

PAST NATIONAL OFFICERS

†JOHN C. ROBINSON.......Commander-in-Chief, 1877–78
†JOHN PALMER ....Commander-in-Chief, 1891
†ALBERT D. SHAW ....Commander-in-Chief, 1899
JAMES TANNER .... Commander-in-Chief, 1905
†JAMES B. McKEAN,
        Senior Vice-Commander-in-Chief, 1866–67
†EDWARD JARDINE. Senior Vice-Commander-in-Chief, 1874
†JOHN PALMER.....Senior Vice-Commander-in-Chief, 1879
ALFRED LYTH......Senior Vice-Commander-in-Chief, 1897
†LEWIS E. GRIFFITH. Senior Vice-Commander-in-Chief, 1907
†NICHOLAS W. DAY..Senior Vice-Commander-in-Chief, 1911
‡JOSEPH HADFIELD. Junior Vice-Commander-in-Chief, 1888

---

† Deceased.   ‡Severed his connection with the Order.

PAST DEPARTMENT COMMANDERS

†James B. McKean......................Saratoga Springs
†Daniel E. Sickles....................... New York City
†Edward B. Lansing...............................Auburn
†John C. Robinson............................Binghamton
†Henry A. Barnum...................... New York City
†Stephen P. Corliss .... Albany
†Edward Jardine .... New York City
†John Palmer .... Albany
James Tanner........................ Washington, D. C.
†William F. Rogers .... Buffalo
†James McQuade .... Utica
†L. Coe Young ....Binghamton
†Abram Merrit .... Nyack
†James S. Fraser......................... New York City
John A. Reynolds ....Fairport
†Ira M. Hedges .... Haverstraw
†H. Clay Hall .... Little Falls
†Joseph I. Sayles .... Rome
†George H. Treadwell .... Albany
†N. Martin Curtis .... Ogdensburg
†Harrison Clark .... Albany
†Floyd Clarkson .... New York City
Charles H. Freeman .... Corning
†Theodore L. Poole .... Syracuse
†Joseph P. Cleary .... Rochester
John C. Shotts .... Yonkers
Edward J. Atkinson..................... New York City
James S. Graham .... Oxford
†Albert D. Shaw............................. Watertown
†Anson S. Wood................................. Wolcott
Joseph W. Kay .... Brooklyn
N. P. Pond .... Rochester
Charles A. Orr .... Buffalo
Allen C. Bakewell....................... New York City
John S. Koster .... Port Leyden
†Henry N. Burhans .... Syracuse

† Deceased.

James M. Snyder .... Troy
John S. Maxwell .... Amsterdam
†Harlan J. Swift .... Cuba
†William H. Daniels........................ Ogdensburg
†M. J. Cummings .... Brooklyn
DeWitt C. Hurd .... Utica
George B. Loud .... New York City
Oscar Smith .... Albany
Samuel C. Pierce .... Rochester
James D. Bell .... Brooklyn
Zan L. Tidball .... Bath
†Solomon W. Russell ....
DeAlva S. Alexander, Buffalo, transferred from Dept. Potomac
†W. L. Palmer, Binghamton, transferred from Dept. Dakota

PAST SENIOR VICE-DEPARTMENT COMMANDERS

†William R. Rogers.   †J. K. Hood.
†James M. Gere.   †Homer B. Webb.
†Edward B. Lansing.   †Edward J. Deevey.
†John C. Robinson.   †William L. DeLacey.
John A. Reynolds.   Edward J. Atkinson.
†Samuel Minnes.   P. C. Soule.
†John Palmer.   †C. Hull Grant.
†Joseph Egolf.   †Frederick Cossum.
†John G. Copley.   †George Chappell.
†Constantine Nitzsche.   †Rufus Daggett.
†Jacob Welsing.   John S. Maxwell.
†Henry Osterheld.   Edward J. Mitchell.
John E. Savery.   †John H. Swift.
†Robert Keith.   Clark H. Norton.
†H. Clay Hall.   †M. J. Cummings.
†L. P. Thompson.   †W. Charles Smith.
C. W. Cowtan.   †E. C. Parkinson.
C. A. Orr.   George E. Dewey.
†J. P. Cleary.   †Daniel J. O'Brien.
Charles H. Freeman.   †Jared W. Wicks.

† Deceased.

George F. Tait.

†William A. Boyd.

James M. Watson.

Samuel C. Pierce.

Daniel H. Cole.

James D. Bell.

Alfred E. Stacey.

Austin H. Stafford.

James A. Allis.

George Hollands.

†Alexander E. Mintee, Buffalo, transferred from Dept. Cal.-Nevada.

Past Junior Vice-Department Commanders

†James M. Geer.

†Bradley Winslow.

†V. Krzyanowski.

John A. Reynolds.

†John W. Marshall.

†Willard Bullard.

†Joseph Egolf.

†A. B. Lawrence.

†Edwin J. Loomis.

†Robert H. McCormic.

†George H. Treadwell.

†J. Marshall Guion.

†James F. Fitts.

†Dennis Sullivan.

†Edwin Goodrich.

Frank Z. Jones.

†J. C. Carlyle.

†W. B. Stoddard.

†G. S. Conger.

†C. Hull Grant.

†Robert Wilson.

†W. L. Scott.

†Gardner C. Hibbard.

Edward A. Dubey.

William F. Kirchner.

Silas Owen.

†Daniel Van Wie.

†John Kohler.

John S. Koster.

N. R. Thompson.

Walter Scott.

Jerre S. Gross.

†Philo H. Conklin.

†Daniel W. Hulse.

†D. C. Bangs.

†David Isaacs.

L. L. Hanchett.

George E. Dewey.

†Edward H. Fassett.

†Daniel J. O'Brien.

†Jared W. Wickes.

James Campbell.

DeWitt C. Hurd.

Robert P. Bush.

†L. O. Morgan.

†Henry E. Turner.

†C. C. Caldwell.

C. J. Westcott.

Nelson Mattice.

David H. Dyer.

Robert Simpson, Jr., M. D.

Isidore Isaacs.

†James Loftus.

John W. Mullens.

---

† Deceased.

HEADQUARTERS DEPARTMENT OF NEW YORK,
GRAND ARMY OF THE REPUBLIC,
SARATOGA SPRINGS, N. Y., *June* 27, 1917.

GENERAL ORDERS, }
   No. 1.   }

Having been elected Commander of the Department of New York, Grand Army of the Republic, at its fifty-first annual Encampment, held at Saratoga Springs, June 26-28, 1917, I hereby assume command and announce the following appointment:

Assistant Adjutant and Quartermaster General—E. J. Atkinson, Post 80, New York City.

Other staff appointments will be announced in subsequent orders.

WILLIAM F. KIRCHNER,
Department Commander.

———

HEADQUARTERS DEPARTMENT OF NEW YORK,
GRAND ARMY OF THE REPUBLIC,
CAPITOL,

ALBANY, N. Y., *July* 30, 1917.

GENERAL ORDERS, }
   No. 2.   }

I. At the Fifty-first Annual Encampment of the Department of New York, Grand Army of the Republic, held at Saratoga Springs, June 26, 27 and 28, 1917, the following named Comrades were elected for the ensuing year:

Department Commander — William F. Kirchner, Post 600, New York.

Senior Vice-Commander — Henry S. Redman, Post 84, Rochester.

Junior Vice-Commander — Frank Johnson, Post 354, Odgensburg.

Medical Director — William Taylor, M. D., Post 49, Canastota.

Chaplain — Rev. Reuben Kline, Post 385, Port Leyden.

Council of Administration

Elias W. Beach, Post 9, Buffalo.

Samuel Irvine, Post 534, Brooklyn.

Henry Lilly, Post 170, New York.

William H. Kilfoile, Post 18, Troy.

Austin H. Stafford, Post 285, Jamestown.

Delegates to the National Encampment

II.   The following Comrades were elected to represent this Department at the Fifty-first National Encampment, to be held at Boston, Mass., August 19th to 25th, 1917, inclusive:

Delegate-at-Large

	Post
Robert Simpson, Jr.	434

Delegates

Louis H. La Vallee	121
George B. Herrick	333
James L. Lyons	136
Chas. Cotton	222
William A. Ramage	45
Ira D. Rowley	523
Robert P. Bush	6
William McKinley	88
Geo. A. Colton	209
George W. Flynn	9
Frank Hammond	9
John Hoppes	254
Daniel H. Cole	17
William H. Lyons	35
John S. Robertson	9
Joseph E. Ewell	2
Thomas H. Kiernan	148

	Post
Charles A. Shaw	10
Timothy T. Donovan	21
Patrick Hayes	362
Lewis S. Pilcher	327
Samuel McAuliffe	391
John H. Deal	33
James Campbell	458
Isidore Isaacs	557
Fred C. Barger	140
Henry L. Swords	103
George Blair	516
Patrick H. Doody	69
Wallace Riley	76
E. A. Wheeler	23
D. F. McOmber	162
Caius A. Weaver	151
Albert B. Wilbur	301
C. J. Westcott	119
John McCloskey	560
John H. Hilliker	368
John E. Vandenburgh	141
H. B. Ormsbee	92
William G. Caw	90
Theo. P. Kellogg	438
Chas. D. Emery	226
Henry J. Redfield	248
James H. Everett	127
E. H. Sentell	109
Edward J. Mitchell	60
John W. Durham	93

Alternate-at-Large

	Post
James R. Silliman	600

Alternates

Henry A. Kraus	32
John M. Nagel	128
Oliver A. Pratt	44
Henry C. Draper	148

Post

William B. Price 435

E. H. Millington 299

John W. Nye 8

James S. Snedeker 466

Louis Finkelmeier 122

Alfred J. Moss 471

James A. Allis 66

William H. Sanger 509

Newell C. Fulton 391

Charles T. Thompson 84

Thomas J. McConekey 499

J. G. Burney 19

Geo. W. Rogers 381

Frank E. Cooley 644

Gilbert W. Peck 5

William A. Howell 222

F. M. Hunting 166

Thos. Berridge 138

John E. Banks 661

B. Franklin Raze 9

Geo. H. Sears 2

Joseph H. Benzino 239

Arthur B. Avery 506

Frederick J. Weber 2

W. O. Myers 2

Nelson Simmons 2

D. S. French 528

Isaac O. Best 289

William H. Deyle 110

John M. Wilcox 441

L. D. Mereness 51

Frederick M. Fosdick 113

Edward C. Case 53

James S. Carson 107

H. J. Knapp 667

Augustus Denniston 543

A. A. Sabin 65

Joel G. White 26

Post

B. L. Dunbar 636
Warren B. Pike 156
Andrew J. Freeman 46
C. M. Woolsey 495
Augustus Kipp 60

Mistakes in spelling of any of the foregoing names, or in the number of the Post, should be sent to these Headquarters for correction at once.

III. The following named Comrades are hereby appointed to positions on the staff of the Department Commander:

Assistant Adjutant-General — E. J. Atkinson, Post 80, New York.

Assistant Quartermaster-General — E. J. Atkinson, Post 80, New York.

Department Inspector — Samuel McAuliffe, Post 391, Rochester.

Judge Advocate — Joseph E. Ewell, Post 2, Buffalo.

Chief Mustering Officer — John McCloskey, Post 560, Richmond Hill, Queens County.

Patriotic Instructor — George L. Hughson, Post 95, Peekskill.

Senior Aide-de-Camp — Isidore Isaacs, Post 557, New York.

They will be obeyed and respected accordingly.

IV. The following Comrades are hereby appointed a Committee on Legislation, to whom will be referred all questions affecting the interests of Comrades:

Oscar Smith, Post 5, Albany.
James D. Bell, Post 435, Brooklyn.
James M. Snyder, Post 141, Troy.
Joseph W. Stevens, Post 63, Albany.
Robert P. Bush, Post 6, Horseheads.

V. All communications relating to the business of the Department should be addressed to E. J. Atkinson, Assistant Adjutant-General, G. A. R. Headquarters, Capitol, Albany, N. Y.

Requisitions for supplies should be directed to E. J. Atkinson, Assistant Quartermaster-General, G. A. R. Headquarters, Capitol,

Albany, N. Y., and all checks, drafts, etc., in payment therefor, as well as for per capita tax, should be made payable to his order.

Posts that have not sent in their A and B reports and per capita tax for the six months ending June 30, 1917, must do so at once.

VI. The following Comrades are hereby appointed as Aides-de-Camp on the staff of the Department Commander and will be obeyed and respected accordingly:

	Post
Charles A. Orr	2
Zan L. Tidball	2
De Alva S. Alexander	2
Nelson Simmons	2
George H. Sears	2
Fred J. Weber	2
Samuel C. Pierce	4
John A. Reynolds	4
Oscar Smith	5
Edward B. Roe	5
G. W. Tompkins	5
Henry Reineck	5
Robert P. Bush	6
G. V. R. Merrill	6
Francis D. Carter	6
Henry L. Keene	6
Fred A. Mathews	6
Charles D. Giles	7
B. W. Austin	7
George H. Stevens	8
Henry J. Kopper	8
M. J. Donovan	8
Alfred Lyth	9
Arthur H. Howe	9
John S. Robertson	9
Walter T. Smith	9
Cola D. R. Stowits	9
George W. Flynn	9
Charles A. Shaw	10
R. R. Lord	12

Post

Robert C. Breese.................................... 45
A. J. Freeman...................................... 46
Adam Niles 46
George E. Neice.................................... 47
Elijah Mosher 48
William J. Kiernan................................. 48
William Taylor ....'................................ 49
William H. Parmele................................ 49
Cornelius Van Alstyne.............................. 51
L. D. Mereness.................................... 51
DeWitt C. Hurd.................................... 53
Alisha B. Baker.................................... 53
Edwin H. Risley.................................... 53
Thomas E. Briggs.................................... 53
Rodolphus H. Tipple.............................. 57
William H. Lay.................................... 59
John C. Shotts 60
Edward J. Mitchell................................ 60
Augustus Kipp 60
Jere S. Clark...................................... 60
George Hendrickson ....'........................... 60
John Schmidling 62
Herman Lange 62
James K. Prosser.................................. 65
A. A. Sabin....................................... 65
James A. Allis..................................... 66
H. Stewart Warner................................ 66
William J. Stewart................................ 66
Edwin Humphreys 67
Francis Bacon 72
John R. Dixon..................................... 74
Wallace Riley 76
Charles W. Flagler................................ 76
Charles E. Hubbard 79
Charles Just 80
George J. O'Reilly 80
James Herron 81

Henry S. Redman, Senior Vice Department Commander

	Post
Chester Stoddard	124
James H. Everett	127
Griffin A. Hart	127
John M. Nagel	128
William J. Barry	128
W. H. Van Cott, Jr.	135
Cornelius Ten Eyck	135
George E. Dewey	135
James L. Lyons	136
Thomas P. Tuite	136
Thomas Berridge	138
Ezra Houghtaling	138
Allan C. Bakewell	140
Francis B. Stedman	140
Henry J. Howlett	140
Josiah C. Long	140
Fred C. Barger	140
L. Curtis Brackett	140
George W. Stokes	140
James M. Snyder	141
John E. Vandenburgh	141
Charles F. Roemer	141
Charles Mitchell	144
William W. Ryder	144
George F. Bryant	147
William M. Gatchell	147
George H. Skym	147
M. J. Cummings	148
Michael Connelly	148
Samuel Kyle	148
H. C. Draper	148
John H. Forey	151
Clark H. Norton	151
Edward C. Fay	151
O. E. Hayden	151
William Busch	152
Warren B. Pike	156
George S. Parsons	156

Post

Post

Edward W. Castell 399
Clinton Beckwith 404
H. C. Martin 418
Edwin U. Kinny 425
Robert Simpson, Jr............................... 434
W. H. Belchamber 434
C. N. Snyder 434
James D. Bell 435
Edwin C. Squires 435
William B. Price 435
Edward J. Hoffman 435
Harry Montague 436
William Finley 436
Robert McGuire 436
Theodore P. Kellogg 438
John L. Ryno 438
John M. Wilcox 441
L. O. Banks 441
John A. Bock 443
James Campbell 458
Andrew Boyd 458
John B. Trainor 458
C. D. Chilson 459
Charles Harding 459
Calvin L. Vincent 461
E. B. Long 466
James G. Snedeker 466
James Newman 467
Z. A. Austin 470
William Rochester 471
Alfred J. Moss 471
Elias Van Steenberg 483
Frank Danes 486
John Whitaker 486
Lewis Hunt 487
John Hines 487
Henry Snyder 491
David H. King 491

Post

Post

James R. Silliman 600
Henry G. Fritsch 600
Edward Roe 600
Chauncey Quintard 600
William Leggett 607
M. Bornstein 607
J. Gill Atkinson................................ 607
John J. Ashman................................. 619
D. H. Bratt.................................... 619
John C. Sweet................................. 623
Charles Schonberg 628
John A. Leek................................... 628
Edward Lafay 630
John P. Davidson............................... 630
B. L. Dunbar.................................. 636
F. M. Bartholomew.............................. 642
L. A. Belden.................................. 642
E. M. Chamberlain.............................. 644
George E. Dutcher.............................. 644
S. Souders 646
N. W. Gaskill................................. 646
John E. Banks................................. 661
Amas C. Rhoades............................... 665
Henry J. Knapp................................ 667
A. R. Walker.................................. 670
George W. Moore............................... 671

Additional Aides-de-Camp will be appointed on the recommendation of Post Commanders. Commissions will be issued on receipt of acceptance. The names of Comrades for appointment should be forwarded promptly.

VII. The bill providing for an appropriation to provide transportation to Comrades attending the National Reunion and Peace Jubilee at Vicksburg, October 16th to 19th, 1917, having failed to pass in the Legislature, therefore Comrades contemplating attendance are advised that applications for reservations be forwarded direct to the National Association of Vicksburg veterans, 4316 North Kildare avenue, Chicago, Ill.

National Encampment

VIII. The Fifty–first National Encampment of the Grand Army of the Republic will be held at Boston, Mass., August 19th to 25th, 1917, inclusive. Department Headquarters will be established at the Hotel Vendome, Room 20, and will be open for business Monday morning, August 20th, at 10 o'clock. Delegates and Alternates will report, with their credentials, to the Assistant Adjutant-General immediately upon their arrival.

Comrade Philip M. Wales is appointed Acting Assistant Adjutant-General in charge of Department Headquarters, Room 20, Hotel Vendome, during the National Encampment.

Registers will be open to all Comrades who desire to make their presence known.

Caucus of the Delegates to the National Encampment will be held in the large dining-room of Hotel Vendome, Tuesday evening, August 21st, at nine o'clock.

The parade will take place on Tuesday, August 21st at 10 A. M., and the formation will be under the direction of Comrade Isidore Isaacs, Senior Aide-de-Camp and Chief of Staff. Comrades in charge of Posts or County Delegations will report to him at the Hotel Vendome, Monday, August 20th, at 5 P. M. for instructions as to their place in line. The Department of New York will form on the north side of Newbery street facing west, right resting on Dartmouth street, left extending easterly to, and if necessary, southerly along north side of Dartmouth street.

Owing to the fact that no one route of travel can conveniently accommodate to even a majority of the Comrades of this Department who desire to visit Boston during the National Encampment, no so-called Headquarters train is announced.

The Trunk Line Association has made a rate of two cents per mile in each direction, going and returning via same route only; tickets to be sold and good, going, August 17, 18, and 19th, and returning to reach original starting point not later than August 29th.

The following schedule of fares and train service has been furnished by the New York Central Lines:

FARES TO BOSTON AND RETURN.

From Albany $7 65
From Amsterdam 9 00
From Auburn 14 65
From Buffalo 19 55
From Geneva 15 65
From Rochester 16 80
From Rome 12 05
From Syracuse 13 60
From Utica 11 45
From Watertown 15 00

Proportionate fares from other points.

The fare from New York to Boston direct, via N. Y. N. H. & H. R. R., will be at rate of two cents per mile.

SCHEDULE OF TRAIN SERVICE.

Leave Buffalo. . . . 7:20 A. M., 9:30 A. M., 5:10 P. M., 9:30 P. M.
Leave Rochester. . 9:00 A. M., 11:00 A. M., 6:40 P. M., 11:02 P. M.
Leave Syracuse. 10:45 A. M., 12:40 Noon, 8:33 P. M., 12:45 A. M.
Leave Utica. . . . 12:00 Noon, 1:52 P. M., 10:11 P. M., 1:55 A. M.
Leave Schenectady. 1:35 P. M., 3:25 P. M., 12:28 A. M., 4:08 A. M.
Leave Albany. . . . . 2:40 P. M., 5:00 P. M., 1:10 A. M., 4:55 A. M.
Arrive Boston. . . . 8:35 P. M., 10:50 P. M., 7:20 A. M., 10:55 A. M.

Your attention is called to Circular No. 2, issued by the National Encampment Executive Committee and sent herewith.

Department Headquarters, Capitol, Albany, will be closed Saturday, August 18th, and remain closed until Monday, September 3rd.

IX. The following resolutions were adopted at the Fifty-first Annual Encampment, held at Saratoga Springs June 26th to 28th, 1917:

Resolved, That the Department of New York, Grand Army of the Republic, in this crisis of our Country's history, heartily endorses the action of the President of the United States and Congress in placing the United States as one of the contestants in the present world war on the side of liberty and democracy and heartily pledges all the influence and efforts of the survivors of the union veterans of the War of the Rebellion, in sustaining our government armies and navies, in the present great contest.

WHEREAS, Through the efforts of Past Department Commander E. J. Atkinson who drafted the bill known as the Smith-Dowling Bill and which has become a law known as chapter 768, Laws of 1917, and

WHEREAS, Said act provides that veterans of the Civil War who have been in service of the State and the several cities and counties thereof for ten years and shall have reached the age of seventy years shall be retired at their own request on half pay and thereafter shall be entitled to half pay, therefore be it

Resolved, That the thanks of the Comrades in this Department are due and hereby tendered to Past Department Commander E. J. Atkinson, the Assembly and Senate for the unanimous passage of the bill and especially to Governor Charles S. Whitman who signed the bill on June 6th.

WHEREAS, The New York State Legislature has decreed that the question of the right of women to vote shall be settled by a referendum to the voters of this State on November 6th, and

WHEREAS, The women of New York State have, through their Suffrage Party and other organizations, undertaken war service in behalf of the nation, and

WHEREAS, Other nations, including our allies, Russia and Great Britain, appreciative of the service given by the women of their countries, have pledged themselves to the cause of greater democracy as expressed by Women Suffrage, be it therefore,

Resolved, That the G. A. R. Department Encampment assembled in Saratoga Springs, N. Y., June 26 to 28, 1917, does hereby recommend that this government, by granting equal suffrage, avail itself of the services of its women as well as of its men in the full efficiency of citizenship.

WHEREAS, The State of New York has established a State Defense Council to meet the present emergency, and

WHEREAS, There is in every county, under the Resource Mobilization Bureau of the State Defense Council, a County Home Defense Committee, designed to co-ordinate all efforts toward mobilization made by all citizens and organizations of the county, and

WHEREAS, It is highly fitting that the New York State Department of the G. A. R., with its great tradition of national service, be closely associated with any State plans in the interests of the national defense, therefore be it

Resolved, That the New York State Department of the G. A. R. should and hereby does assure the Governor of the State and the State Defense Council of its hearty co-operation. And, that the several posts of the New York State Department of the G. A. R. are urged to write to the chairman of the County Home Defense Committees in their respective counties, placing their services at the disposal of the County Home Defense Committee as far as their strength shall permit. And, be it further

Resolved, That a copy of this resolution be sent to the Governor of the State, Chairman of the New York State Defense Council, and to the Adjutant-

General, in whose office the Resource Mobilization Bureau is established, and to the Chairman of the Food Supply Commission.

WHEREAS, The Grand Army of the Republic, Department of New York, assembled in its 51st Annual Encampment at Saratoga, N. Y., June 26 to 28, 1917, desires to put itself on record in appreciation of the more than generous treatment the veterans of the State have ever received at the hands of both Houses of our Legislature, and especially in appreciation of the consistent, stalwart and uninterrupted friendship shown toward them by Governor Charles S. Whitman; and

WHEREAS, This Empire State of ours led all other States in the erection and maintenance of State Soldiers' Homes, the annual appropriations for the support thereof having ever been generous; and

WHEREAS, Liberal legislation has been enacted securing the permanency of our comrades in public position so long as those comrades were enabled to discharge the duties of the places held by them, with further liberal enactments providing for the retirement, with generous compensation, of those who by reason of the infirmities of age were incapacitated for the performance of the duties of the positions held by them; therefore be it

Resolved, That while we can, in recognition of these benefactions say but little more than " Thank You," this we do say with all our hearts as we engraft it in our records; and be it further

Resolved, That we desire and direct that our Department Commander shall see to it that properly certified copies hereof are placed in the possession of Governor Charles S. Whitman, of the President of the Senate, and the Speaker of the House of Assembly, and that due and proper means be taken to insure the widest publicity, through the medium of the public press of the State, of this, our act of grateful recognition.

In Memoriam

James Loftus

Comrade James Loftus died at his home in Albany on June 21, while serving as Junior Vice-Commander of this Department.

At 17 years of age he volunteered his services to defend the Union, as a member of Co. K, 10th N. Y. Heavy Artillery and upon his discharge he re-enlisted in Co. F, 4th U. S. Cavalry, serving in Texas and on the Plains.

For many years he was employed by the State as Custodian of Civil War flags and relics located in the Capitol.

Comrade Loftus was a devoted member of the Grand Army

of the Republic and was always ready to serve a Comrade in any way within his power. He served several terms on the Department Council of Administration and its Legislative Committee.

Comrade Loftus was a member of L. O. Morris Post 121, Grand Army of the Republic.

By Command of
WILLIAM F. KIRCHNER,
Department Commander.

Official:

E. J. ATKINSON,

Assistant Adjutant-General.

INFORMATION WANTED

Mrs. L. S. Clayton, 5528 Osage avenue, Philadelphia, Pa., desires to hear from members of the 66th N. Y. Vols., 2d Corps, Army of the Potomac, of which Orlando H. Morris was Colonel.

Comrade O. Mennet, Adjt. Post 55, Dept. Cal., and Nevada, G. A. R., 1194 W. 31st street, Los Angeles, Cal., has made an urgent inquiry for the address of Comrade J. B. Fincht, last located in Brooklyn, N. Y.

HEADQUARTERS DEPARTMENT OF NEW YORK,
GRAND ARMY OF THE REPUBLIC,
CAPITOL,

ALBANY, N. Y., *Nov.* 22, 1917.

GENERAL ORDERS, }
No 3. }

1. The Fifty-first National Encampment of the Grand Army of the Republic was held at Boston during the week of August 19th, at which the delegates and Past Department Commanders to the number of sixty-seven were in attendance. Headquarters were established at Hotel Vendome, and was at all times during the Encampment the scene of activity, especially in the attendance of a large number of visiting Comrades, as the registration records

will show, thus affording valuable information to many inquiries. In this respect we are much indebted to Comrade Edward J. Mitchell, Acting Assistant Adjutant General, who was in immediate charge at Headquarters. The parade took place on Tuesday, August 21st, and the Department Commander takes this occasion to thank the six hundred Comrades who appeared and who contributed by their presence in line to the splendid showing of the Department, evidenced by the plaudits of the vast multitude which thronged the entire line of march. The delegates met in caucus at Hotel Vendome on Tuesday evening, August 21st, and unanimously recommended the reappointment of our Comrade Cola D. R. Stowits to the office of Quartermaster-General, so ably filled by him for a number of years. Comrade George A. Price, of U. S. Grant Post 327, was unanimously chosen to represent our Department on the National Council of Administration, and it was the sense of the caucus that Atlantic City receive our support as place for holding the National Encampment of 1918, and New York was so recorded in the Encampment. By a bare majority of one vote, however, the city of Portland, Oregon, was selected. The hospitality of the city of Boston, and the provisions made by the Committee for the enjoyment of our Comrades and their families, remain with us a lasting and happy memory, which is most gratefully acknowledged.

.II. *Post Inspections.*— The Regular Annual Inspection of Posts are directed by the Department Commander and the Post Commanders will designate a Past Post Commander of their respective Posts for the performance of this duty. Inspections will be made during months of November and December, and reports of such inspections to be made to Comrade Samuel McAuliffe, Department Inspector, at these Headquarters prior to December 25th on blank enclosed.

III. Patriotic Instructors are expected to seek co-operation of capable civilian advocates of patriotism, to address the public schools and other assemblages, selecting speakers who are known to be in sympathy with the objects and purposes of the Grand Army of the Republic.

The Department Patriotic Instructor, by and with the approval of the Department Commander, has appointed the following-named Comrades Assistant Patriotic Instructors:

ASSISTANT PATRIOTIC INSTRUCTORS, 1917-1918.

County.   Name.   Address.

Albany — John P. Slocum, Albany.
Allegany — George B. Herrick, Whitesville.
Bronx — Thomas P. Tuite, New York City.
Broome — O. A. Kilmer, Binghamton.
Canada — Thomas Hughes, Toronto, Canada.
Cattaraugus — Silas J. Daniels, Olean.
Cayuga — Rev. Charles S. Shurger, Union Springs.
Chautauqua — L. L. Hanchett, Jamestown.
Chemung — Henry L. Keene, Elmira.
Chenango — George W. Payne, Norwich.
Clinton — Moses Bourdon, Plattsburg.
Columbia — Rev. D. William Lawrence, Hudson.
Cortland — I. J. Walker, McGraw.
Delaware — F. C. Ames, Stamford.
Dutchess — Henry Krieger, Poughkeepsie.
Erie — Joseph W. Grosvenor, M.D., Buffalo.
Essex — Daniel S. French, Wadhams.
Franklin — Robert McC. Miller, Malone.
Fulton — George H. Swan, Gloversville.
Genesee — Delos M. Jones, Batavia.
Greene — Algernon S. Thomas, Catskill.
Hamilton — W. D. Jennings, Long Lake.
Herkimer — James G. Burney, Little Falls.
Jefferson — Robert B. Hoffman, Adams Center.
Kings — Miles O'Reilly, Brooklyn.
Lewis — Boardman Persons, Castorland.
Livingston — Charles S. Lynde, Dalton.
Madison — William Taylor, M.D., Canastota.
Monroe — Monroe M. Copp, Rochester.
Montgomery — Seely Conover, Amsterdam.
Nassau — Carlton J. Greenleaf, Freeport.
New York — George Blair, New York.
Niagara — Chauncey Weatherwax, Lockport.
Oneida — Edward C. Cass, Utica.
Ontario — D. F. McOmber, Canandaigua.

County.   Name.   Address.

Onondaga — Albert R. Walker, East Syracuse.

Orange — A. B. Wheeler, Middletown.

Orleans — Edwin L. Wage, Albion.

Otsego — Cyrus J. Westcott, Oneonta.

Oswego — John K. Fox, Oswego.

Putnam — Gilbert D. Bailey, Brewster.

Queens — Geo. E. Tilly, Jamaica.

Rensselaer — Philip S. Vanderzee, Wynantskill.

Richmond — William P. Hagadorn, Mariners Harbor.

Rockland — Edward B. Weiant, West Haverstraw.

St. Lawrence — Robert W. Barrows, Canton.

Saratoga — Jerome Ball, Cohoes.

Schenectady — Albert Reese, Schenectady.

Schoharie — Lyman D. Mereness, Sharon Springs.

Schuyler — J. L. Buck, Watkins.

Seneca — Francis Bacon, Waterloo.

Steuben — John D. Wheeler, Hornell.

Suffolk — Charles Satterley, Patchogue.

Sullivan — Gabriel F. Currey, Liberty.

Tioga — Nathan W. Gaskill, Owego.

Tompkins — Bloom La Barr, Ithaca.

Ulster — Rev. Austin H. Haynes, Kingston.

Warren — Newton S. McOmber, Glens Falls.

Wayne — J. S. Koys, Lyons.

Washington — George S. Scott, Fort Edward.

Westchester — Abraham H. Tompkins, Yonkers.

Wyoming — Holmes W. Burlingame, Warsaw.

Yates — Frank Dancs, Penn Yan.

IV. Post Commanders are requested to forward to the Assistant Adjutant-General the names of Comrades (giving full names and addresses) for recommendation to the Commander-in-Chief for appointment as Aides-de-Camp on National Staff.

V. Under the Rules and Regulations the election of Post Officers will occur at the first meeting in December. The importance of selecting Comrades who will be regular in attendance and earnest in their efforts for the welfare of the Order is strongly urged. Acceptance of office involves responsibility that can only be met by faithful service.

Frank Johnson, Junior Vice Department Commander

VI. Reports of Post Adjutants and Post Quartermaster for the six months ending December 31, 1917, should be in the hands of the Assistant Adjutant and Quartermaster-General on or before January 10, 1918, upon blanks (Forms A and B), herewith enclosed. Special care to ensure accuracy should be exercised in the preparation of these reports, and the Department Commander especially urges the necessity for a prompt compliance and the remittance of the per capita tax at the earliest possible moment. All checks and money orders for per capita tax and supplies should be drawn to the order of E. J. Atkinson and directed to these Headquarters.

VII. Credentials for delegates and alternates and Mortuary Report are enclosed herewith.

Post Chaplains will fill out the Mortuary Report and deliver the same to the Post Adjutant, who will forward it with other reports to Headquarters.

Bond to be executed by the Quartermaster will be furnished on request.

VIII. Inasmuch as amendments to the Rules and Regulations are annually made at National Encampments, attention is called to the necessity of Post Commanders providing themselves with the latest edition, procurable from the Assistant Quartermaster-General on requisition and remittance of ten cents, the cost of same. Much of the correspondence and inquiries made to these Headquarters touching upon questions of Grand Army law and involving replies covering the several sections thereto would be obviated if Posts would secure copies of Rules and Regulations of 1917 for their guidance, and thus lessen the work at Headquarters, and it is directed that every Post Commander comply with these instructions.

IX. Special attention is directed to Paragraph XV, General Orders No. 2, from National Headquarters, in reference to the Southern Memorial fund, and it is urged that the Posts in this Department use every effort by liberal contributions to swell the fund and thus aid our Comrades in the South in the decoration of the graves of our Comrades who died on the battlefield and in Southern prisons. Send donations direct to Comrade Cola D. R.

Stowits, Quartermaster-General, 877 Ellicott Square, Buffalo, N. Y.

X. Special attention is called to the fact that the National Encampment has amended Chapter 111, Article 11, Paragraph 2, of the Rules and Regulations, to provide for Junior and Senior Vice Post Commanders having a seat in the Department Encampment. You will be governed accordingly.

XI. The following Comrades are hereby appointed as Aides-de-Camp on the Staff of the Department Commander and will be obeyed and respected accordingly:

John Shanly 2
Lyman A. Dietrick. 2
Frank Hammond 2
H. J. Hopkins 2
Albert Schoenwald 2
Nicholas F. Smith. 2
Henry Simonds 2
Michael Anstett 2
George Wander 2
Alonzo Brightman 2
Michael Brummer 2
Joseph Deuel 2
John Driscoll 2
Joseph S. Huber. 2
Miles C. Huyette. 2
William Rankin 2
Conrad Egloff 2
John Mullens 5
Thomas M. Valleau. 8
Benjamin Levy. 8
B. Franklin Raze. 9
Harvey B. Dennison. 10
Louis Ruden 14
S. F. Putney. 16
Adolf F. Margraf. 24
John J. Morris. 29
Augustus Meyers 29
David McMunigle. 29

Thomas H. Clayton 135
A. G. Mills 140
Chas. A. Benton 140
Owen J. Brady 140
A. L. Dodge 140
D. H. Dyer 141
James H. Porter 146
John Mulligan 146
William Stuart 146
J. L. Cunningham 147
Nelson Cross 165
George H. Brown 170
E. A. Burgoyne 170
Henry F. Birge 182
George H. Taylor 182
Charles U. Combs 182
George Probst 192
Henry Fera 192
Chas. W. Cowtan 197
Walter Scott 197
Geo. A. Hussey 197
David Scott 204
John H. Thomas 206
John Monroe 207
Orin B. Smith 210
L. B. Sperry 213
Samuel Allen 216
R. C. Albro 222
Andrew Kilbury 226
George Hollands 226
Theodore A. Morse 234
Frank R. Battles 234
P. C. Soule 237
William F. Hickey 239
Robert Hosey 255
Edward B. Dalton 255
James H. Emmons 255
Alexander Mueller 264

B. W. Bonnell 461
Levi Bassett 470
George F. Sawyer 471
L. T. Empey 482
J. H. Bush 483
F. B. Vaughn 491
William Ely 508
Edward Kennedy 516
George H. Miller 509
Robert J. Cooper 509
George Dean 523
Joseph A. Sullivan 524
William H. Patterson 527
Isaac J. Post 527
Henry C. Boadamer 542
Thos. V. Smith 544
T. J. Quidore 557
Adolph H. Feeder 557
Max Neustadt 557
Adolph Pineus 557
Albert K. Broughton 570
D. D. Demmick 576
William S. Sughes 578
Howard Whitney 578
John O'Connell 578
Henry P. Guion 590
Chas. H. Liscom 600
George F. Potter 600
E. B. Demarest 600
Samuel McCallum 600
William Connell 600
W. L. D. O'Grady 600
Charles Evans 623
A. E. Stacey 647
William Storms 669
Aaron Abbey 670
John Faucett 672

In Memoriam.

Solomon W. Russell

It is with sincere regret that we are called upon to announce the death of Past Department Commander Solomon W. Russell, who departed this life at his home in Salem, Washington county, on Thursday, October 18th, aged 81 years. Comrade Russell entered the service and was mustered in as Captain of Company A, Seventh N. Y. Cavalry, on September 7th, 1861. He resigned therefrom, and subsequently became Adjutant of the 49th Regiment of Infantry of New York, and was promoted to Captain and Major, and was grievously wounded at the Battle of Rappahannock Station, on November 7th, 1863, (while on the Staff of his kinsman, General David A. Russell, who was killed at the Battle of Winchester, Va.,) and was mustered out of service in June, 1865. He returned home, took up his chosen profession of law and made a distinguished figure in it; not only that, but in all those civic activities of his home town, where he was recognized as its leading citizen. His departure from our midst creates a void that cannot be filled, and his modest, unobtrusive deportment will long be remembered when all that was mortal of him shall have crumbled to decay.

William A. Filsinger

In great sorrow we announce the death of Commander William A. Filsinger, of Chapin Post No. 2, of Buffalo, who departed this life on October 5th, 1917. He was mustered into Chapin Post July 30, 1869, and had filled with credit nearly every position in the Post. He had served as County Inspector and as Chairman of the Memorial and Executive Committee of the G. A. R. of that city, and was always during his life a prominent figure in the Department. His loss is most sincerely regretted.

Patrick Hayes

In the death of Commander Patrick Hayes, of George Ricard Post 362, and Chairman of the Memorial and Executive Committee, G. A. R., of Kings county, on Tuesday, October 6th, his Comrades will miss the presence with them of one who by his sterling qualities had endeared himself to all who knew him. He was one of the earliest members of our order, and his genial presence at Encampments for more than forty years, and his all-absorbing interest in its affairs, will long be held in the memory of all his Comrades.

By command of

WILLIAM F. KIRCHNER,

Department Commander.

Official:

E. J. ATKINSON,

Assistant Adjutant-General.

INFORMATION WANTED

Comrade J. W. Fletcher, 441 West Side avenue, Jersey City, N. J., a former member of the 105th N. Y. Vols., desires to communicate with Comrades who served in the 105th or 94th N. Y. Vols, from western New York in the vicinity of Rochester, Buffalo or LeRoy. The two regiments consolidated in March 1863.

Edith J. Morris, 94 Queensberry Street, Boston, Mass., is very anxious to communicate with former members of Co. I, 41st N. Y. Vols., who served with and knew her grandfather, the late Corporal Frederick Adams.

OFFICE OF PATRIOTIC INSTRUCTOR,

DEPARTMENT OF NEW YORK, GRAND ARMY OF THE REPUBLIC,

914 PAULDING AVENUE,

PEEKSKILL, N. Y., *November 22, 1917.*

CIRCULAR NO. 1.

To Post Commanders and Patriotic Instructors:

It was with some hesitancy that I accepted the honor of this appointment because of my conception of the great importance of the task imposed, and of the fact that we Veterans cannot be very active personally in carrying out the objects of this office. Yet I am ready to lead my Assistants, and they and myself will be glad to cooperate with Post Patriotic Instructors in whatever direction we may find that we can be useful.

The injunction to us is, that we shall " instruct the youth of our land on the duty of patriotism," and to see that the laws relating to the flag are not neglected or ignored. Our efforts have been mainly confined to the schools; but I am going to urge that you widen the scope of our influences, because in these days that are witnessing a peaceful world thrown into chaos, with destruction of life and property reigning in every conceivable form, with a war involving the whole world, a war waged with a fierceness and barbarity before unheard of, it is of the highest importance that a true spirit of patriotism shall be awakened in the adult as well as in the youthful minds and hearts.

While encouraging the practice of providing handsome flags to the school, I will remind you that every Board of Education and of School Trustees is required by law to provide flags for the school houses. I would impress upon you that there are many Organizations, as Fire Companies and Societies, that appear in public, that neglect to provide themselves with flags, and I have found that it is through thoughtlessness, and they are always ready to listen to and to comply with patriotic suggestions.

I wish particularly to request that you extend your efforts to the churches; for there is no more appropriate place for our banner, representing as it does so much that is pure and holy, than by the pulpits in the churches; and I recommend that you advise that the flag be on a staff with a floor support near the pulpit.

Continue to impress upon men and women the world-wide practice, too largely neglected in this country, of saluting a passing flag and the National Anthem. And bear in mind that our Anthem is the "Star Spangled Banner," made so by army and navy practice, and that the song "America" does not require a salute, or rising of an audience.

Discourage the floating of soiled and tattered flags. A dirty flag on the side of or over a house, or on a pole, or a flag torn to ribbons, or a few fragments of a flag on a staff, are not displays of patriotism, but indicate an indifference to the significance and the glory of the flag.

Each Comrade can exercise a quiet influence within his own circle that may be farther reaching than he would ever imagine, and will often be felt where and when he would least expect it. Every Veteran of the War for the Union, a war that has not yet been equalled in its expenditures of men and money in proportions to the populations, is himself an emblem of loyal AMERICAN patriotism, which stands for "Our Country, right or wrong," embodying a determination to make it always right and secure those victories and that progress that come only through struggles that are right.

Cooperate in all things with the Woman's Relief Corps and all kindred Patriotic Organizations.

Finally, brook no criticism of the Government and its wonderful efforts in the world's contest against Kaiserism and for universal Democracy.

Yours in Fraternity, Charity and Loyalty,

GEO. L. HUGHSON,
Patriotic Instructor, Dept. of New York.

Approved:

WM. F. KIRCHNER,
Department Commander.

GRAND ARMY OF THE REPUBLIC,

CAPITOL,

ALBANY, N. Y., *April* 12, 1918.

To Post Commanders:

The Department Commander calls special attention of the Post Commanders to the following letter received from National Headquarters relative to the Southern Memorial fund, and it is urged that the Posts in this Department make every effort, by liberal contributions, to meet the amount assessed upon this Department, and forward such donations without delay to Cola D. R. Stowits, Quartermaster-General, 877 Ellicott Square, Buffalo, N. Y.

WILLIAM F. KIRCHNER,
Department Commander.

COMRADE WILLIAM F. KIRCHNER,
Commander, Dept. of New York, G. A. R.,
NEW YORK CITY.

MY DEAR COMMANDER:

At the meeting of the National Council of Administration held in the Hotel Vendome at the close of the 51st National Encampment, the question of raising funds for the Southern Memorial Fund was considered at some length. It was finally decided that the Commander-in-Chief should ask the Departments to raise their proportionate amount of the total sum necessary. This he has delayed doing, hoping that the amounts subscribed might be sufficient. The appeals made in General Orders have been so little heeded that it now becomes necessary to ask each Department Commander to secure from the Posts in his Department a specified amount. We estimate that $200.00 will be a fair amount for your Department to contribute.

Will you not appeal to the Posts in your Department to respond liberally and promptly to this request. In the eight Departments which have the care of these graves in the South, there are less than 2500 Comrades to take care of the hundreds of thousands of graves of our Comrades who fell in battle or died from wounds. Some of these southern Comrades have to travel many miles at great expense on Memorial Day — which is not observed by the localities in which they live — to carry on this work and pay this tribute of respect and affection, and we of the large and stronger Departments should do our part by making it possible for them to carry on this work of love.

Will you kindly see that all contributions from your Department reach the Quartermaster-General by May 1st, if possible?

Fraternally yours,

ROBERT W. McBRIDE,
Adjutant-General.

HEADQUARTERS DEPARTMENT OF NEW YORK,

GRAND ARMY OF THE REPUBLIC,

CAPITOL,

ALBANY, N. Y., *May* 7, 1918.

GENERAL ORDERS, }
No. 4. }

I. At a meeting of the Department Council, held at Headquarters at the Capitol, Albany, February 26, 1918, the city of Ithaca was selected as the place and June 25, 26 and 27, 1918, as the dates of holding the Fifty-second Annual Encampment of the Department of New York, Grand Army of the Republic.

II. Department headquarters during the Encampment will be established at the Hotel Ithaca, and will be open for business at 10 o'clock A. M. June 25. Post Commanders and delegates will report to the Assistant Adjutant-General immediately on arrival, that they may be checked and receive their badges. The Committee on Credentials will meet at the same time and place. Commanders must not fail to bring their credentials and thus avoid delays and embarrassment.

III. The Department is taking up with the Trunk Line Association, representing the various railroads in the State, the question of reduced rates for members of the Grand Army of the Republic and associate bodies attending the Fifty-second Annual Encampment at Ithaca, and will be published in future General Orders.

IV. The Committee on Accommodations of the Board of Commerce of Ithaca have assumed the responsibility of providing rooms for all applicants. It will, therefore, be necessary for all Comrades desiring accommodations to communicate with the Committee on Accommodations, Board of Commerce, stating their requirements. Everything is conducted on European plan, with prices ranging from $1.00 to $2.50 per day. Ample provisions will be made to furnish meals at very reasonable prices.

Ithaca Hotels	Will Accommodate
Ithaca Hotel	125
Clinton Hotel	100
Alhambra Hotel	20
Tompkins House	65
Office Hotel	35
Lehigh Valley House	45
Senate Hotel	22
Cayuga House	36
Union Hotel	40
Oriental Hotel	12
Conley Hotel	43
Hub Hotel	24
Exchange Hotel	20
Monk's Hotel	20
Commercial Hotel	36
Y. M. C. A.	56

A large number of rooming houses and private residences are at the disposition of the Local Committee on Accommodations, and are first-class in every respect.

Memorial Day

V. The day of solemn yet happy memory is near at hand, and in accordance with custom May 30th will be observed as Memorial Day. It is a day made sweet by the tender memories it revives, made grand by the solemnity of its ceremonies, made glorious by the revival of heroic deeds, made precious by its inspiring lessons of patriotism.

America will celebrate the coming day of remembrance with a holy fervor heretofore unknown, because upon land and sea our sons and grandsons are offering their lives to the cause of humanity and are to-day battling that Liberty may kindle her altar fires across every valley and on every mountain top of Europe. Seeking world dominion, the mightiest military power on earth has turned fair fields, hallowed homes, peaceful villages and great cities into shambles, and made the civilized world gasp with horror. There is no divided sentiment in the Grand Army as to the righteousness of our nation in aligning itself on the side of the Allies. Glory to the Stars and Stripes — it is fluttering side by side with the flags of England and France in vindication of national honor and the liberties of mankind.

There is but little the Grand Army can do in the way of actual service to frustrate the foul conspiracy to strike down Liberty, but we can do much to inspire our noble boys to do valiant service beneath the flag our blood sanctified.

VI. The National Encampment has directed that General Logan's Memorial Day order shall be read as a part of the public services. The following is a copy of Past Commander-in-Chief Logan's Memorial Day order:

Headquarters Grand Army of the Republic,

Washington, D. C., *May* 5, 1868.

General Order, ⎱
   No. 11.   ⎰

I. The 30th day of May, 1868, is designated for the purpose of strewing with flowers or otherwise decorating the graves of comrades who died in defence of their country during the late rebellion, and whose bodies now lie in almost every city, village and hamlet churchyard in the land. In this observance no form of ceremony is prescribed, but Posts and Comrades will in their own way arrange such fitting services and testimonials of respect as circumstances may permit.

We are organized, Comrades, as our Regulations tell us, for the purpose, among other things, " of preserving and strenghtening those kind and fraternal feelings which have bound together the soldiers, sailors and marines who united to suppress the late rebellion." What can aid more to assure this result than by cherishing tenderly the memory of our heroic dead, who made their breasts a barricade between our country and its foes. Their soldier lives were the reveille of freedom to a race in chains, and their deaths the tattoo of rebellious tyranny in arms. We should guard their graves with sacred vigilance. All that the consecrated wealth and taste of the nation can add to their adornment and security is but a fitting tribute to the memory of her slain defenders. Let no wanton foot tread rudely on such hallowed grounds. Let pleasant paths invite the coming and going of reverent visitors and fond mourners. Let no vandalism of avarice or neglect, no ravages of time testify to the present or to the coming generations that we have forgotten as a people the cost of a free and undivided republic.

If other eyes grow dull and other hands slack and other hearts cold in the solemn trust, ours shall keep it well as long as the light and warmth of life remain to us.

Let us, then, at the time appointed gather round their sacred remains and garland the passionless mounds above them with the choicest flowers of springtime; let us raise above them the dear old flag they saved from dishonor; let us in this solemn presence renew our pledges to aid and assist those whom they have left among us, a sacred charge upon a nation's gratitude — the soldier's and sailor's widow and orphan.

II. It is the purpose of the Commander-in-Chief to inaugurate this observance with the hope that it will be kept up from year to year while a survivor of the war remains to honor the memory of his departed comrades. He earnestly desires the public press to call attention to this Order, and lend it friendly aid in bringing it to the notice of comrades in all parts of the country in time for simultaneous compliance therewith.

III. Department Commanders will use every effort to make this Order effective.

By command of

JOHN A. LOGAN,
Commander-in-Chief.

N. P. CHIPMAN,
Adjutant-General.

It is further directed that the address of President Abraham Lincoln at the dedication of Gettysburg Cemetery be also read. It is as follows:

President Lincoln's Address at Gettysburg, Nov. 19, 1863

Four score and seven years ago our fathers brought forth upon this continent a new nation, conceived in Liberty and dedicated to the proposition that all men are created equal. Now we are engaged in a great Civil War; testing whether that nation, or any nation so conceived and so dedicated, can long endure. We are met on a great battlefield of that war. We have come to dedicate a portion of that field as a final resting place for those who here gave their lives that that nation might live. It is altogether fitting and proper that we should do this.

But, in a larger sense, we cannot dedicate — we cannot consecrate — we cannot hallow — this ground. The brave men, living and dead, who struggled here have consecrated it far above our power to add or detract. The world will little note, nor long remember, what we say here, but it can never forget what they did here. It is for us, the living, rather, to be here dedicated to the unfinished work which they who fought here have thus for so nobly advanced. It is rather for us to be here dedicated to the great task remaining before us — that from these honored dead we take increased devotion to that cause for which they gave the last full measure of devotion — that we here highly resolve that these dead shall not have died in vain — that this nation, under God, shall have a new birth of freedom — and that government of the people, by the people, for the people, shall not perish from the earth.

Edward J. Atkinson, Assistant Adjutant and Quartermaster-General

MEMORIAL SUNDAY, MAY 26TH

VII. Memorial Sunday will be observed on May 26th, and Posts are expected to attend divine service and invite all auxiliary and kindred orders to join them in these services.

VIII. Post Commanders are requested to confer with School Superintendents and teachers in their several localities to hold patriotic exercises in the schools, and that the Comrades co-operate by making addresses to the pupils along patriotic lines that will be instructive and interesting.

MOTHERS' DAY, MAY 12TH

IX. The sacrifices and labors of the Mothers in behalf of the boys at the front during the crucial period of '61 to '65, in the War of '98, and the supreme sacrifice and loyalty of the Mothers who have given their sons to the existing war for humanity can never be appropriately appreciated by expressions of praise. To them is due the Union success in the Great War of the Rebellion, the success of America in the War of '98, and to the Mothers of the boys across the seas will be due the success of our arms, which is assured in the triumphant cause of humanity against which brutality and beastiality cannot long prevail.

It is, therefore, recommended that Mothers' Day, May 12th next, be observed by our Comrades by wearing a white carnation.

FLAG DAY, JUNE 14TH

X. It is directed that Flag Day, June 14th, be appropriately observed, and that Old Glory be flung to the breeze in homes and public buildings, and Comrades are requested to put forth their best efforts to that end.

XI. Post Patriotic Instructors will forward their reports through the Post Commander to the County Patriotic Instructor immediately after Memorial Day and not later than June 7th. County Patriotic Instructors will forward such reports of their respective counties to the Department Patriotic Instructor, Comrade Geo. L. Hughson, Peekskill, N. Y., not later than June 10th. Strict Compliance with foregoing is required.

XII. Post Commanders are directed to turn over Memorial Day blanks (enclosed herewith) to the Post Chaplain, who will have same properly made out and promptly forwarded to the

Assistant Adjutant General, Department Headquarters, Capitol, Albany, N. Y., and not to the Department Chaplain.

XIII. Under an amendment to the Rules and Regulations adopted by the National Encampment, semi-annual reports ordinarily made for term ending June 30th are discontinued. Especial attention is directed to the Rule which provides that per capita tax for the term ending June 30, 1918, and the rate of tax must be based on last report for term ending December 31, 1917; more plainly speaking, the per capita for term ending June 30th will be for number of Comrades in good standing December 31, 1917, and shall be forwarded to the Assistant Quartermaster General.

XIV. Special attention is directed to amendment of Rules and Regulations which provide that the Senior Vice Post Commanders and Junior Vice Post Commanders are by virtue of their offices delegates to the Department Encampment, and it is expected they will show their appreciation of the honor and demonstrate their interest in the well-being of the Grand Army by being present at the Encampment.

NATIONAL ENCAMPMENT

XV. The National Encampment will be held in the City of Potrland, Oregon, the week beginning Sunday, August 18th. The necessary transportation facilities will be at our disposal and at a rate of one cent a mile, the lowest rate given us for many years. The rate applies to members of the Grand Army of the Republic and their families — also members of the Army Nurses' Association, Women's Relief Corps, Ladies' of the G. A. R., Daughters and Sons of Veterans and Sons of Veterans Auxiliary.

It is requested that Posts be prepared to present the names of Comrades and their Posts who will positively attend the Encampment and forward same to Assistant Adjutant General for submission to Department Encampment for election as delegates.

XVI. The following Comrades are hereby appointed as Aides-de-Camp on the staff of the Department Commander and will be obeyed and respected accordingly:

	Post
John H. Davis	8
William L. Young	327
Joseph Wooley	467

In Memoriam.

Michael J. Cummings

Past Department Commander Michael J. Cummings died at his home in Brooklyn on January 3, 1918. He enlisted on January 12, 1864, as a private in Company B, 48th Regiment, New York Volunteer Infantry; was wounded at the battle of Olustee, and was honorably discharged as Sergeant September 1, 1865.

After some years spent in private employment he was appointed clerk in the office of the City Clerk of Brooklyn in 1877, and remained there for fifteen or sixteen years, having arisen to the office of City Clerk, which he held for some years. Under Greater New York, on January 1, 1898, he became Secretary of the Sewer Department, and when that Department ceased to exist he was transferred to the Sewer Bureau, in the Borough President's office in Manhattan, where he remained until his death. In the discharge of his public duties he was careful, prompt and intelligent.

Comrade Cummings was mustered into Thomas C. Devin Post No. 148, Department of New York, on September 12, 1884, and remained an active member until his death. He was Commander of his Post in 1888, and Department Commander of New York in 1909. He was trustee of the Permanent Fund of the Grand Army of the Republic, and Chairman of the board at the time of his death and for a number of years prior thereto. He was for eight years Chairman of the Memorial and Executive Committee, G. A. R., of Kings county.

Comrade Cummings in any body of men was a leader. As a Comrade he was characterized by his readiness and willingness to help a Comrade, regardless of any consideration other than the fraternal tie. Comradeship meant what its name implies to him.

William A. Boyd

Past Senior Vice Department Commander Wm. A. Boyd died at his home in New York City January 24, 1918. He enlisted April 20, 1861, in the 71st N. Y. S. M., and served ninety days. Re-enlisted in the 62d N. Y. Vol. Inf. September 13, 1861, and was discharged December 13, by reason of ill health. Mustered into Lafayette Post 140, July, 1905. He was elected Senior Vice Department Commander in 1908, and served as Judge Advocate of the Department, and at the time of his death was Chairman of the Memorial Committee, County of New York, and Trustee of the W. R. C. Home at Oxford, N. Y.

By command of

WILLIAM F. KIRCHNER,

Department Commander.

Official:

E. J. Atkinson,

Assistant Adjutant-General.

Information Wanted

Gold Badge inscribed J. McCann, 124th N. Y. Vols. is in possession of Com. S. M. Mildenberg, 253 Broadway, New York City, who will gladly deliver same to proper party on application.

A silver rank badge of the Union Veteran Legion has been found in New York City. Owner can have same on proving ownership by applying to Comrade E. J. Atkinson, Assistant Adjutant General, Room 1, City Hall, New York City.

Mr. Louis Birkemeier, 2505 Jefferson Avenue, Cincinnati, Ohio, desires to communicate with former members of Co. B, 28th Reg't, N. Y. N. G. during the Civil War and living in Brooklyn at time of service: Capt. Henry Obusean, Lieut. Joseph Whitman, Orderly Serg't. John Straus, Sergeant John Wagner, Andrew Smidt, Joe Gerber, Messrs. Eff and Boehner; Aides-de-Camp, John H. Davis, Post 8; William L. Young, Post 327; Joseph Wooley, Post 467.

HEADQUARTERS DEPARTMENT OF NEW YORK,

GRAND ARMY OF THE REPUBLIC,

CAPITOL,

ALBANY, N. Y., *June 8*, 1918.

GENERAL ORDERS, }
No. 5. }

I. As previously announced in General Orders No. 4, the Fifty-second Annual Encampment of the Department of New York, Grand Army of the Republic will be held in the City of Ithaca, June 25th, 26th and 27th, 1918.

II. Department Headquarters during the Encampment will be at the Hotel Ithaca, and will be open for business at 2 P. M., June 25th. Post Commanders and Delegates will report to the Assistant Adjutant-General, with their credentials, immediately on arrival, and when checked by the Credentials Committee will receive their badges.

III. The following appointments are hereby announced: Comrade Edward J. Mitchell, Post 60, Acting Assistant Adjutant-General, Comrade Bert F. Parsons, Post 327 and Comrade Caius A. Weaver, Post 151, Committee on Credentials.

IV. The Committee on Credentials will be in session at Headquarters, Hotel Ithaca, main floor, Tuesday, June 25th, from 2 P. M. until 8 P. M. and on Wednesday from 8 to 9:30 A. M., when it will adjourn to meet at the Lyceum Theatre, where the business sessions of the Department will be held during the Encampment.

V. The business sessions of the various organizations will be held at the following named places:

Grand Army of the Republic, Lyceum Theatre, Cayuga St.

Sons of Veterans, Aurora Street M. E. Church, Aurora and Mill Streets

Woman's Relief Corps, State Street M. E. Church, State and Albany Streets.

Ladies of the G. A. R., Unitarian Church, Buffalo and Aurora Streets.

Daughters of Veterans, Episcopal Parish House, Cayuga Street.

Sons of veterans Auxiliary, Aurora Street M. E. Church, Aurora and Mill Streets.

VI. The Department Headquarters of the Woman's Relief Corps, Ladies of the Grand Army of the Republic, and Daughters of Veterans, will be located at the Hotel Ithaca, and the Division Headquarters of the Sons of Veterans, and Sons of Veterans Auxiliary will be located at the Clinton House.

VII. The Department has taken up with the Trunk Line Association, representing the various railroads in the State, the question of reduced rates for members of the Grand Army of the Republic and associate bodies attending the Fifty-second Annual Encampment at Ithaca. The following is the decision of the Trunk Line Association:

" Two cents per mile each direction, with minimum of $1.00 for the round-trip from points in New York State, going and returning via same route only; tickets to be sold and good, going June 23d, 24th and 25th and returning to reach original starting point not later than June 29th."

VIII. The general program of the receptions will be held on Tuesday evening, June 25th, at the Hotel Ithaca at 9 P. M. and the Camp-fire will be held at the Aurora Street M. E. Church, Aurora and Mill Streets, at 8 o'clock P. M. June 26th. Among the speakers on this occasion will be Commander-in-Chief Orlando A. Somers, Governor Charles S. Whitman, Past Commander-in Chief James Tanner and others.

IX. All representatives and Comrades are requested to assemble at the Hotel Ithaca promptly at 9:30 A. M. June 26th, for the parade to the Lyceum Theatre. Automobiles will be provided for Comrades unable to march.

X. The Council of Administration will meet at Headquarters Hotel Ithaca, at 3 o'clock P. M. June 25th, to audit the accounts of the Assistant Quartermaster-General and transact such other business as may be properly brought before them.

XI. Members of Local Committee on Accommodations will be in attendance at Stations on arrival of trains, together with a Corps of Boy Scouts to act as guides.

XII. Department Headquarters at Albany will be closed from Saturday, June 22d to Monday, July 1st, 1918.

XIII. The attention of Post Commanders is called to the amendment of the Rules and Regulations adopted by the last National Encampment, (semi-annual reports ordinarily made for the term ending June 30th are discontinued.) Especial attention is directed to the Rule which provides that the per capita tax for term ending June 30th, 1918, and the rate of tax must be based on the last report for the term ending December 31st, 1917. More plainly speaking, the per capita for term ending June 30th will be for number of Comrades in good standing December 31st, 1917, and must be forwarded to the Assistant Quartermaster-General, Capitol, Albany, N. Y., not later than July 10th, 1918. Blank forms giving the number of members in good standing December 31, 1917, and the amount due June 30, 1918, are enclosed. All checks, drafts, money orders, etc., should be made payable to the order of E. J. Atkinson, Assistant Quartermaster-General.

XIV. The National Encampment of the Grand Army of the Republic will be held in the City of Portland, Oregon, the week beginning Sunday, August 18th, and National Headquarters will be located in the Hotel Multnomah, Portland, Oregon, during the Fifty-second National Encampment; also the Headquarters of the Department of New York will be at the same Hotel.

The Director-General of Railroads has granted a rate of one cent a mile. This is the lowest rate which has been given us for many years, and should assure us a large attendance at the National Encampment in Portland. The rate applies only to members of the Grand Army of the Republic and their families, and members of the Army Nurses' Association, Woman's Relief

Corps, Ladies of the G. A. R., Daughters of Veterans, Sons of Veterans and Sons of Veterans Auxiliary.

By command of

WILLIAM F. KIRCHNER,
Department Commander.

Official:

E. J. ATKINSON,
Assistant Adjutant-General.

INFORMATION WANTED

B. H. Benton, Son of a Veteran and deceased member of Sumner Post 24, wants to trace a poem presented by his mother to the Post. Address Comrade John M. Fisher, Commander Sumner Post 24, 238-240 West 129th Street, New York.

The name and address of surviving Comrades of Co. G, 69th N. Y. Vols. who served with and knew Joseph H. White. Address A. J. Hoitt, 7 Central Square, Lynn, Mass.

HEADQUARTERS G. A. R. PARADE

ITHACA, N. Y., *June* 25, 1918.

GENERAL ORDERS, ⎫
No 1, ⎭

I. By authority of the Executive Committee the following program for the Parade of the Grand Army of the Republic is announced.

1. The Parade will start from the Ithaca Hotel at 9:30 A. M., Wednesday, June 26, 1918, west on State to Geneva, north on Geneva to Buffalo, east on Buffalo to Aurora, south on Aurora to State, to Cayuga, to the Lyceum Theatre.

2. Assembly points are assigned as follows: Ithaca City Band in front of Ithaca Hotel.

Squadron " D," U. S. A. School of Military Aeronautics, west side of South Aurora head at State.

Drum Corps National Guard, New York, east side of South Aurora, head at State.

Company D, 4th Regiment, New York State Guard immediately behind its Drum Corps on east side of South Aurora.

Grand Army of the Republic, west side of North Aurora, head at State.

Sons of Veterans east side of North Aurora, head at State.

Parochial Drum Corps and Boy Scouts, west side of North Aurora, behind the G. A. R.

Troops will assemble at 9:00 A. M.

3. ORDER OF MARCH

Chief Marshal Colonel Frank A. Barton, U. S. Army.

Assistant marshals: First Lieut. John N. Wolfe, A. S. S. C.; 1st Lieut. J. W. Fowler, A. S. S. R. C.; 2d Lieut. F. J. Cummings, A. S. S. R. C.

Ithaca City Band.
Squadron " D," U. S. A. School of Military Aeronautics.
Drum Corps, National Guard New York.
Company D, 4th Regiment New York State Guard.
Sons of Veterans.
The Grand Army of the Republic.
Parochial Drum Corps.
Boy Scouts.

4. The Military Police under the command of Sergeant Andrew Muro, S. C., will be assigned to posts by their commanding officer and will clear assembly points of all traffic and pedestrains by 9:00 A. M., and the line of march by 9:30 A. M.

By order of the Chief Marshal,

JOHN N. WOLFE,

First Lieutenant, A. S. S. C.,

Adjutant.

OFFICIAL PROCEEDINGS.

LYCEUM THEATRE, ITHACA, N. Y., *June* 26, 1918.

The encampment was called to order at 10 A. M., Mr. Joseph F. Hickey, President of the Ithaca Board of Commerce, presiding.

PRESIDENT HICKEY.—Commander Kirchner, members of the Grand Army of the Republic, ladies and gentlemen: To open the program we will ask you to kindly rise and sing "America," after which we will ask you to remain standing until after the invocation by Dr. Griffis.

REV. WILLIAM ELLIOTT GRIFFIS, D. D.—Let us invoke the Divine blessing. Almight God, Father of all Eternity, and Lord of the spirits of the flesh, we give Thee thanks that Thou hast bestowed upon us this beautiful day upon which we come together to recall the memories of the time that tried men's souls, to bring back the days of eager effort and earnest consecration to serve Thee and serve our country, and we glorify Thee that while we age and pass away Thou art the same and Thy years do not fail; time writes no wrinkle upon thy brow, but as thou wert so art Thou now, ready to bless all those who call upon Thee and serve Thee in earnestness of spirit, and we to-day, many of whom have passed the meridian of life, come to consecrate to Thee our bodies and our spirit, our country and our dear ones, our friends who are on the sea and beyond the sea, struggling that the people might live and that the Government which is of the people and by the people and for the people may not perish off the earth. God bless our sons, our brothers, who are maintaining the cause for which our fathers lived and died, and may they ever uphold the honor of that flag which our fathers died to plant over their graves. And now, Almighty God, we ask especial blessing upon the Grand Army of the Republic. Be with the veterans. Be with the old men. Be with them in their loneliness. Be with them in their joys and sorrows. Bless all who love them and take care of them, and make their declining days sweet with the ministration of affection. Almighty God, bless the women. Keep our boys from the bad ones, bring the good woman with all her powers of blessing and aid and comfort to sustain our army so that it may be one of purity and of righteousness. Bless the President of the United States and all associated with him in power, our Congress and all who are carrying out the will of the people, from the greatest to the smallest. Pardon all our sins; love us freely; go with us when we walk through the valley of the shadow of death, and on the bright camping grounds of the other world may we answer to the call and sit down with Thee in heavenly places in Christ Jesus, in whose name we begin and end all our petitions, giving glory to the Father, and the Son and the Holy Spirit, now and forevermore, Amen.

PRESIDENT HICKEY.— Commander, members of the Grand Army of the Republic, ladies and gentlemen: A few months ago a committee of the Grand Army of the Republic met in Albany to decide on the place to hold the convention. The Board of Commerce of the city of Ithaca sent a delegation to Albany and they were earnestly requested if possible to get that convention for the city of Ithaca. On that committee were Judge Kent and Comrade George W. Hunt, of this city, and we felt if anybody could persuade the G. A. R. to come to Ithaca that committee could. I am informed by a comrade this morning that after a plea made by three different cities unanimous choice was made for Ithaca.

We are glad to have you with us, particularly at this time, for we need inspiration at this critical period of the world's history. I am not going to take your time. There are speakers here on the program, but I want to thank the G. A. R. on behalf of the people of the city of Ithaca, and particularly on behalf of the Board of Commerce, for responding to our request. We are proud of the city. You are accustomed to meeting in a larger place, but we feel a particular pride in this little city, and we believe that after you have spent a few days with us that you will agree that we have reason to be somewhat proud. It is a well regulated city and a well governed one, and for this we have reason to thank our very efficient Mayor, whom I now have the honor to introduce, Frank B. Davis, Mayor of the City of Ithaca.

MAYOR DAVIS.— Mr. President, Commander Kirchner, members of the Grand Army of the Republic, ladies and gentlemen:

I want to thank you most sincerely for this invitation to welcome you to our city. It is indeed a genuine pleasure that has come to this city in entertaining the state encampment of the Grand Army of the Republic. In extending your comrades a hearty welcome from Ithaca it is unnecessary to remind you that your deliberations will be somewhat shadowed, more or less, by our national and international affairs, for we are engaged in the greatest of all wars since the beginning of time. It is a war that has tested and tried us and a war that is still going to try and test us as we have never been tried or tested before. We are going to win this war. (Applause.) That is absolutely certain, because we are right and because we are strong.

But as this war has already demanded sacrifice from us we have still got to make more and more sacrifices of money and of blood. We have got to thoroughly understand that the country needs us now as she never needed us before. We have got to understand that every man, woman and child has a duty to perform in our country's great need, and we have got to conscientiously learn what we can best do toward winning this war. Some must go over there; some have already gone; and still more must go. We have got to make sacrifices of money as we have already done. Some must help in the production of food and munitions and ships, as they have done, and are doing, and must still do. But in some way or another every last one of us, every man, woman and child has got to do their utmost to make this nation and the allied nations victorious in this great struggle for the ideals of free government. I am proud that I can stand here to-day as a citizen of this great state, of your state, of my state, and say that New York is a loyal and patriotic state. I am proud that I can stand here as an official representative of the people of this city and say that Ithaca is a loyal and patriotic city, and in this war will measure up to its full duty.

I feel that every man, woman and child in Ithaca is heart and soul with our Government in this great struggle, and we are enthusiastically with our fellow-countrymen in upholding the honor of our country whenever its integrity is assailed.

When the American flag goes up all others must come down. (Applause.) Wherever it leads us, on land or sea, on this continent or in Europe, our hearts are with it and we willingly sacrifice our lives in its defense. That is your spirit, my spirit, and the spirit of seventeen thousand loyal, patriotic Ithacans who are behind our Government, and it is such a city that bids you a hearty welcome. I thank you. (Applause.)

PRESIDENT HICKEY.— Now I am sure you will be pleased to listen to your beloved Commander, Commander Kirchner.

COMMANDER KIRCHNER.— Mr. Mayor, on behalf of the comrades of the Grand Army of the Republic of this state, whom I have the honor to represent as the Department Commander, I thank you for your patriotic and kind words of welcome. When I look around and see our ladies and our comrades and the good citizens of Ithaca I am sure that your words of welcome came from them through their heart, and we appreciate your kind words. (Applause.)

When the council of administration met at our Headquarters in the Capitol at Albany and the matter was taken into consideration where we were to hold our 52d annual encampment of this great Department, representatives of three different cities in this state appeared there, presented their invitations, and when Judge Kent offered the city of Ithaca, and after we had listened to his eloquent address, the concensus of opinion of the council at once was that the city of Ithaca was the place to hold the 52d annual encampment of this Department.

The welcome that we have received, and the friendship of the people of Ithaca certainly recompenses the Grand Army of the Republic for coming here, and we are glad that the council of administration so decided.

Mr. Mayor, I want to thank you, and I am sure that I express the sentiment of every veteran in the Grand Army of the Republic of this great state, for your kind welcome to this city. (Applause.)

THE PRESIDENT.—" Ithaca in military history " is the subject of the address which will be delivered by Rev. William Elliott Griffis, D. D. Dr. Griffis is a lifelong student of history, and I am sure you will appreciate his address.

REV. WILLIAM ELLIOTT GRIFFIS, D. D.— Commander, comrades, Mr. Mayor, Mr. Chairman, ladies and gentlemen: In our city, where you honor us to-day by being our guests, we have the memories of more than one man of white skin, for here was one of the hearthstones of the great Iroquois confederacy, founded by the noblest type of savage man who ever stood on the continent. It is named after a great hero and traveler, Ulysses, and the name Ithaca has been in the civilized languages of the world for over 4,000 years, so we at least are proud of the name, and the sponsor, who gave the name to this city, was no less a personage than Sineon DeWitt, a general on the staff of Washington's army, the first graduate of Rutgers College, which, when the Revolutionary War broke out, enlisted, faculty and students, in one body for the army of freedom, and who was present at the surrender of Burgoyne and made the fortifications at Yorktown, and who in his later life was Surveyor General of the State of New York, and surveyed that great military tract by which the Continentals were in some measure repaid for their long effort.

Now, one word as to these Iroquois Indians. Some day our colleges and school books will do them justice. They were a forest republic. They were cruel. So was the white man. They gave the white man many things for his good. Before the white man with his theodolite and sections had found out the topography of this wonderful state, the Iroquois had built the Long House extending from the Hudson to the Niagara river on that wonderful highland that stretches all through central New York like a natural castle, has Lakes Erie and Ontario for its northern boundary, the Hudson for its eastern boundary, has the Monongahela and the other river which links the Ohio, has the Potomac and Delaware for its main natural line, and on this land she built a confederacy, a nation of tribes which had in it eloquence and diplomacy and many things which we have been glad to keep and improve upon.

Now, when the time came that the English House was divided against itself, and our Continental fathers hoped to have fourteen stripes in the flag, and they tried hard to get Canada in, they went among these Iroquois Indians and tried to get them neutral, but where the Continental Congress could spend one dollar Great Britain could spend one hundred, and the Indian is a conservative man. In his theology, which he had, and his ethics, which he had, and his ideas which he had, he held on to the old father in Great Britain, and when the Indians met our men at Oriskany the most stubbornly contested battle of the whole Revolution was fought, for the Revolution was fought chiefly on New York soil. It carried such mourning into the Long House that these warriors of the forest determined on revenge and they went down the Susquehanna and destroyed Wyoming, and went down through Cherry Valley and destroyed that; and, sir, in order that Washington's army, for he never had more than 15,000 drilled or disciplined troops, so that the frontier could be protected and the time come when they might march to Yorktown, it was necessary to destroy this Indian country. How should it be done? To build forts on the frontier and garrison them was entirely beyond the resources of the Continental Congress, so Washington just for this work took 5,000 of his best troops and sent them into this part of the country under the command of General Sullivan.

Now, I do not pretend to be a profound student of strategy and tactics, but I have noticed that the man who is of Scotch blood or Scotch-Irish blood generally makes strategy and tactics one thing — get at the enemy as quickly as possible and annihilate him. (Applause.) And so Washington and Sullivan in the Revolution, Grant and Sheridan in our Civil War, and Sir Douglas Haig, all English-speaking men of to-day, have one idea — to get at the army of the enemy and destroy it. This war will never be settled until that job is finished. (Applause.) Finished it will be. Now, Sullivan led 5,000 Continentals into this region when there were nothing but Indian trails and very few people had ever been here except captives or hunters. How to get at these people was the problem, from the Mohawk valley, from Oswego, from Pittsburg? Now, I have taken the trouble to go down to the city of Washington to see how Washington fought out from the beginning the whole expedition, which I do not so lightly compare with Saratoga and Yorktown in its decisive power to win the war. Washington took the opinions of the captives, missionaries, traders and hunters. He put them all down on a page and finds there is so much water in this river at a certain time, woods here, open country there, and by and by he fixes his plan so that the left wing started from Pittsburg, the right wing started from Schenectady and goes up the

Mohawk valley, and the center comes from Easton, with the artillery.

Now Washington was jeered at and laughed at and crucified by criticism just as men are to-day with our lying newspapers, which we do not have in Ithaca (laughter), and Washington was jeered at because he took artillery, but I know among these veterans there are artillerymen, and I tell you it was the artillery that decided the day at the great decisive battle on the 29th of August, 1779, which gave the death blow to the Iroquois confederacy, so that after Sullivan had finished his march they were never able to put anything in the field but a scalping party and they ravaged the Mohawk Valley. It opened the pathway to civilization.

Now on the way back there was a festival at Elmira. They had lived on succotash for six weeks, and every bit of food was carried on the 2,000 horses that went with them, and at that festival for the first time they tested beefsteak in the woods. On the way back two Continental regiments visited Ithaca. Do you wonder we are proud? Do you wonder that our Chairman's head and our Mayor's head are swelled a little to-day? Why, we had the 4th Pennsylvania regiment come down the other side of the lake and pass through our city, and into the wilderness, and also the 3rd New Hampshire that saved the day. So then this was a great victory, a great and decisive point in the history of the Revolution.

Now we pass by many years until in 1789 we had a general government for the first time, when the hunter sovereignity gave way to a constitution, one of the noblest ever penned, under which we as a nation have lived while growing from one million to one hundred million. It is a constitution that can well bear emulation and copying in other lands.

But Ithaca not only has a military history. It not only sent men to the war of 1812, but we have powder mills along the streams that had falls, and it was our country's namesake, Daniel D. Tompkins, who was able to borrow millions of dollars on his personal credit and to equip 12,000 men, by which New York State was saved from British invasion. Ithaca also counts it to her credit that it was from Ithaca that Dr. Parker and Whitman went out taking the first white men and women across the Rocky

SAMUEL MCAULIFFE, Inspector

Mountains to settle the great states of Washington and Oregon, and if I could take you around the town I could show you many things that might draw tears, and one is an old blacksmith shop where the first vote was taken that Ithaca should support a missionary out in Washington and Oregon which opened civilization on the Pacific coast.

We had men in the Mexican War. There died only a few weeks ago a Cooper in Captain May's Dragoons at the battle of Resaca de la Palma. It was one of the greatest cavalry charges known until Custer came along, and we are glad to-day to welcome these red necktie sons of Custer and we are glad we remember Sheridan's 20,000 cavalry. (Applause.)

But friends, we not only had men in the Spanish War, where there was hardly enough war to go around, but every time we marched up to that cemetery we can dip the flag in honor of the graves of every soldier that died in any of the wars, and I would to God there were introduced into the ritual of the Grand Army the dipping of the flag to the soldiers of all the wars by which our country has been preserved.

And now and last we have come to the final struggle of democracy with autocracy, and we have sent our sons and our brothers across the sea, and our prayers have gone with them, and the good women have prayed and worked and toiled, and we are all hoping and praying and believing that autocracy shall down and democracy shall live. (Applause.)

Mr. Commander, I talked to-day with a veteran 88 years old. I look into the faces of these men and I doubt whether there is anyone here or could be anyone here under 65. I look into the faces of men whom God Almighty, because of their temperate lives, has allowed to live to three score years and ten. I am proud to look into the faces of clean, healthy men who may not have the strength they had when they were called on sometimes to march 40 miles a day with 40 rounds and a gun and knapsack; I am glad to look into the faces of such clean lived men, but I say to you, Mr. President, Mr. Mayor, Mr. Commander, that if by some powerful miracle of the Almighty we every one of us could lay off 55 years what would we do? Well, I know one man, what he would do, and when I say that I think all the men here also,

3

about 800, I think I know what they would do. They would stand forth in the ranks of those who have gone from Scotland and England and Ireland and Wales to hold up the cause of freedom. (Applause.) I think all would go with France, the hero nation, and be willing to lay down his blood, his life, in the soil where Lafayette sleeps; and I for one, and no doubt there are many of you, if I could lay aside 55 years I should enlist for Belgium. (Applause)— Belgium, the nation that with only 68,000 men kept back for six weeks a horde of 500,000. It was six weeks before England fired a shot, and France was occupied in the south, and little Belgium with only 68,000 men held back the whole horde of them. And my final reason, and here I close my address, thanking you for your kind attention, my final reason for wanting to enlist for Belgium is this: It hasn't got into our school histories, but some day we will have better school histories than we have now, some day the old prejudice against England will go; some day we will realize his need and that it is a hero nation; some day we will realize that Japan, whom I have known for 60 years — I taught the Japanese students who came to our country in 1866 — I had the honor of beginning the public school system of the United States in Japan; I had the honor of unfurling the stars and stripes first in the capital cities of the United States — I know the Japanese. They are good allies, but my final reason for wanting to fight for Belgium is this: It is generally told in our school histories that the Dutch, God bless them, were the first people that settled the State of New York. That is not true. You cannot settle a country until you have women and children to make homes. (Applause.) We will never win this war unless the women stand by us. And the first shipload of people that made home, wives and children and babies in cradles, who cultivated the soil — who was it came over in the good ship New Netherland in 1623, and how about the Walloons Bout who settled Manhattan Island, settled where Albany is now, settled on the shores of Gloucester, N. J.? The first homes established in New York, New Jersey, Delaware were by Walloons, French speaking Protestant people, driven out of Belgium by the Spaniards in 1567, when Belgium was desolated as it is now. That is the reason why, in honor of New York State and those who first held up the banner with its millions, I should enlist for Belgium. (Applause.)

PRESIDENT HICKEY.— Owing to illness Prof. C. L. Durham is not able to appear before you to-day, and I have to announce that Prof. Samuel P. Orth of Cornell and Ithaca has kindly consented to address you in his stead on the present war. I have the honor to introduce Prof. Samuel P. Orth.

· PROFESSOR ORTH.— Mr. Chairman, members of the Grand Army of the Republic: I am one of those very unfortunate persons who was too young to be one of you and too old to be one of those on the other side, and beleive me, those of us of middle age are the victims of this war, for we have no glorious recollections to carry our memories back over fields heroically won as you have, and we have no anticipation. Whether we can be in at the death of the modern Nero on the other side of the banks of the Rhine I don't know, and I want you to pity me.

I went up to the doctor when war was declared. My family doctor happens to be the one who examines the boys here. He was partly to blame, probably, for the derelict he was examining, but he said he would not commission me to carry toothpicks for a Sergeant. (Laughter.)

All the background of those who belong to my generation was made by men like yourselves. The background of the new generation is made by your sons and your grandsons and my brothers. Those of us who for many years have been told that wars were over and had taken the anasthesia prepared by the camouflagers on Wilhelm Strasse now realize that the heroic in human nature, thank God, has not died and that we are not a soft nation (applause), for our war program says our war, and when I was called up on the 'phone last night I was told that Bull Durham — we call him that because we like him — was to talk about our war. It is our war. It was our war when the inpertinent Bernstorff called a sacred international agreement a scrap of paper; it was our war when the plains and beautiful valleys of Belgium were devastated so that not even a rose bush or a strawberry plant could smile to God's recurring sun. It was our war when the Gulf Light Sunk it was our war when Edith Cavell, God bless the women, when Edith Cavell was shot by the Hun for being an angel of mercy. (Applause.) It was our war — ah, how we remember the sleepless nights that followed it when the Lusitania was sent to the bottom of the sea with 300 babies — 300 infants, into a great eternity whence they had but recently come. What kind of an enemy is it that will kill the babies in warfare? Go back to the days of Attila, the Hun. Why, the Iroquois, Dr. Griffis, would not have been guilty of such a barbarous act. Do you want to outsavage the savage? You do not need to read the history of the great pioneers who paved the way across our continent. Read the history of modern Germany and you will outsavage all the savagery that the world has ever seen. They are worse than the savage because they claim the laboratory and the library and the church as their own — claims which no savage ever made. It is our war, finally, when the demons of the deep, disregarding every claim of humanity and every written portion of international law, it was our war when they began that ruthless warfare. My friends, it was our war, written in the book of destiny, and it is our war to-day. It will be our war until that old flag is carried through the streets of Berlin (applause), by the boys in khaki. (Applause.) Do you know what color khaki is? It is a mingling of the blue and the gray. (Applause.) It is a sun kissed color. It will not fade. It will not waver, it will never know defeat. (Applause.) And then — then it will be the world's war forever and it will be written across the pages of history in golden letters that the constellation of hope for mankind was a cluster of stars in the red, white and blue. (Applause.)

Lloyd George in his last two speeches has said we are waiting for America to come, and we are all saying for God's sake let's hurry up. Clemenceau, the grand tiger of the magnificent French, has said in his last three interviews that it depends on America. Poincaire, the doughty and scholarly president of our sister republic in France, has admitted it. The eyes of sunny Italy are upon us. All the world is waiting with abated breath what America is going to do. Why, of course, it is our war, isn't it? (Cries of Yes.)

My friends, I have often heard my father tell of the great suspenses of the Civil War. He told how he did not sleep during all the nights of the Battle of Gettysburg. Where he lived they could not get long distance telephone communication then. He told me how he held his breath, he and his neighbors, when it was doubtful whether or not the Mississippi was going to be open to the gunboats of Farragut and to the heroes of Grant. He told me how it was dubious how the Battle of Mobile Bay was going to eventuate. We may also now hold our breaths. Two more thrusts of the Hun army and the long reach of the artillery will demolish the capital of modern art — Paris. We must hold our breath for those brave Frenchmen, God bless them all, being determined that they will send their children and their aged now, and they are doing it this very minute, out of their beautiful and resplendent capital and sacrifice its historic buildings, its magnificent boulevards, its works of art, everything that it stands for in 2,000 years of history rather than give in to the Hun. Ladies, you ought to have a warm place in your hearts for Paris. But, ladies, if Paris falls where are you going to get the design for the next spring bonnet? (Laughter.) I will tell you, gentlemen, and ladies. If Paris falls the French are not going to give up, and we, while we will gird the belt a couple of inches tighter and we will go across, because Paris must be avenged as Belgium must be avenged, and if Paris falls, and the charge to Paris is a symbol of the world charge, if Paris falls it means that the Germans must anticipate a like result for every Bourgeoise town on the other side of the Rhine.

Now, why is it, why is it? I am going to answer the question very briefly why it is our war. First of all because this is a very different world from that which George Washington lived in. Why, when he gave the advice to the 13 struggling states not to engage in entangling foreign alliances — we are disentangling foreign alliances by the way — Benjamin Franklin's electric spark was still a plaything, and to-day the telephone, electricity of all kinds, in all manner of useful methods, is being applied — when he gave that advice, the steam running out of a cooking pot upon the stove was still merely a matter of amusement. Nobody thought of harnessing it. To-day we cross the ocean in a week, the continent in five days. Why, it was our war from the beginning because we are all neighbors now, and when you have got a neighbor whose chickens scratch up your garden, whose dog fights your cat, and who calls you names over the back fence, you are going to do something to him. (Laughter.) We are all neighbors now, and if there is one in the family of nations who carries a dirk hidden in his pocket and is ready to stab you in the back, that bully must be put somewhere where he cannot use the dirk on us. (Applause.)

But there is another reason. The Kaiser for once told the truth — it took him a long time to get to it — in his anniversary announcement the other day. He said, sir, it was a war between two ideals. I hate to call his side of the fence an ideal, but I am using his words. It was a war between two ideals, the ideal of dynasty and the ideal of democracy. Now a dynasty is everything that a democracy is not. A dynasty can make plans from generation to generation and hide them beneath the cloak of dissimulation until the favorable moment comes. Then it can cast aside the cloak and strike — exactly what the Prussian has done now. Democracy — De Tocqueville, the first and greatest camouflager, said it is the weakness of democracy that it cannot persist in a plan. Why, we cannot even plan from one administration to another. A dynasty is above law; a democracy is built upon law; a dynasty can hide its sins beneath the glittering favor of splendor; a democracy can only do humble penance in sackcloth and ashes for its mistakes; a dynasty exploits the people a democracy lifts the humblest into the golden realm of opportunity; a dynasty is a reactionary system against which our fathers fought in the battles of the Revolution, and it was the system of dynasty that President Monroe had in mind when he issued the famous manifesto which now bears the name of the Monroe Doctrine when he said their system, the dynasty system, established upon our continent would be looked upon by us with fear and aversion. You cannot have to-day, men and women, you cannot have to-day with the modern inventions, the modern methods of getting about from one continent and one place to another, you cannot have to-day with the lightening exchange of information, two such antagonistic systems of government standing side by side. There are now two ideas of government. When this war is over there will be only one idea of government. (Applause.)

That is the reason why it is our war. If the Kaiser puts his foot upon the necks of civilization you and I will suffer and our children and our children's children will suffer. The next peace that is made, the peace after this war, is not going to bear the legend that we found in all the manufactured goods that flooded our markets " Made in Germany "; it is going to be made in Washington, if I am any kind of a prophet, and that peace, gentlemen of the Grand Army and ladies, that peace, Mr. Chairman, that peace is going to be an insurance policy to our children, to our grandchildren, to our great grandchildren, because it will be our way of ending our war. (Applause.)

Just one final word. (Cries of go on.)   Gentlemen, I have said it is our war, and I have said that collection of stars in the azure of the greatest banner that kisses the breeze is the constellation and hope of the world. What would have happened to that collection of stars if you had not won the Civil War? Have you thought of that? Well, then why isn't it your war? (Cries of It is.)

And how it must please you to-day, you who have come here, every one of you with the snows of many years resting upon your brows, to find the vindication of Chancellorsville and Gettysburg, of all that march of heroic events, to find its vindication now, that over on the other side of the ocean were men who wondered what you were fighting for. And do you know what fills me with more pride than anything else? I have been in England a good many times. I was over there when they began their great debate what to do with the House of Lords, whether to pull its wisdom teeth or all the teeth. And a couple of the members of the House of Commons carried around with them the Federalist, which contains the writings particularly of Alexander Hamilton on the question of a bicameral or unicameral parliament. And I said " I am glad to see you are reading from an American statesman," " Oh, no," one of the gentlemen said, "Alexander Hamilton was born an Englishman." " Oh," I said, " but he died an American."

Now it pleases it me more than anything else to see the Saint of this war, the prophet of this war — who is he — Abraham Lincoln, quoted more than any other single statesman by Lloyd

George and all the British parliamentarians at this time. You can hardly read a speech that Lloyd George makes or that Clemenceau makes, and he was in this country a number of years — was a school teacher down in Connecticut somewhere, but what they are saying something that Abraham Lincoln said, and if my faith and yours is based upon reality the spirit of the greatest American who ever lived, and one of the greatest men ever made in the image of God, is looking down with benign satisfaction that a united republic is marching in the van of the battle of civilization in our war, in the war which you helped make victorious for youth, saved the constellation in the flag from disintegration and made it a United States of America. God bless you all.

(Prolonged applause.)

(Three cheers were called for and given for Prof. Orth.)

President Hickey.— Sir Commander and comrades, we will close the program by simply extending to you a very warm invitation to come again.

The Commander.— Comrades and delegates, I desire to state that we now adjourn and will meet in this hall at two o'clock precisely, when the opening session of our encampment will begin.

Comrade Tanner.— It is now half-past 11. Let us have the opening of the encampment, the Commander's address and the appointment of committees. Won't the Commander accept that suggestion?

Commander Kirchner.— I will.

Comrade Tanner.— Then I so move.
The motion was duly seconded and carried.

Commander Kirchner.— I want to say to the visiting comrades and ladies that we wish them to retire so that we can enter upon our duties as delegates to this encampment. Now all persons who are not delegates to this encampment will please retire.

The Acting Assistant Adjutant-General.— Is the officer of the day present?
(No response).

ACTING ASSISTANT ADJUTANT-GENERAL.— Commander, I would suggest that you select two or three comrades to go along the line and take up the countersign. The officer of the day isn't present nor has he his guards here.

THE COMMANDER.— Is the officer of the day present?

(There was no response).

THE COMMANDER.— Comrade McCloskey, Comrade Michael Woods will step up here. I want a couple of more comrades to take up the countersign. Comrade Cole and Comrade Irvine. Now each of you comrades take an aisle and take up the counter-sign, and the quicker you do it the sooner we will get ready.

After taking the countersign from the delegates the comrades reported to the Commander, who announced that all present were members of the Grand Army.

THE COMMANDER.— Comrades, this is the 52d annual encamp-ment of the Department of New York of the Grank Army of the Republic. We meet in fraternity, charity and loyalty, and may our hearts beat as one in sustaining the great objects of our asso-ciation. The Chaplain will invoke the Divine blessing.

Rev. D. T. McMillan, Acting Department Chaplain, then invoked Divine blessings as follows:

Almighty God, most merciful Father, we thank Thee for that kind protecting providence that has brought us together to-day. Thou art the source of light and wisdom. We pray that Thou wilt direct us in the exercises of this encampment, to Thy glory, to the welfare of Thy people and the great interests which we represent. Quiet our hearts and minds, we pray Thee, with the assurance of the progress of that war beyond which so disturbs us, where our sons have gone. Give them, we pray Thee, victory, and may they return with songs of victory in Thine own good time, but do not grant peace, Oh God, until it shall come to us permanently to bless the human race. We have but one Master, and that is God, the Father, here and everywhere. Hear us and bless us for Christ's sake. Amen.

THE COMMANDER.— I now declare the 52d annual encampment of the Department of New York, Grand Army of the Republic, open in due form. The first order of business is the report of the Committee on Credentials.

The Chairman of the Committee of Credentials reported that up to the present time 451 comrades had received their badges as delegates to the encampment.

THE COMMANDER.— Comrades, you have heard the report of the Committee on Credentials; what is your pleasure?

On motion duly seconded the report was adopted.

Department of New York
GRAND ARMY OF THE REPUBLIC
ROLL CALL OF THE DEPARTMENT

DEPARTMENT OFFICERS

*WILLIAM F. KIRCHNER.........Department Commander
*HENRY S. REDMAN.............Senior Vice-Commander
*FRANK JOHNSON..............Junior Vice Commander
WILLIAM TAYLOR...................Medical Director
REV. REUBEN KLINE.......................Chaplain

OFFICIAL STAFF

EDWARD J. ATKINSON } Assistant Quartermaster-General
Assistant Adjutant-General
*JOSEPH E. EWELL.....................Judge Advocate
*SAMUEL McAULIFFE ....Inspector
*JOHN McCLOSKEY..............Chief Mustering Officer

COUNCIL OF ADMINISTRATION

*Elias W. Beach   *Henry Lilly
*Samuel Irvine   *William H. Kilfoile
Austin H. Stafford

PAST DEPARTMENT COMMANDERS

†James B. McKean ....Saratoga Springs
†Daniel E. Sickles ....New York City

---

† Deceased.   * Present.

†Edward B. Lansing ....Auburn
†John C. Robinson ....Binghamton
†Henry A. Barnum ....New York City
†Stephen P. Corliss ....Albany
†Edward Jardine ....Albany
†John Palmer ....Albany
*James Tanner ....Washington, D. C.
†William F. Rogers ....Buffalo
†James McQuade ....Utica
†L. Coe Young ....Binghamton
†Abram Merritt ....Nyack
†James S. Fraser ....New York City
 John A. Reynolds..............................Fairport
†Ira M. Hedges ....Haverstraw
†H. Clay Hall ....Little Falls
†Joseph I. Sayles ....Rome
†George H. Treadwell ....Albany
†N. Martin Curtis ....Ogdensburg
†Harrison Clark ....Albany
†Floyd Clarkson ....New York City
*Charles H. Freeman ....Corning
†Theodore L. Poole ....Syracuse
†Joseph P. Cleary ....Rochester
×John C. Shotts ....Yonkers
 Edward J. Atkinson.......................New York City
†James S. Graham ....Rochester
†Albert D. Shaw ....Watertown
†Anson S. Wood ....Wolcott
 Joseph W. Kay.................................Brooklyn
 N. P. Pond..................................Rochester
*Charles A. Orr................................Buffalo
*Allan C. Bakewell ....New York City
*John S. Koster ....Port Leyden
†Henry N. Burhams ....Syracuse
*James M. Snyder ....Troy
*John S. Maxwell ....Amsterdam
†Harlan J. Swift ....Cuba

---

† Deceased.   * Present.

†William H. Daniels ....Ogdensburg
†M. J. Cummings ....Brooklyn
*DeWitt C. Hurd ....Utica
*George B. Loud ....New York City
*Oscar Smith ....Albany
*Samuel C. Pierce ....Rochester
*James D. Bell.................................Brooklyn
*Zan L. Tidball ....Brooklyn
†Solomon W. Russell ....Salem
   DeAlva S. Alexander, Buffalo, transferred from Dept. Potomac.
†W. L. Palmer, Binghamton, transferred from Dept. Dakota.

PAST NATIONAL OFFICERS

†John C. Robinson ....Commander-in-Chief, 1877–78
†John Palmer ....Commander-in-Chief, 1891
†Albert D. Shaw ....Commander-in-Chief, 1899
*James Tanner ....Commander-in-Chief, 1905
†James B. McKean........Senior Vice-Com.-in-Chief, 1866–67
†Edward Jardine.......Senior Vice-Commander-in-Chief, 1874
†John Palmer.........Senior Vice-Commander-in-Chief, 1897
*Alfred Lyth..........Senior Vice-Commander-in-Chief, 1897
†Lewis E. Griffith......Senior Vice-Commander-in-Chief, 1907
†Nicholas W. Day......Senior Vice-Commander-in-Chief, 1912
‡Joseph Hadfield......Junior Vice-Commander-in-Chief, 1888

PAST SENIOR VICE DEPARTMENT COMMANDERS

†William F. Rogers   †Joseph Egolf
†James M. Gere   †John G. Copley
†Edward B. Lansing   †Constantine Nitsche
†John C. Robinson   †Jacob Welsing
   John A. Reynolds   †Henry Osterheld
†Samuel Minnes   †John E. Savery
†John Palmer   †Robert Keith

---

* Present.
† Deceased.
‡ Severed his connection with the Order.

†H. Clay Hall
†L. P. Thompson
C. W. Cowtan
C. A. Orr
†J. P. Cleary
Charles H. Freeman
†J. K. Hood
†Homer B. Webb
†Edward J. Deevey
†William L. DeLacey
Edward J. Atkinson
P. C. Soule
†C. Hull Grant
†Frederick Cossum
†George Chappell
†Rufus Daggett
John S. Maxwell
*Edward J. Mitchell
†John H. Swift
Clark N. Norton

†M. J. Cummings
†W. Charles Smith
†E. C. Parkinson
George E. Dewey
†Daniel J. O'Brien
†Jared W. Wickes
*George F. Tait
†William A. Boyd
*James M. Watson
Samuel C. Pierce
*Daniel H. Cole
James D. Bell
*Alfred E. Stacey
*A. H. Stafford
*James A. Allis
*George Hollands
†Alenander E. Mintee, Buffalo,
    transferred from Dept., Cal.
    and Nevada.

PAST JUNIOR VICE DEPARTMENT COMMANDERS

†James M. Geer
†Bradley Winslow
†V. Krzyanowski
John A. Reynolds
†John W. Marshall
†Willard Bullard
†Joseph Egolf
†A. B. Lawrence
†Edwin J. Loomis
†Robert H. McCormic
†George H. Treadwell
†J. Marshall Guion
†James F. Fitts
†Dennis Sullivan
†Edwin Goodrich

Frank Z. Jones
†J. C. Carlyle
†W. B. Stoddard
†G. S. Conger
†C. Hull Grant
†Robert Wilson
†W. L. Scott
†Gardner C. Hibbard
Edward A. Dubey
William F. Kirchner
Silas Owen
†Daniel Van Wie
†John Kohler
John S. Koster
*N. R. Thompson

---

† Deceased.   * Present.

Walter Scott
Jerre S. Gross
†Philo H. Conklin
†Daniel W. Hulse
†D. C. Bangs
†David Isaacs
*L. L. Hanchett
George E. Dewey
†Edward H. Fassett
†Daniel J. O'Brien
†Jared W. Wicks
*James Campbell

DeWitt C. Hurd
*Robert P. Bush
†L. O. Morgan
†Henry E. Turner
†C. C. Caldwell
*C. J. Westcott
Nelson Mattice
David H. Dyer
Robert Sumpson, Jr., M. D.
*Isidore Isaacs
†James Loftus
*John W. Mullens

Post No. 1 — Rochester

Com., James H. Splaine
S. V., Jeremiah D. Smith
*J. V., Michael Murphy
Delegates:
*James H. Graham
Robert Forristal
Alternates:
John A. Schuey
Watson K. Benjamin

Post No. 2 — Buffalo

*Com., Nelson Simmons
*S. V., Frank Hammond
*J. V., Fred Webber
Delegates:
*Conrad Egloff
*Geo. H. Sears
Joseph E. Ewell
William Rankin
Geo. Wander
*Frank K. Robert
Alternates:
Conrad Fisher

E. E. Joseph
*E. H. M. Bamburg
Frank Myers
Chas. R. Sweet
William Brack
F. Fleming
Lyman A. Dietrick

Post No. 4 — Rochester

Com., John A. Reynolds
S. V., Samuel C. Pierce
J. V., William C. Morey
Delegate
*Chas. E. Benton
Alternate:
S. B. Williams

Post No. 5 — Albany

Com., John E. Jones
S. V., Geo. Messer
J. V., Chas. H. Billson
Delegates:
*Gilbert W. Peck
*Richard M. Barber

---

* Present.   † Deceased.

Alternates:
James M. Erwin
George Tompkins

Post No. 6 — Elmira
*Com., Sanford D. Haines
S. V., James H. Loughridge
J. V., Schuyler Beers
Delegates:
*Frank P. Frost
Henry L. Keene
Alternates:
*G. V. R. Merrill
Francis D. Carter

Post No. 7 — Clifton Springs
*Com., Chas. D. Giles
S. V., Frank Wunderlen
J. V., J. M. Cooley
Delegate:
*B. W. Austen
Alternate:
E. D. Coff

Post No. 8 — New York
Com., Geo. H. Stevens
S. V., Michael J. Donovan
J. V., Charles A. Grant
Delegate:
Henry J. Kopper
Alternate:
*A. B. Ostrander

Post No. 9 — Buffalo
*Com., Calvin A. Brainard
*S. V., E. N. Bowen
*J. V., John Maxwell
Delegates:
*Arthur H. Howe
*Geo. W. Flynn
*Cola D. R. Stowits

*Walter T. Smith
Alternates:
Albert H. Adams
John S. Robertson
T. Augustus Budd
Geo. M. Booth

Post No. 10 — Brooklyn
Com., Jacob Callas
S. V., Jacob H. Fredericks
J. V., George W. Reed
Delegate:
Charles A. Shaw
Alternate:
James H. Nason

Post No. 11 — Brooklyn
*Com., Robert H. Davis
S. V., John C. Rennert
J. V., Joseph Doyle
Delegate:
*John B. Mendell
Alternate:
Henry Peasell

Post No. 12 — Afton
Com., R. R. Lord
* S. V., Geo. W. Johnson
J. V., P. M. Shaw
Delegate:
P. F. Cole
Alternate:
Geo. A. Haven

Post No. 14 — Utica
Com., Robert J. Clark
S. V., Lansing Fowler
J. V., Moses Ellwood
Delegate:
Joseph Tessy

* Present.

Alternate:
Moses D. Ellwood

Post No. 15 — Schenevus
Com., W. H. Colegrove
S. V., Mordecia Knapp
J. V., D. P. Lappens
Delegate:
Rev. D. P. Lappens
Alternate:
Mordecia Knapp

Post No. 16 — Cleveland
*Com., Louis Wanner
S. V., Thos. D. Dean
J. V., F. G. Terpenny
Delegate:
S. F. Putney
Alternate:
Gaylord Horkins

Post No. 17 — Gloversville
Com., Daniel H. Cole
S. V., Leonard Cooper
J. V., William H. Hare
Delegate:
Edgar J. Best
Alternate:
*William M. Harris

Post No. 18 — Troy
Com., W. H. Kilfoile
S. V., Giles Pease
J. V., John Carnick
Delegate:
*Henry Pease
Alternate:
John Foster

Post No. 19 — Little Falls
Com., James G. Burney
S. V., Benjamin Lane
J. V., Phillip Gressman
Delegate:
Lewis Hart
Alternate:
Wm. H. Suits

Post No. 20 — Poughkeepsie
Com., Harry E. Murray
S. V., Theo. Van Kleeck
J. V., John L. Osborn
Delegates:
Henry I. Williams
Wm. S. Plummer
Fred N. Norris
Alternates:
Chas. E. Chase
Almon B. Beneway
Wm. H. Millard

Post No. 21 — Brooklyn
*Com., Timothy T. Donovan
S. V., James B. Tooker
J. V., Townsent Bragaw
Delegate:
*Thomas E. Holt
Alternate:
George W. White

Post No. 23 — Waterville
Com., Rowland Roberts
S. V., J. W. Hartley
J. V., S. Templeton
Delegate:
*E. A. Wheeler
Alternate:
Robert Carlin

* Present.

Joseph E. Ewell, Judge Advocate

Post No. 24 — New York

*Com., John M. Fisher
S. V., Adolph F. Masgraf
J. V., Lewis Deion
Delegate:
John W. Dick
Alternate:
*Wilson Berryman

Post No. 25 — Worcester

Com., S. M. Flint
S. V., Charles Wilsey
J. V., A. D. Phillips
Delegate:
A. D. Phillips
Alternate:
Chas. Wilsey

Post No. 26 — Cooperstown

Com., Joel G. White
*S. V., Charles J. Tuttle
J. V., Cornelius Vandervoort
Delegate:
W. H. Martin
Alternate:
*Charles J. Tuttle

Post No. 27 — Coxsackie

Com., Newton A. Calkins
S. V., David Hoffman
J. V., John Van Wormer
Delegate:
J. B. Cole
Alternate:
John S. Hiscerd

Post No. 29 — New York

*Com., Edward M. Griffiths
*S. V., John J. Morris

J. V., Philip Brady
Delegates:
*Louis N. Aarons
John C. Zimmerman
Alternates:
Robert M. Sterritt
Edward Meehan

Post No. 30 — Binghamton

Com., Alfred A. Lord
*S. V., W. S. Ruger
J. V., C. S. Rogers
Delegates:
*S. J. Palmer
W. S. Ruger
*Nicholas Martin
Alternates:
Frederick Yingling
George Raymond
Jacob Lester

Post No. 31 — New York Mills

*Com., Rev. George B. Fairhead
S. V., George M. Gregory
J. V., Warren Penfield
Delegate:
*Joseph Kepworth
Alternate:
Robert Cooper

Post No. 32 — New York

*Com., Jacob Parr
S. V., Charles Sieler
J. V., Francis Ficke
Delegate:
*Henry A. Kraus
Alternate:
Charles Schoen

* Present.

Post No. 33 —Amsterdam

Com., John L. Abeling
S. V., Alfred Casler
*J. V., Frank Ross
Delegates:
John Howell
*Augustus Myers
Alternates:
William Hayse
William Rylands

Post No. 34 — Troy

Com., David Hilton
S. V., Charles Huntington
J. V., Hiram N. Wager
Delegate:
*Parker P. Nicholas
Alternate:
Charles Huntington

Post No. 35 — Brooklyn

*Com., Wm. H. Lyons
*S. V., Wm. H. Ridgway
J. V., George Lacker
Delegate:
Wm. H. Ridgway
Alternate:
*Edward S. Upson

Post No. 38 — New York

Com., Isaac H. Fuhr
S. V., James Kerrigan
J. V., James C. Angus
Delegate:
Thomas R. Tettey
Alternate:
George Miller

Post No. 39 — Prospect

*Com., James Hane
S. V., Willet Thayre
J. V., E. P. Comstock
Delegate:
A. T. Orvis
Alternate:
Joseph Trimble

Post No. 40 — Oxford

*Com., John Few
S. V., Alonzo Heyes
J. V., Alfred Ayers
Delegate:
*F. E. Dunham
Alternate:
Alonzo Heyes

Post No. 41 — Ithaca

*Com., Edward A. Willson
*S. V., James Wallace
*J. V., J. V. McIntyre
Delegate:
*John LaFrance
Alternate:
*D. W. Burdick

Post No. 42 — New York

*Com., Henry Witthack
S. V., Felix Short
J. V., Charles L. Hughes
Delegate:
†John J. Young
Alternate:
John Marshall

Post No. 43 — Cohoes

Com., C. S. Travis
S. V., M. Steenburg

---

* Present.

† Deceased.

J. V., C. N. Greene
Delegate:
*Jas. H. Van DeMark
Alternate:
James E. Stephens

Post No. 44 — New York

*Com., James C. Montgomery
S. V., Thos C. Lawrence
J. V., William Reiber
Delegate:
George A. Drew
Alternate:
*Oliver A. Pratt

Post No. 45 — Auburn

*Com., Thos. Tallman
S. V., E. Sailsbury
J. V., D. B. Robbins
Delegates:
*Ransom Fletcher
*Levi Palmer
Alternates:
Robert C. Breese
Wm. Stalker

Post No. 46 — Ballston Spa

Com., A. J. Greeman
S. V., Adam Niles
J. V., Henry C. Dye
Delegate:
Geo. M. Hoyt
Alternate:
Geo. W. Gardner

Post No. 47 — Rome

Com., L. A. Martin
S. V., Hiram Palmer
J. V., Wm. Hughes

Delegate:
*S. C. Baldwin
Alternate:
William Rose

Post No. 48 — Beacon

*Com., Elijah Mosher
S. V., D. J. Barrett
J. V., Levi Hadfield
Delegate:
*William J. Kiernan
Alternate:
Hezekiah Cullen

Post No. 49 — Canistota

Com., William Taylor, M. D.
S. V., Abram Betsinger
J. V., Harmon Wagoner
Delegate:
*Wm. H. Parmelee
Alternate
Lyman L. Martin

Post No. 50 — Flushing

Com., R. W. Carman
S. V., Philip H. Knighton
*J. V., Henry C. Dunham
Delegate:
R. W. Carman
Alternate:
*J. J. Smith

Post No. 51 — Canajoharie

*Com., C. Van Alstine
S. V., George Reynolds
J. V., Chas. Hilderbrant
Delegate:
*A. Parsons
Alternate:
A. B. Frey

* Present.

Post No. 52 — Newburgh

Com., Curtis Stanton
S. V., Joseph M. Sterling
J. V., Wm. C. Goodrich
Delegate:
Patrick J. McDonald
Alternate:
Thomas Hewitt

Post No. 53 — Utica

Com., Jacob P. Yakey
*S. V., Phillip Graff, Jr.
J. V., Edward C. Case
Delegates:
Eugene C. Ferry
Charles W. Scharff
Alternates:
John C. Bauer
Edward C. Case

Post No. 55 — Wolcott

*Com., Albert Wamsley
S. V., Nicholas V. Bigelow
J. V., Henry Wamsley
Delegate:
*Joseph E. Lawrence
Alternate:
James G. Cook

Post No. 56 — Lee Center

Com., David French
S. V., F. H. Wait
J. V., Elon Fenton
Delegate:
David French
Alternate:
Wm. Brown

Post No. 57 — Fonda

Com., John A. Hubbard
S. V., Jacob V. Smith

J. V., P. V. Colgrove
Delegate:
R. H. Tipple
Alternate:
Phillip V. Colgrove

Post No. 58 — Newburgh

Com., Charles Beck
S. V.; John N. Milligan
J. V., H. H. Bates
Delegate:
Alternate:

Post No. 59 — Oswego

*Com., Geo. R. Resseguie
*S. V., Jason Robertson
J. V., Wesley Van Over
Delegate:
Chas. M. Wade
Alternate:
Harvey Neal

Post No. 60 — Yonkers

*Com., Augustus Kipp
S. V., John F. Cronin
J. V., Fred Gugel
Delegate:
George R. Hendrickson
Alternate:
*Jerome D. Barnes

Post No. 62 — New York

*Com., John Schmidling
S. V., Herman Lange
J. V., John Thiele
Delegate:
Herman Lange
Alternate:
William Rohling

* Present.

Post No. 63 — Albany
Com., A. J. Hinman
S. V., R. C. Folger
J. V., W. H. Terrill
Delegate:
C. M. Hyatt
Alternate:
E. M. McCamman

Post No. 65 — Oswego
*Com., James K. Prosser
S. V., Henry C. Jacobs
J. V., John H. McGraw
Delegate:
*George H. Lester
Alternate:
Richard Bowers

Post No. 66 — Syracuse
Com., James A. Allis
S. V., Adam Smith
*J. V., H. Stewart Warner
Delegates:
*Adam Metzger
*Chas. Umbrich
Alternate:
Lawrence McCarthy

Post No. 69 — New York
*Com., Patrick H. Doody
S. V., Charles H. Reilley
J. V., John Molloy
Delegate:
Michael Lynch
Alternate:
John Molloy

Post No. 70 — Fort Plain
Com., Abram H. Sweet
S. V., Henry Seeber

J. V., James Anson
Delegate:
W. B. Hokork
Alternate:
Henry Seeber

Post No. 72 — Waterloo
Com., Warren E. Lerch
*S. V., Abram M. Schott
J. V., Joseph Huntington
Delegate:
A. M. Schott
Alternate:
Francis Bacon

Post No. 73 — Lyndonville
Com., Henry H. Vosler
S. V., Corrall Phipany
J. V., Samuel Lewis
Delegate:
Corrall Phipany
Alternate:
Mickle Gephart

Post No. 74 — Naples
Com., Geo. Rackham
S. V., I. S. Wilson
J. V., Philip Dinzler
Delegate:
John R. Dixon
Alternate:
*B. I. Preston

Post No. 76 — Lockport
*Com., Wallace Riley
*S. V., Chauncey Wetherwax
J. V., Joseph Deball
Delegate:
*F. A. Brown

---

* Present.

Alternate:
Peter J. Rabb

Post No. 77 — New York
Com., Thomas Hamilton
S. V., William T. Lewis
J. V., George Wenner
Delegate:
Richard H. Bermingham
Alternate:
Roderick R. Ryan

Post No. 78 — Seneca Falls
Com., William Durnin
S. V., William Marvin
J. V., Thomas Casey
Delegate:
*Henry H. Jones
Alternate:
P. W. Bailey

Post No. 79 — New York
Com., Lucius E. Wilson
S. V., Michael Gormley
J. V., George W. Taylor
Delegate:
Chas. E. Hubbard
Alternate:
George C. Cuttle

Post No. 80 — New York
Com., Charles Just
S. V., George J. O'Reilly
J. V., Edward Long
Delegate:
George J. O'Reilly
Alternate:
Robert Kelly

Post No. 81 — Bath
*Com., Rozel Seager
S. V., James M. Thomas
J. V., James Herron
Delegate:
James Herron
Alternate:
*Fred Cooper

Post No. 82 — Nyack
Com., Alonzo Jewell
S. V., Winfield S. Requa
J. V., Isaac S. Wallace
Delegate:
Henry E. Smith
Alternate:
Conrad Hoffman

Post No. 83 — Norwich
*Com., Geo. W. Payne
*S. V., Harvey Trass
J. V., John Gridley
Delegate:
James Brownell
Alternate:
Harvey Trass

Post No. 84 — Rochester
Com., Henry S. Redman
*S. V., James H. Noyce,
*J. V., Henry G. Gauer
Delegate:
William H. Whiting
Alternate:
*Charles T. Peck

Post No. 85 — Portville
Com., L. E. Carr
S. V., Joseph C. Cole

---

* Present.

*J. V., A. O. Burdick
  Delegate:
*Joel A. Burdick
  Alternate:
  Geo. Baker

Post No. 86 — Belfast

Com., Elmer Hitchings
S. V., W. Hicks
J. V., W. Kelley
  Delegate:
Wallace Vaughn
  Alternate:
Willard Elmer

Post No. 87 — Springville

Com., Geo. H. Barker
S. V., F. S. Smith
J. V., Norton Baker
  Delegate:
Wm. Block
  Alternate:
F. S. Smith

Post No. 88 — Wappingers Falls

Com., George Ruch
S. V., George Abbott
J. V., John Thompson
  Delegate:
Wm. McKinley
  Alternate:
John W. Babcock

Post No. 89 — Brooklyn

Com., Chares H. Lunt
S. V., Robert Keirs
J. V., John McAvey
  Delegate:
John E. Evans

* Present.

  Alternate:
John McAvey

Post No. 90 — Schenectady

Com., Lewis Cohen
S. V., Park Van Aernam
J. V., James F. White
  Delegate:
*Wm. G. Caw
  Alternate:
W. D. Davis

Post No. 91 — Medina

Com., Ziba Roberts
S. V., Wm. Traw
J. V., John Lewis
  Delegate:
Gaine Ball
  Aternate:
William Loads

Post No. 92 — Saratoga Springs

*Com., H. B. Ormsbee
S. V., Henry Cunningham
J. V., Edwin B. Duell
  Delegates:
*Robert F. Knapp
Patrick McDonald
  Alternates:
J. E. Clark
*Robert S. Remington

Post No 93 — Penn Yan

*Com., John W. Durham
*S. V., John Harris
J. V., John McGough
  Delegate:
Amasa E. Church

Alternate:
*Stephen B. Dunton

Post No. 94 — Geneva
*Com., John H. Stevens
*S. V., Geo. A. Carr
*J. V., Wm. Genther
Delegate:
*George H. Bearnish
Alternate:
Rush Probasco

Post No. 95 — Peekskill
Com., Geo. L. Hughson
S. V., Odell Dyckman
J. V., Elias G. McChain
Delegate:
Henry S. Free
Alternate:
Samuel Take

Post No. 96 — New York
*Com., Theodore Weberg
S. V., Joseph Stumpf
J. V., Wm. Walters
Delegate:
Theodore Weberg
Alternate:
Henry Lerch

Post No. 97 — Boonvlle
*Com., G. O. Bridgman
S. V., Henry Lockwood
*J. V., Stephen Klinck
Delegate:
James H. Fitch
Alternate:
Benjamin Griffiths

Post No. 98 — Portland
*Com., Geo. W. Edgcomb
S. V., David C. Beers
J. V., Elijah Adams
Delegate:
*Elijah Adams
Alternate:
J. C. Seamans

Post No. 99 — Newark
Com., Wm. B. Vosburg
S. V., Geo. H. Mills
*J. V., Conrad Weh
Delegate:
Chas. Burchard
Alternate:
*Victor La Reaux

Post No. 100 — New York
Com., James T. Walker
S. V., George A. Teller
J. V., J. Augustus Brill
Delegate:
John Hassall
Alternate:
John W. Jacobus

Post No. 101 — Perry
Com., Wm. K. Selden
S. V., James Russell
J. V., W. C. Hendershott
Delegate:
. . . .
Alternate:
. . . .

Post No. 102 — Moriah Center
Com., Charles Acome
S. V., A. H. Woodruff

* Present.

J. V., Daniel Cannon
Delegate:
A. H. Woodruff
Alternate:
James Cota

Post No. 103 — New York
*Com., Henry L. Swords
S. V., James N. Allison
*J. V., Adolph E. Dick
Delegate:
George Brack
Alternate:
A. E. Dick

Post No. 104 — Rhinebeck
Com., A. C. McCurdy
S. V., Douglas Marguardt
J. V., Edward Luff
Delegate:
C. A. Nichols
Alternate:
Norman Killmer

Post No. 105 — Homer
Com., Frederick Monk
*S. V., Theron Gutcher
J. V., E. A. Williams
Delegate:
George C. Saterlee
Aternate:
Smith Wright

Post No. 106 — Rochester
*Com., J. J. Augustine
S. V., Stephen Miller
J. V., John Ropelt
Delegate:
*Justus Beisheim

Alternate:
Geo. Stehler

Post No. 107 — Shortsville
*Com., Ira M. Dibble
S. V., Charles M. Sisco
J. V., Charles Haas
Delegate:
Chares M. Sisco
Alternate:
J. V. Peacock

Post No. 108 — Binghamton
Com., N. E. Rowe
*S. V., B. P. Harper
J. V., Leroy Bostwick
Delegate:
*S. F. Black
Alternate:
J. B. Lucas

Post No. 109 — Sodus
*Com., Edward H. Sentell
S. V., William H. Allen
J. V., Eli Darling
Delegate:
*Morris J. Seymour
Alternate:
Walter Shaver

Post No. 110 — Ilion
*Com., Theodore Harter
S. V., L. B. Colburn
J. V., Wm. H. Keeler
Delegate:
Wm. S. Cox
Alternate:
M. D. Hartford

* Present.

Post No. 111 — Pulaski
Com., John E. Bentley
S. V., Thomas R. Stewart
J. V., B. D. Burdick
Delegate:
*Hartwell Douglass
Alternate:
Aaron N. Burr

Post No. 112 — New Brighton
Com., Edward Openshaw
S. V., M. F. Ball
J. V., John Bostrom
Delegate:
*Jacob Knoblock
Alternate:
John Bostrom

Post No. 113 — New York
*Com., Matthew B. Brennan
S. V., Louis L. Felkir
*J. V., Bartholomew Oehmen
Delegate:
*George Messemer
Alternate:
Isaac Brown

Post No. 114 — Albion
Com., L. E. Griswold
S. V., Edwin R. Fuller
J. V., Henry B. Cleveland
Delegate:
*Henry J. Babbitt
Alternate:
Lewis Galarnean

Post No. 116 — Schuylerville
Com., C. H. McNaughton
S. V., A. C. Hammond

J. V., Geo. W. Potter
Delegate:
Miles H. Delong
Alternate:
Dewitt W. Thomas

Post No. 118 — Philmont
Com., J. I. Spoor
S. V., Albert E. Edwards
J. V., James Robertson
Delegate:
Robert H. Brandow
Alternate:
Myron Wheeler

Post No. 119 — Oneonta
*Com., W. H. Brown
S. V., Chas. Morrison
J. V., Geo. Mackley
Delegate:
A. Munson
Alternate:
*W. H. Morenus

Post No. 120 — Katonah
Com., J. A. Tuttle
*S. V., J. B. Turner
J. V., John Cargan
Delegate:
J. T. Lockwood
Alternate:
Joseph Flood

Post No. 121 — Albany
Com., Charles Fisher
*S. V., John W. Hewitt
J. V., David J. Crounse
Delegate:
*Chas. Donnelly

---

* Present.

*William Johnston
Alternate:
William M. Chatham
John P. Slocum

Post No. 122 — Brooklyn
*Com., Louis Finkelmeier
S. V., August Bothe
J. V., Philip Fensterer
Delegate:
John Kromer
Alternate:
Mathius Eberhardt

Post No. 123 — Newfield
Com., Jonathan Underdown
S. V., M. E. Van Ostrand
J. V., Alonzo Palmer
Delegate:
*Aaron Poyer
Alternate:
George W. Peck

Post No. 124 — Unadilla
Com., W. G. Hotaling
S. V., Louis Gundlach
J. V., S. Phillips
Delegate:
*C. C. Stoddard
Alternate:
W. W. Cleaver

Post No. 125 — Sanborn
Com., Oliver Velzey
S. V., Robert Hiam
J. V., A. J. Harley
Delegate:
Geo. B. Suick

Alternate:
Chauncey Wichterman

Post No. 126 — Wilson
. . . .

Post No. 127 — Kingston
*Com., James E. Everett
*S. V., Griffin A. Hart
J. V., H. S. Jennings
Delegate:
*Chas. H. Styles
Alternate:
Edward W. Matheson

Post No. 128 — New York
*Com., John M. Nagel
S. V., Adolph Goldfish
J. V., John Flaherty
Delegate:
*William J. Barry
Alternate:
Jacob Jacobs

Post No. 129 — Tonawanda
Com., Charles B. Parker
S. V., Jay Collins
J. V., Edgar Magbee
Delegate:
Geo. Brunner
Aternate:
Jay Collins

Post No. 130 — Warsaw
Com., Mills W. Marchant
S. V., Wm. H. Cornell
J. V., Judson U. Gaige
Delegates:
Jacob M. Smith

---

* Present.

Alternate:
*Wm. H. Cornell

Post No. 132 — Franklin
. . . .

Post No. 133 — Niagara Falls
. . . .

Post No. 134 — Johnson City
Com., I. W. Butler
S. V., E. B. Williams
J. V., Gardner Brown
Delegate:
E. B. Williams
Alternate:
E. S. Rozell

Post No. 135 — New York
S. V., Dennis Farrell
J. V., Robert Dickey
*Com., John W. Noble
Delegate:
*Corneilus Ten Eick
Alternate:
W. H. Van Cott, Jr.

Post No. 136 — New York
*Com., James L. Lyons
*S. V., Thomas P. Tuite
J. V., James Farrell
Delegate:
Thomas P. Tuite
Alternate:
None given

Post No. 137 — Greene
. . . .

Post No. 138 — Hudson
Com., Thomas Berridge
S. V., Joseph Way

J. V., Jonas M. Plass
Delegate:
John J. Plass
Alternate:
Joseph Way

Post No. 140 — New York
Com., George W. Case
S. V., Ora Howard
*J. V., Albert L. Dodge
Delegates:
*Fred C. Barger
Josiah C. Long
*Francis B. Stedman
*Edwin A. Whitfield
Alternates:
John H. Palmer
L. Curtis Brackett
Ora Howard
Geo. S. Foder

Post No. 141 — Troy
*Com., John E. Vandenburgh
S. V., Wm. J. Nelson
J. V., Henry Waterman
Delegate:
*Charles F. Roemer
Alternate:
Charles F. Fahl

Post No. 142 — Delhi
Com., M. S. Capack
S. V., R. A. S. McNee
J. V., Wallace Crosby
Delegate:
George W. Grant
Alternate:
John Ferguson

* Present.

Post No. 144 — Ossining

*Com., Charles Mitchell
S. V., Wm. W. Ryder
J. V., John A. Cowie
Delegate:
*Wm. W. Ryder
Alternate:
J. Arthur Tompkins

Post No. 145 — Phoenix

*Com., E. A. Crandell
S. V., C. F. Brainard
J. V., J. W. Parker
Delegate:
*T. C. Taggart
Alternate:
A. B. Ross

Post No. 146 — New York

Com., John Mulligan
S. V., William Stuart
J. V. George W. Collier
Delegate:
Christian Diehl
Alternate:
David Clark

Post No. 147 — Glens Falls

Com., George F. Bryant
S. V., Newton A. McOmber
J. V., Edward Dickinson
Delegates:
Clarence M. Cool
Stephen Simons
Alternates:
George H. Skym
Anson A. Scoville

Post No. 148 — Brooklyn

*Com., Thos. H. Kiernan
*S. V., S. Kyle
*J. V., A. Hatfield
Delegate:
*H. C. Draper
Alternate:
*G. O. Jenney

Post No. 150 — Harpersville

Com., G. E. Hurlburt
S. V., Y. Sherwood
J. V., E. W. Linga
Delegate:
R. Lovejoy
Alternate:
Theodore Sherwood

Post No. 151 — Syracuse

*Com., Henry C. Ransom
*S. V., Robert McArthur
J. V., Thomas R. Scott
Delegates:
*John H. Forey
*Caius A. Weaver
*Edward C. Fay
*Isaac Depew
Alternates:
John Standon
Oscar E. Hayden
H. D. Benjamin
Milo Rosenthal

Post No. 152 — Brooklyn

*Com., William Busch
S. V., Elmer Chaphy
J. V., Robert H. Brant
Delegate:
Coleman Cohen

* Present.

Alternate:
Simon Nager

Post No. 153 — Lyons
Com., Henry Alford
S. V., H. W. Harrington
J. V., H. Bramer
Delegate:
John H. Cosart
Alternate:
R. D. Pudney

Post No. 154 — Marathon
. . . .

Post No. 155 —Moravia
Com., Benjamin Wilson
S. V., Elijah Greenfield
J. V., W. H. Baker
Delegate:
E. E. Palmer
Alternate:
A. Hutchinson

Post No. 156 — Gouverneur
*Com., Warren B. Pike
S. V., Lorenzo Smith
J. V., Silas W. Payne
Delegate:
*George S. Parsons
Alternate:
Silas W. Payne

Post No. 157 — Esperence
Com., John Hunter
*S. V., William Landers
*J. V., M. J. Tompkins
Delegate:
M. J. Tompkins
Alternate:
William Landers

Post No. 158 — Brookton
. . . .

Post No. 159 — Fair Haven
*Com., E. R. Robinson
S. V., George Adams
J. V., E. N. Andrews
Delegate:
*Charles Howland
Alternate:
Alex. Campbell

Post No. 160 — Cazenovia
*Com., Otis Jillson
S. V., C. W. Barrett
J. V., J. L. Lawson
Delegate:
E. A. Peck
Alternate:
O. P. Snyder

Post No. 161 — Brooklyn
Com., Joseph G. Morrell
S. V., George A. Baldwin
J. V., David Baisley
Delegate:
John R. Wofield
Alternate:
William C. Johnson

Post No. 162 — Canandaigua
Com., Orson L. Babbitt
S. V., J. W. Booth
J. V., Leroy Ingraham
Delegate:
*D. F. McOmber
Alternate:
A. F. Avery

Post No. 163 — Tottenville
Com., Hubbard R. Yetman

---
* Present.

Post No. 164 — Skaneateles
Com., H. H. Loss
S. V., E. D. Gillett
J. V., Warren Youker
Delegate:
J. A. Barber
Alternate:
E. D. Gillett

Post No. 165 — Elmira
Com., A. B. Cornell
S. V., Henry Newman
J. V., Henry Perry
Delegate:
Chas. C. Spaulding
Alternate:
W. R. Jenkins

Post No. 166 — Weedsport
Com., T. S. Barker
S. V., James Harrington
J. V., E. Van Etten
Delegate:
F. M. Hunting
Alternate:
F. D. Barnard

Post No. 167 — Norwood
Com., H. H. Bailey
S. V., J. A. Rutherford
J. V., Ralph Amos
Delegate:
Ralph Amos

Post No. 168 — Highland
Com., Edmund Paltridge
S. V., Henry Elting
J. V., Joseph Simpson

Delegate:
Aaron Rhoads
Alternate:
Mark Rose

Post No. 169 — Hermon
Com., F. A. Stalbird
S. V., Tyler Spencer
J. V., A. P. Thurston
Delegate:
W. A. Leonard
Alternate:
Tyler Spencer

Post No. 170 — Mt. Vernon
Com., Abraham Minnerly
S. V., Charles W. Van Court
J. V., William H. Caine
Delegate:
*Edward A. Burgoyne
Alternate:
Max W. Korhammer

Post No. 172 — Lafayette
. . . .

Post No. 173 — Clyde
Com., C. H. Bowman
S. V., Abram L. Wood
J. V., Edward Gridley
Delegate:
Abram L. Wood
Alternate:
Edward Gridley

Post No. 174 — Oneida
Com., Orange F. Smith
S. V., Volney Isbell
J. V., Stephen C. Waterman
Delegate:
William S. Leete

---

* Present.

Alternate:

Norman L. Cramer

Post No. 175 — Port Byron

*Com., William H. Root
S. V., Frank P. Hicks
J. V., James H. Moss
Delegate:
Harry B. O'Neil
Alternate:
*Frank Garrity

Post No. 176 — Goshen

. . . .

Post No. 177 — Sidney

*Com., Charles Wood
S. V., R. J. Nechols
J. V., Milton Burrows
Delegate:
C. P. Tryon
Alternate:
O. A. Gifford

Post No. 178 — Middleport

*Com., Squire Wiser
S. V., Alonzo Smith
J. V., Charles Taylor
Delegate:
J. K. Bidleman
Alternate:
F. M. Shelp

Post No. 179 — Haverstraw

Com., Alonzo Bedell
S. V., James M. Floyd
J. V., George W. Mott
Delegate:
*Edward B. Weiant
Alternate:
None given

Post No. 180 — Forks

. . . .

Post No. 182 — New York

*Com., Rev. D. J. McMillan
S. V., Alfred H. Baiseley
J. V., Paul Kaiser
Delegate:
Charles U. Combes
Alternate:
James M. LaCoste

Post No. 183 — Cuba

Com., G. W. Baldwin
S. V., H. F. Clapp
J. V., N. C. McElheney
Delegate:
Marvin Brown
Alternate:
H. F. Clapp

Post No. 184 — Deposit

Com., Milton D. Whitaker
S. V., D. E. Burrows
J. V., Starr B. More
Delegate:
D. K. Dibble
Alternate:
M. C. Russell

Post No. 186 — Alton

. . . .

Post No. 188 — Dexter

*Com., Charles M. Blair
S. V., Chas. Underwood
J. V., Robert Essington
Delegate:
George W. Wood
Alternate:
Albert L. Morgan

* Present.

JOHN McCLOSKEY
Chief Mustering Officer

Post No. 190 — Dalton
Com., C. S. Lynde
S. V., Henry Swender
J. V., Daniel Stieh
Delegate:
Wm. Holmes
Alternate:
B. F. Town

Post No. 191 — Ellenville
Com., John Powers
S. V., Wm. F. Loren
J. V., Wm. H. Bradford
Delegate:
Wm. H. Bradford
Alternate:
L. F. Hall

Post No. 192 — New York
Com., Henry Fera
S. V., Chas. Koehler
J. V., Nicholas Pisbach
Delegate:
Jostrow Alexander
Alternate:
Richard B. Morgner

Post No. 193 — Palmyra
Com., Robert M. Smith
S. V., Clark Barron
J. V., Charles E. Nelson
Delegate:
Joseph S. Benedict
Alternate:
Martin Randolph

Post No. 194 — Canisteo
Com., W. W. Howell
S. V., H. Crane

J. V., O. Doty
Delegate:
O. B. Goff
Alternate:
Albert Summers

Post No. 195 — Belmont
Com., James Johnson
S. V., Wm. Lathram
J. V., Wm. E. Crary
Delegate:
Wm. E. Crary
Alternate:
Hugh Johnson

Post No. 196 — Oxford
*Com., A. B. Bennett
S. V., L. G. Lindsley
J. V., Edgar Waters
Delegate:
Geo. Lamb
Alternate:
*James D. Smith

Post No. 197 — Brooklyn
*Com., John E. Norcross
S. V., Richard A. Maddren
J. V., Joseph McGregor
Delegate:
Wm. L. Griffiths
Peter S. M. Munro
Alternate:
James H. Hopper
Geo. Alex. Hussey

Post No. 198 — Altamont
*Com., John T. Stafford
S. V., David Relyea
J. V., Wm. H. Ketcham

* Present.

4

Delegate:
Newton Ketcham
Alternate:
*Charles W. Wright

Post No. 199 — Whitney Point
. . . .

Post No. 200 — Lowville
*Com., Wm. W. Stevens
S. V., Geo. P. Holmes
J. V., Felix McConwell
Delegate:
Emory Steele
Alternate:
*Wm. A. Rosebush

Post No. 201 —King Ferry
Com., S. C. Bradley
S. V., F. A. Dudley
*J. V., E. W. Stark
Delegate:
*J. B. Dickinson
Alternate:
Chas. H. Hardy

Post No. 202 — Angola
Com., Charles Harper
S. V., Edward Barry
J. V., Charles Wooderson
Delegate:
*C. C. Robinson
Alternate:
Emil Rock

Post No. 204 — Rensselaer
*Com., James E. Johnson
S. V., Jacob Snyder
J. V., Theodore Rhodes
Delegate:

*David Scott
Alternate:
Theodore Rhodes

Post No. 205 — Monticello
*Com., Wm. B. McMillen
S. V., John Waller
J. V., David Dunn
Delegate:
John H. Davis
Alternate:
David Dunn

Post No. 206 — Brooklyn
Com., Jacob Bestetter
S. V., Thomas F. Boyle
J. V., Samuel E. Burr
Delegate:
Charles G. Hall
Alternate:
William Weisner

Post No. 207 — Brooklyn
*Com., Theo. Whiting
S. V., Henry Savage
J. V., Solomon John

Post No. 209 — Walton
*Com., Albert Smith
S. V., Thomas B. Clark
J. V., John R. Beagle
Delegate:
Chas. A. Hubbell
Alternate:
David Hammond

Post No. 210 — Patchogue
Com., Chas. Satterley
S. V., Isaac T. Moore
J. V., Wm. P. Kaler

---

* Present.

Delegate:
Orin B. Smith
Alternate:
Chas. W. Everetts

Post No. 211 — Fairport
Com., J. S. Kelsey
S. V., Ira Brown
J. V., Fred Sinamoos
Delegate:
*Henry M. Grawbarger
Alternate:
A. T. White

Post No. 212 — New Paltz
Com., Wm. H. D. Blake
S. V., Samuel Paltridge
J. V., George H. Mackey
Delegate:
Moses G. Young
Alternate:
Zadoc G. Rhodes

Post No. 213 — Malone
*Com., Robert McC. Miller
S. V., Henry J. Merriam
J. V., Albert C. Hadley
Delegate:
C. H. Totman
Alternate:
E. S. Kelsey

Post No. 214 — Potsdam
*Com., M. M. Corbin
S. V., John McGilveny
Delegate:
*M. V. B. Ives
Alternate:
James Fox

* Present.

Post No. 215 — Saugerties
. . . .

Post No. 216 — Dansville
Com., Oscar Woodruff.

Post No. 217— Sandy Creek
Com., John J. Hollis
S. V., R. G. Soul
J. V., O. J. Woodard
Delegate:
F. D. Tiff
Alternate:

Post No. 218 — Arcade
Com., W. A. Howard
S. V., R. J. Tilton
J. V., A. M. Norton
Delegate:
R. J. Tilton
Alternate:
George Haskell

Post No. 219 — Attica
Com., Elon P. Spink
S. V., John Corey
J. V., Henry Radder
Delegate:
Paul Glor
Alternate:
D. S. Spring

Post No. 220 — North Collins
Com., E. G. Fenton
S. V., James Reed
J. V., Fred Lindon
Delegate:
A. S. Barker
Alternate:
J. S. Warner

Post No. 222 — Olean
Com., S. J. Daniels
S. V., Sylvester Frank
*J. V., W. A. Howell
Delegate:
*B. S. Yard
Alternate:
George H. Lott

Post No. 223 — Gilbertsville
Com., Perry Springer
S. V., W. Scott Gilbert
J. V., Wm. E. Stebbins
Delegate:
*F. H. Musson
Alternate:
S. A. Silvey

Post No. 225 — East Bloomfield
Com., C. E. Taylor
S. V., E. J. Springsteen
J. V., Geo. Gains
Delegate:
E. J. Springsteen
Alternate:
Henry Homes

Post No. 226 — Hornell
*Com., Charles D. Emery
S. V., Thomas A. Williams
J. V., Charles E. Hackett
Delegate:
George Hollands
Alternate:
J. K. Chapman

Post No. 227 — Clinton
Com., W. E. Bowen
S. V., H. H. Milber

J. V., B. F. Bates
Delegate:
C. A. Austin
Alternate:
B. F. Seely

Post No. 228 — Ransomville
*Com., Wm. Luff
S. V., Samuel Traviss
J. V., Mark A. Schoonmaker
Delegate:
George Woods
Alternate:
*W. A. Coulter

Post No. 231 — Brooklyn
Com., Wm. J. Courtney
S. V., Henry Larson
J. V., Thomas McNally
Delegate:
Geo. R. Cranz
Alternate:
Charles Rischoff

Post No. 232 — Ellicottville
. . . .

Post No. 233—Brooklyn
Com., Charles Montgomery
S. V., Frederick K. Altvater
J. V., Ernest Wagner
Delegate:
Adolph H. Schumann

Post No. 234 — New York
Com., Frank R. Battles
S. V., Chas. Lewis
J. V., Geo. E. Bennet
Delegate:
Theo. A. Morse

* Present.

Alternate:
Fred Lewis

Post No. 235 — Avon
Com., Henry A. Nott
S. V., M. C. Watkins
J. V., E. M. Royce
Delegate:
A. H. Smith
Alternate:
M. C. Watkins

Post No. 236 — Brockport
Com., George Williams
S. V., Christian Miller
J. V., Henry Deo
Delegate:
*James Larkin
Alternate:
Henry Schram

Post No. 237 — Fillmore
Com., P. C. Soule, M. D.
Delegate:
Len Hacket
Alternate:
Wm. Rearwin

Post No. 238 — Johnsonburg
Com., J. W. Jones
S. V., F. L. Head
J. V., F. C. Reiber
Delegate:
F. L. Head
Alternate:
Belus Calkins

Post No. 239 — Buffalo
Com., Charles McDowell
*S. V., Charles Weyler

J. V., John Schultz
Delegate:
*Wm. F. Hickey
Alternate:
Joseph Benzino

Post No. 240 — Cohocton
Com., N. J. Wagner
S. V., Wm. H. Rex
J. V., Jacob Wagner
Delegate:
Wm. H. Rex
Alternate:
Edwin H. Wetmore

Post No. 241 — Friendship
Com., Alvia Jordan
S. V., Lewis Stickney
J. V., Marshall Deen
Delegate:
Z. H. Margin
Alternate:
T. C. Carrier

Post No. 246 — Little Valley
Com., C. P. Rice
S. V., M. B. Jones
J. V., Joseph Cullen
Delegate:
*D. H. Gibson
Alternate:
M. B. Jones

Post No. 247 — Bolivar
Com., J. Dunning
S. V., C. W. Williams
J. V., Thomas McKay
Delegate:
Geo. H. Parker

* Present.

Alternate:

J. M. Thompson

Post No. 248 — Bath

Com., Henry J. Redfield

*S. V., Joseph F. Morrison

J. V., John W. Dysert

Delegate:

*John H. Cochrane

Alternates:

Robert Miller

John W. Dysert

Henry C. Koon

Post No. 250 — Ithaca

*Com., George W. Hunt

*S. V., Lafayette Crum

*J. V., W. H. Birdsall

Delegate:

*Ebenezer Miller

Alternate:

John McIntosh

Post No. 251 — Red Creek

Com., D. N. Hunter

S. V., C. Cortright

J. V., H. Wellott

Delegate:

D. D. Peterson

Alternate:

O. J. Frost

Post No. 252 — Ticonderoga

. . . .

Post No. 253 — Gansevoort

Com., A. D. Lord

S. V.,

J. V., J. H. Brown

Delegate:

G. H. Brown

Alternate:

D. Steenburgh

Post No. 254 — Buffalo

Com., John Hoppes

S. V., Edward Smith

*J. V., Radge O'Connor

Delegate:

*M. F. Hutchinson

Alternate:

Henry Waterburg

Post No. 255 — New York

Com., Samuel W. Carr

S. V., Peter W. Mulford

J. V., Hezekiah Bridelman

Delegate:

James H. Emmons

Alternate:

George W. Titus

Post No. 256 — Richfield Springs

Com., W. H. Cadwell

S. V., H. Wolcott

J. V., Wm. Goodridge

Delegate:

Jay Winnie

Alternate:

H. Wolcott

Post No. 257 — Johnstown

Com., James H. Parks

S. V., James Britton

J. V., Jacob Keck

Delegate:

Jeremiah Keck

Alternate:

Jacob Keck

---

* Present.

Post No. 258 — Barker

Com., Wm. S. Thompson

†S. V., W. P. Hoffman

J. V., F. L. Bristol

Delegate:

S. E. Armstrong

Alternate:

L. J. Gross

Post No. 259 — New York

*Com., Theodore H. Ernst

S. V., John J. Tuttle

*J. V., Morris Hauff

Delegate:

*John W. England

Alternate:

Charles Dickinson

Post No. 260 — Groton

*Com., Thomas B. Hopkins

S. V., B. F. Hatch

J. V., D. O. Clough

Delegate:

*George B. Close

Alternate:

Oliver Avery

Post No. 262 — Redfield

Com., S. J. Griffith

S. V., Norman Randall

J. V., Joseph Bammert

Delegate:

S. J. Griffith

Alternate:

Norman Randall

Post No. 263 — Hunter

Com., F. A. Barber

S. V., George B. Goodrich

J. V., George Ruoff

Delegate:

Jacob Stotz

Alternate:

E. W. Fisher

Post No. 264 — New York

*Com., John P. Heintz

*S. V., Herrman Lange

*J. V., Charles J. Martin

Delegate:

Arnold Dalon

Alternate:

Alexander Mueller

Post No. 266 — Middletown

Com., A. B. Wheeler

S. V., A. S. Wilson

J. V., N. M. Bredhead

Delegate:

Joseph Kniffin

Alternate:

Stephen Slater

Post No. 267 — Granville

Com., William Cooper

S. V., A. Leffingwell

J. V., Leroy L. Barnard

Delegate:

Leroy L. Barnard

Alternate:

William Miller

Post No. 269 — Carthage

Com., William Ohoro

S. V., George Christman

J. V., Samuel M. Knowles

Delegate:

J. M. Corwin

* Present.

Alternate:
David Ash

Post No. 270 — Spencerport

*Com., Jacob Schaffer
*S. V., Sigmund Stettner
*J. V., Warren Nelson
Delegate:
Charles Noble
Alternate:
....

Post No. 271 — Fulton

*Com., J. H. Stewart
S. V., George Coles
J. V., Patrick Casey
Delegate:
Philip Dietrick
Alternate:
....

Post No. 272 — Hamilton

Com., David Williams
S. V., Isaac Marsh
J. V., Thomas Smith
Delegate:
R. A. Risley
Alternate:
L. J. Martin

Post No. 273 — Henderson
....

Post No. 274 — Sag Harbor

Com., G. C. Morris
S. V., A. E. Topping
J. V., —————
Delegate:
Albert E. Topping
Alternate:
Theo. F. Haines

Post No. 275 — West Webster
....

Post No. 276 — Corning

*Com., A. A. King
S. V., S. B. Shaddock
J. V., F. M. Copp
Delegate:
Jerome Billington
Alternate:
J. C. Hakes

Post No. 278 — Baldwinsville

Com., Alonzo C. Taylor
S. V., Patrick Hurley
J. V., Jerry Reals
Delegate:
A. R. Failing
Alternate:
William Rodgers

Post No. 279 — Port Jervis

Com., F. S. Goble
S. V., C. D. Frazer
J. V., E. Loureaux
Delegate:
Charles D. Frazer
Alternate:
John Sheane

Post No. 280 — Downsville

Com., S. E. Hunter
S. V., W. P. Hotchkiss
J. V., M. C. Radeker
Delegate:
W. S. Sprague
Alternate:
M. C. Radeker

* Present.

Post No. 281 — North Tonawanda
*Com., J. P. Christgau
S. V., W. J. Howard
J. V., Ed. Ball
Delegate:
A. P. Austen
Alternate:
J. P. Christgau

Post No. 282 — Kennedy
Com., Sumner A. Smith
S. V., Chas. H. Taylor
J. V., Nathan C. Cobb
Delegate:
Chas. B. Sturdevant
Alternate:
Alonzo Bain

Post No. 283 — Long Island City
Com., K. F. Macfarlane
S. V., Geo. W. Smith
J. V., Henry Kelley
Delegate:
Joseph M. Zarmon
Alternate:
Henry Kelley

Post No. 284 — Malone
Com., Thomas Denio
S. V., Luke Tebo
J. V., Peter Roberts
Delegate:
H. N. Barrett
Alternate:
Luke Tebo

Post No. 285 — Jamestown
*Com., Robert Little
S. V., F. E. Pennock

J. V., Adam Ports
Delegate:
Julius M. Shaw
John A. Brown
*S. J. Woodward
Rev. M. V. Stone
Alternate:
William Callahan
Adam Ports
*Cyrus W. Lord
Samuel W. Willard

Post No. 286 — Brooklyn
*Com., Alonzo D. Mohr
S. V., Andrew Johnson
J. V., Peter T. Francisco
Delegate:
Rev. Thomas J. Whitaker
Alternate:
Isaac C. Osborne

Post No. 287 — Cattaraugus
. . . .

Post No. 288 — Pittsfield
Com., John B. Bacon
S. V., Wm. S. Williams
J. V., Imos Sweeten
Delegate:
A. M. Newton
Alternate:
Imos Sweeten

Post No. 289 — Broadalbin
Com., J. O. Best
S. V., Wm. Dingman
J. V., David Mulligan
Delegate:
Lorenzo Ecker

* Present.

Alternate:
Wm. Davis

Post No. 290 — Corinth
Com., Thomas Peak
*S· V., Ransford Densmore
J. V., George Holmes
Delegate:
Ransford Densmore
Alternate:
D. W. Kendell

Post No. 291 — South Butler
. . . .

Post No. 292 — Brocton
Com., A. Mathews
S. V., T. K. Titus
J. V., S. P. Mors
Delegate:
A. A. Fay
Alternate:
D. T. Raub

Post No. 293 — Rockland
Com., Joseph Cammer
S. V., John Gray
J. V., Lewis Snyder
Delegate:
J. D. W. M. Decker
Alternate:
M. P. Bennett

Post No. 294 — Hoosick Falls
Com., John Gibson
*S. V., J. H. Lapins
J. V., Alonzo Lohnes
Delegate:
Giles Brown

Alternate:
Philip Walters

Post No. 295 — Sherman
Com., Henry Mina
S. V., Peter Castles
J. V., William Robins
Delegate:
. . . .
Alternate:
. . . .

Post No. 296 — Canaseraga
Com., Byron Bennett
S. V., I. I. Green
J. V., Charles Chappel
Delegate:
Geo. R. Dolloph
Alternate:
N. S. Fay

Post No. 297 — Randolph
Com., G. F. Gould
S. V., D. M. Graves
J. V., James Helms
Delegate:
S. Z. Fisher
Alternate:
A. G. Dow, Jr.

Post No. 298 — Kendall
. . . .

Post No. 299 — Batavia
Com., W. J. Gilboy
S. V., W. H. Hunn
J. V., John Stavely
Delegate:
*D. M. Jones

---

* Present.

Alternate:
W. H. Hunn

Post No. 300 — Black River
Com., W. J. Horton
S. V., Geo. A. Dyer
J. V., A. S. Gibson
Delegate:
J. St. Temis
Alternate:
M. M. Catwell

Post No. 301 — Middletown
Com., Louis Wientz
*S. V., Francis A. Clarke
J. V., A. J. Hornbeck
Delegate:
*A. B. Wilbur
Alternate:
Francis A. Clarke

Post No. 302 —Brewster
J. V., Com., Frank Wells

Post No. 303 — Cheshire
Com., T. C. Townsend
S. V., R. W. Jameson
J. V., ————
Delegate:
Rudolph Senn
Alternate:
S. E. Nott

Post No. 306 — Theresa
*Com., W. F. Swann
S. V., Geo. Chaumont
J. V., Simeon Dayly
Delegate:
George Chaumont

Alternate:
John Seymore

Post No. 307 — New York
Com., John K. Darragh
S. V., James Grove
J. V., Cornelius Curtin
Delegate:
Andrew J. Walling
Alternate:
Henry J. Humphreys

Post No. 309 — Cambridge
Com., Willard Lawton
S. V., Gardner Bentley
J. V., Albert Corbett
Delegate:
John Haslem
Alternate:
James Leigh

Post No. 310 — Leon
Com., Orin W. Bump
S. V., H. B. Holister
J. V., H. J. Trumbell
Delegate:
C. D. Kelley
Alternate:
Henry Cunningham

Post No. 311 — Liberty
Com., Joel C. Fisk
S. V., Dubois J. Vanwagner
J. V., Ira Porter
Delegate:
*John A. Darbee
Alternate:
Joseph Rampey

* Present.

Post No. 313 —New York
*Com., Christopher A. Farrell
S. V., James O. Connor
J. V., Maurice D. Mendoza
Delegate:
Isaac Costa
Alternate:
*James J· Flood

Post No. 314—Wayland
. . . .

Post No. 316 — Luzerne
Com., E. George Dunklee
S. V., James H. Olds
J. V., Elias Ives
Delegate:
Andrew J, Aldrich
Alternate:
Henry Lafayette

Post No. 317 — Sinclairville
. . . .

Post No. 320 — Williamson
Com., H. N. Burr
S. V., C. C. Hudson
J. V., Henry Briton
Delegate:
C. L. Tassell
Alternate:
H. N. Burr

Post No. 323 — Watertown
Com., Orville J. Van Wormer
S. V., Z. B. Merriam
J. V., James McCauley
Delegate:
Simeon W. Sargeant

Alternate:
*Thos. T. Ballard

Post No. 324 — Westfield
Com., James Bond
S. V., Jere Mahle
J. V., B. H. Beadle
Delegate:
*W. H. Walker
Alternate:
Jere Mahle

Post No. 325 — Ovid
*Com., Henry Covert
S. V., Wm. T. Balbay
J. V., D. C. Marvin
Delegate:
*John W. Swarthout
Alternate:
D. C. Marvin

Post No. 326 — Greenwich
Com., George L. Tucker
S. V., Edwin R. Mosher
J. V., Martin Bennett
Delegate:
Frank Drogan
Alternate:
Edward Gleason

Post No. 327 — Brooklyn
*Com., Donald A. Manson
S. V., John W. Reid
*J. V., Charles L. Clark
Delegates:
*Lewis S. Pilcher
William D. Dickey
*Birt F. Parsons

* Present.

*Alexander Barnie
*Henry C. Broas
  Alternates:
George W. Brush
*William C. Peckham
Miles O'Reilly
Crighton B. French
John Murphy

  Post No. 330 — New York
*Com., Thos. H. Stritch
*S. V., Michael J. Cummerford
J. V., George A. Stewart
  Delegate:
John Rotchford
  Alternate:
Christian Nelly

  Post No. 332 — Standards
Com., Seth Graves
S. V., John Bestner
J. V., Dan Cornwell
  Delegate:
E. Van Nostrand
  Alternate:
John Lestner

  Post No. 333 — Whitesville
Com., Albertus Burr
*S. V., Ransom Fish
J. V., Elias Ketcham
  Delegate:
*George B. Herrick
  Alternate:
Albert L. Robbins

  Post No. 335 — Fort Ann
Com., H. B. Coleman
S. V., H. W. Harrington
J. V., James Cunningham

  Delegate:
A. C. Vaughan
  Alternate:
O. J. Belden

  Post No. 336 — Wellsville
*Com., George H. Blackman
*S. V., Ira S. Crandall
*J. V., Edwin H. Easton
  Delegate:
Adelbert D. Lewis
  Alternate:
*Francis Barnes

  Post No. 338 — Troy
Com., George M. Lemon
*S. V., Rice C. Bull
J. V., A. D. Hobbs
  Delegate:
Ezra Stillman
  Alternate:
Henry S. Scofield

  Post No. 341 — Odessa
*Com., John L. Halpin
S. V., Reuben Graves
J. V., O. O. Gardner
  Delegate:
*O. O. Gardner
  Alternate:
Wm. Fitzgerald

  Post No. 346 — Canton
*Com., R. W. Barrows
S. V., H. J. Cook
J. V., Wm. Heckles
  Delegate:
*D. W. Sherwin
  Alternate:
H. J. Cook

* Present.

Post No. 349 — Hartland
*Com., George Humphrey
S. V., O. B. Hays
J. V., James Mayne
Delegate:
O. B. Hays
Alternate:
A. K. Welsher

Post No. 350 — Union
*Com., P. N. Pierson
S. V., Nelson Baird
J. V., Theodore Bayless
Delegate:
*H. T. Dunbar
Alternate:
James Monroe

Post No. 352 — Saranac
Com., J. H. Brissette
S. V., H. Fifield
J. V., Rufus Robinson
Delegate:
F. J. Ayers
Alternate:
C. W. Ormsby

Post No. 353 — Greenport
. . . .

Post No. 354 — Ogdensburg
*Com., James C. Birge
S. V., David H. Lyon
J. V., George A. Tann
Delegate:
Charles Snyder
Alternate:
Obadiah C. Platt

Post No. 356 — St. Johnsville
Com., C. W. Scudder
S. V., J. A. Barker
J. V., John Coy
Delegate:
C. M. Lambert
Alternate:
Daniel Clemons

Post No. 357 — Great Valley

Post No. 358 — Marietta
*Com., Elijah H. Baker
S. V., I. W. Davey
J. V., Seymour Pierce
Delegate:
Patrick Heenan
Alternate:
Abram Waldron

Post No. 359 — Gowanda
Com., L. W. Henry
S. V., A. T. Groat
J. V., M. Matthews
Delegate:
Melvin Matthews
Alternate:
Geo. Weiser

Post No. 360 — Sackett's Harbor
. . . .

Post No. 362 — Brooklyn
Com., John S. Hayes
S. V., James E. Morgan
J. V., David T. While
• Delegate
John S. Hayes
Alternate:
Chas. T. Latimer

* Present.

Post No. 363 — Brushton
Com., H. P. Steenberge
S. V., Standish Steenberge
J. V., J. B. Greene
Delegate:
A. B. Allen
Alternate:
H. J. Johnson

Post No. 364 — West Winfield
Com., Dennis A. Dewey
S. V., Evan Evans
J. V., O. H. Wilcox
Delegate:
J. A. Jones
Alternate:
James Patterson

Post No. 365 — Glen Cove
Com., John W. Campbell
S. V., W. M. Searing
J. V., Wilbur Southern
Delegate:
John W. Campbell
Alternate:
James Harroll

Post No. 366 — Plattsburg
Com., John H. Moffit
S. V., Moses Bourdon
J. V., B. Myers
Delegate:
Moses Bourdon
Alternate:
W. H. Harris

Post No. 367 — Mexico
Com., W. S. Sweetland
S. V., Daniel Barnard

*J. V., Wm. Tilepaugh
Delegate:
Wm. E. Wanik
Alternate:
E. P. Stevens

Post No. 368 — Jamaica
Com., William H. Beers
S. V., LeRoy W. Swartwood
J. V., John H. Hilliker
Delegate:
John H. Hilliker
Alternate:
Thomas S. Rider

Post No. 369 — Honeoye Falls
*Com., Edwin Warren
S. V., Marvin Peck
J. V., C. W. Hudson
Delegate:
Charles S. Chambers
Alternate:
C. W. Hudson

Post No. 370 — Argyle
Com., James A. Harsha
S. V., J. H. Woodcock
J. V., Robert Smith
Delegate:
. . . .
Alternate:
. . . .

Post No. 372 — Addison
Com., M. E. Crane
S. V., D. O. Keefe
J. V., Geo. Osborne
Delegate:
Eugene L. Alben

* Present.

Alternate:
Edward P. Seamon

Post No. 373 — Antwerp
. . . .

Post No. 374 — Mooers Forks
. . . .

Post No. 376 — De Ruyter
Com., D. C., Clark
*S. V., Eugene Rider
*J. V., James Hunt
Delegate:
E. Rider
Alternate:
James Hunt

Post No. 378 — Port Chester
*Com., William Croft
S. V., Nicholas Fox
J. V., John E. Weed
Delegate:
*William H. Hyler
Alternate:
Clark S. Higgins

Post No. 379 — Jay
. . . .

Post No. 380 — Salamanca
. . . .

Post No. 381 — Adams
Com., Daniel D. Bassett
S. V., Peter Sheldon
J. V., Geo. L. Bannister
Delegate:
*A. C. Dack
Alternate:
- Albert G. Glass

* Present.

Post No. 382 — Livonia
. .'. . . . .

Post No. 383 — Candor
Com., John H. Wheeler
S. V., Geo. B. Pumpelly
J. V. D. P. Jackson
Delegate:
J. K. Holly
Alternate:
Geo. B. Pumpelly

Post No. 385 — Port Leyden
Com., C. M. Thomas
S. V., C. J. Gookins
J. V., Patrick Keahane
Delegate:
Harris Schell
Alternate:
E. H. Sanyer

Post No. 386 — South Dayton
Com., Charles Shults
S. V., D. O. Yates
J. V.,
Delegate:
Charles Eadick
Alternate:
Charles Shults

Post No. 387 — Orwell
. . . .

Post No. 389 — Panama
Com., Josiah R. Casselman
S. V., Milo J. Tripp
J. V., William Stevens
Delegate:
Ambrose Cross

Alternate:

Milo Tripp

Post No. 390 — Delevan

. . . .

Post No. 391 — Rochester

Com., Albert R. Fowler

S. V., Horace G. Osborne

J. V., Fred B. Albro

Delegate:

*N. C. Fulton

Alternate:

Samuel McAuliffe

Post No. 392 — Geneseo

Com., George S. Williams

S. V., Richard M. Jones

J. V., Minard Arville

Delegate:

James W. Wadsworth

Alternate:

Gilbert I. Dean

Post No. 393 — Dunkirk

Com., Thos. J. Arevill

S. V., Peter Cadro

J. V., F. B. Kinner

Delegate:

Oscar Wheelock

Alternate:

Chas. E. Fell

Post No. 394 — New York

*Com., Michael B. Wood

S. V., William Hoening

J. V., Thomas Quinlan

Delegate:

*David Thom

Alternate:

Augustus Sharp

Post No. 395 — Schroon Lake

. . . .

Post No. 397 — Rochester

Com., Henry Elson

*S. V., Alfred J. Stone

*J. V., John Warren

Delegates:

*C. C. Brownell

*J. B. Teller

Alternates:

G. A. Lent

J. P. Denniston

Post No. 398 — Akron

. . . .

Post No. 399 — Brooklyn

Com., W. P. Eshleman

S. V., William Keck

J. V., Martin Elbert

Delegate:

*Edward W. Castell

Alternate:

Henry Staples

Post No. 402 — New York

Com., S. H. Milddenberg

S. V., Thomas Donohue

J. V., Alfred M. Graff

Delegate:

Alfred M. Graff

Alternate:

Wm. Elkinhans

Post No. 403 — Fredonia

Com., Jesse Putnam

S. V., Charles E. Randall

J. V., Clark Wilcox

* Present.

Delegate:
Charles E. Randall
Alternate:
George Harris, M. D.

Post No. 404 — Herkimer

Com., S. C. Clobridge
S. V., Thos. R. Petrie
J. V., James F. Whiting
Delegate:
*Clinton Beckwith
Alternate:
John Q. Adams

Post No. 406 — Ontario

Com., J. W. Speller
S. V., Finley Finkle
J. V., Alfred Esley
Delegate:
Wm. Birdsall
Alternate:
H. E. Stanford

Post No. 408 — New York

Com., John Muller
S. V., Adam Wurster
J. V., John H. Reinwell
Delegate:
John T. Haas
Alternate:
. . . .

Post No. 409 — Rochester

Com., William McVeen
S. V., Martin A. Vickery
J. V., Thomas W. Wark
Delegate:
James Hason
Alternate:
Richard Kingston

Post No. 410 — Clayton

Com., John B. Bezna
S. V., Merick Wiley
J. V., Darwin V. Olney
Delegate:
Daniel D. Butts
Alternate:
John B. Bezna

Post No: 411 — Mooers

Com., E. J. Steinburge
S. V., Geo. Kaufman
J. V., Chas. Bosroth
Delegate:
E. J. Steinburge
Alternate:
Charles Deal

Post No. 412 — Bergen

Com., Alfred F. Bennett
S. V., S. K. Green
J. V., George Redenger
Delegate:
Thomas Clare
Alternate:
Samuel Parnell

Post No. 413 — Sanquoit

Com., William E. Kimball
S. V., Richard Gillonen
J. V., Henry A. Fisk
Delegate:
L. E. Vinegar
Alternate:
Henry Dwyer

Post No. 414 — Bliss

Com., J. D. Eager
S. V., James S. Austin

* Present.

J. V., Milton Burnap
Delegate:
James S. Austin
Alternate:
Milton Burney

Post No. 415 — Morristown
Com., Simon Plumsteel
S. V., John Lavine
J. V., John Lavine
Delegate:
C. C., Fitch
Alternate:
John Lavine

Post No. 416 — Millport
Com., R. B. Davidson
S. V., Chas. Knott
J. V., A. L. Kenyon
Delegate:
A. L. Kenyon
Alternate:
Chas. Knott

Post No. 417 — Nunda
*Com., E. L. Cook
S. V., H. P. Burnell
*J. V., John Halleran
Delegate:
*C. K. Sanders
Alternate:
R. K. Bergen

Post No. 418 — Central Square
Com., Lyman Morgan
S. V., Cowen Ladd
J. V., Wm. Shrader
Delegate:
*Wm. Church

Alternate:
W. A. Scudder

Post No. 421 — Winthrop
Com., Milo H. Felton
S. V., James Campbell
J. V., Hugh Cusser
Delegate:
....
Alternate:
....

Post No. 423 — Valois
....

Post No. 424 — Alexandria Bay
Com., David H. Taylor
S. V., S. Makepease
J. V., C. Ahles
Delegate:
Oliver H. Perry
Alternate:
S. Makepease

Post No. 425 — Massena
Com., Edwin W. Kinney
S. V., Levi Carbino
J. V., Orick M. Hosmer
Delegate:
Benjamin Nichols
Alternate:
John A. Shampine

Post No. 426 — Northport
Com., N. S. Ackerly
S. V., Wm. E. Mulford
J. V., Geo. Gerard
Delegate:
Chas. L. Smith

* Present.

Alternate:

A. C. Tillitson

Post No. 427 — Rushford

Com., Byron Van Name

S. V., A. L. Litchard

J. V., P. A. Taylor

Delegate:

A. L. Litchard

Alternate:

W. W. Bush

Post No. 428 — Alfred

Com., Thos. T. Burdick

S. V., A. C. Rogers

J. V., H. M. Davis

Delegate:

Isaac M. Langworthy

Alternate:

J. F. Langworthy

Post No. 429 — Stockton

Com., J. D. Wilder

S. V., T. C. Williams

J. V., Israel Raymond

Delegate:

T. C. Bloomfield

Alternate:

Frank Pangborn

Post No. 431 — Grahamsville

Com., C. D. Hall

S. V., H. A. Everitt

J. V., J. C. Donaldson

Delegate:

G. F. Curry

Alternate:

*W. A. Briggs

Post No. 432 — Clarence

*Com., I. U. Miller

S. V., D. S. Fuller

J. V., O. Fanner

Delegate:

John Fidinger

Alternate:

C. A. Tucker

Post No. 434 — Vermillion

*Com., W. H. Belchamber

S. V., V. Dubois

J. V., W. W. Fish

Delegate:

*C. Sherman

Alternate:

W. W. Fish

Post No. 435 — Brooklyn

Com., James D. Bell

*S. V., Wm. J. Thompson

*J. V., Alfred L. Bennett

Delegates:

*Edwin H. Squires

*William B. Price

Alternates:

Edward J. Hoffman

William Constans

Post No. 436 — New York

*Com., Henry Montague

S. V., Wm. H. Allen

J. V., August Hoffman

Delegate:

*William Finley

Alternate:

John S. Nallay

---

* Present.

Post No. 438 — Interlaken

*Com., Theo. P. Kellogg
S. V., John L. Ryno
J. V., Darwin McDuffie
Delegate:
*John L. Ryno
Alternate:
E. K. Holton

Post No. 439 — Forestville

. . . .

Post No. 440 — Hamburg

Com., Samuel R. Saunders
S. V., Henry Michael
J. V., Joseph Taylor
Delegate:
Dr. C. W. Bourne
Alternate:
Andrew Stein

Post No. 441 — Three Mile Bay

*Com., John M. Wilcox
S. V., Henry Selter
J. V., Byron Persons
Delegate:
L. C. Angell
Alternate:

. . . .

Post No. 442 — McDonough

Com., H. L. Bentley
S. V., H. A. Jackson
J. V., Harrison Phillips
Delegate:
James S. Tennant
Alternate:
Harrison Phillips

Post No. 443 — Brooklyn

Com., John H. Bock
S. V., Charles A. Lester
J. V., John T. Strube
Delegate:
Charles H. Hawxhurst
Alternate:
*Jeremiah Costello

Post No. 444 — Marion

Com., F. E. Peck
S. V., L. P. Deuel
J. V., Isaac Morrison
Delegate:
W. W. Moon
Alternate:
L. P. Deuel

Post No. 445 — Lodi

*Com., Wm. B. Clawson
*S. V., Wallace Sears
*J. V., A. L. Beach
Delegate:
Wallace Sears
Alternate:
O. E. Slaght

Post No. 448 — Brookfield

Com., Elmer Langworthy
S. V., J. N. Morgan
J. V., H. E. Sprague
Delegate:
L. D. Morgan
Alternate:
N. A. Crandall

Post No. 450 — Macedon

. . . .

* Present.

Post No. 451 — College Point
Com., Charles Buser
S. V., Fred Wilkins
J. V., Edwin A. Snyder
Delegate:

. . . .

Alternate:

. . . .

Post No. 455 — Rochester
*Com., I. H. Chatfield
S. V., Hiram Krill
J. V., G. Bohlman
Delegate:
*James B. Williams
Alternate:
W. A. Ricker

Post No. 456 — South Otselic
*Com., D. M. Webster
S. V., Leroy Soule
J. V., Harvey Stearns
Delegate:
Harvey Stearns
Alternate:
Cyrus R. Warner

Post No. 457 — Cicero
*W. B. West
S. V., W. F. Hamilton
J. V., John Rauscher
Delegate:
*R. E. Luce
Alternate:
D. Smith

Post No. 458 — New York
*Com., Andrew Boyd
S. V., Chas. J. Evers

J. V., H. P. Niebuhr
Delegate:
J. B. Trainer
Alternate:
Chas Troy

Post No. 459 — Mount Morris
*Com., Chas. D. Chilson
S. V., John S. Baker
J. V., H. G. Chamberlain
Delegate:
*Charles Harding
Alternate:
Richard Redmond

Post No. 461 — Waverly
Com., J. W. Emblem
S. V., Jacob F. Edick
J. V., Richard Evans
Delegate:
B. W. Bonnell
Alternate:
*George M. Paige

Post No. 464 — Spencer
*Com., Wm. Tucker
*S. V., A. Southwick
J. V., J. T· Hyers
Delegate:
*J. H. Alderman
Alternate:
A. Southwick

Post No. 466 — White Plains
*Com., E. B. Long
S. V., P. Gilroy
J. V., C. LeViness

---

* Present.

Delegate:
*James S. Snedeker
Alternate:
D. W. Bogart

Post No. 467 — Amenia

Com., James Newman
S. V., Joseph Wooley
J. V., Lewis Buckley
Delegate:
Bernard Gilroy
Alternate:
James Newman

Post No. 470 — Hammondsport

*Com., Hiram Morrison
S. V., G. F. Lane
J. V., G. A. Austin
Delegate:
*Levi Bassett
Alternate:
Robert Beck

Post No. 471 — Troy

Com., Wm. Rochester
*S. V., Alfred J. Moss
J. V., James Fagin
Delegate:
Alfred J. Moss
Alternate:
*Frederick Weaver

Post No. 472 — Hamilton, Canada

. . . .

Post No. 475 — Caton

. . . .

Post No. 476 — McGrawville

Com., John W. Adams
S. V., N. W. Smith

J. V., Geo. W. Chapin
Delegate:
N. W. Smith
Alternate:
I. J. Walker

Post No. 477 — Grand Gorge

. . . .

Post No. 478 — Glenwood

. . . .

Post No. 481 — Andover

Com., John Deming
S. V., F. C. Davis
J. V., I. Remington
Delegate:
U. W. Stratton
Alternate:
Wm. McDonough

Post No. 482 — Camden

Com., W. W. Elden
S. V., John Lobdell
J. V., A. H. Keningson
Delegate:
L. F. Empey
Alternate:
Warner Yeomans

Post No. 483 — Hancock

Com., W. H. Smith
S. V., Levi Biggs
J. V., James Rose
Delegate:
*Elias Vansteenberg
Alternate:
Robert Gill

Post No. 484 — Keeseville

. . . .

* Present.

Post No. 486 — Penn Yan

*Com., Frank Danes
S. V., Chas. W. Morgan
J. V., James Tames
Delegate:
*John Whitaker
Alternate:
Geo. F. Mahon

Post No. 487 — Schaghticoke

*Com., Lewis Hunt
S. V., John Hines
J. V., Henry Simmons
Delegate:
John Hines
Alternate:
S. V., Edgar F. Fields

Post No. 488 — Castile

J. V·, Com., E. D. H. Laird
Delegate:
H. T. Castle
Alternate:

. . . .

Post No. 491 — Fort Edward

Com., George Scott
S. V., Henry Snyder
J. V., Fred Aubrey
Delegate:
David H. King
Alternate:
Henry Snyder

Post No. 493 — Sherburne

*Com., Richard H. Griffin
*S. V., Wm. Friar
J. V., Curtis Coggeshall

Delégate:
Wm. Friar
Alternate:

. . . .

Post No. 494 — Union Springs

*Com., Chas. L. Shergur
S. V., Ed. Powers
*J. V., L. Hoff
Delegate:
Martin Myders
Alternate:
Nathaniel Hoaglan

Post No. 495 — Milton

*Com., C. M. Woolsey
S. V., L. C. Beam
J. V., J. C. Merritt
Delegate:
E. R. Martin
Alternate:
J. C. Merritt

Post No. 496 — Tarrytown

*Com., Arthur Humphreys
S. V., Sylvester Gesner
J. V., Peter See
Delegate:

. . . .

Alternate:

. . . .

Post No. 499 — Brooklyn

*Com., Thos. J. McConekey
*S. V., Henry M. Maguire
*J. V., Chas. D. Myers
Delegate:
Henry M. Maguire
Alternate:
John Stack

---

* Present.

Post No. 500 — Brooklyn
*Com., Wm. Knappmann
*S. V., John A. Williams
*J. V., James F. O'Hara
  Delegate:
James F. O'Hara
  Alternate:
Chas. F. Wilcox

Post No. 501 — Savannah
. . . .

Post No. 502 — Angelica
Com., S. D. Travis
S. V., J. N. Deming
J. V., Daniel Deming
  Delegate:
*L. S. Crandall
  Alternate:
*Alex Lytle

Post No. 504 — St. Regis Falls
Com., Adnor Somers
S. V., Charles Gnac
J. V., O. F. Brabon
  Delegate:
B. C. Somers
  Alternate:
Antwine Young

Post No. 505 — Halsey Valley
Com., Francis A. Cooper
S. V., C. M. Taylor
J. V., W. H. Goodwin
  Delegate:
. . . .
  Alternate:
. . . .

Post No. 506 — East Aurora
*Com., Arthur B. Avery
S. V., George Edwards
*J. V., Joseph C. Kent
  Delegate:
Abram Dimon
  Alternate:
James B. Pattingell

Post No. 507 — Avoca
*Com., Marcus S. Walker
S. V., John Heimrath
J. V., W. H. Wood
  Delegate:
J. M. Willis
  Alternate:
J. S. Overhiser

Post No. 508 — Franklinvlle
Com., James Dempsey
S. V., Allen Williams
J. V., Valories Swift
  Delegate:
William Ely
  Alternate:
Allen Williams

Post No. 509 — New Rochelle
. . . .

Post No. 514 — Catskill
Com., John W. Van Leuven
*S. V., A. Sidney Thomas
J. V., John N. King
  Delegate:
A. Sidney Thomas
  Alternate:
*William C. Tice

---

* Present.

Post No. 515 — Watkins

*Com., E. M. Morse
S. V., Henry Wait
J. V., J. L. Terrill
Delegate:
*C. W. Hurd
Alternate:
S. B. Brown

Post No. 516 — New York

*Com., George Blair
*S. V., Henry J. Karney
J. V., John D. R. Keenan
Delegate:
Henry J. Kearney
Alternate:
John D. R. Keenan

Post No. 518 — Springwater

Com., Harrison E. Allen
S. V., Abraham J. Swarts
J. V., John Steffy
Delegate:
Scott W. Snyder
Alternate:
Abraham J. Swarts

Post No. 521 — Suffern

Com., Thomas W. Hilyer
S. V., Gustave Hart
J. V., Judson Young
Delegate:
John G. Turrill
Alternate:
Wm. F. Mann

Post No. 523 — Silver Creek

*Com., W. H. Bartlett
S. V., George Dean

J. V., Christian Ave
Delegate:
*Ira D. Rowley
Alternate:
Lafayette Green

Post No. 524 — Port Richmond

Com., Bernard Mullin
S. V., John S. Dougherty
J. V., John McCrum
Delegate:
Joseph A. Sullivan
Alternate:
R. D. Waldo

Post No. 525 — Copenhagen

Com., A. C. Bickford
S. V., John White
J. V., D. B. Ely
Delegate:
C. E. Chamberlain
Alternate:
Judson C. Hart

Post No. 526 — Vernon

Com., George G. Clark
S. V., F. G. Pepper
J. V., Geo. T. Earl
Delegate:
Fred Graves
Alternate:
*Jessie Fort

Post No. 527 — Freeport

Com., William H. Patterson
S. V., William N. Tabb
J. V., James H. Johnson
Delegate:
Elbert B. Rose

---

* Present.

Alternate:
R. S. Seckerson

Post No. 528 — Elizabethtown
Com., D. S. French
S. V., S. A. West
J. V., A. J. Durand
Delegate:
Lawrence Redmond
Alternate:
S. A. West

Post No. 531 — Long Lake
Com., W. D. Jennings
S. V., B. F. Emerson
J. V., Geo. Wilson
Delegate:
Geo. Wilson
Alternate:
C. B. Harmer

Post No. 532 — Toronto
Com., Thomas Hughes
S. V., John Boyce
J. V., J. H. Davidson
Delegate:
. . . .
Alternate:
. . . .

Post No. 533 — Crown Point
*Com., E. J. Barker
S. V., E. H. Bailey
J. V., W. H. Cook
Delegate:
R. W. Whitford
Alternate:
Henry Ruin

Post No. 534 — Brooklyn
Com., Samuel Irvine
*S. V., Francis J. Raye
*J. V., David Lloyd
Delegate:
*Wm. H. Cornell
Alternate:
Francis J. Raye

Post No. 535 — Pulteney
*Com., J. C. Albright
S. V., G. S. Prentiss
J. V., J. H. Gibson
Delegate
John Prentiss
Alternate:
*E. A. Prentiss

Post No. 538 — Bay Shore
*Com., William W. Hulse
S. V., ——————
J. V., Frank W. Dorsee
Delegate:
Frank W. Dorsee
Alternate:
. . . .

Post No. 539 — Chatham
Com., P. H. Garrity
S. V., D. F. Bunk
J. V., W. H. Watson
Delegate:
John E. Mattoon
Alternate:
James Lunnen

Post No. 542 — Buffalo
Com., Gregory J. Langmeyer
S. V., George L. Waterman

* Present.

J. V., Andrew Schmitz
Delegate:
*Adam J. Wagner
Alternate:
Garrett Breier

Post No. 543 — Washingtonville
Com., Francis R. McGreen
S. V., James H. Smith
J. V., Howard Youngblood
Delegate:
Augustus Denniston
Alternate:
John G. Brooks

Post No. 544 — Hempstead
*Com., Thos. V. Smith
S. V., William Seaman
J. V., Joseph P. Reed
Delegate:
George Beil
Alternate:
Thos. P. Smith

Post No. 546 — Cornwall-on-Hudson
Com., Thomas Taft
S. V., Geo. Chatfield
J. V., Geo. F. Dobiecki
Delegate:
James C. Haggerty
Alternate:
Eli McCreery

Post No. 549 — Savona
Com., Adam Vose
S. V., M. R. Westcott
J. V., J. I. Helm
Delegate:
A. S. Gould

Alternate:
D. F. French

Post No. 551 — Taberg
Com., Frank Bassett
S. V., Abram Bergy
J. V., Alfred Barker
Delegate:
Joseph Chisam
Alternate:
Chancy Banning

Post No. 553 — Holland
Com., B. M. Stanton
S. V., H. Selleck
J. V., A. J. Sweetapple
Delegate:
Wm. H. Burnett
Alternate:
H. Burlingame

Post No. 555 — Wellsburg
Com., D. Morley
S. V., J. S. Wilcox
J. V., C. Ostrander
Delegate:
D. Morley
Alternate:
J. S. Wilcox

Post No. 557 — New York
Com., Isidore Isaacs
S. V., Adolph H. Feeder
J. V., Thomas J. Quidor
Delegate:
Wm. V. G. Riblet
Alternate:
Wm. P. Skiffington

* Present.

Post No. 559 — New York

*Com., J. H. Lounsberry

S. V., A. F. Clausen

*J. V., George Eagles
  Delegate:

*Frank D. Meres
  Alternate:
Washington Katen

Post No. 560 — Elmhurst

Com., John McCluskey

S. V., James Smith

J. V., John H. Loskan
  Delegate:

*John G. Scheper
  Alternate:
James Smith

Post No. 562 — Chateaugay

Com., A. H. Rushford

S. V., John Laclair

J. V., James N. Smith
  Delegate:
John Meagher
  Alternate:
John Laclair

Post No. 563 — Whitehall

Com., Thomas Covil

S. V., A. Culver

J. V., John Scott
  Delegate:
L. H. Carrington
  Alternate:
J. W. Allen

Post No. 564 — Walden

Com., C. G. Hunt

S. V., Chas. G. Hunt

J. V., J. H. Tompkins
  Delegate
Geo. W. Crist
  Alternate:
Alonzo Carson

Post No. 565 — Woodhull

Com., J. B. Brown

S. V., J. D. Slade

J. V., H. J. Howard
  Delegate:
J. D. Slade
  Alternate:
. . . .

Post No. 570 — Salem

Com., Wm. J. Cruikshank

S. V., Edgar Ladd

J. V., Frederick Henn
  Delegate:
Albert K. Broughton
  Alternate:
Merritt Larabee

Post No. 572 — Trumansburg

*Com., F. B. Fish

*S. V., Robert Cannon

*J. V., Wm. F. Ball
  Delegate:

*H. C. Burdick
  Alternate:
Geo. Whipple

Post No. 573 — Scriba

Com., David Wright

S. V., Z. M. Randel

J. V., Freeman Brazeau
  Delegate:
Harvey Dubois

* Present.

Alternate:
Henry Hubbard

Post No. 575 — Warwick
Com., W. J. Rounsavell
S. V., Wm. Dolson
J. V., P. D. Howell
Delegate:
*John S. Springer
Alternate:
Melvin Green

Post No. 576 — Smyrna
*Com., Geo. W. Crumb
S. V., F. M. Sanders
J. V., A. Frazier
Delegate:
*Josiah Miles
Alternate:
Francis M. Sanders

Post No. 578 — New York
Com., Thos. H. Robertson
S. V., John O'Connell
J. V., John Heney
Delegate:
Dennis Downey
Alternate:
John Thain

Post No. 581 — Parishville
. . . .

Post No. 582— Bainbridge
Com., Daniel T. Banner
S. V., James L. Hyde
J. V. Chauncey Alger
Delegate:
J. V., T. E. Searles

Alternate:
J. L. Hyde

Post No. 583 — Jasper
Com., A. Murphy
S. V., T. V. Moore
Delegate:
. . . .

Alternate
. . . .

Post No. 587 — Hudson Falls
Com., Hiram Hyde
S. V., L. J. Severance
J. V., A. J. Blake
Delegate:
James McCarty
Alternate:
H. N. Rogers

Post No. 588 — Natural Bridge
Com., Fred A. Simser
S. V., Wm. Williamson
J. V., Luther Wright
Delegate:
Wm. Williamson
Alternate:
L. H. Wood

Post No. 589 — Frewsburg
Com., W. H. Sears
S. V., Robert Fuller
Delegate:
W. H. Sears
Alternate:
P. E. Miller

Post No. 590 — Yonkers
Com., William Riley
S. V., Abram C. Leviness

---

* Present.

J. V., Abraham C. Gould
Delegate:
Theodore Van Ness
Alternate:
Samuel Archer

Post No. 593 — Tully

Com., W. L. Earle
S. V., Horace Russell
J. V., Lester Estey
Delegate:
James H. McGahen

Post No. 594 — Keene Valley

S. V., J. E. Henry
J. V., James A. Hall
Delegate:
James A. Hall
Alternate:
John W. Otea

Post No. 597 — Phelps

Com., Alonzo Spears
S. V., H. C. Severance
*J. V., Ed. P. Hicks
Delegates:
*Geo. M. White

Post No. 598 — Highland Falls

. . . .

Post No. 599 — Parish

. . . .

Post No. 600 — New York

*Com., James R. Silliman
S. V., Chas. H. Liscom
J. V., Henry G. Fritsch
Delegate:
*Chauncey Quintard

Alternate:
Edward Roe

Post No. 603 — Short Tract

Com., John S. Pitt
S. V., Eli W. Drury
J. V., S. B. Luckey
Delegate:
S. B. Luckey
Alternate:
Albert H. Dorey

Post No. 604 — Frankfort

Com., M. K. Ellsworth
S. V., Adam J. Miller
J. V., George H. Storms
Delegate:
A. G. Getman
Alternate:
Henry Joubin

Post No. 607 — New York

*Com., William Leggett
S. V., Oscar H. Riker
J. V., Camden O. Rockwell
Delegate:
J. K. Atkinson
Alternate:
Thos. R. Murray

Post No. 608 — Manlius

Delegate:
Chas. D. Brown
Alternate:
M. J. Flanders

Post No. 609 — S. W. Oswego

Com., George Farnham
S. V., James Prosser

* Present.

J. V., Alexander Elder
Delegate:
Simeon Stevenson

Post No. 613 — Apalachin

Com., P. A. Foster
S. V., Pulaski Kent
J. V., Uri Short
Delegate:
Charles Baker
Alternate:
Pulaski Kent

Post No. 615 — Verona

Com., F. T. Sleight
S. V., M. S. Crossett
J. V., B. Wood
Delegate:
M. S. Crossett
Alternate:
B. Wood

Post No. 617 — Millerton

*Com., Silas Wilkinson
S. V., Gilbert Hunt
J. V., Horace Griswold
Delegate:
Gilbert Hunt
Alternate:
Watson D. Marsten

Post No. 619 — Mechanicville

Com., John J. Ashman
S. V., M. Tripp
J. V., T. Washburn
Delegate:
Levi Hydorn
Alternate:
M. Tripp

Post No. 621 — Saranac Lake

Com., Warren Flanders
S. V., Peter Sequa
J. V., Edward Riley
Delegate:
Nelson Foster
Alternate:
Joseph Leggett

Post No. 623 — Elmira

*Com., James N. McAllister
S. V., Thos. Waters
J. V., Richard Kennedy
Delegate:
*John C. Sweet
Alternate:
A. F. Packard

Post No. 624 — Georgetown

Com., James Vanhovenburgh
S. V., Charles Bliss
J. V., John Snell
Delegate:
Charles Bliss
Alternate:
John Lines

Post No. 627 — Port Jefferson

Com., A. Bentley
S. V., G. W. Kinner
J. V., Albert Walker
Delegate:
C. F. Stertevant
Alternate:
G. M. Dayton

Post No. 628 — Long Island City

*Com., Chas. Schonberg
S. V., Joseph E. Brown

* Present.

George L. Hughson, Patriotic Instructor

J. V., William Hewitt
Delegate:
John A. Leek
Alternate:
James J. Ryan

Post No. 630 — Waterford
*Com., Edward Lafay
S. V., Nathan Munn
J. V., Hiram Coons
Delegate:
*Jerome Ball
Alternate:
Nathan Munn

Post No. 632 — Scippio
Com., Francis Flynn
S. V., J. P. Northway
Delegate:
*J. B. Hitchcock
Alternate:
J. P. Northway

Post No. 633 — Belleville
. . . .

Post No. 636 — Rockaway Beach
*Com., B. L. Dunbar
S. V., Cyrus Lawrence
J. V., John Bieth
Delegate:
B. L. Dunbar
Alternate:
James A. Molinari

Post No. 640 — North Cohocton
. . . .

Post No. 641 — Huntington
Com., James Wright
S. V., David A. Baldwin

J. V., John S. Carr
Delegate:
George F. Barr
Alternate:
Alonzo B. Dodge

Post No. 642 — Clemons
*Com., F. M. Bartholomew
S. V., Nelson Steluir
J. V., Eph. Sheldrich
Delegate:
*L. A. Belden
Alternate:
Gardner Harvey

Post No. 643 — Amityville
Com., George W. Lyon
S. V., William P. Roe
J. V., Z. Hendrickson
Delegate:
Z. Hendrickson
Alternate:
George W. Trenchard

Post No. 644 — Albany
Com., Frank E. Cooley
*S. V., Charles P. Hoag
J. V., Edwin Hall
Delegate:
*George E. Dutcher
Alternate:
*Charles A. Taggart

Post No. 646 — Owego
*Com., Eli Hutchins
*S. V., Emanuel Decker
J. V., James L. Prince
Delegate:
*Clay Knickerbocker

* Present.

5

Alternate:
J. D. Degroat

Post No. 647 — Elbridge

Com., Alfred E. Stacey
S. V., J. R. Robinson
J. V., William Welch
Delegate:
T. C. Knight
Alternate:
Charles Newell

Post No. 648 — Liverpool

Com., Oscar Forger
S. V., John R. More
J. V., Charles E. Swords
Delegate:
Charles Edwards
Alternate:
John R. More

Post No. 649 — Prattsburg

Com., J. H. Potts
S. V., George O. Parker
J. V., E. Drum
Delegate:
None elected
Alternate:
None elected

Post No. 652 — London, Canada

Com., William T. Peel
S. V., George W. Pitt
J. V., William J. Laskey
Delegate:
Charles Cox

Post No. 654 — Roslyn

Com., William H. Wood
S. V., Henry B. Hendrickson

Delegate:
None elected
Alternate:
None elected

Post No. 655 — Otto

Com., Edward Smallman
S. V., Robert C. Beach
J. V., Nicholas Whittmyer
Delegate:
George H. Wayne
Alternate:
Robert C. Beach

Post No. 656 — Riverhead

Com., Albert H. Terry
S. V., William H. Dayton
J. V., James A. Fletcher
Delegate:
Henry H. Preston
Alternate:
William H. Dayton

Post No. 659 — Morrisonville

Com., Nicholas Lawliss
S. V., Cashmere Russell
J. V., James Redmond
Delegate:
J. H. Good
Alternate:
B. N. Curtis

Post No. 660 — Leicester

Com., Michael McMahon
S. V., John M. Fiero
J. V., R. B. Ingersol
Delegate:
R. G. Moses

* Present.

Alternate:
R. B. Ingersol

Post No. 661 — Pawling
Com., John E. Banks
S. V., Solomon Woodin
J. V., George W. Toffy
Delegate:
*Perry W. Chapman
Alternate:
Solomon Woodin

Post No. 663 — Lysander
. . . .

Post No. 664 — Dolgeville
Com., Levi Helmer
S. V., John Vedder
J. V., John Vedder
Delegate:
John Vedder
Alternate:
L. Hutton

Post No. 665 — Middle Grove
Com., George Dingmon
S. V., John Winney
J. V., Judson Ecker
Delegate:
Amos C. Rhoades
Alternate:
None elected

Post No. 666 — East Randolph
Com., L. L. Morton
S. V., S. A. Monroe
J. V., E. R. Jones
Delegate:
T. H. Hinman
Alternate:
N. W. Miller

Post No. 667 — Fayetteville
*Com., Duane P. Babcock
S. V., Edward F. Hopkins
J. V., William Amerman
Delegate:
*Henry J. Knapp
Alternate:
William S. Babcock

Post No. 669 — Brooklyn
. . . .

Post No. 670 — East Syracuse
Com., Daniel Stryker
S. V., C. H. Burlingame
J. V., Eugene Cole
Delegate:
*A. R. Walker
Alternate:
Eugene Cole

Post No. 671 — Watervliet
Com., George W. Moore
S. V., John Evans
J. V., John Burke
Delegate:
Michael Ryan
Alternate:
Edwin Mandeville

Post No. 672 — Elmira
*Com., W. H. Hathaway
S. V., Eugene Root
J. V., Lafayette Farr
Delegate:
*John Faucett
Alternate:
Levi Low

---

* Present.

THE COMMANDER.— I would ask the Senior Vice-Commander to take the Chair. He is not present, So I will ask the Junior Vice to take the Chair. In his absence I will request Past Commander Bell to please take the Chair.

The Commander then read his address, which is as follows:

ADDRESS OF THE DEPARTMENT COMMANDER

COMRADES.— In compliance with the Rules and Regulations of our Order, and following the example of my predecessors, I have the honor to submit for your consideration a report of my action as Commander of this Department during the past year.

I wish to congratulate the Comrades for the harmony in our ranks, and the evident desire on their part to carry on the work of the Grand Army of the Republic in accordance with the established Rules and Regulations of our Order.

In accepting the honorable office to which I was chosen by your unanimous vote a year ago, I pledged myself to act as far as I was able for the best interest of every Comrade of this Department — whether that pledge has been fulfilled is for you to decide.

The past year has been crowded with National and International questions of grave importance affecting the well-being of the civilized world, and while the American people were reluctant to enter this great war, yet the force of circumstances leading to that end were irresistible. Our Army and Navy are now ranged with the Allies in the great battles in Europe for justice and humanity. The continued insolence of the German Imperial Government could not longer be tolerated by our people, and now that we are in this war, and our Soldiers and Sailors are showing to the world their fighting qualities, there is but one course for our Country to pursue, and that is to fight with all its powers for victory in this holy cause. We have not entered this war through any selfish motives, nor do we look for any reward. We have entered this war in the defense of our rights as a Nation, and in favor of the oppressed people of Europe who have appealed to us for help. The Grand Army of the Republic is to-day more highly esteemed than ever before. The present war has turned the thoughts of the people more keenly to the scenes of our Civil War, and the memories of that terrible conflict have been revived. The people of our Country are again brought face to face with what war means, and realize what the Veterans of that war passed through to save our glorious Union and Flag, which now holds such an honored place among the Nations of the world.

VISITATIONS

During the year I have visited a number of Posts in different parts of the State, also attended reunions and other celebrations of Veterans and their Auxiliaries, where I met many of our Comrades and was at all times well received and hospitably entertained. I found everywhere a desire on the part of our Comrades to exemplify the principles of Fraternity, Charity and Loyalty, and to advance the interests of our Order. In addition, I have kept in close touch with others through correspondence on various matters of interest appertaining to our Order, and gave instructions and advice when needed. In this important duty I was ably assisted by Past Department Commander Edward J. Atkinson, my Assistant Adjutant-General, whose familiarity with the requirements of our Order greatly facilitated our work.

FIFTY-FIRST NATIONAL ENCAMPMENT

The Fifty-First National Encampment of the Grand Army of the Republic was held in the city of Boston, Mass., during the week of August 19, 1917, at which the delegates and Past Department Commanders to the number of sixty-seven were in attendance. Headquarters of the Department were established at the Hotel Vendome, and was at all times during the Encampment the scene of activty, especially in the attendance of a large number of visiting Comrades, as the registration records show, thus affording valuable information to many inquirers. In this respect we are indebted to Comrade Edward J. Mitchell, Acting Assistant Adjutant-General, who was in immediate charge at Headquarters. The parade took place on Tuesday, August 21st, and the Department Commander was very much gratified that the six hundred Comrades who appeared contributed by their presence in line to the splendid showing of the Department, as evidenced by the plaudits of the vast multitude which thronged the entire line of march. The hospitality of the city of Boston, and the provisions made by the local committee for the enjoyment of our Comrades and their families will remain with us a lasting and happy memory.

The delegates met in caucus at the Hotel Vendome on Tuesday evening, August 21st, and unanimously endorsed Comrade Orlando A. Somers, of Indiana, for Commander-in-Chief. They also recommended the reappointment of our Comrade, Cola D. R. Stowits, to the office of Quartermaster-General, so ably filled by him for a number of years. Comrade George A. Price, of Post No 327, was again chosen to represent our Department on the National Council of Administration, and it was the sense of the caucus that Atlantic City receive our support as the place for holding the National Encampment of 1918, and New York was so recorded in the Encampment, but by a bare majority of one vote, however, the city of Portland, Oregon, was selected. The week of August 18th has been the time fixed, and the rate of fare at one cent per mile, the lowest rate given in many years. We bespeak for those who attend a magnificent excursion, and trust that our Department will be fully represented.

SOLDIERS AND SAILORS' HOME AT BATH

On October 16, 1917, I visited the Soldiers and Sailors' Home at Bath, N. Y., in company with the Assistant Adjutant-General, and devoted part of two days to the inspection of that institution. We were cordially received by Col. S. M. Morgan, the Commandant, and Past Department Commander Zan L. Tidball, the Adjutant of the Home. The day after our arrival being the regular monthly meeting of the Board of Trustees, we were accorded an opportunity to meet, and were greeted by the members of that body.

The Commandant being officially engaged with the Board of Trustees, we were escorted by Adjutant Tidball through all the departments of the home, and given every opportunity for our inspection. Particular inspections were made of the subsistence and dormitory departments. The food furnished to the members of the Home is of the best quality and well prepared. The dormitories are supplied with clean and comfortable beds and bedding, and all whom we came in contact with expressed themselves well satisfied with their surroundings and treatment. The hospital was visited and found well equipped for the proper care and comfort of the sick.

The building that was destroyed by fire some time ago, I was informed, was to be rebuilt in the near future, which will add very much to the comfort of our Comrades at the Home.

WOMAN'S RELIEF CORPS HOME

My visit to the Woman's Relief Corps Home at Oxford, N. Y., in company with the Assistant Adjutant-General, was most pleasant and satisfactory. Past Department Commander James S. Graham, Superintendent of the Home, met us at the station, and extended every courtesy and opportunity to inspect the buildings and their beautiful surroundings, and the various arrangements for the care and comfort of the old men and women under his charge. The buildings are so constructed and connected as to afford recreation during the bad weather, so that at all times the inmates have an opportunity to exercise. The private rooms are commodious, clean and comfortable. The bill-of-fare contains a well assorted variety of substantial food of excellent quality, which is well prepared and served. The kind attention and treatment bestowed by Comrade Graham and his good wife upon these old people must create in their hearts a home-like feeling.

MOUNT MCGREGOR

My visit to Mount McGregor was an interesting and enjoyable trip. I was received by Comrade Robert F. Knapp, of Saratoga Springs, a member of the Board of Trustees of the Mount McGregor Association, and Comrades Ormsbee and Remington, who accompanied me to the Grant Cottage and presented me to Mrs. Clarke, the widow of Comrade O. P. Clarke, and now the custodian of the Cottage, since the death of her husband, having been appointed to that position by the Board of Trustees. The present and future welfare and interest of this historical spot and Cottage wherein the great General passed the last moments of his life is carefully looked after by Mrs. Clarke, the official custodian.

On my visit I found that there was no flag-pole on the grounds to display the flag of our country. I recommend that the Legislature be requested to make an appropriation to provide for the placing of a pole and flag at the Grant Cottage at Mount McGregor.

MEMORIAL DAY

Memorial Day of 1918 will pass into history as among those of the most eventful in the history of the Grand Army of the Republic. While the membership of our Order is diminishing, the observance of the day, and the popular interest in it at this time, while our Country is engaged in this world war, its sacred memories have never been more generally observed.

FLAG DAY

Flag Day this year has been usually well observed in our Department, and especially under the present conditions, while our Country is engaged in this world war. The celebration of the day appears to all our people as a public duty, and the display of the flag in this Department has been very general during the past year. It is now seen upon every public building and private residence throughout the country.

VETERANS' RIGHTS

At the last Department Encampment held at Saratoga Springs, 1917, the Committee on Resolutions presented to the Encampment the case of Comrade Edwin A. Doty, of Albany, who was demoted and whose salary was reduced, in violation of law. His counsel, Wm. T. Byrne, having been retained by the Comrade, and who is engaged in fighting the case in the Court of Claims against the State of New York, for which the said Wm. T. Byrne presented the following bill: " For professional services and disbursements in the matter of the claim of Edwin A. Doty against the State of New York, being Claim No. 9981 in said court, the sum of $250.00."

The matter was referred to the Council of Administration with the recommendation that they be authorized to take such action as they may deem proper.

The matter was brought before the Council at the meeting in Albany on January 26, 1918, and by a unanimous vote appropriated the sum of $250.00 from the defense fund to carry the case through the court, Comrade Doty pledging himself to return said amount to the Department if successful, of which his counsel seemed to be assured.

I recommend that this encampment confirm the action of the Council in this case.

WOMAN'S RELIEF CORPS

The close fraternal relations existing between the Grand Army of the Republic and its Auxiliary, the Woman's Relief Corps, under the able leadership of Department President Mrs. Ada T. Gardinier, of New York City, convinces us that we are under great obligations to these noble women for their faithful services, not only in the present, but in the years past. I trust we fully appreciate the work they are doing for us. Many Posts of this Department, as well as throughout the country, have been able to retain their membership and organization because of the financial aid and encouragement the Woman's Relief Corps has given by their co-operation, and I cannot too strongly recommend its expansion.

LADIES OF THE GRAND ARMY OF THE REPUBLIC

The Ladies of the Grand Army of the Republic are composed of the wives, mothers, sisters and daughters of the Veterans of the Civil War. Although they are a separate and distinct organization from the Woman's Relief Corps, yet they are doing a good and noble work in assisting our Comrades and their families in every possible way, and in so doing merit our lasting obligations for their noble and loyal support, under the leadership of Mrs. Mary J. Campbell, of Penn Yan, N. Y., the Department President.

DAUGHTERS OF VETERANS

This organization is one in which the Grand Army of the Republic is and should be specially interested, since it is composed exclusively of the daughters and granddaughters of the Civil

War Veterans. It is deserving, and should receive every encouragement to strengthen and firmly establish itself for the future, and it has during the past year made good progress under the leadership of Miss Lillian G. Dyas, of Binghamton, N. Y., the Department President.

SONS OF VETERANS

The Sons of Veterans are making good progress in many sections of the State. They seem to have been very active during the past year under the able leadership of Division Commander J. Harris Loucks, of Albany, N. Y., and are realizing that they must soon take up the work of their fathers. Their organization will, we hope, in the near future grow in number as rapidly as that of the Grand Army of the Republic must decrease. Their work will soon be the work now done by the Grand Army. This they are beginning to realize, and I believe we have every reason to feel that when the time comes, they will take up our work and do it well.

SONS OF VETERANS AUXILIARY

The Sons of Veterans Auxiliary are to the Sons of Veterans what the Woman's Relief Corps are to the Grand Army of the Republic. I am pleased to say that they are doing good and patriotic work under the influence of their Department President, Mrs. Harriet A. Pettinger, of Rochester, N. Y.

DEPARTMENT OFFICERS' REPORTS

I respectfully call your attention to the reports of the different Department Officers for the year just closed. There is one item in the report of the Assistant Adjutant-General that I deem important and proper to call to your attention, and that is the losses by suspension. Doubtless these suspensions are for causes deemed proper, but it seems to me that much charity could be exercised in the matter of suspension for non-payment of Post dues. We cannot hope at this late day to obtain recruits from those who have held aloof from our ranks all these years, but we can retain in membership those now on our rolls. We should not drop or suspend any Comrade for non-payment of dues. If he is worthy, we should see that his name remains on the Post roster until the summons comes that cancels all his debts.

IN MEMORIAM

It is with sincere regret that I report the loss of several of our Past Department Officers during the past year:

Past Department Commander Solomon W. Russell died at his home in Salem, Washington County, N. Y., October 18, 1917. Age, 81 years.

Past Department Commander Michael J. Cummings died at his home in Brooklyn, New York City, January 3, 1918. Age, 73 years.

Past Senior Vice-Department Commander William A. Boyd, died at his home in New York City, January 24, 1918. Age, 76 years.

Past Judge Advocate Horace D. Ellsworth died at his home in Canton, St. Lawrence County, N. Y., February, 1918.

The Department Commander and members of his Staff were present and attended the funeral services of Comrades Russell, Cummings and Boyd.

CONCLUSION

Before concluding this report, I desire to express my sincere appreciation to the members of my Official Staff who so faithfully and loyally assisted me in upholding the standard of our great Order. To the members of the Council of Administration, to my Aides-de-Camp, and to all my Comrades who so loyally assisted me in the discharge of my duties my sincere thanks are due. While my obligations to these Comrades are great, yet I feel under special obligations to some members of my Staff. Permit me to especially mention the faithful services of my Assistant Adjutant and Quartermaster General Comrade Edward J. Atkinson. His close attention and clear perception of the duties of his Office were of the greatest value to my administration.

To my Senior Aide-de-Camp Comrade Isidore Isaacs are due my sincere thanks for his faithful and ever loyal services during my term of Office.

I cannot let this opportunity pass without a word of commendation for the services of Miss Bernice Case, our Clerk at Department Headquarters. Her faithfulness and devotion to duty have been of untold value and her ability in systematic office work cannot be excelled and those who have experienced the need of such services can more fully appreciate their value.

Comrades, my duties as Commander of this great Department are about finished. I have done my best to render faithful service for the distinguished honor conferred upon me one year ago. While the duties of the Office have been exacting, yet they were very pleasant. I have had an opportunity to meet more Comrades and knowing them better than otherwise would have been possible.

I again thank you for the honor bestowed upon me and the kind consideration and cheerful assistance rendered me throughout the past year.

WILLIAM F. KIRCHNER,

Department Commander.

Comrade Bell — The Commander's address will be referred to a committee when appointed.

Commander Kirchner.—As the next order of business the Acting Assistant Adjutant-General will announce the committees.

The Acting Assistant Adjutant-General then read the following list of committees:

COMMITTEES FOR ENCAMPMENT

Commander's Report

James D. Bell, Chairman

John C. Shotts	Zan L. Tidball
Charles A. Orr	John S. Maxwell
James M. Snyder	DeWitt C. Hurd
James D. Graham	Samuel C. Pierce
Charles H. Freeman	

Resolutions

James Tanner, Chairman

Oscar Smith
James D. Bell
Alfred Lyth
Samuel C. Pierce

John C. Shotts
John S. Maxwell
Chas. A. Orr

Senior Vice Department Commander

Austin H. Stafford, Chairman

Daniel H. Cole
James A. Allis

C. W. Cowtan
George F. Tait

Junior Vice Department Commanders

Robert P. Bush, Chairman

John W. Mullens
C. J. Westcott

James Campbell
Robert Simpson, Jr., M.D.

Assistant Adjutant-General

Henry C. Draper, Chairman

Philip M. Wales
George H. Lester

B. Franklin Raze
John Conway

Assistant Quartermaster-General

Philip M. Wales, Chairman

Edward J. Mitchell

J. R. Silliman

Department Patriotic Instructors

Edward B. Long, Chairman

A. B. Ostrander

John Quincy Adams

Department Chaplain

George B. Fairhead, Chairman

H. Clay Wood

Ezra Stillman

Medical Director

Robert Simpson, Jr., M.D., Chairman

Lewis S. Pilcher   Robert P. Bush

Legislative Committee

John C. Shotts, Chairman

B. Franklin Raze   William H. Hyler

Judge Advocate

James D. Bell, Chairman

Alfred Lyth   George Blair

Special Committees to Visit Associate Societies

To visit Woman's Relief Crops — Past Commander James S. Graham, Joseph E. Ewell, Elias W. Beach, Acting Assistant Adjutant-General Isidore Isaacs.

To visit Ladies of the G. A. R.— Past Commanders Geo. B. Loud, Zan L. Tidball.

To visit Sons of Veterans — Past Commanders Samuel C. Pierce and Oscar Smith.

To visit Daughters of Veterans — Past Commanders John C. Shotts and John S. Maxwell.

To visit Sons of Veterans Auxiliary — Past Commanders Charles H. Freeman and Zan L. Tidball.

Committee on Delegates, Alternates and Council of Administration

James D. Bell, Chairman

Charles A. Orr   Samuel C. Pierce
Oscar Smith   James M. Snyder
Robert P. Bush   John C. Shotts
John McCloskey   A. H. Stafford
James R. Silliman   George Hollands

COMMANDER KIRCHNER.— Comrades, what is your pleasure?

COMRADE TANNER: You have announced my name as chairman of the Committee on Resolutions. I want to give notice to my fellow members that I now call a meeting of that committee for nine o'clock to-morrow morning. When I say nine o'clock it means nine o'clock and it means much more discomfort to me than it can to them, for I cannot get much, if any, sleep until long after midnight and my sleep will be abridged in the morning, and I would call the meeting of the committee for room No. 4 over in the Ithaca Hotel, which is the headquarters room of Grand Army Posts which has been placed at our service for that purpose, and we would like whatever resolutions there may be, that will go to that committee, if they can be handed in now so that we can measure up as to the quantity of work we will have to do we shall be very glad. I take it that all the comrades are anxious to do the business of this encampment, do it thoroughly and as soon as possible and get back to their homes as soon as they can.

Now, sir, every one will agree that there is a shadow on this encampment, and I think they will agree with me, sir, that it is proper that we should take notice of it in our opening to-day. Our able, genial and efficient Assistant Adjutant-General and Quartermaster-General, Eddie Atkinson, is not able to be with us, and in my opinion I doubt most seriously if he will ever be with us again. I hope so. But he is lying in his home down in Yonkers, and I think, sir, that one of the first things for the Acting Assistant Adjutant-General should be an authorization to prepare a resolution to be telegraphed to him this afternoon to let him know that we miss him, and that though absent he is not forgotten. Eddie Atkinson and I have disagreed often in Grand Army matters but we have ever held the grasp of comradeship and there has been a close friendship between us, and to me, coming to Ithaca, sir, with the knowledge that for once I cannot have Eddie recite the " Dandy Fifth " is a sorrow to me now, sir, and if we have a stenographer here I will take the liberty of dictating to the stenographer.

COMMANDER KIRCHNER.— Yes, we have one here.

Comrade Tanner.— Then let him take this:

E. J. Atkinson, 90 Bruce Avenue, Yonkers, N. Y.

Your Comrades of the Grand Army, assembled in their 52d Encampment at Ithaca, N. Y., meet and miss you and mourn your absence. Our hearts go out to you in the affliction that is upon you, which we know you are bearing with the same steady nerve and splendid spirit that carried you through the bloody years of the 60's. We hope that Providence will grant you surcease of pain and complete recovery and reunion with us at some future day. We give you this message, buck up and hold fast.

That is to be signed by the Department Commander, if you please.

On motion duly seconded the resolution of Comrade Tanner was adopted, and the acting Assistant Adjutant-General was directed to send the telegram.

Commander Orr.— I offer the following resolution and ask that it be read and referred to the Committee on Resolutions.

Comrade Tanner.— Under our rule the resolution is to be read and referred to the committee without debate.

The resolution, as read, is as follows:

Whereas, The war news from the front indicates that the tide of battle in the Great World War is turning in favor of our allies. Now, therefore,

Resolved, That we congratulate our sons and grandsons. That they are honored in serving in such a cause.

We served to uphold the flag of this nation and preserve it a "United Republic," but they are serving in a war waged to preserve the liberties of all the nations of the earth, small and great, against the tyranny of autocracy and militarism.

It has been said that republics are ungrateful. We veterans of the Civil War are living examples of the falsity of this charge, so far as the Republic of the United States is concerned. Our government has made the most liberal provision for its soldiers, veteran soldiers, and their widows, of any nation in history.

We send a message of good cheer to our boys at the front and remind them that this nation has never been defeated in any war it has entered upon, and does not propose and must not be now. (The Central Powers will please take notice of this.)

We pledge ourselves anew to the great principles for which this republic stands and will back " Our Boys " at the front to the last dollar and will, if necessary, join them on the firing line. Further

" *Resolved,* That the Stars and Stripes is concededly the flag joined with those of our allies to win the world from ruthless and unspeakable cruelty as waged by our enemies, to light the pathway of a righteous civilization throughout the world and to crush out of existence the last vestige of Prussianism."

Comrade Bell.— I desire to ask the Committee on the Commander's Address to meet immediately after the adjournment upon the platform here, and also the Committee on the Judge Advocate's Report. We will have room enough on the stage for both committees and it won't take long.

Comrade Zan S. Tidball.— I offer the following resolution:

" Whereas, The recent acts of the Congress of the United States, increasing widows' pensions and the pensions of the veterans of the Civil War, have brought relief to the men and the families of those who risked their lives in defense of the flag;

" *Resolved,* That the Department of New York, Grand Army of the Republic, in Annual Encampment held in the city of Ithaca June 25–27, 1918, expresses its gratitude to the Congress for its generous and praiseworthy action;

" *Resolved,* That we sincerely appreciate the prompt approval of said acts by President Wilson;

" *Resolved,* That we are under deep and lasting obligation to Senator Smoot for his untiring work in securing the enactment of the laws affording this relief;

" *Resolved,* That a copy of these resolutions, properly authenticated, be sent to the President of the Senate, Speaker of the House of Representatives, President Wilson and Senator Smoot, and that copies thereof be furnished to the Associated Press and the United Press."

Commander Kirchner.— This resolution will be referred to the Committee on Resolutions.

Commander Kirchner laid before the Convention the following communication:

Headquarters Robert G. Shaw Post 112,

Department of New York, G. A. R.,

New Brighton, Staten Island, N. Y., *April* 16, 1918.

General William Kirchner, *Commander, Department of New York, G. A. R.:*

Dear Comrade.— At the last meeting of this Post the following resolutions were adopted:

"Whereas, The membership of our beloved Order is fast passing away in death; and

"Whereas, The Comrades of the Post desire, above all related things, that the object and principle for which the Grand Army of the Republic fought — the preservation of the union, one and indivisible — should be remembered and revered by future generations; and

"Whereas, The Comrades of the United Spanish War Veterans and the Comrades now fighting for the existence of our country, served or are serving practically for the object and principle of our foundation, inasmuch as if foreign military despotism should defeat our army and navy our splendid sacrifices would have been made in vain; therefore

"*Resolved*, That we suggest and recommend that the Constitution and By-Laws of our Order, in order to secure its perpetuation, be, for the reasons offered above, amended to provide that:

"All honorably discharged soldiers, sailors, and marines of the Spanish-American War and of the present European War are eligible for admission to the comradeship of the Grand Army of the Republic; and

"*Resolved,* Further that we earnestly request our Department Commander to so favorably consider our suggestion and recommendation as to advocate its indorsement by the next State Encampment for transmission to, with recommendation for adoption by, the National Encampment at its its next annual session.

"We are, General, very respectfully, yours, in F., C. and L,.

Post Commander, EDWARD OPENSHAW,

Adjutant JAMES BUCKEL,

Quartermaster, JACOB KNOBLOCK.

"When their cause in effect and in fact is the same,
    Comrades all may unite in one glorious name!"

COMRADE TANNER.— We have no power to do anything with that except to refer it to the delegation to the next annual encampment. We cannot uproot the rules and regulations that are the very foundation of the Grand Army.

COMMANDER KIRCHNER.— I refer that to the Committee on Resolutions. I want to say that a request is made there that the Commander of this Department should endorse it. I want to say now in the presence of every comrade here that I will not endorse it. (Applause.)

COMRADE OSCAR SMITH.— I offer the following resolution:

"WHEREAS, Learning there was to be a vacancy on the Board of Trustees of the Soldiers' and Sailors' Home, at Bath, N. Y., the comrades in Albany were advised that it would be of great advantage to the Board and the Home if one of the Trustees were from Albany or its immediate vicinity. That the appropriations and supplies required by the Home made it necessary that one or more of the Trustees should come to Albany frequently to look after these matters, and as they were serving without compensation, except to cover actual expenses, less labor and better results could be attained by a resident member of the Board. That Albany and its vicinity had not been represented on this Board for eighteen years. Comrade Past Department Commander

James M. Snyder, of Troy, was induced to become a candidate for this position. He is a most capable business man, a member of the firm of Earl & Wilson, one of the oldest shirt and collar manufacturers of Troy, N. Y. Comrade Snyder is one of the best and most favorably known in the capital district. He resides but six miles from the capital; he is a most worthy comrade, and would be at the service of the Board at all times. His candidacy was endorsed by his comrades of Rensselaer, Albany and Schenectady counties, by the Mayors of the city, city officials without regard to party, also by many respected and influential comrades about the State. It was later learned that one other candidate had asked for this appointment, one Comrade George B. Loud, of New York city, to succeed himself. In order to have the Comrade appointed that could render the best service and satisfy the largest number of veterans of the State, the Governor has left it to the vote of this encampment and will appoint the one you select. Therefore,

" Resolved, That we believe that Comrade J. M. Snyder is the one that can render the best service; that his locality has a prior claim; that a comrade located there can render the best service for the Board, and thru them for the Home and its inmates; and we therefore pledge him our votes and most loyal support in this encampment, and ask the Governor to appoint him to fill the vacancy now existing in the Board of the Bath Home."

Commander Kirchner.— Referred to the Committee on Resolutions. Are there any further resolutions or communications to be offered?

Comrade Orr.— Yes, Commander Kirchner, I have a resolution which I ask to be read.

"Whereas, There is pending in the Congress of the United States a bill known as the Volunteer Officers Retired bill, said bill having passed the Senate; now, therefore,

" Resolved, That the thanks of this Encampment be hereby extended to the members of the United States Senate for their favorable action upon this bill.

"We earnestly urge the House of Representatives to concur with the action of the Senate upon the same, feeling assured as we do, that President Wilson will complete this act of justice to the few surviving officers who led our boys to victory over fifty years ago, by signing the same."

COMMANDER KIRCHNER.— Referred to the Committee on Resolutions.

COMRADE LYTH.— I would move that the reports of Department officers, other than that of the Department Commander, be received and referred to committees for their action without debate and without reading.

The motion was duly seconded and carried.

THE ACTING ASSISTANT ADJUTANT-GENERAL.— Reports have been received from the following:

Department Commander.
Senior Vice Department Commander.
Junior Vice Department Commander.
Judge Advocate.
Medical Director.
Department Chaplain.
Assistant Adjutant-General.
Assistant Quartermaster General.

COMMANDER KIRCHNER.— It is now half past 12. It is suggested that we take a recess until two o'clock. Is that satisfactory to the comrades?

COMRADE DR. BUSH.— Before that motion is put, I have one request to make. On the Committee of the Department Chaplain's report is the name of Past Department Chaplain Wood. I am informed that he has passed beyond and is no more, and I request that Comrade Charles L. Scherger be substituted, that his name be substituted, for that of Past Department Chaplain Wood.

COMMANDER KIRCHNER.— I accept that.
At this point a recess was taken until 2 p. m.

REPORT OF SENIOR VICE=DEPARTMENT COMMANDER

ROCHESTER, *June* 6, 1918.

EDWARD J. ATKINSON, *Assistant Adjutant-General:*

DEAR SIR AND COMRADE.— I have the honor to submit herewith my report as Senior Vice-Department Commander for the past year.

In July last I attended the annual meeting in Rochester of the Monroe County Veterans' Association, which was honored by the presence of Commander Kirchner and several members of his official staff. In January I installed the officers of Peissner Post No. 106, making the twentieth time I have had the honor and privilege of inducting into office the officers of a Post composed entirely of German veterans, conducting both services and ritual in German, and than whom no more loyal and patriotic veterans and citizens exist in our broad land.

While in attendance at the National Encampment at Boston I was taken seriously ill, and from that time until recently I have been able to give but little time to either business or Grand Army affairs.

On last Memorial Day I was able to perform the duties of Chief Marshal. The parade was the largest seen in Rochester on any Memorial Day within my remembrance. There were about 7,500 in the line. The veterans occupied automobiles, nearly one hundred machines being used. Teachers and pupils from the public and parochial schools to the number of 1,500 formed an entire division and were greeted with applause all along the line of march.

In conclusion, I desire to express my sincere thanks to the Comrades for the honor conferred upon me and to the Commander and the members of his staff for their unfailing courtesy.

Health, happiness and prosperity to each and all is my earnest wish.

Yours in F., C. and L.,

HENRY S. REDMAN,
Senior Vice-Department Commander.

REPORT OF JUNIOR VICE-DEPARTMENT COMM

OGDENSBURG, *June* 6, 1918.

COMRADE EDWARD J. ATKINSON, *Assistant Adjutant-General:*

AND COMRADE.— I have the honor to submit my report of services as Junior Vice-Commander of the Department of New York for 1917–18.

I have attended all meetings of the Council of Administration during this time and acted, in my judgment, for the best interests of the Comrades of this Department at such meetings and did all I could to make the administration of the Department Commander a successful one.

In August, 1917, I was in attendance at the National Encampment at Boston, Mass., and assisted at Department Headquarters to the best of my ability during its continuance.

I have been at the service of our Comrades or their dependent ones and presented all their grievances to our Congressman, Hon. Bertrand H. Snell, who has done much to assist them in having justice done them.

I was in charge of our memorial services and secured Governor Charles S. Whitman to make our memorial address, which was a cheering one to our remnant of Comrades and a good loyal one to all citizens of our country.

I have to thank you for your courtesy and my Comrades for the honor they have conferred upon me.

Fraternally yours in F., C. and L.,

FRANK JOHNSON,
Junior Vice-Commander.

UDGE=ADVOCATE

BUFFALO, N. Y., *June* 25, 1918.

.KINSON, *Assistant Adjutant-General,*
ork, G. A. R.:

DE.— Pursuant to the requirements of the
I have the honor to submit the following
report .. ate of the Department of New York,, Grand
Army of the Ro........, for my term ending on the 25th inst.

Only three questions have been submitted to me by the Department Commander during my term, in each of which I wrote an opinion, copies of which are attached hereto as a part of this report.

Question 1:

Has the Veterans' Relief Committee representing the Grand Army of the Republic power to determine the amount to be raised by the municipality for the relief of indigent veterans?

The answer is in the negative, the committee having only advisory power.

Question 2:

Is it against the law to have the name of the Post printed on the flag?

The answer is, Yes. The law makes no distinction in the matter.

Question 3:

Is a city liable for the care of an indigent veteran residing outside the municipality?

Answer, No.

In case number one it would seem from the wording of the statute that the Relief Committee has full power to determine the amount to be raised for indigent relief, and the lower courts so held; but on review the higher courts in each instance reversed the lower courts and held to the contrary doctrine.

Permit me through you to thank the Department Commander for expressing his confidence in me by appointing me to the position of Judge-Advocate for this Department, my fifth term in the office, and to extend assurance of my great appreciation of his many courtesies and that of other Comrades and officers.

Yours in F., C. and L.,

JOSEPH E. EWELL,
Judge-Advocate.

DEPARTMENT OF NEW YORK, GRAND ARMY OF THE REPUBLIC.

In the Matter of the Relief of Indigent Veterans of the City of Middletown, New York.

JOSEPH E. EWELL, *Judge-Advocate.*

Decision No. 1, September, 1917

STATEMENT OF FACTS

The Veterans' Relief Committee of the city of Middletown, having complied with all the requirements of law regarding the relief of indigent veterans, determined and decided that certain sums of money were necessary for that purpose and requested the proper authorities of the city of Middletown to provide the same as required by section 80 of the Poor Law. The city refused to provide the amount requested, and provided a lesser amount, presumably under claim that the lesser amount would be sufficient for the purposes required.

CONCLUSION OF LAW

The city acted within its legal rights. The conclusions of the Relief Committee as to the amount required for relief of indigent veterans is not binding upon the city. The municipality has full power to determine the amount of money necessary to be provided by it for the relief of veterans.

Chapter 706 of the Laws of 1887 provided for the relief of " poor and indigent " veterans, and together with amendments to the acts subsequently made, specified with great particularity the methods, manner and proceedings necessary to effect such relief. Upon one point, however, the law was not clear. It provided that certain officials should provide such " sum or sums of money as may be necessary " for veteran relief, but does not distinctly specify who has authority to determine what that amount shall be. A controversy arose on this point immediately after the original law was enacted, which could only be decided by the courts. The lower courts held that the Relief Committee had full power in the matter, and that the municipality had no authority to overrule its action; but the higher courts on appeal refused to sustain this contention, and held that the municipality had power to modify and revise the action of the Committee, and was required to appropriate only such sum or sums of money for veterans' relief as in its judgment was necessary.

There are two cases in the higher courts covering this point, viz.: People ex rel. Crawford v. City of Rome (136 N. Y. 489–1893), and People ex rel. Conde v. Meyers as Comptroller of the City of Schenectady, 161 A. D. 315–1914, both cases holding that the municipality has full power of revision over the action of the Relief Committee in determining the amount to be raised and provided for relief of veterans. This must therefore be accepted as the law. It is believed, however, that in case an inadequate amount should be appropriated an alternative writ of mandamus could be obtained and the question of fact tried out and if the Committee's contention is sustained a peremptory writ would issue compelling payment as requested by the Committee.

Department of New York, Grand Army of the Republic

In the Matter of the Desecration of the Flag of the United States of America.

Joseph E. Ewell, *Judge-Advocate*

Opinion No. 2

Query by Comrade James W. Smith, Post No. 619, Mechanic-ville, N. Y.:

Is it " against the law to have the name of the Post printed on the United States Flag ? "

The answer must be in the affirmative. Chapter 54 of the New York State Laws, 1917, is so definite and clear that no comment is necessary. It contains the following provisions:

> " Any person who in any manner, for exhibition or display, shall place or cause to be placed, any word, figure, mark, picture, design, drawing or any advertisement, of any nature upon any flag, standard, color or ensign of the United States of America, or state flag of this state or ensign, or shall expose or cause to be exposed to public view any such flag, standard, color or ensign, upon which after the first day of September, nineteen hundred and five, shall have been printed, painted or otherwise placed, or to which shall be attached, appended or annexed, any word, figure, mark, picture, design or drawing, or any advertisement of any nature, or who shall expose to public view, manufacture, sell, expose for sale, give away or have in possession for sale, or to give away, or for use for any purpose, any article or substance, being an article of merchandise, a receptacle of merchandise or article or thing for carrying or transporting merchandise upon which after the first day of September, nineteen hundred and five, shall have been printed, painted, attached, or otherwise placed a representation of any such flag, standard, color or ensign to advertise, call attention to, decorate, mark or distinguish, the article or substance, on which so placed, or who shall publicly mutilate, deface, defile, or defy, trample upon, or cast contempt, either by word or act, upon any such flag, standard, color or ensign, shall be deemed guilty of a misdemeanor."

It will be seen from the above that no word, figure, mark, picture, design, drawing or any advertisement can lawfully be placed upon the flag for exhibition or display.

DEPARTMENT OF NEW YORK, GRAND ARMY OF THE REPUBLIC

In the Matter of the Relief of Indigent Veterans of the City of Port Jervis, in Same County.

JOSEPH E. EWELL, *Judge-Advocate.*

Opinion No. 3, February, 1918.

SYLLABUS

A city is not required to relieve or care for an indigent veteran who is not a resident thereof.

Dr. Raphael H. Medrick of Port Jervis, N. Y., submits an inquiry as to whether a city is liable to pay an order given by a doctor on the city treasurer by the Commander and other members of the Relief Committee for caring for an old soldier and his wife residing outside the city limits, the soldier being a member of the city Post in good standing, and the Commander not having filed a bond with the town board of the township surrounding the city.

Section 80 of the Poor Law provides in part as follows:

> " No poor or indigent soldier, sailor or marine who has served in the military or marine service of the United States and who has been honorably discharged from such service nor his family nor the families of any who may be deceased, shall be sent to an almshouse, but shall be relieved and provided for at their homes *in the city or town where they reside.*"

It is clear therefore that no liability would attach on the part of the city in the matter referred to by Dr. Medrick. Steps, however, should be taken to procure relief of the Comrade under the provisions of the above law.

Reference is made to Opinion No. 1 of this series under date of September, 1917, in the matter of the relief of indigent veterans of the city of Middletown bearing upon this subject, but not necessary to the determination of this case.

REPORT OF MEDICAL DIRECTOR

OFFICE OF MEDICAL DIRECTOR, DEPARTMENT OF N. Y., G. A. R.

June 13, 1918.

E. J. ATKINSON, *Assistant Adjutant-General Department of N. Y., G. A. R.:*

I have the honor to transmit the following report as Medical Director of the Department of N. Y. G. A. R.

There being no reports from the various Posts of this Department curtails very materially the value of the report of the Medical Director of the Department

The history of the Grand Army of the Republic will be a bright page in the annals of the great American Republic, and sad to contemplate, will in a few years become an accomplished fact, as the membership is fast decreasing in the posts located in all parts of the State, and many Posts are obliged to surrender their charters for want of sufficient members to properly conduct the ordinary business relating to our order.

It is now 53 years since the Civil War came to an honorable close and the flag waived over the whole extent of the United States and Territories as our Country then existed.

The Spanish-American War added immensely to our territory and responsibility as a nation advocating pure democracy which in a large measure has prepared us as a nation to espouse the cause of the allies now battering for the very existence of democracy throughout the world.

Our assistance as a nation comes none too soon in men, munitions, money and machinery so essential in this world wide war, which will, let us hope, prove the utter annihilation of Prussianism so the world will be entirely rejuvenated from its moral leprosy.

The Empire State of New York has generously aided its veterans in many ways. First in the way of tax exemption on property purchased with pension monies, also providing homes for indigent veterans. The Bath Home gives comfort to 1,047 of our country's defenders.   Two hundred and eleven being absent on furlough.

The Women's Relief Corps Home at Oxford gives pleasant homes to 29 veterans' wives.

Veterans' widows	107
Veterans' mothers	1
Army nurses	2
Total	168

The Women's Relief Corps Home is a veritable paradise for indigent couples and widows of veterans.

The laws of our State gives every Post authority by complying with the law to secure an appropriation for the relief of veterans and widows who are in needy circumstances.

Respectfully submitted in F., C. and L.,

WILLIAM TAYLOR,
Medical Director.

REPORT OF CHAPLAIN

PORT LEYDEN, *June* 10, 1918

EDWARD J. ATKINSON, *Assistant Adjutant and Quartermaster General, Department of New York, G. A. R.:*

DEAR SIR AND COMRADE.—As the Department year is near its close I submit this as my report of Department Chaplain: My duties have been very light; no deaths have occurred in my own Post, neither have I been called upon to officiate at the funeral of any Civil War Veterans, but I have interested myself in the matter of getting headstones for the unmarked graves of soldiers' wives and widows. I have found in my own county " Lewis " that while the law provided for them no provision to pay for them had been made by our Board of Supervisors, but I was assured this was an error and would be corrected at the next session. I also found one unmarked grave of a soldier of 1812, and a headstone is being prepared for that. I do not recall as having seen in Memorial Day orders anything in regard to placing flag or flowers on the graves of the wives and widows of Civil War Veterans, and would suggest that in the future the attention of Posts be called to this fact and that flags and flowers be placed upon these graves at the same time they are placed upon those of deceased Comrades. Not being called upon to make a tabulated mortuary report I am not able to state how many have been mustered out during the year 1917; neither have I received the Posts Chaplain's Memorial Day Report, so have no data as to attendance on that day — and now, Comrades, again thanking you for the honor conferred in my re-election I commend you and yours to the love and care of Him Who has provided for all our needs, and brought us safely through another year. With the hope and prayer that when we are mustered out of this life we shall be mustered into the Grand Army above where God is the Supreme Commander.

Yours in F. C. L.,

REUBEN KLINE,
Department Chaplain.

AFTERNOON SESSION.

June 26, 1918, 2 p. m.

Commander Kirchner.— Comrades, we are now ready to proceed with the business of this encampment. I take great pleasure in presenting to you this afternoon the Commander-in-Chief of the Grand Army of the Republic, who is here to participate and to visit this encampment officially. I now have the pleasure of presenting to you Commander-in-Chief Orlando A. Somers.

Comrade Isaac.— Three cheers for the Commander-in-Chief.

The Comrades arose and cheered enthusiastically for the Commander-in-Chief.

Commander-in-Chief Somers.— Commander, Comrades of the Department of New York, I bring to you the greetings of your Comrades from the other Departments of the United States. Everywhere that I have been, with one exception, I have met a lot of Comrades who look just about like you look.

A Voice.— What was the exception?

Commander-in-Chief Somers.— The exception was New Orleans where they were all as black as midnight. (Laughter.)

A Voice.— That is only skin deep.

Commander-in-Chief Somers.— The difference was that these men had passed over the auction block and had fought for their freedom and had achieved it, and writing home to my people I told them they had all been field hands and the relief corps did not have a white face among them, and I said the relief corps had all been field hands and subject to sale to the highest bidder upon the market, and my good wife wanted to know how I knew they had all been field hands, and I said if there had been those there who had been house servants some of them would have been of a lighter shade of color. (Laughter.) That is the difference between the Department of Louisiana and Mississippi and New York. Other departments have men who look just like you

WILLIAM TAYLOR, M. D., Medical Director

look. They are men who have seen similar services. They belong
to that peculiar type of men and temperament of men very
similar. Fifty years have winnowed out those of the different
variety from among our ranks, and when I go among the Comrades frequently I see men who look like brothers as well as
Comrades, showing that there is a certain type of us who have
achieved long life, and I sometimes say we are the survival of
the fittest. (Applause.)

Physically that is true. Many of us have been buried upon the
battlefields, and the cause of their not being here to-day is not a
question of the survival of the fittest.

A year ago over here at Boston where I was honored with the
position of Commander-in-Chief I had some little doubts about
the propriety of having allowed my department to have presented
my name for that high honor. I had my doubts whether I would
be able to make good or not, and I have still enough of that
doubt in my mind to be trying to make good every day since the
encampment adjourned at Boston.

One of the things, two and three of them, that I had in my
own mind I thought to accomplish, yet I made no mention of it
to any person for fear I might fail. I did not want this position
just to hold it for the honor that was in it, but for the opportunity
that would come to me to do something for my Comrades.
(Applause.) I had in mind the splendid men who had preceded
me in this office and the high standard at which they had kept the
great Grand Army of the Republic, and I had feared that I
might fail to worthily be their successor. I had in my mind a
matter that was fresh in my memory, because on the Memorial
Day preceding the Boston encampment, for some reason or other
that I had never been able to define letters came to me from the
South appealing to me personally for funds with which to bear
the expenses of Memorial Day in the South land. Now I do
not know why that should be. I was not noted for my means.
I was not different from the other Comrades, but they did come
in numbers, appealing for money to buy flowers to place upon
the graves of our dead Comrades in the South land. I was so
impressed with their action that I made up my mind, if possible,
if I ever received the honors of that office, that I would provide

6

some way or other by which that fund might be raised and our Comrades not have to beg for money with which to buy flowers to put on the graves of our dead Comrades.

At the first meeting of the committee — the committee representing all the departments — which assembled immediately upon the adjournment of the encampment, I brought the matter before them, suggesting that if we would apportion the sum among the various departments that were able to give they would give it willingly, and asked estimates from our efficient Quartermaster-General as to what sum would be necessary, and having ascertained, the matter was apportioned between the departments, and this last Memorial Day, without any hardships to anybody or any Post, we had plenty of money to attend to that affair, and the Quartermaster-General says we have enough to do it again. (Applause and cries of good.) I was very much gratified about that.

Another thing I had in my mind, and that was, inasmuch as the encampment was to go to the far West that a reduced rate of fare ought to be procured. I mentioned that to some of my friends, some of the Past Commanders-in-Chief, and they said Somers, it is not worth while to waste your time and energy on that. We have tried that out. You cannot do anything. Notwithstanding that I said I am going to make a try, and before I had been at home one week I was in correspondence with the railroad corporations, I didn't wait until the eve of the convention, and it was not two weeks until I had delegations of railroads hammering on my front door every hour of the day nearly wanting that you should go west over their roads, and I asked them what inducements they had. They answered superior equipments. Superior equipment — we can care for you better than the other fellows, and that was the statement of each one of them. I said, men, the Grand Army of the Republic is not asking for superior equipment; the Grand Army of the Republic when it went to the war if it was fortunate it went in cattle cars, (Applause), and we were pretty well content then. Ordinary equipments will do us, but give us a reduced rate, that is what we are asking for, don't mention the equipment. Well, I hammered along that way until there was a congestion in the railroad traffic passenger service of the country, and one morning the papers said the Government had taken over the railroads, and all my work had been for nothing, just as I had been told it would be, and I laid awake that night, and next morning before I sat down to breakfast I got it through my clumsy noddle that it would be easier to do business with the Government that we had saved than it would be to do it with the railroad corporations, and I got busy and called my very efficient committee together, or a majority of them, Washington Gardner, our distinguished road chairman, and at the risk of spending some of the Grand Army's small amount of money we repaired to Washington to see Secretary McAdoo, to see what Mac-a doodle-do. We went there, and to make a long story short we got everything we wanted or asked for in the way of a reduced rate. When we called upon the Secretary he was in a jolly good humor, and there is nothing like having a man in a jolly good humor when you want to ask a favor of him. First get him in a good humor. My friend, the Quartermaster-General, knows just how to do that. I sometimes do it a little differently, but he was in a jolly good humor and we had only been introduced when he commenced talking, not like a great dignified Secretary of the Treasury in a nation of one hundred million, but more like a schoolboy than anything else, and he said, " Men, I am just feeling in such a good humor that I have to let something go." He said, " Yesterday I sent out 27,000 telegrams, that is a good many telegrams to send in one day, to the banks of this country asking them if they would loan me 10 per cent. of their reserve fund, three billions of dollars, for ninety days, until I could float a new Liberty Loan, and here are the answers," and on the long table in the office there, there were hundreds and thousands of answers, and he read some of them, and they were very brief. Sometimes the bank would say " Sure " and that would be all. Sometimes "You bet." Sometimes " Twice that much." And one said, "Yes, come down and get everything we have got excepting the fixtures," and he was so pleased, and he had a right to be, that he was in splendid good humor. As soon as opportunity offered I told him the purpose of our visit. I told him that for a number of years we had been unable to secure a reduced rate over the railroads to our National

Encampment north of Mason's and Dixon's line. That south of it the men who wore the gray had invariably secured a one cent rate and I had only proceeded that far when he said " Yes, yes." He is the son of a confederate soldier himself. He said " Yes, they were just in here last week, they wanted to know if I would give them the same rate the railroads had been giving them to their meetings, and I told them of course I would." Well, men, my case was made that minute. It was just made then. I said to him, Well, Mr. Secretary, I am going to ask you if you won't grant the same favor to the men who fought to save the Republic that you have granted to the men who fought to destroy it," and there was but one answer and it came quickly, " Of course I will," I didn't have to be wise at all. It was just as easy as taking candy from a baby. So I went out of that office and I think I was six inches taller than when I went in. I had done something to favor every man who wants to go to Portland, and I hope every man in the Grand Army of the Republic wants to go.

A voice.— We all want to go.

Well, one cent a mile it is now, with some trimmings that have been added since then, but without that it would have been three cents and a half a mile and still some trimmings, but the way it is, it is one cent a mile. Of course, the Pullmans come extra, and this half-cent a mile extra for riding on the Pullman makes another little frill. I don't know that I can do anything with the secretary about that added half cent. I am going to try to make him believe that we were to have the fare without that if I can, but I don't know how that will be.

Well, another thing, men. Soon after I came into office letters commenced coming to me from Comrades scattered all over the Republic telling me that the increased cost of living had so absorbed their funds that they were not able to buy food and fuel and pay for medical services, and many of them were sick, and by reason of our increased age and infirmities had lost their earning capacity, so that they relied solely upon their pensions, and with these changes there was much suffering. It may not be that way in your department. You people look like you are able to take care of yourselves; but, friends, there are thousands of our Comrades who do not have the means of subsistence and who have lost their earning capacity, so we concluded we would see the Senate Committee on Pensions and see if we could not have a meeting of them, and our friend Senator Smoot (applause), the widows' friend, Senator Smoot, said yes, he would call the committee together and they would hear us, and he called the committee together, and with them came Representative Sherwood, our Comrade from Ohio. Now, men, in appointing that committee I gave it all the thought and judgment that I had to secure a proper committee, and I had reasons for naming every man that is a member of that committee. I named Washington Gardner because of his relations to the Grand Army of the Republic and because of his experience in legislation and because he is a splendid man with a very agreeable presence and a very persuasive voice, and I made him chairman of that committee. I put Colonel Royce of Washington on because he is on the ground and had experience on the committee. I put Colonel McElroy on that committee because he edits the National Tribune and is everlastingly talking and sometimes doing things, too, and I found him to be a very useful man. But I put General Sherwood on because he was my Comrade and because he was in Congress, and for another reason that I do not often use when I am doing things, and that was because he was a Democrat. (Laughter and applause.) You know we don't have any politics, but it is about the first time I ever found one that I could put in a proper place and use him. (Laughter.) And then I came down to Indiana and put Judge Hensch on because he was a Democrat and Department Commander. Now, I want to say this: I have observed that I am unable to distinguish any difference when these men are just Comrades. When they are Comrades a Democrat looks just as good to me as a Republican does, and I have respect for them and for their politics, because in this Republic every man has a right to do as he pleases, and I respect the fellow who opposes me if he is sincere just as much as if he is for me. Let him make his fight, stand up and give and take, and I wanted Judge Hensch because he was a good friend of " Tommie " Marshall, the Vice-President, and a number of other distinguished Congressmen, and so I made up this kind of a committee and happened to be ex officio a member of the committee myself, and I thought that was a pretty good thing, too. (Laughter.) Well, we had the Senate Committee and presented the matter to them, and, men, they listened just as carefully as if they were going to be beneficiaries of the bill themselves, and when I told them of a number of cases there could be no question but what they were convinced. I took one of my near neighbors, a man who had served four years, and who was such a sufferer from asthma and phthisic that he spend his hours on his elbows and knees because that was the only position in which he could get his breath, gasping all the time nearly, and with medical attention two or three times a week, and he was getting $25. He had an old wife trying to nurse him. He had an orphan grandchild, and they were trying to live in a four-room house for which they paid $10 a month. Their doctor's bills averaged $5 to $10 a week. Coal was $10 a ton. Clothing and food was proportionately high. And I said: Gentlemen, how is that man to live, how is he to live, and are you going to let him go to his grave for lack of medical attention, fuel or food. Is that the way the men who saved the Republic are to end their days? And one of them said, and it was my own Senator, too, he said, You make an application for a special pension and I will see that it is granted. I said, Senator New, I know fifty men in my neighborhood who are in just as distressing a condition as that man; will you grant all of them special pensions? And there are thousands of them in the Republic. And, suffice to say, men, it was made clear to them, so clear that they could only see one course, and our friend, Senator Smoot, says, " I will take the matter up immediately, and I think I can have the Senate Committee pass on it to-morrow." Well, that was early enough. But that night, before I slept, someone called me on the 'phone and said, " The Senate Committee passed on that to-day and it was unanimous." (Applause.)

And I was greatly encouraged, but my friend Sherwood had his bill in the lower house and he was very tenacious, and General Sherwood is a very old man and very deaf, and, after all my talking to him, and after my telling him that I did not like his bill and did not want it to become enacted into law, he afterwards said I told him I was in favor of it. Now, that was only caused by his lack of hearing, and it is very unfortunate for him, because General Sherwood is a great soldier and a brave man and our friend, and so it was just unfortunate. Well the Sherwood bill passed the House. I did not want it. It said that this bill shall not apply to any soldier whose income exceeds $1,000, including his pension. That is, if your income was $1,000 and $5 you were not entitled to a pension under it. If your income was $995 you were entitled to a pension under it. If you were a little better off next year and it went over the thousand dollars you lost your pension. If you were a little poorer next year or had to call the doctor twice more you would be entitled to it, and I didn't want something that I had and I did not have. I did not want it. And then it said it shall not apply to a man if he was a member of a Soldiers' Home. Now, men, it looked too much like placing the stigma of pauperism upon my comrades, and I said this to my Senator, " Senator New, if it comes to the question of starvation or being denominated as a pauper let them starve." (Applause,) " If this Republic wants them to end their days that way let them end it that way." Suffice it to say that when the Sherwood bill went to the Senate the Smoot bill was substituted for it and the Smoot bill passed the Senate, and to make it short when it went back to the House the Smoot bill was substituted for the Sherwood bill in the House upon General Sherwood's motion (applause), and 15 minutes after the bill was laid upon the President's desk it had been signed (applause), and became a law to be enforced from and after its passage, and next time you get your pension I just want you to remember that I had something to do with it. (Applause.)

And that is more gratification to me than anything else there is in the commandership of the Grand Army of the Republic, that I believe I have been able to do something for my comrades who most needed help. (Applause.)

Those are the three things I had in my mind when I was elected Commander in Chief. Another thing I have in my mind now — I don't know whether I will be able to accommmplish anything in that matter or not — but there are two men outside of the Grand Army of the Republic who might be in it to every one that is inside of it, and if these men who have been the beneficiaries of the legislation procured by the Grand Army of the Republic are not in they should be with us. And any soldier who has any regard for his comrades, or any gratitude, if he don't become a member of the Grand Army he is a slacker. Now it is up to the Department of New York to get after these fellows. There are some of them that ought to be with us. There are a few of them probably we do not want. Scrutinize their record carefully. But we ought to add at least one-third to our numbers within the next year. Now if that shall be accomplished I will feel fully satisfied with my administration.

Now in going to Portland I wish every man on the Atlantic coast could go to the Pacific coast. It would be like I said to the people over at Boston — probably some of you heard me say it — that I was proud of the city of Boston with its 300 years of history, and if I could I would have every citizen of the Republic go to Boston and visit that most historic city with all of its patriotic monuments and tablets and everything else that is good in American history, because I said I believed they would be better American citizens if they would do that. Well, that pleased my Boston friends very much. Then I said to them, and if I could I would have every citizen of Boston go and visit this vast empire that stretches away out to the Pacific ocean, and I believe the people of Boston would be better American citizens. I do say that any man who travels this country in its great dimensions will feel like he is a better American citizen than if he had stayed at home. (Applause.) It is a wonderful empire that stretches away off to the Pacific slope, and it would be a grand thing if in our closing days we could visit that country that we had saved and made so glorious. I hope we will just strain a little to see our way clear to go there. If you have the one cent rate and the pension furnishing money to pay that rate why not blow it in, boys, and go?

I expect I will have opportunity to talk to you again, and I thank you for the time and ask pardon for having taken so much of it. (Great applause.)

(Three cheers were given for the Commander-in-Chief.)

COMMANDER-IN-CHIEF.— I thank you all heartily.

COMMANDER KIRCHNER.— The Assistant Adjutant-General will read the communication from the National Headquarters.

The communication was read as follows:

HEADQUARTERS GRAND ARMY OF THE REPUBLIC.

INDIANAPOLIS, IND., *May* 29, 1918.

EDW. J. ATKINSON, ASSISTANT ADJUTANT-GENERAL,

Department of New York, G. A. R., State Capitol, Albany, N. Y.:

MY DEAR COMRADE.— The Commander-in-Chief and I have just had a conference in Chicago with the Chairman of the Trans-Continental Passenger Association, and he desires from us certain information.

It has been decided that no tickets will be sold except on presentation of a certificate countersigned by the Commander-in-Chief and Adjutant-General. These certificates will be issued to the Assistant Adjutant-General of each Department, and will be distributed by him to the various Posts of his Department.

Members of the Grand Army of the Republic, Woman's Relief Corps, National Association of Army Nurses of the Civil War, Ladies of the G. A. R., Daughters of Veterans, Sons of Veterans, and Sons of Veterans' Auxiliary, who purpose attending the National Encampment, and members of their families, who are entitled to the reduced rates, must secure their certificate from the Adjutant of their respective Posts, or of the Post nearest them. Further information as to the issuing of these certificates will soon be promulgated in General Orders.

Will you kindly let me know by return mail the approximate number of certificates which will be required in your Department. It will be better to make the number higher than expected. This information is desired so that the Passenger Association may know how many certificates to have printed, and it is necessary that we hear from you at once.

Fraternally yours,

ROBERT W. MCBRIDE, *Adjutant-General.*

"*June* 10, 1918.

COMRADE ROBERT W. McBRIDE, *Adjutant-General,*
G· A. R., 1224 *State Life Building, Indianapolis, Ind.:*

MY DEAR COMRADE.—Yours of 'May 29th received and in
reply to same would say that this Department will need 400
certificates.

Very truly yours in F. C. & L.,
EDWARD J. ATKINSON,
Assistant Adjutant-General."

COMMANDER KIRCHNER.—Are there any other communications?

THE ACTING ASSISTANT ADJUTANT-GENERAL.—A lady outside
wished to be admitted and she was informed that no ladies will be
admitted this afternoon and so handed this communication in to be
read:

"DEAR COMMANDER.— Convey to the Comrades in convention my heart whole greetings, and best wishes for your
convention. May the name of G. A. R. be emblazoned forever
upon the Flag that is going forward to bless the nations of the
earth. The women who are your kin will never fail you, and
in the years of the ages will keep your spirit alive to bless
humanity. America sent its Pershing across but America
had it 69th Regiment, and among the Blue Devils they
showed the spark that lights the line that may bend but will
never break, God won't let it.

Yours in F. C. & L.,
LAURA B. PRISK,
Mother of Flag Day."

COMRADE BELL.— I have one or two reports from committees
ready, if you will take them up now.

COMMANDER KIRCHNER.—We are ready to take them up
now.

COMRADE BELL.— I will present one in the first instance on the
Judge Advocate's report. The committee direct me to report as
follows:

"Your committee on the report of the Judge Advocate
respectfully reports that it has examined that report and

finds that the work of the office has been faithfully and intelligently performed and therefore recommend the adoption of the following resolution:

Resolved, That the report of the Judge Advocate be approved and the Judge Advocate commended for faithful service.

(Signed)   JAMES D. BELL, Chairman.
ALFRED LYTH,
GEORGE BLAIR,
Committee.

On motion duly seconded the report was adopted.

COMRADE BELL.— The Committee on the address of the Department Commander is ready to report.

To the Department Encampment Comrades.— Your Committee on the address of the Department Commander respectfully reports:

That it has carefully considered that address and commends it for its brief and comprehensive presentation of the work of the Department Commander during his term. The excellent condition of the Department is most convincing proof of the constant care of the Department Commander and the good judgment by which he has been guided in the discharge of his onerous duties. This committee desires particularly to recommend to the consideration of Posts the suggestions of the Department Commander in regard to the exercise of more care and more charity in the matter of suspensions. The suspended list should be shortened, instead of being lengthened. Your committee further reports that the action of the Council of Administration in appropriating the sum of $250 from the defense fund for the prosecution of Comrade Doty's case should be confirmed. The following Resolutions are presented for adoption:

Resolved, That the address of the Department Commander be approved and the labors of the Department Commander be commended and that he carry with him in his retirement from his great office our love and admiration.

Resolved, That the action of the Council of Administration at its meeting in January last in appropriating $250 from the defense fund to aid in the prosecution of the case of Comrade Edwin A. Doty of Albany be confirmed.

Signed by the Committee.

James D. Bell, *Chairman.*
John C. Shotts
Charles A. Orr
James M. Snyder
John S. Maxwell
Samuel C. Pierce
James S. Graham

On motion duly seconded the report of the committee was adopted unanimously.

Comrade Fairhead.— From the Committee on Chaplain's report:

We have considered the report of Chaplain Kline. No Post reports were sent to him. These went to headquarters. He suggests more care for headstones for veterans' graves. With this we agree. He further suggests the decoration of graves of veterans' wives. This seems to us impracticable as a general plan and better be left to localities and home sentiments.

Respectfully submitted by the committee,

George B. Fairhead
Rev. Chas. L. Scherger
Ezra Stillman

On motion duly seconded the report of the committee was adopted.

Comrade Bush.— Your committee to examine the report of the Junior Vice Department Commander is ready to submit its finding. The Committee on the Report of the Junior Vice Department Commander respectfully reports that they have read his report, that they commend the patriotic activities of the Junior Vice Department Commander and approve the report.

(Signed) ROBERT P. BUSH
C. J. WESCOTT
JOHN W. MULLINS

On motion duly seconded the report of the committee was adopted.

COMRADE STAFFORD.— Department Commander, your committee on the report of the Senior Vice Commander respectfully reports that they have read the same and approve it and recommend its adoption.

(Signed) AUSTIN H. STAFFORD
DANIEL H. COLE
JAMES A. ALLIS
                    Committee

The report of the committee was adopted.

COMRADE PILCHER.— This is the report of the committee on the Report of the Medical Directors. Your Committee desires to express approval of the patriotic sentiments contained in the report of the Department Medical Director, and recommends that the report be placed on file.

(Signed) LEWIS L. PILCHER
ROBERT P. BUSH

The report of the committee was adopted.

COMRADE LONG.— I am making a report for the Committee on Patriotic Instruction. The committee, to whom was referred the report of the Patriotic Instructor, would respectfully recommend that the report be approved and printed in the minutes.

(Signed) E. P. LONG
A. B. OSTRANDER
JOHN QUINCY ADAMS
                    Committee

The report of the committee was adopted.

COMRADE DRAPER.— I have a report on the Assistant Adjutant-General.

The report of the Assistant Adjutant-General was read in full and is as follows:

Report of the Assistant Adjutant-General,

Albany, N. Y., *June 25, 1918.*

Comrade William F. Kirchner, *Department Commander, New York, G. A. R.:*

I herewith submit my report as Assistant Adjutant-General of this Department during your administration:

The following table shows the membership at the close of the year 1917, and the changes during that year:

```
Number of members in good standing January 1, 1917. . 14,045
Loss during the year.........................  2,056
Gain during the year........................    427
                                                     ——————  1,629

    Total membership January 1, 1918.............. 12,416
```

```
Loss by death during the year, January 1, 1917, to Jan-
    uary 1, 1918 ....................................  1,195
Loss by honorable discharge ........................     25
Loss by transfer ..................................     52
Loss by suspension ................................    544
Loss by delinquent reports .........................    124
Loss by surrender of charter........................    116

    Total loss .....................................  2,056
Gain by muster ............................    142
Gain by transfer ............................     91
Gain by reinstatement .......................    166
Gain by reinstatement from delinquent reports..     28

    Total gain ....................................    427

    Net loss ......................................  1,629
```

The following Posts have surrendered charters from June, 1917, to June, 1918:

Post No.		Number member
37	Located at Auburn, N. Y.	28
64	Located at Chittenango, N. Y.	6
67	Located at New York.	8
115	Located at Middlesex, N. Y.	10
154	Located at Marathon, N. Y.	9
158	Located at Brookton, N. Y.	10
396	Located at LeRoy, N. Y.	15
401	Located at Rose, N. Y.	17
447	Located at Hannibal, N. Y.	13
543	Located at Washingtonville, N. Y.	10
591	Located at New Haven, N. Y.	9
669	Located at Brooklyn, N. Y.	7
	Total	142

Your committee have examined the within report and recommend its adoption.

HENRY C. DRAPER, *Chairman*
GEORGE H. LESTER."

Unanimously adopted.

COMRADE TANNER.—Commander, in this Encampment we hear a great deal about conservation of food. I am interested at the present moment in the conservation of time. Your Committee on Resolutions will meet to-morrow morning at nine o'clock and be in here very soon after that to make their report. It won't be much trouble I imagine from what I have in my pocket to dispose of that order of business. Under our rules and regulations the election and installation of officers comes as the last thing of the encampment. Now let us get the candidates before us and get through with the report. Let us have the nominations now and then a good many of us can get away about noon to-morrow. I move you, sir, that we go into nomination of officers and that election be made a special order for to-morrow morning at 10 o'clock.

The motion was duly seconded and carried.

Quartermaster-General Stowits.— The time of the Commander-in-Chief is very short. He has several visitations to make among our allied associates in this city, and I therefore ask that he be excused.

Commander Kirchner.— According to the rules and regulations the first office for which there are to be nominations is that of Commander for the ensuing year. We are now prepared to hear them.

Comrade Bell.— Comrades of the Encampment, on behalf of my comrades of Kings County it is my honor and pleasure to nominate for Commander of this great department for the ensuing term Comrade Lewis S. Pilcher of U. S. Grant Post 327 of Brooklyn. (Applause.)

At the outbreak of the Rebellion Comrade Pilcher was a student in the University of Michigan. After his graduation in 1862 he entered the medical school to fit himself for the practice of the profession of medicine in which he was destined to be so distinguished. Early in 1864 the call for troops was so pronounced that he abandoned his studies and enlisted in the 2nd United States Colored Cavalry in February, 1864, as hospital steward for which his training has fitted him to give good service. He remained in the army in the faithful discharge of his duties until his honorable discharge in September, 1865. He then returned to his studies, which he completed in 1866, receiving his degree of M. D. In 1867 he was commissioned as an assistant surgeon in the navy. In the harbor of Havana, while on his first cruise, he was ordered to take the place of the surgeon of of the training ship Saratoga who was dying of yellow fever, the first victim of an epidemic of that great plague which had broken out on that great ship. Thirty-seven of her crew, numbering in all 224, were attacked and 17 died on the homeward voyage. Surgeon Pilcher stuck to his task with heroic fortitude, ministering to all sufferers with entire self forgetfullness and when his ship reached New York and he was relieved from responsibility he fell in the sick ward and had to make a fight for his own life which fortunately proved successful.

After five years' service in the navy Comrade Pilcher resigned his commission and began the practice of his profession in Brooklyn, and in that he soon became distinguished, and in time reached the front rank as a surgeon, not only in Brooklyn, but in the entire country.

Comrade Pilcher's work in the Grand Army has been notable. He was successfully Commander of his Post and was chosen as Surgeon General of the Grand Army of the Republic. Comrade Pilcher has made good wherever he has been placed. He was a good soldier. He is a good citizen, a distinguished surgeon, and in our ranks he has been noted for his comradeship, for learning, for standing for those things which were of advantage and interest to his comrades.

Now, Comrades of the Encampment, without further elaboration, I desire to say that the Kings County comrades assure you that Comrade Pilcher is worthy of your election as Commander of this great Department, and ask you to compliment them by his election, in the full confidence that the interests of our great order will thereby be promoted. (Great applause.)

Comrade Snyder.— Commander and comrades, I do not believe that it is necessary for me to say one word to you, who have been coming to these encampments all these years, and who are acquainted with Dr. Pilcher. You know his worth, you know his ability. Dignified, interested in comradeship and in every effort that he has made he has proven himself worthy of the honor that this encampment ought to bestow upon him. I cannot say one word more than already been said in his favor, but I do, representing the delegates from Rensselaer, Schenectady and Washington Counties, who are here, and who would manifest their appreciation for a comrade who has been with us all these years, second his nomination for the office of Department Commander. (Applause.)

Comrade Smith.— There is nothing that I can say but what has been said by Comrades Bell and Snyder; consequently I simply rise to say that the Albany County delegates are delighted and instruct that I shall say for them that they will vote for Comrade Pilcher for Department Commander.

Comrade Lyth (of Buffalo).—At the request of numerous comrades from the City of Buffalo, and from others, neighbors of ours, I rise to second this nomination. We do it, knowing the conscientious work that has been put in by our Comrade Pilcher, and we hope and trust to see him successful at the head of this organization and we will never regret it. (Applause.)

Comrade Bush.— Commander and comrades, at the request of delegates from Baldwin Post No. 6 I rise to second the nomination of Comrade Pilcher for the office of Department Commander. (Applause.) Two years ago I suggested it to his son when he told me of the interest that his father took in the Grand Army, of his pleasure in being elected Commander of his Post, and I suggested it to the son that his father allow me to present his name for Commander, but the comrades of the department had been promised and pledged, and we finally thought it was not wise to present his name at that time. I have hugged this desire ever since and am only too pleased now to second his nomination. One reason is that he is a doctor, and that calls on me to tell a story of a gentleman of Irish decent that was in my office the other day and war topics came uppermost in our conversation. He said, " Were you a doctor during the war?" " No, I was a private." Yes, you were making wounds instead of curing them ?" " Yes." " You got in the habit of killing people down there?" " Well, we were expected to if we had a chance." " And so when you got that habit you came home and studied medicine?" (Laughter.) In the same line as he suggested it. But I want to say of our Comrade Pilcher that his fights since he came out of the navy have been against disease and that he has evinced the same interest for the health of his comrades that he has for the success of the Grand Army, and I take pleasure in seconding his nomination.

Comrade Stafford.— On behalf of the delegates from Chautauqua County I take great pleasure in seconding the nomination of Dr. Pilcher for the office of Department Commander.

COMRADE MITCHELL.— On behalf of the delegates from Westchester County we take great pleasure in seconding the nomination of Comrade Pilcher.

COMRADE WEAVER.— Representing Post 151, of Syracuse, I have been selected to present to this department the name of a comrade for the high office of Department Commander. This comrade of mine as a boy of 19 in August, 1862, enlisted in Company K of the 10th New York Heavy Artillery, and he served three years. He left to look after his business, making arms for the Government at that time. He was a tool maker and was earning his share of the profits of from two to three hundred dollars a week. He left that to go with his boys into the army. He has been a successful business man. He is connected with the Commercial Travelers Association and is Senior Vice-President of that organization of some 90,000 men. He has been a comrade of the Grand Army for 48 years. For four successive years he was commander of his Post, President of the Memorial Association of our city, and he is a trusted, worthy comrade.

Now, comrades, I am one of the countrymen. I do not believe in New York having the office of commander all the time. They have it at the present time. Only a little while ago Comrade Bell was Commander from Kings 'County, and there are other comrades whose claims should be considered, and we are entirely opposed in our section, and many of my comrades who are here assembled are of the same feeling, that we do not like to see the office of Commander selected a year in advance. We are now comrades engaged in a great war, to demonstrate whether democracy shall prevail or aristocracy. Now let us take it up here in the Grand Army and fight it out on that line. Let the delegates selected and the officers of the department come here and select their officers. That is the way to do it. If not, you may just as well be a rubber stamp and stay at home if these nominations are to be made and ratified, then what is the use of our coming here to ratify their work? Half a dozen can do it as well as for us to come here, if we are to have nothing to say. You will make no mistake, comrades, in endorsing the man whose name I shall present for Commander, John H. Forey of Post No. 151. (Applause.)

COMRADE PARSONS.— I am from U. S. Grant Post 327. Commander and comrades, I have never had any idea that there was any aristocracy in the Grand Army of the Republic. I have belonged to it a great many years. I graduated from the public school at the age of 14. I didn't have any education. Our comrade whom we present for Department Commander Louis S. Pilcher — Comrade Bell in stating some of his good qualifications failed to make this statement: At the age of 14 he entered college in the Michigan University and at the age of 17 he graduated, the youngest graduate that ever went out of Michigan University. He is a comrade as we all are. There are no aristocrats. We do not elect our delegates from one part of the state but from every part of the state because of their qualifications for the office. I speak for Comrade Pilcher as hundreds of my comrades do. I speak for Comrade Pilcher for the Post to which I belong, which has 200 members, and every member of that Post heartily endorses him because they know he will make a great Commander of the Department of the State of New York. We hope that the comrades here will elect Comrade Pilcher and we will be responsible for him. If he fails to make such a Commander as we expect him to make we will court martial him.

COMMANDER KIRCHNER.—Are there any other nominations?

COMRADE DEPEW (Root Post 151).— I am not Chauncey Depew but I suppose I am somewhat connected with him, but I am not such a talker as he is. I rise to second the nomination of Comrade Forey. I do it because I know the man. I have been in the Grand Army with him for a good many years and I know from the record that he is a good man and a good comrade. I do not say he is any better than any other comrade, (but I do say he is as good as any other comrade whether he comes from Buffalo, Brooklyn or New York. We are all supposed to be good men. If we were not we would not be in the Grand Army to-day. We would not have the Grand Army badge on us if we were not considered good men to-day by our Government that we help to support, as we do support, and which we helped to save. Comrade Forey did as much as any other comrade could do, and if he is elected Commander this Grand Army convention will make no mistake. You will find him a true man in every respect, and let me say this, that the lowest, if there is one, comrade in the post has just as much favor from Comrade as the highest one. He knows no difference in that respect.

We have colored men in our Post, colored men that we are proud of, that helped to throw off the shackles of slavery. John H. Forey's right hand is out to meet them on every occasion the same as it is to meet our own. It is a pleasure for me to second the nomination of such a man. I began to think there was nobody here but Brooklyn men and New York men, but I guess there are a few others. Now we ask that the Commander of this department for the coming year be selected from the central or western part of the state. There is in the central and in the western part of this state just as good men as you can find in any other part of the state, and so I ask you, comrades, you who are delegates to this convention, to stand firm for the central and western part of the state by electing ohn H. Forey. (Applause.)

Comrade D. W. Burdick (Post 41).— I rise to second the nomination of John H. Forey. My knowledge of John H. Forey is that in 1862 on the 30th of August he enlisted in my battery. He served with me during the war, until I was promoted to another command. He is a faithful, honest straight forward Grand Army man. (Applause.)

Thomas H. Stritch.— Department Commander and comrades, I want to say to this comrade who spoke a while ago that there are some comrades from New York City who are willing to go outside of their own city and vote for a comrade that comes from another section of the state. I am here to represent myself. I am not authorized to cast a vote for this candidate or that candidate. I ame here to represent myself and in that way I am going to second the nomination of Comrade Forey for Department Commander, for this very reason, Commander and Comrades: Time after time we come to these different conventions, you know it as well as I do, and we have no choice in the selection of candidats for the different offices. They are selected ahead of us. We come here and we are supposed to do as we are told. On this occasion, comrades, you who are members of Posts, who are delegates, you have your chance now to show whether you will vote for the selected candidate or the candidate that is chosen by the comrades of the Grand Army of the Republic of the State of New York. That is why I am here to second the nomination of Comrade Forey. (Applause.)

Comrade Ballard (of Watertown).— I rise to second the nomination of Comrade Forey. Our Post is entitled to five votes in this encampment. I am the only man to represent the Post. I could not get the Commander, nor the Senior Vice-Commander, nor the Junior Vice-Commander, nor the other delegates to come. They said there was no use to come, the selection for the future for the office of Commander was made last year at Saratoga. I am not here to make a speech, but that is the truth, and not only that, but for a fact my Post instructed me, instructed the delegates that should come to this encampment to support Comrade Forey. They knew him, they knew him as a young man, they knew him as a soldier, they were comrades with him, and they know what is said in his favor here to-day is every word true, and I know that the efferson County delegates, who are entitled to be here but are not here, because they say it is no use to come, because the elections are all fixed up the year beforehand.

Comrade Bell.— I desire to say that I attended the encampment at Saratoga last year and I know for a fact that Comrade Pilcher's name was not mentioned there and he was not a candidate there; that the name of another comrade was mentioned, and that it was only long aferward that Comrade Pilcher was named as candidate and he had nothing to do with what the comrade says.

Comrade Doody (Post 69).— Commander, I will state that consistency is a jewel, and I have been here, coming many and many occasions to the different encampments of this great state. I have always been an independent, and those of you who know me pretty well know that I have opposed certain restrictions as to nominations but, as I said, consistency thou art a jewel, and there is but very little consistency in some of the statements made here in regard to nominations. When I am asked to go into a caucus or a conference I am honorable enough to state my opinions, I am honorable enough when I state them to stand to them, I am honor-

able enough to know that when a nomination is made and I am
bound to do so I will do it. That is an honorable trait in a gentleman and in a comrade of the Grand Army of the Republic
especially.

Now then when you go into a caucus you will support your
nominees, won't you, as men? I say to a man who goes into a
caucus, if he opposes that caucus when he comes here, I call him
nothing but a sycophant and a treacherous man. That is my
expression of this, and hence when a man comes to me and says,
" Comrade Doody, are you in favor of a certain man? " I say I
have to consider that and I have considered carefully, and I have
done it here independent of the caucus and I have succeeded.
This time I say to you, comrades, that it is no more than just and
right that when a man is asked to go into a caucus and he does it
and then chooses to break it, that is a treacherous act of conduct
on his part, and it would be on my parrt, hence I will second the
nomination of the man from Brooklyn because I was bound to do
it as an honorable man and will do it, and I second the nomination of Comrade Pilcher.   (Applause.)

COMRADE BLAIR.— Commander and comrades, it is indeed
refreshing to those of an independent mind to have listened to the
discussion here within the last few minutes, but I feel in all my
experience of nearly 12 years of active work in the Grand Army
that I have failed to discover any revelations of autocracy.   There
has been a great deal said, and there is no man within the sound
of my voice who is more hostile to autocracy than I am.   I believe
in a square deal, and I also believe in preparation, and without
experience, without consultation, and without weighing the things
that are apt to crop up from time to time you will not succeed, and
when you call a caucus that caucus gives you a chance, you independent men I am appealing to now—it gives you a chance to say
what you feel and you can act accordingly.   But when you go into
a caucus, and I was Chairman of the New York County caucus of
the City of New York, and I represent 67 votes who have been
pledged to the candidate from Brooklyn, and I want to tell you,
comrades, that this argument of autocracy is a catch penny argument that counts for nothing with fair-minded fighting men.   If
I go into a caucus I am a free man, I go there to abide by the

vote of the majority. This is the rule of the American Republic everywhere. Otherwise we would have anarchy all over this land. The minority has always submitted to the majority, and you might call it by whatever name you please you must recognize the fact that there cannot be any success in any department of life, including convention work, without some preparation and without weighing the conditions as they confront you, and the reason I rise, Commander, is that I was Chairman of the caucus in New York City and I felt justified in taking the floor and defending the caucus of which I was chairman. (Applause.)

COMRADE STRITCH.— I do not want any wrong impression to go out that the Post I was commander of was represented at that caucus by me. I want the comrades to understand I did not attend the caucus. If I was healthy enough to do it I would have done it, but the caucus I am attending is the caucus of accredited delegates. That is you. You know the object of a caucus. It is simply the gathering of a few. It is not a representative body by any means. The idea of a comrade standing up here and saying he has the authority to cast the vote of 67 Posts of New York. (Cries of he did not say that.) I want this understood, that my Post was not pledged in that caucus. I have always been a consistent comrade. I have always attended meetings of the department and many of the National Encampments for many years, and have done my work there. However, I am doing my work now and I am doing it on the floor.

(Several voices moved that nominations be closed.)

COMMANDER KIRCHNER.—A motion has been made and duly seconded that nominations be closed. Are you ready for the question?

(Cries of question.)

All those in favor of the motion that nominations be closed will say aye, and those opposed no.
The motion is carried.

COMMANDER KIRCHNER.—We are now ready to receive nominations for Senior Vice Department Commander.

COMRADE MERES (Post 559).—Comrades, I want first to direct your attention to a branch of the service on whom rested the initial force of this rebellion. The regular army of the United States was composed of commissioned officers largely from the South, in sympathy with a cabinet and President who were in favor of dissolution. That body of commissioned officers, to a large extent, when the opportunity offered, hauled down the old flag and put up 'l:ce the stars and bars. But there was a little company of the rank and file that was down in the wilds of Texas who when they were parading up and were asked to step three paces to the front and join the Confederacy with the promise of promotion and rapid advancement — one of the comrades who is a member of my Post stepped forward and said to Joe Johnston, " I enlisted under that flag, I enlisted to serve the Constitution of the United States and to take such pay and allowances as Congress from time to time might offer. Now, Colonel, if you will take that flag with you we are with you to a man." And the truth of what is verified by the fact that it came from Joseph E. Johnston's lips at the time of the funeral of General Grant when I presented Comrade Mood in the carriage where Johnston sat along with General Sheridan. Another comrade of my Post was a Sergeant Major. His wife was a company laundress. She took the flag and pinned it around her skirts and the Sergeant was condemned by a Court Marshal to be shot because he cut a flag staff down, and Johnston was the one that interceded and saved his life. These are the regular army boys. These are the men that were first in the field and last in the field, and I come to-day before you boys to ask you to do your duty by the regular army. I know how you regarded us during the times of strife. I know that the regular army man with the scales on his shoulders was despised, but we have proved ourselves loyal comrades. We do not get the benefit that you have by mingling with your associates who went to the front and came back with you. For fifty years I never met a man who served in my company, and yet I was a faithful member of the Grand Army of the Republic, and now I ask you to consider the name of one man who served in the regular army during the last period of the war, was sent after the war to the frontier, received a medal from Congress for services in the Indian War, and so I say with Webster, Comrade Ostrander needs no eulogy. There is Comrade Ostrander. You need no eulogy, you are a comrade, and therefore I take great pleasure in placing you in nomination. (Applause.)

COMRADE NAYLAND (Post 259).—Without any oratory or further talk, from my personal knowledge of Comrade Ostrander, knowing him to be a good man and true, and loyal and true member of the Grand Army of the Republic, I take great pleasure at this time in seconding his nomination for the office of Senior Vice Department Commander. (Applause.)

COMRADE NACHTMAN (of Middletown Post).— I rise to second Comrade Ostrander.

COMRADE STRITCH (Post 330).— I rise to second the nomination of Comrade Ostrander, for this reason: I like the way he began his fight.. He began canvassing, seeking comrades individually for a year or more, asking their suffrage. He has gone about his work independently. He has gone about it cleverly and to-day he has convinced most of the comrades that he deserves this office and I am very glad to be here and second this nomination.

COMRADE NACHTMAN (of Middletown Post).— I rise to second the nomination of Comrade Ostrander.

COMRADE ALLIS (Post 66).— I rise to place in nomination for Senior Vice of this Department a member of my Post who has occupied the various chairs, who has been a member for years without number, who has devoted the last 10 or 12 years of his entire time to patriotic work, being as luck would have it so situated that he can devote his time to that way. He has been patriotic instructor of our Post for the last 10 years and also of the County of Onondaga. Having held these various offices he certainly is qualified, as all those who know him will certify, to hold any position in the Grand Army of the Republic, and I have the honor of presenting the name of H. Stewart Warner of Post 66 for Senior Vice Commander of this Department.

COMRADE METZGER (of Lily Post).— It gives me great pleasure to have the opportunity to second the nomination of this comrade, whom I know as a comrade is entitled to that office. He is willing at any time to spend his time when there is anything wanted for the benefit of the Grand Army, and I am glad I have the opportunity of seconding his nomination — Comrade Henry Stewart Warner.

COMRADE BLAIR.— Commander, in behalf of the delegates that met in caucus from the County of New York I am authorized to cast to-morrow and therefore naturally will second this nomination for Comrade Warner — and we have this to say, that we recognize that the upper part of the State, and especially the central part of the State should have recognition on the ticket. Now we did not come here from New York asking you for the Commander because we had the Commander last year, and I wish, Commander, to remind the delegates that it is no longer a question of territory, for if it was considered — the number of men that this State sent to the front in the 60's, you must not lose sight of the fact that New York city furnished 250,000, and the balance of the State furnished an equal number, therefore when we do get a little more at our end of the State you should always remember that we did half the work so far as following the call of Abraham Lincoln is concerned. I therefore second the nomination of Comrade Warner for Senior Vice on behalf of 67 delegates from the County of New York.

COMRADE STRITCH.— I want to know if my post, the post I represent is named?

COMRADE BLAIR.— It is not.

COMRADE LOUD.— I do not rise to second any nomination but simply to correct a misstatement. I was present at the caucus of the New York delegates. They acted upon the recommendation of the Department Commander to decline to act upon any other nomination. A motion was made to endorse candidates for Senior and Junior Vice Commander, and no action was taken, and the comrade who has made a statement to the contrary is mistaken. I would like to ask the comrade if I am not stating the truth.

COMRADE BLAIR.— Not exactly.

Comrade Isaacs.— I wish to state, comrades, while it is hardly right for the Department Commander or the Adjutant-General to interfere with either candidate — unfortunately I was selected secretary of the caucus committee. Ed Atkinson was elected chairman. Under instructions from the chairman I called a caucus of the delegates from the Posts of New York. Every delegate was notified to be present. Against my wishes and desires I was re-elected secretary. The question came up on the adoption of a report or recommendation whom the Posts of New York should endorse for Department Commander. Forty-nine we:c cast for Comrade Pilcher. No other name was mentioned. Seven posts declined to vote. There was a committee appointed of five by the chairman to meet here and make a recommendation to the conference for New York city, whom they should support for Senior Vice Commander. They performed that duty, and I wish to state that Comrade Blair is perfectly right — 67 comrades signified their intention of voting for Comrade Warner. (Applause.)

Comrade McAuliffe.— I rise to second the nomination of Comrade Stewart Warner. I have known the comrade for many years. I have known him to be an honest, faithful comrade of the Grand Army of the Republic, and I am going to say that I appeal to the aristocracy, the aristocracy of the citizenship of the United States of America that is composed of the Grand Army of the Republic — the men who saved this Republic in the time of peril. That matchless cavalry leader, George A. Custer, and also Philip Sheridan and you dough boys always felt contented when you knew that Sheridan was on the way and Custer on the flanks, and therefore it gives me great pleasure to second the nomination of Comrade Stewart Warner.

Comrade McConekey (of Kings).— On behalf of the delegates from Kings county I rise to heartily endorse and second the nomination of Comrade Warner.

(On motion duly seconded nominations for Senior Vice Commander were closed).

The Commander.— Nominations for Junior Vice Department Commander are in order.

COMRADE TANNER.— Commander and comrades, in the Grand Army I live in Washington and shall until the Grand Army lays me away. I am disposed to go a good ways from home on this occasion, clear from Brooklyn to Buffalo. I have been amused here this afternoon, living in Washington as I have for 29 years, I sometimes go up to the Capitol and sit preferably in the gallery of the House of Representatives. You can hear a great deal of talk and if you are posted fairly well you can know how little sincerity there is in the speaking. Before this war broke out, sir, I had no knowledge of the meaning of the word camouflage. We are getting very much accustomed to it now. We know what it is, and I have heard a great deal of it here this afternoon. While I am inclined to think, if I may accept the judgment and expression of some, that I am a low down " ornery " sort of a cuss in the Grand Army, notwithstanding my membership running back to the year 1868, because if certain things be true I must believe that I am an autocrat. A year ago at Boston propositions were made to me, and you would have thought that I had the Grand Army of New York in my pocket. And yet the gentlemen who made that proposition, and there were several of them, are denouncing autocracy to-day, and they are claiming a great individual wrath. Any man who can take my right from me as a Grand Army man has got to be a better man than I am. I never entered a Grand Army or political convention but what I owned all that was under my hat. It is my business to do as I do and it is not for you to denounce as autocrats those who differ from you. It is not for you to denounce when a year ago you were ready to go into a combination that would cover not only one year but two years. Enough of that.

A matter of form — yes — your badges show it, your expressions show it. Dr. Pilcher is going to be your next Department Commander. Perhaps if there is one of us here that ought to have any shadow of reason for voting against him it might well be me. As I told the National Convention of the Grand Army, when I nominated him for Surgeon-General, way back he held the knife on me, and with a little carelessness he could have let the blood out of me and I would have been saved many years of pain, but I thank God that I have lived to be here and take part in this, the finest encampment of this department that we have had for years.

I have heard one statement made here from the Mayor of the city of Ithaca that I doubt. He says they have only 17,000 population. I say we saw 35,000 at least on the streets. So, boys, don't think that any of this rough stuff goes outside of the hall. We will be exchanging cigars and in the old days we would have been taking a drink together. It all disappears when the ballot is counted and the smoke is wafted away.

Now I have been on my feet many times in the Grand Army to nominate and to second, and of course, we always have joy in serving our friends, and sometimes it is deeper and goes back farther than it does in others, and I am at this moment, sir, to dip into the memory of many years, away back in the early 70's, when I first became acquainted with a comrade of the Grand Army whom I have always held in the deepest affection ever since, and that is George W. Flynn of Buffalo for Junior Vice Commander of this Department. If you want his record — he joined the 85th New York in 1861 and followed the trail to July, 1865, all along the bloody trail that that regiment trod. When his term of enlistment expired he re-enlisted in the same regiment. If you want his educational qualifications I say to you that he was a graduate of the Universities of Andersonville and Florence. In the Grand Army he has been one of the most faithful comrades we ever had. I would have been delighted long years ago, sir, to have asked my comrades to give him even a higher position than he now aspires to, or has consented to be a candidate for to-day, but I never could get his consent. I congratulate, while I am on my feet, sir, you for the splendid record you have made, the Grand Army for the way in which you have upheld its character and dignity and for those who may be disappointed I would say be patient — perhaps under suffering of greater or lesser length of time, if God Almighty will spare your lives long enough we will take you up with joy in turn, but to-day for Junior Vice Commander of the Department I ask you all to take George W. Flynn of Buffalo. (Applause.)

COMRADE ADAM J. WAGNER (Post 542).— I rise to say a few words in favor of the remarks just made by Comrade Tanner. At the installation of officers of Post 9 of Buffalo this year, Comrade Flynn celebrated his 40th anniversary. On that day he was mustered in as Commander of Post 87 in the city of Buffalo. I have known him for 50 years or more, and a more honored and more enthusiastic and more worthy comrade of the Grand Army of the Republic we haven't got. I take great pleasure in seconding the nomination of Comrade George W. Flynn. (Applause.)

COMRADE HOLLAND.— I rise to second the nomination of Comrade Flynn. Comrade Flynn belonged to my brigade. He was captured with me at Plymouth, North Carolina, taken to Andersonville and to Florence with me, and a man that lived through those two places, to stand on this floor ought to be with us to-day, is entitled to some consideration, therefore I am glad to second the nomination of Comrade Flynn.

COMRADE COSTELLO (Post 443).— Commander, I move that the nominations be closed, and that we nominate Comrade Flynn unanimously.

The motion was duly seconded and carried·

COMRADE COSTELLO.— I move that the rules be suspended and that the Adjutant-General cast one ballot for Comrade Flynn for Junior Vice Department Commander.

The motion was duly seconded and carried and the Adjutant-General under the direction of the Commander cast one ballot for Comrade George W. Flynn of Buffalo for Junior Vice Commander.

COMMANDER KIRCHNER.— I declare Comrade George W. Flynn duly elected Junior Vice Commander of this department.

The next order of business is the nomination for Chaplain.

COMRADE TANNER.— I did not intend to be a repeater so quickly, but you know I have deep concern for the spiritual condition of you boys. I know you are in need of it. I have my own ideas about it. I carried a National Encampment for Chaplain-in-Chief once when there were four candidates by saying that I knew the Grand Army so well, and how much intercession they would need at the throne of God, that my favorite for Chaplain-in-Chief was the man who lived 5,000 feet nearer God than any of the rest of the candidates, and splendid old P. C. Iliss.

of Salt Lake City, who went to his grave less than a year ago was elected just because of that little thing that got them. Now then I am concerned to have a Chaplain of the Grand Army of the Republic of the Department of New York who can measure up to the remark, who can appear as our Chaplain in the coming days with christian fervor, a man who when he is before the public we shall be glad to have the citizenship judge of the Grand Army of the Republic, and so, sir, I nominate a comrade that I have got acquainted with since I came to this encampment. I do not know even his first name, but the Commander and I fixed it up in the absence of the Chaplain that he should lead the prayer at the opening of the encampment. I nominate for Chaplain of this department for the ensuing year the Rev. Duncan J. McMillan of Alexander Hamilton Post 182 of New York.

On motion duly seconded nominations for Chaplain were closed.

On motion duly seconded it was ordered that the rules be suspended and that the Adjutant-General cast one vote for the Rev. Duncan J. McMillan as Chaplain of this department for the ensuing year.

Comrades Orr and Draper having been appointed tellers the Adjutant-General announced that he had cast one ballot for the Rev. Duncan J. McMillan as Chaplain of this department for the ensuing year.

COMMANDER KIRCHNER.— The tellers having reported the name of Rev. Duncan J. McMillan of Post 182 as being on the ballot cast by the Acting Assistant Adjutant-General for the office of Chaplain of this department I declare him elected for the ensuing year.

The next order of business is the nomination for medical director.

COMRADE LAWSON (Post 7).— I would nominate Comrade Taylor from Canastota.

COMRADE TANNER.— There is a comrade we all love, and in a large conference last evening we named him as one we would be glad to support. I allude to Comrade Robert P. Bush of Elmira. I say of Dr. Lush, with all my heart, that with all his

Rev. Reuben Kline, Chaplain

faults I love him still.   Sometimes he hasn't kept still enough
to suit me, but it is all in the wash.   The Grand Army of the
Republic owes Dr. Bush more, I think, than it will ever have to
repay.   For the thirteen years he was in the Legislature of this
State he did a great deal for it, and in our conference last night
we thought it was time to give some recognition there.   I had
supposed that somebody from Baldwin Post would be here and
from his intimate knowledge of the record of Dr. Bush and his
Grand Army work would place him in nomination and state those
things which are to his credit, all of them, from 1861 to 1918.
I nominate Dr. Bush.

COMRADE LAWSON.— I withdraw the name of Comrade Taylor
and heartily endorse the nomination of Comrade Bush.

It was moved and seconded, and the motion was carried, that
the Adjutant General cast one ballot for the nominee.

The same comrades acting as tellers reported to the Commander
that the Acting Assistant Adjutant-General had cast one ballot
bearing the name of Robert P. Bush for medical director of this
department for the ensuing year.

COMMANDER KIRCHNER.— The tellers having reported that the
name of Robert P. Bush appears upon the ballot cast for medical
director for the ensuing year, I declare Comrade Robert P. Bush
elected medical director for this department for the ensuing year.

COMRADE MITCHELL.— I have a report here from the committee on examining the accounts of the Quartermaster General:
"We have examined the report of the Assistant Quartermaster
General and we find it correct, comprehensive in form, and we
desire to commend Comrade Atkinson for the admirable manner
in which he has performed the duties of his position.   Signed,
respectfully submitted, Edward J. Mitchell, James R. Silliman,
committee."

The report is as follows:

7

REPORT OF THE ASSISTANT QUARTERMASTER GENERAL

Headquarters Department of New York, G. A. R.
Office of the Assistant Quartermaster General
Capitol, Albany, N. Y., *June* 22, 1918.

Comrade William F. Kirchner, *Department Commander:*

Dear Sir and Comrade.— In compliance with the Rules and Regulations of the Grand Army of the Republic, I submit to you the following statement and detailed report in full of the business transacted in this office from June 23, 1917, to June 22, 1918.

Yours in F. C. and L.,

EDWARD J. ATKINSON,
Assistant Quartermaster General."

RECEIPTS

1917.

June 23. Received from P. M. Wales, A. Q. M. General	$747 83	
June 27. Received from Daughters of Veterans..	25 00	
July 13. Received from State of New York (balance due last administration).	228 29	
Per Capita Tax		
First term, 1917. . . . . $1,311 10		
First term (delinquents). 19 80		
Preceding terms (delinquents). 6 00		
Second term, 1917. . . . . $1,211 30		
Second term (delinquents) 25 50		
		$2,573 70
Supplies		
June 22, to August 1, 1917. . . . . $39 03		
August, 1917 . . . . 11 35		
September, 1917 . . . . 18 29		
October, 1917 . . . . 17 04		
November, 1917 . . . . 18 46		
Carried forward	$104 17	$3,574 82

Brought forward	$104 17	$3,574 82
December, 1917	28 99	
January, 1918	63 94	
February, 1918	28 03	
March, 1918	13 00	
April, 1918	14 05	
May, 1918	32 09	
June, 1918	11 02	
		295 29

Oct. 9, 1917. Received from State
New York $1,137 02
June 2, 1918. Received from State
New York 1,466 13

		2,603 15

Total receipts (General Fund)............ $6,473 26
Due from State New York on appropriation of
$3,000 to July, 1918...................... 396 85

$6,870 11

On deposit Albany Savings Bank
July 1, 1917................... $2,166 83
Nov. 14, 1917. Deposited (withdrawn
from account Home Savings Bank). 200 00

$2,366 83
Interest, January 1, 1918.......... 45 32
Interest, July 1, 1918............. 48 24

2,460 39

On deposit Albany Savings Bank
(Defense Fund), July 1, 1917.... $259 21
Interest to January 1, 1918........ 5 18

$264 39
To Edwin A. Doty, March 20, 1918, to
defray attorney's fee in claim
against State 250 00

Carried forward	$14 39	$9,330 50

Brought forward	$14 39	$9,330 50
Interest to July 1, 1918...........	28	
		14 67

On deposit Home Savings Bank July 1, 1917	$5,093 78	
Oct. 1, 1917, withdrawn to deposit account, Albany Savings Bank....	200 00	
	$4,893 78	
Interest to January 1, 1918........	97 86	
	$4,991 64	
Interest to July 1, 1918............	99 83	
		5,091 47

Receipts for the year and cash on deposit.......	$14,436 64

Value of supplies turned over by Philip M. Wales.	$273 56
Value of supplies on hand June 22, 1918.......	292 26

DISBURSEMENTS

Voucher

1.	Bernice Case, clerk, June, 1917 ..	$125 00
19.	Bernice Case, clerk, July, 1917 ..	125 00
29.	Bernice Case, clerk, Aug., 1917 ..	125 00
35.	Bernice Case, clerk, Sept., 1917 ..	125 00
41.	Bernice Case, clerk, Oct., 1917 ..	125 00
45.	Bernice Case, clerk, Nov., 1917 ..	125 00
51.	Bernice Case, clerk, Dec., 1917 ..	125 00
57.	Bernice Case, clerk, Jan., 1918 ..	125 00
69.	Bernice Case, clerk, Feb., 1918 ..	125 00
74.	Bernice Case, clerk, Mar., 1918 ..	125 00
78.	Bernice Case, clerk, Apr., 1918 ..	125 00
83.	Bernice Case, clerk, May, 1918 ..	125 00
		$1,500 00

Carried forward	$1,500 00

Voucher

Brought forward		$1,500 00
18. E. J. Atkinson, A. A. and Q. M. General, July, 1917..........	100 00	
28. E. J. Atkinson, Aug., 1917	100 00	
34. E. J. Atkinson, Sept., 1917	100 00	
40. E. J. Atkinson, Oct., 1917	100 00	
44. E. J. Atkinson, Nov., 1917	100 00	
50. E. J. Atkinson, Dec., 1917	100 00	
56. E. J. Atkinson, Jan., 1918	100 00	
68. E. J. Atkinson, Feb., 1918	100 00	
73. E. J. Atkinson, Mar., 1918	100 00	
77. E. J. Atkinson, Apr., 1918	100 00	
84. E. J. Atkinson, May, 1918	100 00	
89. E. J. Atkinson, June, 1918	100 00	
		1,200 00
17. Wm. F. Kirchner, Dept. Com'dr.	$100 00	
36. Wm. F. Kirchner, Dept. Com'dr.	100 00	
49. Wm. F. Kirchner, Dept. Com'dr.	100 00	
71. Wm. F. Kirchner, Dept. Com'dr.	100 00	
85. Wm. F. Kirchner, Dept. Com'dr.	100 00	
		500 00

DEPARTMENT ENCAMPMENT, SARATOGA, N. Y.

Bills of Former Administration

7. The Sun Printing Co., to window cards	$3 00	
10. Philo M. Wales, office expenses..	3 25	
11. Henry Pease, color bearer.......	5 00	
12. Bernice Case, railroad fare and hotel bill	7 90	
13. Leroy L. Barnard, Credential Committee	10 00	
14. Wm. H. Kilfoile, Credential Committee	10 00	
15. John B. Trainer, Credential Committee	10 00	
		49 15

Carried forward		$3,249 15

Voucher
Brought forward $3,249 15

Council Meeting, Saratoga, June 26, 1917

2. Wm. F. Kirchner $12 00
3. Austin H. Stafford 20 00
4. George Hollands 21 75
5. Henry Lilly 12 00
6. Elias W. Beach 17 90
8. Edwin H. Risley 8 75
9. Philip M. Wales 6 35
                                  _____
                                                            98 75

Council Meeting, Albany, February 27, 1918

62. Frank Johnson $21 44
63. Elias W. Beach 18 18
64. Henry Lilly 10 00
65. Samuel Irvine 10 00
66. Austin H. Stafford 27 91
67. E. J. Atkinson 14 00
                                  _____
                                                           101 53

Office Expenses

21. July, 1917 .... $31 82
30. August, 1917 ....   28 60
39. September, 1917 ....   28 77
42. October, 1917 ....   22 31
47. November, 1917 ....   30 90
53. December, 1917 ....   29 34
60. January, 1918 ....   33 55
70. February, 1918 ....   15 05
76. March, 1918 ....   15 10
79. April, 1918 ....   27 77
87. May, 1918 ....   17 40
90. June, 1918 ....   23 05
                                  _____
                                                           303 66
                                                      _____

Carried forward $3,753 09

Voucher

Brought forward $3,753 09

Printing, Stationery, etc.

23. S. H. Wentworth	$113 23	
33. S. H. Wentworth	74 74	
38. Gavit & Co....................	59 00	
46. S. H. Wentworth	54 50	
52. S. H. Wentworth	13 00	
59. S. H. Wentworth	6 00	
75. S. H. Wentworth	12 00	
80. S. H. Wentworth .'............	12 75	
81. Oliver A. Quayle	32 20	
86. S. H. Wentworth	38 00	
88. S. H. Wentworth	14 25	
		429 67

National Per Capita Tax

20. Cola D. R. Stowits (1st term, 1917)	$234 35	
58. Cola D. R. Stowits (2d term, 1917)	217 28	
		451 63

Supplies

32. Cola D. R. Stowits	66 75	
43. Cola D. R. Stowits	3 50	
48. Cola D. R. Stowits	10 50	
54. Cola D. R. Stowits	6 00	
55. Cola D. R. Stowits	11 00	
61. Cola D. R. Stowits	4 75	
82. Cola D. R. Stowits	51 45	
		153 95

Miscellaneous Bills

16. Chas. H. Gardner, to bonds for Q. M. General and clerk.....	$15 00	
22. Heiser, Muhlfelder & Co., to ribbon for badges	27 50	
31. Chas. H. Bailey, reporting proceedings at Saratoga	125 00	

Carried forward $167 50 $4,788 34

Voucher

Brought forward $167 50 $4,788 34
37. Cadby & Son, mailing tubes.....   12 50
72. Edward J. Atkinson, A. A. and
     Q. M. General, expense to
     Ithaca in connection with
     Department Encampment 20 64
                                                        200 64

National Encampment Expense, Boston, Mass.

24. Boston City Band $125 00
25. Isidore Isaacs, headquarters ex-
     pense 5 25
26. Hotel Vendome 123 10
27. Wm. F. Kirchner, headquarters
     expense 6 00
                                                        259 35

        Total disbursements $5,248 33

Receipts (General Fund) $6,870 11
Disbursements 5,248 33

    In National Commercial Bank and on hand. . $1,621 78

Digest of Disbursements

Paid officers' salaries $3,200 00
Paid bills of former administration............   49 15
Paid council meetings (2)..................   200 28
Paid office expenses 303 66
Paid printing, stationery, etc................   429 67
Paid national per capita tax................   451 63
Paid supplies 153 95
Paid miscellaneous bills 200 64
Paid National Encampment expense..........   259 35

                                               $5,248 33

ASSETS

Cash in bank and on hand	$9,188	31
Value of supplies on hand...................	292	26
Due from State New York July 1, 1918, to July 1,		
1919, as per annual appropriation bill	3,000	00
Total	$12,480	57

COMRADE LILLY.— I move that a committee be appointed to nominate the Council of Administration and the delegates and alternates to the National Encampment.

COMMANDER KIRCHNER.— The motion is that a committee be appointed to nominate the Council of Administration and the delegates and alternates to the National Encampment for the ensuing year. Is that motion seconded?

The motion was duly seconded.

COMMANDER KIRCHNER.— The number of representatives to the next encampment from this department is 42. That means 41 delegates with one delegate at large and the same number of alternates to be elected. Are you ready for the question? All those in favor will signify by saying aye and those opposed no.

(After a pause.) The motion is duly carried.

The Adjutant General will announce the names of that committee.

The Adjutant General then read the names as follows: James D. Bell, Chairman, Charles A. Orr, Samuel C. Pierce, Oscar Smith, James M. Snyder, Robert P. Bush, James S. Maxwell, John C. Schotts, John McClosky, A. H. Stafford and James R. Silliman.

COMRADE TANNER.— You will have to change the name of Maxwell. He has had to go home.

THE COMMANDER.— In place of Comrade Maxwell please insert the name of Past Senior Vice Commander Hollands from Hornell. As Comrade Maxwell was selected as a member of the Committee on Resolutions and since he was compelled to go home,

I substitute the name of Charles H. Freeman, Past Department Commander, in his place.

COMRADE BLAIR.— Commander I move we take a recess until 10 o'clock to-morrow morning.

COMRADE BELL.— The committee just named in regard to selecting candidates for the Council of Administration and for the National Encampment will meet to-night at nine o'clock in the room known as No. 4 in the Hotel Ithaca. All the members of the committee kindly be present. We make it late on account of the camp fire.

COMMANDER KIRCHNER.— If there is any comrade here that desires to be placed upon that ticket to the National Encampment as a delegate and who has in mind going there he will hand his name to the chairman of that committee the name and number of his post and the county that he represents.

COMRADE BLAIR.— I move that we take a recess until 10 o'clock to-morrow morning and before you put that motion I would like to know whether we have passed any resolutions fixing the date for the election of officers.

THE COMMANDER.— At 10 o'clock to-morrow morning.

All those in favor of taking a recess until to-morrow morning at 10 o'clock will say aye and those opposed no.

(After a pause.) The motion appears to be carried and accordingly the encampment will be in recess until 10 o'clock to-morrow morning except for the camp fire which takes place to-night.

CAMP FIRE.

June 26, 1918, 8 p. m.

The Camp Fire was opened by singing the Star Spangled Banner by the entire assemblage.

COMRADE STOWITS, *Chairman.*— In the eternal revolving of the cycle of time three score years are but an infinitesimal part, but in that small number of years there is fraught events which will change the life of a nation or the life of a people. A little less than three score years ago a throng of young men in this land assembled for the purpose of trying to establish and settling for all time whether a free nation could exist. How well they succeeded is known to you all. Past years have demonstrated fully what they started to do and what they carried out. Even to-day the very principles that our boys stood for are now the principles of the allied nations of this world and they are going to finally establish the fact that democracy is settled forever. (Applause.) I do not propose to take up your time with any further remarks as we have quite a long program, and I therefore call on the doctor for the invocation.

REV. DR. KLINE.— Let us pray. Our Lord Jesus Christ, we pray Thee that we may realize Thy presence in our midst to-night; we thank Thee that the Kingdom of Heaven means democracy in the largest and best interpretation of that term; we thank Thee, Lord, for what the men of the Grand Army fought for in the 60's, and we are glad Lord, that because they fought so well and so bravely and so chivalrously that we are gathered here to-night under the flag that we love better than we love our own lives, a free nation, an undivided nation, and we are glad, Lord, that their successors their grandsons are out on the front to-night battling for the same cause, that liberty and justice and a true fraternity may obtain in this world, that it may be delivered once and for all from Prussian militarism and from German tyranny; God bless our boys on the fighting front to-night; we are proud of them; we are glad because they have shown the very spirit that the men in the 60's showed, that they are willing to give their lives bravely and heroically for the very same cause for which these very men and those whom we buried in the cemeteries all over this country gave their lives so long ago; we thank Thee for our nation; we thank Thee because in Thy providence Thou hast called us to take this providential part in this great world struggle. God give us victory, help us to make whatsoever sacrifice is necessary to that end. May we be willing to pay the price as this nation paid the price in the 60's, and may we count no sacrifice too great that this war may be won and that victory once more may be ours. God bless this encampment that has met in our city. We thank Thee for the splendid sessions of to-day, for the spirit of the delegates, and now, Lord, in this great Camp Fire to-night may we feel that Thou art with us. God bless our Governor. We thank Thee for his presence on this platform to-night. Speak through him, O Lord, and may the message just touch our hearts, burn within us, and may his words not be forgotten, and may we go away from this service with a higher degree of patriotism than we had before, with a realization of the responsibilities of citizenship greater than we had before. There is Corporal Tanner, Oh Lord. We thank Thee for his life and for the place he has in the affections not only of the Grand Army of the Republic but of this entire nation. Bless the others that take part in this program to-night, and may we feel when it is over that we are better for having been here, from the lowest to the greatest. We cannot forget, Lord, to pray for the President of the United States. We thank Thee for his life. We thank Thee for his wise statesmanship that he has manifested in this critical juncture of our nation's history, and God bless him, and those in authority under him, and those associated with him in this great war. God be with them all. Bless our Army and Navy, and may we feel that God is with us, and may we not forget, Oh Lord, that righteousness exalteth a nation, and may we ever put that before us and may we strive to be a nation ever whose object is the Lord. We ask it in Christ's name. Our Father who art in Heaven hallowed be Thy name; Thy Kingdom come, Thy will be done on earth as it is in Heaven. Give us this day our daily bread and forgive us our trespasses as we forgive those who trespass against us, and lead us not into temptation but deliver us from evil, for Thine is the kingdom and the power, and the glory, forever and ever, Amen.

Comrade Stowitts.— My friends, especially those outside the Grand Army of the Republic, I wish to say that this great organization at its birth, when the first gun was fired upon Fort Sumter, 52 years ago, a plan was formulated to organize the Grand Army of the Republic, and from that day to this hour comrades have met in annual session throughout the various departments in this land, also in National Encampment. The great Empire

State of New York has had a department since 1866 and this is the 52nd encampment that we have had. We are here enjoying the hospitalities of this beautiful city, for which we thank you very much. I will now present the Department Commander of the State of New York, Comrade William F. Kirchner.

COMMANDER KIRCHNER.— Mr. Chairman and Governor, comrades, ladies and friends: As the Commander of this great department of the Empire State, and in behalf of the comrades who represent that state, I want to thank the good people and citizens of Ithaca for this wonderful entertainment that they are giving to the delegates and their auxiliaries· at this time at our 52nd annual encampment of the Grand Army of the Republic. I assure you that every veteran's heart beats with gratitude. We have come here amongst you to continue our deliberations and we hope that while we are here that our deliberations will be a success and that our encampment will also be a success to the good people who are entertaining us in the City of Ithaca. As the presiding officer said, 52 years ago the Grand Army of the Republic found its organization in a little town in the State of Illinois known as Decatur, organized by a Reverend gentleman who was a veteran of that Civil War on the 4th day of April 1866 and, from that one post every state in the United States added from time to time. The department of New York was organized in 1866. It held its first encampment at that time, and year after year we have met to legislate for the interests and the benefit of our organization and our principal foundation was patriotism, and we have taught that from that day to this, so that our rising generation could realize what it meant after four years' hard fighting during the 60's. To-day, the sons and grandsons of that great organization, that great army that fought the battles in the 60's, are now fighting for the same principles that we did in the 60's. They are on the other side doing what we did at that time, and from all the reports that we have got to the present time the American boys are making good. (Applause.) We have lived a lifetime and we thank God that he permitted so many of us to remain, and I hope that he will allow us a little longer because we want to receive our boys when they come back with the Stars and Stripes. (Applause.)

It was a glorious sight in 1865, on the 23d and 24th of May, when the Grand Army of the Republic after its victories, and the surrender at Appamatox passed in review to the President of the United States and our great captain, U. S. Grant. We want to live to receive our boys in the same way. We want to be the reviewing officers and we are satisfied that they are our sons and grandsons, the present generation of young men who have done this.

Now I do not want to detain you any longer; I do not want to say any more, because you are going to have a wonderful number of good and able speakers, and I am only wasting your time, and I want you to enjoy the evening. I thank you. (Applause.)

COMRADE ISAACS.— Mr. Chairman, ladies and gentlemen, I will not take up your time. I am well aware of the distinguished gentlemen who are present this evening who will entertain you better than I. I am simply here to perform a pleasant duty. Commander Kirchner, when all the good comrades at Saratoga elevated you to the highest position in the gift they made no mistake; you made good. (Applause.) For the past year you have rendered valuable services to your comrades. I wish to state in my membership of 50 years in the Grand Army with no reflection on the illustrious comrades who have preceded you, I do not know of one who has done better work than you have performed, and in behalf of the comrades, your official staff and your many friends who are comrades of the Grand Army of the Republic, I wish to present to you this slight token of our affection and esteem. Wear it on your heart. It is a symbol of the highest order of patriotism, so vigilant and so grave. Wear it that it may be to the other comrades who may aspire to the position which you now hold, and who may follow in your footsteps, an inspiration to do the higher and the nobler things, as I here say to you well done, good and faithful servant. (Applause.)

(Comrade Isaacs then pinned upon the breast of Commander Kirchner a beautiful jewelled emblem.)

My duty as chief aide was to see that the boys put up, and they put up very liberally. In fact they responded better than I expected they would, and, Commander, as you are now to retire

— to-morrow at this time you will be as I am, you will be a high private in the ranks, and when you get back and go down to that place in Jersey called Asbury Park, and as you sit there on your veranda and you gaze at the names of your friends you will say as I say here to you for he was a jolly good fellow, and in behalf of your official staff and your comrades I present you this slight token of our esteem. You will find here the names of all of your comrades who were your friends, and I want to tell you you had a big pile of them. (Applause.)

COMRADE KIRCHNER.— I want to say to you and through you to my comrades who have been so generous to me that there is nothing in the world that I appreciate more than the high honor that was conferred upon me one year ago by the unanimous choice of my comrades, and to-night to receive this great token of friendship, the insignia of my office as a member of the Grand Army of the Republic, I do not know what to say, but I sincerely thank you, sir, and my comrades for this great surprise. It was not a surprise in one way. It has been a custom for years that when the Commander retires after doing his one year's duty, and we only had on one or two occasions a comrade who succeeded himself and Comrade James Tanner, was one of those, because we needed him. (Applause.) Comrade Tanner was the man who fathered and established the home for the poor soldiers at Bath, and the work that he commenced in his first term we certainly had to retain him to complete in his second, so I thank you, sir, from the bottom of my heart, I thank my comrades one and all. We are here to-night, we may be somewheres else a year from now, but my wish is that we may all meet again at our 53rd annual encompment. I thank you. (Great applause.)

COMRADE ISAACS.— I would request Mrs. Ellis, daughter of our Department Commander to step forward. I simply wish to say, Mrs. Ellis, you are about to undertake quite a trip across the continent, to attend the National Encampment at Portland. You are not aware that I heard you express yourself that you would like to have a certain thing when you started over, so that you could do some good work for the boys who are doing and giving their all on the other side, and having more money than we knew what to do with I now present to you on behalf of the official staff of your father this token of our esteem. (Applause.)

COMRADE ISAACS.—Mrs. Gaudineer, is she present? Mrs. Gaudineer, the comrades down in New York City, knowing full well the good work you have done in the past year helping our poor comrades down there, and their widows, have authorized me in their behalf to present to you this slight token of affection and esteem, and with it goes our best wishes for your future prosperity and welfare.

MRS. GAUDINEER.— Comrade Isaacs, I can hardly find words to thank you for this token. I do not know what it is, but whatever it is it will always be a pleasant reminder of my year in office when I had the assistance of my comrades of the Grand Army of the Republic on each and every occasion, and I thank one and all. (Applause.)

COMRADE ISAACS.—Mrs. Demarest will please step forward. We all know in New York City what this lady has done. We appreciate it. A few years ago she held the proud position of President of the Women's Relief Corps. To-day she holds the office of secretary, and Mrs. Demarest, we know what you have done in the past and we do not know of any woman in the Women's Relief Corps that has done the work and is able to do the work that you have performed. In behalf of the comrades in New York City please take this and God bless you. (Applause.)

MRS. DEMAREST.— You know and I hope the comrades in New York City know that whatever work my hands can do, my head can think of, my heart can dictate for the veterans of the Grand Army of the Republic I am always ready and willing to do as long as God lets me live. (Applause.)

THE CHAIRMAN.— The quartette will sing The Battle Hymn of the Republic.

COMRADE STOWITS.— Comrades, it will hardly be necessary for me to even mention or eulogize the next speaker. He is our superior officer. He is the Commander in Chief of the Grand Army of the Republic, a position second to the highest possible in the land. (Applause.) You have heard from him many times.

You have read his documents that have been sent out in General Orders, you know what he has meant and you know after his career is nearly over how well he has succeeded. Now we will just demonstrate to the citizens of Ithaca what he is by presenting him — the Commander in Chief, Orlando A. Somers.

COMMANDER IN CHIEF SOMERS.—Your Excellency, comrades of the Grand Army of the Republic, members of the Relief Corps, ladies of the Grand Army of the Republic, Sons of Veterans, Daughters of Veterans and Sons of Veterans Auxiliary — American citizens all — and there is no higher title in this republic to-day than that of American citizen. (Applause.) It means more to America and more to mankind than any other occasion in the history of the republic. I am here representing the Grand Army of the Republic and I am proud of them. I have been in almost every nook and corner of the republic and everywhere I am proud of them, and having met them and the people of the republic on occasions like this I am not only proud of my comrades, but I am proud of the American citizens who are their friends. (Applause.)

It is difficult in this day to confine one's remarks to the Grand Army of the Republic and its history. It has a glorious history. I am sometimes asked, I was over in Boston not long ago, and I was asked by a newspaper man if I expected to say anything about the present war. I said to him, my friend, have you listened to a prayer any time lately that did not speak of the present war; have you listened to a sermon that did not mention the present war; I said if you have you had better change your place of worship. (Applause.) I am pleased to say to you that, as here, every nook and corner of this great republic is wide awake and full of patriotism, and it means more now than in any other period of its history, but I am going to confine myself for a little while to what has been done, and while our history is and has been history, most of it, we are just as proud of our comrades who are absent as we are of the history they made. The Grand Army of the Republic, to me, is composed of the grandest citizens of the republic, and after the winnowing of 50 years I can present to you to-night the most dignified looking body of men that ever assembled in this city. (Applause.) I am asking the men of the Grand Army of the Republic to respond to the gavel that the people of Ithaca may take a look at you.

(Upon the rapping of the gavel the delegates arose amidst the applause of the assemblage.)

I think it was when the Huns overran Rome some time in the past centuries that a squad of them broke into the Roman Senate who were then in session counseling as to what was the best means to preserve the republic, notwithstanding the city was in the hands of the enemy, and having broken into the Senate Chamber they stood in awe before them and retired and reported to their King that they had just found an assembly of Kings. The Roman Senate was never comprised of a more dignified body than that of the members of the Grand Army who are assembled here this evening, and it was the boast of Rome that to be a citizen of Rome was a greater honor than to be a king in any other land. And I say to-night that to be an American citizen is a prouder boast than ever to have been a Roman. (Applause.)

Speaking of the Grand Army of the Republic and its accomplishments briefly — I want the people who are here to bear in mind something of what these men have done. I want to talk history a little. I heard some professor say very recently that when the history of the republic was written it would read a little differently from now. The truth of it is our school histories sometimes give so much space as five lines to a great battle. They are afraid they will offend somebody, and for half a century we have been trying to reconcile our enemies. That is not the way we settled the question. It was unconditional surrender. (Applause.) And men of New York when we settle the question with Germany the Germans will be unconditionally surrendered. (Great applause.) And Uncle Samuel will sit at the head of the table, and when he has signed his name to that document it will mean democracy for all lands. (Applause.) The American flag never recognized any other conditions than unconditional surrender. Now we have no trouble with our former enemies because our victory meant more to them than to any other people in the republic, and they are enjoying greater blessings on account of it than they ever could have enjoyed in our defeat. Sometimes the people now think that it was not much of an army we belonged to. I want to speak a moment about that for fear when you are considering the present army you will think it was just a squad of foragers or something of that kind. I want to say to these young people in figures and terms that they can understand and which they cannot forget that our army was composed of 1700 regiments of infantry, a thousand men to the regiment. Frequently more than half of this number was lost in battle, in hospital, in prison pen, and the regiments were re-graded and their roster finally gave them twice as many. Now you cannot forget the 1700 regiments of infantry, and if you can just get that in your mind you will know more about the army of the Civil War than you have ever known before. And we had 270 regiments of cavalry, 1200 men in a regiment, and if you will ask some of these boys that had to give the road while the cavalry regiments scurried by them, giving out the dust, they will tell you the procession was a mile long and they never would get by, but there were 270 regiments of cavalry, 1200 men in a regiment, and re-graded to fill their losses.

Now you have the infantry, that is the men that walked and carried the muskets, and you have the cavalry, the men that carried the sabres and carbines, and I guess you cannot forget the numbers. If anyone has forgotten raise your hand. (Laughter). I am glad to see you remember. You will remember to-morrow, and we had 900 batteries of artillery, six guns to the battery, 5,400 guns. Now you have an idea of the army we belonged to.

Oh, but they say they are numbering them by millions now. Well, we had 2,800,000 enlistments, and after the war was over we discharged a million and more of men whose terms were not expired, the finest army that ever trod the earth; and we had accomplished more than had been accomplished in any other war, in any other nation or in any other age than had been accomplished in all history. We had saved the republic and freed a race from slavery. (Applause.)

Now you may search sacred or profane history for any other war in which so much was accomplished. Well, that is something for the Grand Army to be proud of, something for the Grand Army to be remembered for, and something that the world now begins to appreciate more than ever. Why, there never has been a time, I do not suppose, in the history of Ithaca when the Department of New York could have brought together such a splendid audience as this, full of patriotic fervor, ready to give anything they may have for the republic.

Well, something else the Grand Army has achieved. For more than 50 years the Grand Army and its auxiliary and allies have been the only organized force in the republic that has kept alive the forces of patriotism. (Applause.) Well, you have got to think awhile to know just what that means. The American people for half a century have been a nation of pacifists, and if you tell a fellow he is a pacifist now he don't take it very well, he don't consider it an honor. The Grand Army of the Republic have been trying to keep the people alive to the necessity of preparedness, but the people thought we were kind of vain dreamers. They didn't understand the price of a republic or they would not have come to that conclusion. For 50 years the American people have been getting rich chasing the almighty dollar, and the Grand Army of the Republic have been trying to keep the forces of patriotism burning upon the altars of the republic. Every 4th of July we have heaped the fagots on the smouldering embers and fanned them into a flame. We have put on there the fagots of the history of the Revolution, of the Declaration of Independence and of their victories and the splendid history made by our forefathers, and we have awakened the people, awakened some of the business men long enough for them to close their business doors, the banks and the stores, for two hours until the speaker could be heard. (Laughter.)

On Washington's birthday sometimes we could get some of them to close for a few minutes and go around the corner to hear the orator, but I never saw a crowded house and have not seen it in 50 years, and on Lincoln's birthday it was little better. When you got around to the meeting you found there the comrades of the Grand Army of the Republic, the women of the Relief Corps, the ladies of the Grand Army, the Sons of Veterans, the Daughters of Veterans, and the Sons of Veterans Auxiliary, and the minister to invoke the divine blessing, and he usually gave way and looked after his other duties while another minister closed the services. (Laughter.) If they had both been there in the beginning one of them would have served the purpose. Well, the Grand Army on such occasions as that, and their allies, have again put the fagots on the smouldering embers and fanned it into a flame and it blazed up and a few people saw the flame and we kept the fire alive.

And on Memorial Day again, we have come with flags and flowers to the graves of our comrades, to honor the memory of the men who saved the republic. And sometimes the people gathered along the streets and watched our procession go by. (Laughter.) And then returned to their business after we had gone to the cemetery and everything resumed its normal conditions. And then my friends, at the graveside or more than a million of men, of our comrades, we have been a living sermon of patriotism and sometimes there was nobody present excepting the Grand Army and their allies and the families of the dead comrades the grieving relatives, and not a store in the city would be closed nor banks, nor a lawyer leave his office, nor anything of that kind, and we have been uneasy about the republic, and we have had our allies, the Relief Corps, the ladies of the Grand Army and others go into the public schools with their flags and their flag salute to see if we could not work on the children before they got into business, and we have succeeded so well that we are sending the children across the seas to fight the battles of the republic now, (applause) and every mother that taught that kind of a lad a lesson was serving this republic just as well as if she had been on the battle line. And every Grand Army Post has each day been just as before serving their country as they were able to serve it on the battle line. The truth of it is if it had not been for our organization I doubt very much whether the response to the call for men to defend the flag would have been answered without riots in our great cities, I doubt it. But as it is there is no party objecting to the war. Each party is vieing with the other and seeing who shall do the most for the republic. Now if we had not been able to keep alive the forces of patriotism and if our people had not been imbued with it by this great army, these millions of men would have been useless, because without patriotism they would have been little better than a mobilized mob and a menace to the republic, and without patriotism our great navy would be no better than junk, there would be no men to fight them, to command them to obey, so we are taking to ourselves the fact that we have been serving our country every day since '61 and we are serving it to-night. (Applause.)

Now about the present war, just a minute. I was over at Washington and because I had four stars on my badge the doors opened there out of regard to the Grand Army of the Republic that I was representing and there was no trouble. No matter what the hurry was at the White House or at the cabinet offices, no matter how they were pressed for time we were admitted, and the things we went there for were accomplished, and among other things we wanted to get on good terms with the President and his cabinet and the United States Senate. We had a reason for it and we succeeded. Among other things we said to the President of the United States that in all his efforts to prosecute the war to a successful conclusion he would find the Grand Army of the Republic behind him. (Applause.) And that there would not be a slacker among them. (Applause.) Having gotten through with the business at Washington we took a run up to Philadelphia, an historic city, a city of which every American ought to be proud, and we went into the old hall there and looked at the tables and the chairs and the ink bottle of which the declaration was written and thought of the great men who had assembled there and of their achievements, and one other point in Philadelphia that interested me more than either of these was a grave of a man who had had much to do with the formation of my convictions about what one's duty is to the republic, and I hunted among the stones there and found the grave of Commodore Stephen Decatur, for I wanted to read myself the inscription on the stone of the toast he gave when there was counsel among the wise men about what to do about certain complications, and you know our officers in the army and in the navy cannot be Democrats, cannot be Republicans, they just have to be soldiers. They are not expected to have any opinion on politics. They are to do the fighting, and when Commodore Stephen Decatur was asked his opinion he raised his glass and said, " My country, may she ever be right;

right or wrong, my country." (Applause.) And I have believed and obeyed that without question, sir, since I had that conviction. And when ever this country declares war, whether its constituted authorities then, no matter what my conviction has been, nor no matter what your conviction has been, when his country declares war it is your duty not to raise any question about this or that, because right or wrong you are for your country or you are against it. (Applause.) If you are against it in time of war the Grand Army has but one name for that, and we call it treason, and we say the penalty for treason is death. (Applause.) And reserving my rights to criticize the public servants in a friendly way I go Stephen Decatur one better, I say this administration, may it ever be right, but right or wrong I am behind this administration. (Applause.)

Of course in a democracy the people come together once in a while in a capacity and say what shall be the policies of the country, and until the people say we demand a change, we must either be for the administration or against the administration. In all of its laudable efforts to prosecute this war to a successful conclusion we are behind the administration.

As my guide was driving me about Philadelphia he pointed to a house sitting on a hill and said that mansion is the former home of Benedict Arnold. Well, I had forgotten that Arnold ever had a home, but Arnold had had a home, and Arnold had been a patriot and one of George Washington's most trusted Generals, and the story of how he ceased to be a patriot and how his very name became a hissing is a pathetic one. You remember that he led that army up through the woods of Maine in the winter time and with General Montgomery assaulted Quebec. Montgomery was killed and the army defeated. Arnold had a limb shattered, was grievously wounded, and he retreated, came down here on the Hudson, and in the battle there at Saratoga after he had obtained leave of absence to heal his wounds and had not yet left, when the battle was on and our army was being defeated Arnold mounted his horse and rode to the head of his troops, his former command, and charged the Red Coats repeatedly, and the Battle of Saratoga was won. It would have been lost had he not done that. And in those charges he again had a limb shattered and asked to be retired to Philadelphia to heal his wounds. Meanwhile his wife had died and left him with some orphan children. Meanwhile six officers of inferior rank and service had been promoted over him, and feeling the sting of disgrace and humiliation on account of this and suffering greviously for the loss of his wife he was put in command at Philadelphia and for some minor trouble there was court martialed and was subject to a reprimand by George Washington. George Washington reprimanded him just as slightly as possible and said to him, "General Arnold, I have complete confidence in you and I will share the command of my own army." Arnold meanwhile had been environed by the loyalists of Philadelphia and he had made love to Mary Chapin's daughter, a loyalist lady, and married her and being surrounded by loyalists who kept not only his wounds of mind opened but his other wounds unhealed, Arnold after all his glorious history plotted treason and undertook to deliver West Point to the enemy. You know the further story of it. It shows this, men, and if any of you have had any greater cause to turn against your government than Arnold had I have never read of it — I have never read of it — but it shows this, no matter what the cause nor what your service has been if you are not loyal now you are a traitor to your country. (Applause.)

I went on up further and saw another example that I want to call your attention to, upstanding, near the window of a room at Yale College there is a splendid statue, a statue of a splendid American officer, nobility stamped in every line and expression. The man to whom that was erected was a captain in Washington's army and he desired to get information from within the enemy's lines, and Captain Nathan Hale, a graduate of Yale University, undertook to secure the information disguised as a school teacher. He secured the information and was on the point of returning when he was captured. He was tried by court martial, if I remember, at night, condemned to be shot at daylight, and standing there with his hands tied behind him he was asked if he had anything to say. He said "yes, I have this to say, that my only regrets are that I have but one life to give for my country." (Applause.)

It has been an honor to bear the name of Hale in all the days since.

I have met a relative of Benedict Arnold, a splendid citizen, and he is yet under the shadow of the disgrace of his ancestor. It ought to be a warning to every American citizen against leaving any shadow of doubt as to his loyalty.

Now as to our boys beyond the sea, I have no fears but what they will bring that flag back untarnished; I have no fears but what it will float over Berlin. (Prolonged applause.) I have no fears but what Prussianism will be crushed. It may take years. It may take millions of men. If you will take out the same per cent. of our young men that was taken out during the Civil War you will have 12 millions of young men in our army, and no matter what England may do, no matter if their army is driven back on the straits and their towns destroyed, no matter if the Prussian flag floats over Paris, the war has become our war, (applause) and these people are our allies, and when this war is settled, as I have said before, we are going to dictate the terms of peace, and that is an assurance to all mankind that they will be altogether righteous and just.

Now I thank this great audience for having listened to a representative of the Grand Army of the Republic, I think the grandest body of men that ever marched to war in any land. I thank you. (Long continued applause.)

COMRADE STOWITS.— Fellow citizens all, especially those of the great Empire State, it is now my happy privilege to present the Governor of the State of New York, which has been my lot three times before. We all love Governor Whitman for what he is, for what he has been and what he will be. He is the soldiers' friend. (Applause.) And I yet fail to remember an instance where he has not to the best of his ability granted every reasonable request that we have asked. Without further ceremony I present His Excellency, the Governor of the State of New York. (Applause.)

GOVERNOR WHITMAN.— Corporal Tanner just remarked to the Commander in Chief and to me that he did not feel at all gloomy to-night, that he never felt better or happier in his life than he does to-night.   I believe that the members of the Grand Army of the Republic of the United States, notwithstanding the fact that the world is still in the shadow of an awful war, I say I believe that you and each one of you have reason to be proud and to be happy so far as we can be happy when men are being killed and giving up their lives for the things that we love — this great country of ours — although it does love the soldier of to-day; although it is tremendously proud of this army steadily growing of the first born of every generation; although we are devoted to this army, the army of to-day, we have not forgotten, and we never can forget, the Grand Army of the Republic.   (Applause.)

Why, if it were not for you, if it had not been for you and the kind of men you were and are, and the things that you did, there would not be anything for these soldiers of to-day to fight for at all.   (Applause.)   They would not have any country, or at least any such country as we have; they would not have the flag without one stripe dishonored or polluted, without one star obscured.   You kept it what it was and you made it what it is. (Applause.)

And don't you think for a moment, notwithstanding what one or another may say; don't you think for a moment that the Americans of to-day do not understand that, because they do understand that.   This splendid gathering to-night of the citizens of Ithaca — and I don't altogether agree with the Commander in Chief — I have seen a good many Memorial Day parades, and it has been my observation that the peoples of our cities and of our towns look with reverence upon these lines, these thinning lines of the nation's heroes, and always have, as they have passed down our streets and away to the cemeteries or holy places of our land to dedicate the graves of those whose wasted bodies filled the patriot graves of the nation.   You live and you ever will live, and the comrades whom you have laid away live in the hearts and in the love and in the reverence of a great people who realize that the very life of the nation which they love has been preserved for us, and God grant for our children's children by your heroism, by your devotion, by your sacrifice and suffering, and by the death of many of those who walked side by side and shoulder to shoulder with you in the time that tried men's souls, even as they are being tried to-day. But you have reason to be happy in the fact that when the crisis has come, when the life of the nation, or rather the very things that you struggled for and the things that you offered up life for, whether the offering was accepted or not; when those things are imperilled again, that the land which you saved is ready and able and willing and proud to save again for their children's children. (Applause.)

Volumes have been written as to the causes of the war of the American Revolution. You remember in our school histories there were chapters always headed — and I suppose there are now — the causes of the Civil War. Volumes will be written as to the causes of the conflict in Europe. In the Declaration of Independence there are twenty-seven specifications. Our grandfathers charged the sinful old head of George the Third, and he was a German, with twenty-seven different offenses which justified their rebellion. They might have omitted them all. Three lines in the Declaration of Independence told the story, and the same cause existed eighty years later, the same cause exists to-day — we hold these truths to be self-evident, that all men are created equal, that they are endowed by their Creator with certain inalienable rights, that among these are life, liberty and the pursuit of happiness. The pursuit of happiness — that is what everything is for that is worth while, that is what our homes are for, our schools are for, our churches are for, that is what our businesses are for and our allies are for — to increase the sum of human happiness, to make life and living in the nations happy for the people of the world, and for the support of this declaration — don't let us forget that — we are committed to this thing long before we are born, any of us — the nation which grew out of these gatherings or groups of men which threw off the bondage under which they lived — for the support of this declaration with reliance on the protection of Divine Providence we do mutually pledge to each other our lives, our fortunes and our sacred honor.

Two systems of government existed even then in the world and over here under the natural conditions in this great wonderful new land a people had grown up to realize that the teaching that God had anointed a man in London to direct their affairs was absurd, that God could anoint any man to control, direct and guide and influence and impress his will and his power and his ideas and his thoughts to dictate to them or any group of men that they should do and what they should believe and what they should think — that the principle of the Divine right of a human being to control a nation or a people was absurd. It is about all there is to the Declaration. There was not room in this new world for the idea that our forefathers had gotten hold of, that all men were created equal, and the idea of English tyranny. They could not live together.

Now a funny thing happened. It seems incredible now, that the men who should sign their names to the Declaration of Independence and be told when they were doing it by their friends they were signing their death warrant, that men who should be willing to face death — everything to be sacrificed if failure ensued — for the proposition that all men are created equal and that liberty was a divine right, should themselves go right home after signing that document and hold human beings in slavery. It is really one of the most incredible things in history that our ancestors should be willing to die for a proposition that God gave liberty to everybody and themselves hold slaves. There was not room enough in the United States of America, there wasn't room enough in this great new free country that those men brought into being for the Declaration of Independence and for African slavery. The two things could not last.

A great New York statesmen said it was an irrepressible conflict; it had to come. It might have been delayed, perhaps. It might have been brought about earlier perhaps under other conditions, but the Emancipation Proclamation was just as naturally the product of the Declaration of Independence and followed it just as inevitably as to-morrow's sunlight follows to-night's darkness. It had to come.

But the idea had gone far beyond the boundaries of this great land of ours. Here it finds its fullest fruition. The world has got hold of the idea. One man is not made by Almighty God to impress his will upon millions and millions of people. If he is a benevolent monarch people will stand it a little while longer, but if he is the kind of creature, if he is a monarch gone mad like the creature to-day upon the imperial throne of the German

Empire it cannot last. (Applause.) Why? There isn't room
enough in the world for the idea for which you men struggled and
sacrificed and many of those near and dear to you died, there isn't
room enough in the world for the things which you and I have
been taught from our cradles that are worth while, there isn't
room enough in this world for the teachings of the Christ of
Bethlehem and the evil and abominable thing which has grown
up in Central Europe during the last forty years. It is going
to go down. (Applause.)

I know there is a Germany of literature and of art and of
poetry and of songs and of music; there is a Germany of folk love
and folk song there is a Germany that lives in the hearts of hundreds and thousands and millions of descendants of Germany;
they look back and love it and have every reason to, and in years
gone by have loved it too. But that Germany is no more. It
has given place to the Germany of the quickening sabre and the
iron heel, to the Germany committed to the obsession that brutal,
physical might makes right and nothing else; that treaties are
scraps of paper; that international law is to be disregarded;
that the sacredness and sanctity of womanhood and manhood
mean nothing to the human race; that art is not to be respected;
that infancy can be sacrificed; that that nation is the greatest
that can slaughter the most — the nation that in blind devotion
to a despot gone mad is hurrying a mighty people to their
destruction.

But don't make any mistake. The German people are with
their government. The German people are with their Emperor.
The German people believe that his is the voice of God. The
German people are satisfied that through his lips the Almighty
is speaking to them. They are meeting the test. There is no
question about it. They have been trained to believe what they
do believe. It has been taught to them from their cradles as
the things we love have been taught to us, and when the test has
come they are true to the things which they have been taught
and the government to which they have looked up to from their
childhood. The German people are with their government.
Their wonderful willingness to sacrifice life, their devotion to
the things, misguided and misdirected as they are, cannot be

questioned. It is a whole nation that is menacing the world. It isn't the Royal family alone. Terrible as it is, however great the sacrifice, however long the time, if that system is not destroyed, then the sacrifices which you men made were made in vain. If we cannot win this war, if this thing is going to be allowed to go on and increase in strength and power, as it will if it isn't beaten now, then these holy dead did die in vain. But it is not going on. We think we have made some sacrifices. We think we have done pretty well as a state, and we have. They asked us for 122,000 men a little over a year ago when the first selective draft law went into effect, and I want to say right here I believe that selective draft law in its conception and operation has been the best consription law ever devised. I believe it has been faithfully carried out, and I believe it is to the everlasting credit of the Wilson administration that this law has been so successful everywhere, in every State in this Union.

They asked us for 122,000 men. Do you know how many we gave them in this State? They asked us for 122,000 men and we gave them 176,000 men under the first draft. (Applause.) Of course they could not all be taken in the draft. Some were too old, some did not meet the conditions, but many were so anxious to go that thousands volunteered in the army and navy reserve, so that there were up to four months ago 176,000. Under the second call we have to-day in all 235,000 men from this State wearing the uniform of the armies and navies of the United States, and by the first of January next if the present plans are accomplished, as no doubt they will be, there will be 300,000 men from the State of New York enlisted, not for three months, but enlisted until the close of the war. (Applause.)

Now that seems pretty good, doesn't it? But I know what these men are thinking about. They know a good deal better than I did up to a few months ago, but I have been studying, I have been looking up the records. We are eleven millions of people in this State to-day. We will have given by the first of January 300,000 men. Do you know how many we would give if we should give now in like proportion to the numbers which our grandfathers gave and our grandmothers too when they gave their sons in the 60's? How many this wonderful State of ours would give if we should give in like proportion as the State gave then to the holy cause for which you fought? We would give 1,100,000 men out of the State of New York alone. (Applause.) Now you think that over. It was a wonderful time in the history of this country. Never in the history of the world did men and women acquit themselves so like men and women, worthy of everything that we love to call American, as did those peoples in these little towns, for most of them were comparatively small then — one in ten of the population, men, women and children — not one in ten men — one in ten of the population, men, women and children, of this great State went out ready to die that the nation and State might live. We think we have done something. Why, ladies and gentlemen, we haven't done anything yet compared with the thing that was done when these men went out, but we know this, that we have the men and we have the means and the same kind of heroic spirit characterizes the boy of to-day as characterized the boy of the 60's, and we are going to give, and we are going to keep right on giving and we are going to answer every call, we are ready to do it, we are willing to do it, we are proud to do it, because the New Yorker of to-day is the descendant of the New Yorker of the days which were the greatest day you men have ever known. (Applause.)

Now when we are asked to give for the Red Cross, when we are asked to buy Liberty Bonds, I want some of my generation to look up the record, to find out how much those bonds that the people took all through our state in the 60's, how much they were worth. We do not have any doubt that these bonds we are buying are as good as gold. There was a good deal of doubt as to whether the United States bonds in those days were as good as gold. But they sold them just the same. Your great country met its obligation then just as it is going to meet its obligation now. We are not going to hesitate. We are not going to grumble either. I like that remark of Corporal Tanner. He isn't gloomy. No, we are not gloomy. He is proud and happy and we have reason to be proud and happy. We have a great country with a splendid opportunity to render this tremendous service to humanity and civilization that we can here in 1918 save the world for the things for which you saved the Nation 50 years ago. (Applause.)

Our test has come. We have been teaching our children loyalty to the flag. We have been persuading ourselves and telling our friends from every stump all over this country on the 4th of July and on Decoration Day that it is nobler to die for the right than to live for the things that are wrong. Have we grown stiff as a people? Do not we love our country as you men did in the days gone by? Don't we believe the things we are saying? The trial has come and so far there has been no question, no hesitancy, no holding back. When the call went out under the draft there were no draft riots anywhere though we were warned they were going to be. The boys came in from all over the state. There were only a few absentees. One man wrote me he was called to go on Thursday but he could not go Thursday because he was busy, he would try to come around Sunday. Another man wrote me he was called to come on Friday. He was going to be married on that day and it would take more than Uncle Sam to stop him but he would come another day of the week. There was another man, a colored man, a fine fellow. You have heard the story, published in New York. He was asked if he claimed exemption and he said, " Exemption, what is that? " and it was explained to him. He said, " Not for mine. The next stop for this nigger am Berlin." (Laughter and applause.) Rather a homely way of putting it, but you know I like that. It represented in a homely English sentiment that course of our people all over our state and all over our land, and they won't stop short of Berlin either. (Applause.)

We sing, and oh, how impressive that song was tonight. We have a right to feel in this cause we have waited a good while. We weren't any too quick to come in, but we have the right to feel now that we are fighting for no selfish purpose. There is nothing sordid or mean or unworthy. There is no desire for aggrandizement or territorial acquisition. I know we are not as a people seized with any desire for revenge or to retaliate. We are not vindictive though we have suffered injury and indignation. We are going out in a cause which we believe is a righteous

Isidore Isaacs, Senior Aide-de-Camp

cause. Our boys are going out to fight in a war which from our
souls we know is a holy war. You have read of the gospel written
in burnished rows of steel. You men know what those words
mean. Right has prevailed sometimes. It did in the 60's at the
point of the steel bayonet, yes, at the cannon's mouth. Our God
is marshing on. I have seen Him in the watch fires of a hundred circling camps, our God is marshing on. You can see Him
to-night in the camps of the Nation where our boys are, those
from your homes, those from your city, those from the university
up here on the hill, those from every home throughout the length
and breadth of our great state and land. I can see Him in those
watch fires where those boys are waiting to be taken across to
pay, if in the infinite wisdom of God they shall be called upon
to pay, the last full measure of devotion, and you can see Him
in these camps on the other side of the sea back of the trenches
perhaps where our boys are waiting the call forward. He has
sounded forth the trumpet that shall never call retreat. Our God
is marching on.

And he is my friend, He is marching with those wonderful
chaps from Italy, and oh, how differently we feel for them, fighting the Austrian from their territory — He is marching too with
those wonderful men from Canada. You know what Canada has
done, they with eight millions, we have eleven millions — I mean
the State of New York has eleven millions. With eight millions
of people in the entire Dominion of Canada they have sent 500,-
000 men across. Our God is marching with them and with those
millions of others following the Cross of St. Andrew and St.
George to protect the British Empire and to give her victory
again. Our God is marching with those soldiers, those heroes of
France who singing as they bleed and smiling as they die have
made a place for their country in the hearts of mankind which no
nation has ever held before, and our God is marching too with
another army, it is a little army yet, but if it shall please His will
to prolong this war it is going to be a mighty army, the Army of
Americans, (Applause.) that are going across the sea following
our holy banner of the Stars and the Stripes of the land of the
free and the home of the brave, a banner which has never known

8

defeat and which, please God, it never shall. (Prolonged applause.)

Ladies and gentlemen, just one moment. On behalf of the Sons of Veterans, I am very proud of the privilege, I am very proud of the request which has been made of me as the Governor of the State of New York, to present to the Grand Army of the Republic of this state — I think we may go further and say to the Grand Army of the Republic of the Nation, the service flag, the very beautiful service flag which hangs at the back of the stage. It represents — every star represents the 968 sons of veterans, the boys in whose veins flow the blood of the heroes of Gettysburg and Antietam and Chancellorsville, the sons of the soldiers who to-day either on the sea or in France, most of them are on the way over from this state who are going over to offer the same sacrifice which you offered for the same cause. (Applause.)

Comrade Stowits.— Friends, it will hardly be necessary to say anything in presenting the next speaker. He is known and loved by the Grand Army of the Republic perhaps better than any other single comrade in the United States. He is the silver-tongued orator of this great organization. I therefore take great pleasure in presenting Corporal James Tanner. (Applause.)

Comrade Tanner.— Mr. Chairman, Commander-in-Chief, Governor, one and all — I come here in your presence to-night from a dinner where we limited the talk to the lips of the Governor, and he in an apologetic way told a story which it seems to me is 100 times more proper for me to tell here at 13 minutes past 10 than it was for him there. It was the story of a couple of countrymen coming out of a Court House where they had been listening to the trial of a man arraigned for murder, and one of the men said to the other, " They will hang that fellow." The other one said, " No, you are mistaken, New York don't hang men any more, they elocute them to death." (Laughter.)

I do feel good to-night and I live up to the prohibition sentiments of this Nation. I have had occasion to tell no less a personage than our Department Commander one thing. I have told it to my boys before Kirchner started to tell me of some of his ailments, and I said " Shut up, I have troubles of my own," but I have stood up under it for 56 years and I am here yet and I will see many of them off to bed before I seek my couch.

The years have been many and they have been full of pain and much sorrow. I have not been particularly in love with life for a good while. There are cords that draw mightily to the other side. Now I pray God that I may live until I see this world trouble settled and settled right. (Applause.)

I wonder — born and brought up under the eaves of the Methodist Church that preaches the doctrine of eternal damnation — I wonder that an outraged and just God has not looked down from the Heavens and opened to its bottommost depths the pit and sent down there to eternal damnation the only rival the devil can ever have, and that is his representative on the throne of Germany to-day. (Laughter and applause.)

The things that produce this state of feeling are unspeakable. Men hesitate to speak of them among themselves. Our lips are closed in the presence of the respectable womanhood of the nation.

I got a message the other day from the son of a glorious old comrade of the Grand Army, Judge Collins of Minnesota, who has gone to his rest, and this message comes from the trenches in Picardy, and there was a sentiment in it that pleased me immensely: " The highest hope we boys have over here is that we can measure up to the record our daddies made in the 60's. We are over here, and we won't come back till its over over here." (Applause.) I am a little reminiscent in my thoughts.

I have been a member of the Grand Army fifty years and somehow or other the boys have been getting me to talking all those years. I want to remind them to-night of one thing — in those early years of the Grand Army of the Republic certain fellows spruced up and you kept step and you bowed gracefully — none of you limped unless you had lost your limb. You felt immensely proud of yourselves and of the great youths that you were the representative of. I told you then not to arrogate to yourselves in your thoughts all the patriotism and all the courage that American manhood could ever contain, for I told you then that as the years ran away and boys were born to us that they would step as steady, they would stand as bravely on the field of battle, if occasion came, and they would hold Old Glory as firm as we ever held it, and carry it as far, and the day has come. We had that feeling then because we knew the mothers that bore the boys, and never has the womanhood of the United States of America stood in nobler splendor than she stand to-day. (Applause.) We see them knitting, knitting, knitting, day and night, the first thing in the morning in many cases, and the last thing at night, sitting in theatres knitting, sitting at home and saying don't talk to me I am purling (Laughter,) or they would drop a stitch, but did you ever stop to think how as the woman knits the socks and the sweaters and all those things that she is knitting into those garments her heart's high hope, her prayers, but above all her faith that the manhood of America will measure up to all that is required and not disgrace womanhood?

We have had a splendid time in Ithaca. I must remember that I am charged by the Grand Army not to overlook some things.

Oh, it was a great address we listened to to-day — two of them — historically from Dr. Griffis and the War of To-Day by Professor Orth.

I heard one statement made from the platform over at the Lyceum that I think conveyed more misinformation to us, even though it fell from the lips of the Mayor, than any statement I have heard in a long time. He told us that the population of this city was 17,000. I will swear to it that I saw at least 35,000 on the streets to-day. (Laughter and applause.) And every face beamed their good will and their good nature, and the little tots that could not stand wiggled their hands as they stood in the carry-all greeting us. Oh, yes, there is another thing about Ithaca. Last night I found in your local paper — I tore out that column — My comrades ever since the war have nailed the "Corporal" to me. I have often been asked if I was christened Corporal. The plain statement is it was the highest rank I ever got, so you may imagine my pleasure when I read the paper last night: "According to a special despatch in the New York Sun to-day Corporal Duncan C. Hutchinson, son of Mr. and Mrs. Stephen G. Hutchinson, of 104 East Falls street, Ithaca, has been noticed for individual honors by the French and the American Governments for the following brave feat: After two officers and two non-commissioned officers of his unit had been killed he took command of the platoon, consolidated the ground they had occupied and held it." (Applause.) I am glad to know that. there is a corporal from Ithaca who is holding up the records and doing his level best. (Laughter and applause.)

I have seen considerable of the Presidents of the United States in my time. I have reflected upon what inadequate compensation they have for taking that great burden upon their shoulders. Even in times of profound peace and prosperity it is a hard place to fill. They are pulled and hauled and solicited by friends who court their favor and want to persuade them to do things, whether they are just the things for the President to do or not, if it will be for that friend's personal advantage. How much heavier it is in war time? I have lived in the days of three great Presidents of the United States who met death by assassination; I have been by the bedside of the first of those martyrs, and the greatest of all, by the death bed of Abraham Lincoln — I stood on that awful morning of 1865 and saw him for the last time. Now, then, my heart goes out in sympathy to President Woodrow Wilson who is carrying to the best of his ability the gigantic burden that rests upon his shoulders. Some of us thought in the past we did not get into this thing quite as quickly as we ought to, but that is in the past. We are in it, and the President sees and saw a good while ago that we had to go into it for all we may. Our good friend Colonel Roosevelt when they were talking about putting half a million or a million said we must put five million over, and then in the parlance that I quote from some of you old fellows, President Wilson said " Why keep the limit down to five millions?" He was ready to make our numerical strength the limit of the game. (Applause.)

We are proud of the fact to-day that the nation stands behind our President as solidly as the North stood behind Abraham

Lincoln in the sixties, and even more so. You talk about slackers? We will make their names as infamous in the next generation as we made that of Copperheads. Did you ever hear why we did not call them rattlesnakes? Because the rattlesnake is a gallant reptile. It sounds a warning before it strikes. The copperheads do not do it. That is why we named them — for that class of people.

We are getting compensation out of this war. It is no mere figure of speech. Our people are living nearer to God to-day because this war is on us. Men are going to church more. If you could read the secrets of their minds you would find them praying more. Our loved ones are over there and all we can say is " into Thy hands, Oh God, we commit them." We want them to do their full duty. We want them to teach the Kaiser a great lesson. He needs education. (Applause.) He said to our Ambassador, Judge Gerard, before we got into the war, that when this war was over he would not receive any further nonsense from the United States of America. I wonder if he does not think he is receiving something now that isn't exactly nonsense. (Laughter.) It may get so hot that some of the hostile forces, hostile to the Kaiser, can reach him or one of his six sons. Families devastated in their membership in Germany but no casualities in the Kaiser's family. From his impious lips there falls the declaration time and again that he is the spokesman of God Almighty on this earth and that he is authorized to dictate what shall govern this world. He then proceeds to countenance the evil and unspeakable outrages that we never dreamed it was possible for human beings to bring about; murderers of womanhood and worse; no respect for age or innocence — all sacrificed to this Moloch of whom I hope it will be true, as you do, that when the conditions of peace are to be determined those conditions will be placed before him, if he is alive then, with the command, " Sign, or you go to St. Helena, as Bonaparte did."

I am one of those who is ready to do without anything made in Germany for the future. (Applause.) The proposition to excuse our children from learning the German language; the proposition to exclude its teaching in our educational institutions is taking great hold on the people. There are those who are opposed to it, but it is being abolished. They talk that German is the language of culture and they quote Goethe and Wagner and Heine and others that represent a Germany that is as much different from the blood-thirsty policy of the Hun as day is from night. I am one of those who would gladly welcome the abolishment of the teaching of that language in all our educational institutions, but based on my Christian faith I can give a little consolation to those who would preserve it by assuring them that when this thing is over, aye, from this time on, German will be the prevailing language spoken in hell for all time to come. (Great laughter and applause.)

THE CHAIRMAN.— Now if you will remain quite just a few moments the remainder of this program will be short. The speeches are limited to five minutes, therefore they will not detain you. The first is an address by the Commander-in-Chief of the Sons of Veterans. I find he is not here so we will omit that. I have pleasure in introducing the President of the Women's Relief Corps, Mrs. Lois M. Knaus:

MRS. KNAUS.— Mr. Chairman, Commander, Your Excellency, Comrades and friends: We are are told that the Comrades of the Grand Army of the Republic are the remnant of a mighty host. I want to say to the Comrades here you are a mighty good looking remnant. (Laughter.) I want to say to the Comrades here that I was proud of every one of you as you stood up to-night, to think of this great number of your Comrades here to-night when they tell us you are a remnant. I am proud to come to you to-night as the representative of 160,000 women, the auxiliary of the G. A. R., the Women's Relief Corps, the organization that for 35 years has stood side by side with you doing what we could for you and your Comrades. We are proud to do it. It has been a privilege to do it, and I want to say to you to-night just this: Your Commander-in-Chief said they stood back of the administration and I want to say the Women's Relief Corps stands shoulder to shoulder with the Grand Army of the Republic back of the administration. And further, I want to say, Comrades, while we are going to do all possible for you, and we are not going to say anything about the time when we will have no G. A. R., for we are going to have a G. A. R. for a long time — you are too healthy looking for us to.say it is near the end, but we have adopted the boys in brown and we are going to do exactly the same for them that we have been doing for you for 35 years. (Applause.) Just as long as there is a boy in brown on the other side that needs our attention, just as long as there is a boy here that needs our attention, we are going to give him all he wants.

We have learned of the Corporal that did well, we give all honor to the high officers — we know what that means — we have to have them, but is is the Corporals and the men behind the guns that have done the work, and we honor every one of you for it. It is the boys in the trenches to-day that are doing the work. We never say if we win the war, we say when we win the war, because we know our boys are going to do it. The American boys have not gone over there to come back defeated. We are going to be able to welcome them and we hope to do so before long.

To-night there came to mind the expression of an old German laundress when she was having trouble in her home, and we said why do you suppose the Good Lord allows those people to live, and she said, " Oh, that's nothing to do with it. God has no use for them and Devil he does better by keeping his here," and that's the way I presume with the Kaiser. He is doing better by keeping here, but we hope he won't keep him here too long. We don't want too many of our boys to go, and I want to say I am so glad to be with you and look into your faces, because you are men we love, and when we see what you have done for us and that you have made it possible for this land and this government to go into this war as we have, the Grand Army of the Republic, the Women's Relief Corps and the allied organizations have been preparing our boys and girls for this, for the girls are doing with their mothers all that is posible. And the women are to be a big factor in this war. We have been a big factor in every war. When you were out you did not have the Red Cross; you did not have the Women's Relief Corps, but you had the women of that time doing all possible, and the women of to-day are going to do all possible and go over the top with the boys.

There is a limit to what we have to say so I am going to leave you with a little toast I am very fond of:

Here's to the people of the wind-tossed north as we meet on the fields of
    France;
May the spirit of Grant be over them all as the sons of the north advance.
Here's to the grey of the sun-kissed south as we meet on the fields of France;
May the spirit of Lee be over them all as the sons of the south advance.
Here's to the blue and the grey as one as they meet on the fields of France;
May the spirit of God be over them all as the sons of our flag advance.

(Applause.)

THE CHAIRMAN.— We will next have an address by Mrs. Mary E. Tarbox, the National President of the Ladies of the G. A. R.

MRS. TARBOX.— It is one of the most delightful things to-day that as we enjoy the blessings of the privilege of religion, the privileges of education, the privileges of thought, and that we do not for one moment forget the men who in the greatest crisis the world ever knew gave to us these blessed privileges. We cannot forget them; we do not forget them; we will not forget them. In fact I think from what I have seen in the last two months they are just beginning to live, for we see reflected in the faces of the boys who have gone across that we women of the organization have been educating them in patriotism all these years and teaching them what these men gave to us — this beautiful heritage which we are enjoying in this country, and as we see all this reflected in their faces, the faces of their fathers, their grand-fathers and others, we cannot for a moment think that these men will ever be forgotten. No, they are just beginning to live. The heart may lie withered in the dust but that which He warmed will live on forever. When they brought this flag home fifty-three years ago which they fought for, untarnished and unblemished, it was a vastly different proposition then, with its thirty-six stars, from the flag that is calling to-day with its forty-eight stars, representing countries from the Atlantic to the Pacific, with the world calling for help, and these boys with the same spirit as their fathers have gone forth to defend it. They will come back with it just the same as did their fathers and grandfathers fifty-three years ago. The same impulses move them, the same God, the same flag, the same country.

> The God to whom Columbus in reverence bent the knee;
> The God who brought the Pilgrims in safety over the sea,
> The God their fathers worshipped they worship still today.
> The God to whom brave Washington at Valley Forge did pray,
> One God, one flag, one country, that flag the red, white and blue
> And a country that is the grandest the centuries ever knew.
> The flag that in the sixties flew in triumph to the breeze,
> That same flag today is a token to our boys across the seas,
> It points the way to Liberty, to men from shore to shore,
> The flag that stands for freedom is the flag we all adore,
> One God, one flag, one country, that one the red, white and blue,
> And the country that's the grandest the centuries ever knew.
> Emblems and history may fade from the portal,
> Keystone may crumble, pillows may fall,
> You are the comrades whose work is immortal,
> Crowned by the dome that is over us all.

(Applause.)

THE CHAIRMAN.— We will now hear from the Daughters of Veterans, the National President, Miss Anna B. Dunham, and Department President, Miss Lillian G. Dyas.

MISS DUNHAM.— Mr. Chairman, Commander-in-Chief, Your Excellency, allied organizations and friends: I am certainly proud to be one of the New York Department. It gives us great pleasure. I bring to you the cordial and loving greetings of every Daughter throughout the United States, and they are greetings that come from the heart. To-night we meet as one large patriotic family around this camp fire, and although the Daughters are among the younger organizations we are by no means the least. We claim the same place as a daughter in the household, for it to to her the rest of the family look for everything.

Our order was organized at Massilon, Ohio, on the 30th day of May, 1885, for the purpose of assisting the Grand Army of the Republic, and to keep green the memory of those who participated in that heroic struggle to save and preserve the Union. Ours is a permanent organization and will last so long as history records the Civil War. We have passed the age of creeping and are able to stand alone. Instead of the daughters leaning on the Grand Army, the Grand Army will lean on the daughters.

As the flower of our young manhood has again been called out history repeats itself. Patriotism is not dead, neither does it slumber. Every age had had its patriot. Every student of history recalls Leonidas and his three hundred brave Spartans who fell at Thermopylae that their country might be saved. How many a school boy has declaimed on the bravery of the young French martyr who fell fighting. His name was always called at the roll call and the soldier standing next would answer " Dead on the Field of Honor." Who has not stood with reverence before the statue of the unknown dead in Arlington cemetery where twenty-one hundred soldier boys are buried, their names and regiments unknown, who laid down their lives that their country's honor might be preserved. And so we might go down the annals of history. We are just beginning to realize more and more what the Civil War really accomplished. Had it not been for the battles of Cedar Mountain and Chancellorsville and others the world would know nothing of democracy. Had General Meade lost at Gettysburg General Pershing would be out of business. Gettysburg is not only the decisive battle of the Civil War but the one upon which present history is living. We will never know the suffering that has been endured, nor the blood that has been shed on the many battlefields of our country, in order that we might sing "My Country Tis of Thee, Sweet Land of Liberty," and I am proud to-night to be at the head of an organization that stands for so much. We are doing our best to help the boys over the top right, but we are doing no more than we ought to do, for these boys are as true to us as our fathers were to our mothers in the sixties, for our fathers were the soldier boys of the sixties and our boys are the soldier boys of to-day.

Our prayer is for peace. The Hun and Imperial Germany must be beaten into submission first before we can have peace. Comrades, we cannot pay you too high an honor for the work you have done, and your work will not cease until every member of the Grand Army of the Republic has answered the last call of the Great Commander. The Daughters will go on from where you left off, for you know when a woman makes up her mind to do a thing she does it, for she has the determination, and it is this determination that is bringing about the conditions whereby she is accompanying her husband to the polls on election day. ·

Now while we are enjoying the cordial hospitality . of the citizens of Ithaca it is my wish that we will all meet again at our National Encampment in August.

> The daughters, the daughters forever,
>   Our glorious nation's defense,
> May the wreaths we have twined never wither
>   Nor the fame of our fathers grow dim,
> May the daughters united ne'er sever,
>   But for our country prove true,
> The sons and the daughters forever,
>   Three cheers for the red, white and blue.

THE CHAIRMAN.— We shall now have the pleasure of hearing from Miss Lillian G. Dyas, Department President, Daughters of Veterans.

MISS DYAS.— Commander-in-Chief, Commander Kirchner, Governor, visiting officers and friends: You have had many speakers to-night and are weary. I am not going to weary you more by repeating what has been told you so many times, but I am here to say to you, Commander Kirchner, that you have been very kind to the New York Department, and it has been appreciated by every member, so I have the honor to-night to thank you for your kindness to us, and to ask you to accept this gift as a token of love and esteem from every daughter of the New York Department, and their wish to you is a life filled with love, peace and contentment. (Applause.)

COMMANDER KIRCHNER.— I am hardly able to say anything now, because this certainly is one of the most unexpected tokens of my friendship towards the daughters, because I have a daughter myself, and there is nothing better in this world for an old man when he loses his side partner than his daughter, and I thank you. (Applause.)

THE CHAPLAIN.— Now may the grace of our Lord Jesus Christ, the love of God, the fellowship and communion of the Holy Spirit

rest upon and abide with each one of you now and forevermore.
Amen.

THURSDAY, *June* 27, 1918.

COMMANDER KIRCHNER.— Comrades, we will now proceed with
the business of this Encampment. The first order of business will
be to receive the report from the Committee on Resolutions.

COMRADE TANNER.— The Committee on Resolutions won't
occupy very much of your time, for I am happy to say on these
propositions the action of the committee in every instance has been
unanimous. The first resolution we present to you is the resolution endorsing Comrade Past Department Commander James M.
Snyder, of Troy, for Trustee of the Soldiers' Home at Bath. The
committee was unanimous in its report, with the exception of
Comrade Smith, Past Department Commander, of Albany, who
did not vote because he had offered this resolution.

COMMANDER KIRCHNER.— It has been regularly moved and
seconded that the report of the Committee on Resolutions be
adopted. Are you ready for the question?

COMRADE LOUD.— As that resolution concerns me I would like
the attention of the Department for three or four minutes only.
That resolution is for the purpose of retiring me as Trustee of the
Home and the appointment of Comrade Snyder, of Troy. The
wording of the resolution indicates that it is the wish of the Governor of the State that the matter be referred to the Encampment.
When I heard that, two weeks ago, the Governor was interviewed
and he stated he had made no suggestion to anyone and no one
was authorized to speak for him, I have been holding over since
February, by instruction of the Governor, who advised me I was
legally a Trustee, sustained by the opinion of the Attorney-
General, until an appointment was made. Comrades, I was never
an applicant for appointment as Trustee. In May, 1915, when
the Comrades of New York gave me a public reception at the
Hotel Majestic, that appointment of Trustee in place of Congressman Goulden, of my state, by the Governor, was a surprise to me
and came to me as a complete surprise. I have served as Trustee
for three years. The officers of the Home and everyone have

asked for my reappointment, and there are other endorsements which I do not need to mention, but among them the Association of Nurses of the Civil War, learning of this matter, had recommended my reappointment, because the president of that association and her mother nursed me when I was carried from the battlefield in 1863 wounded and supposedly mortally wounded. Now, Comrades, the purpose of that resolution is to appoint a Trustee from near Albany, so that the Comrade will be more convenient for the service of the Board.   Comrade Maxwell, the President of the Board, lives at Amsterdam, and can be had in Albany at any moment on call.   The Greater New York Comrades are represented in that Home by 438 members out of the 1,005. Below Poughkeepsie and including Poughkeepsie there are 606 members in that Home.   It is purposed to take one of the Trustees from that Home and give it to Rensselaer, when it has one in the adjoining county of [Montgomery, having 31 members, the two counties having 61 members as against 606 below Poughkeepsie represented by two trustees, one of which it is purposed by this resolution to take away.

As for my claim to reappointment, I have nothing to say.   Most of you know me and those that know me best know there is no man in the United States that has ever worn the button of the Grand Army of the Republic that has fought the number of battles I have fought, and successfully, during the past few years.   I do not want to take the time of the Encampment further.   I am still your Comrade and have worn the badge probably longer than any man in this Encampment — since December, 1866, fifty-two years next December.   I do not think there is a man in the Encampment that outdates me and I do not think there is a man in the Encampment who has been more active than I have and always in the interest of the Comrades.

COMRADE SMITH.— The statement by Comrade Loud that Comrade Maxwell resides in an adjoining county shows that he is not up in geography.   The facts are that he is a busy lawyer residing in Amsterdam, thirty odd miles away.   Those of you who know anything about legislation at Albany know it requires a man on the job there and a man who can be there on call.   It is pretty important at times to have a man at the Capitol to look after the special appropriations they require at the Home, and also to procure the supplies they need. Comrade Snyder was put forward by Albany for the reason that we have not had a man there at the Capitol for eighteen years — not since Comrade Palmer was one of the Board of Trustees, and the Board itself for some years have been asking that we put forward a resident who could be on the ground at all times in the interest of the Home. We have not seen fit to do it. We had no candidate we wanted to put forward. But again asked this year by numerous comrades to forward a man in Albany, or near it, they selected Comrade Snyder as the best man we could get. He is a member of a large manufacturing concern in Troy, only six miles away, and he can look after the interests of the Home very much better than Comrade Maxwell, a very good man, who lives 38 miles away, and who is compelled even now to leave the encampment on account of business. Comrade Snyder is not tied up that way. Comrade Loud was a candidiate before the Governor and is a candidiate before the Governor, and told me after we had Comrade Snyder in the race that the Governor had agreed to appoint him. The Governor says he did not. The matter was held up so long by reason of the very strong endorsements of Comrades Snyder coming from all over the State by prominent and influential comrades, that he was in doubt what to do, and it was suggested that the matter be referred to this encampment and let the boys here decide who in their judgment could best serve the Home. It isn't a question of Comrade Loud or Comrade Snyder, but a question of having somebody on the ground to do the work, which is important, and no one knows it better than those familiar with politics in the city of Albany, as I have been for forty-odd years. We simply ask that the Home and its best interests be taken care of by Comrade Snyder who is fully able to do it. The Governor has stated he has made no promises, as stated by Comrade Loud. Comrade Loud told me he had. He is awaiting your action.

COMRADE BLAIR.— I rise to speak in favor of the resolution reported by the Committee on Resolutions. I will be very brief. We have heard so much about autocracy that we now have a chance to repudiate all that has been claimed by those who believe that this organization is controlled by some mysterious power under the name of autocracy. The law gives us the right to name a Board of Trustees, and for the first time in the history of my attendance at these encampments, going back only ten or twelve years. There has always been wire pulling to succeed in having the Governor appoint trustees for the Bath Home and for the Oxford Home. The Governor has the right to appoint these trustees at the Bath Home, and we are asked for the first time that I can remember to have something to say as to who shall be the Trustee, and therefore I rejoice as a Grand Army man, and active for the past ten years, that we have at last an opportunity to voice the sentiments of the Grand Army of the Republic in encampment assembled of declaring our choice for the man that should be a Trustee at the Bath Home, and I move, if it has not been already moved, the adoption of the resolution reported by the Committee on Resolutions.

COMRADE TANNER.— I suppose there are some of you who remember that I might very consistently ask your attention to say a word about the Bath Home. When in 1876 I went on the platform in Albany to accept my first election as Department Commander I paralyzed my friends and champions in that encampment by telling them that while I was Commander of this Department there would be no special effort made to increase our membership. They confessed to me afterwards they thought I had a brain storm. I let it sink in and then I added for the reason that I have official documents that show me that in many houses in this State there are honorably discharged old soldiers whose only crime is their poverty, who cannot under the terms of admission to the National Home be admitted, and there is no State home, and I propose to give you while I am Department Commander of the State of New York for breakfast, dinner and supper, a soldiers' home in the State of New York, and I had the pleasure of laying its corner stone, and I saw the roof put on I am proud of it. Having gone over the State for two years, until we had raised $60,000, and then having gone before the legislature and got the legislature by unanimous vote to take charge of that home the people did maintain it, and I have a right when its interests are concerned to say something.

Now, then, there seems to be an idea among a few that this is persecution of Comrade Loud. Never a greater mistake made in the world. He has had a term —

COMRADE LOUD.— Not half a term.

COMRADE TANNER.— Many of his comrades desire another to succeed him. We in the committee voted unanimously on the basis of Snyder's near residence to Albany, and his life since the war, making familiar with business matters. The contention about whether the Governor promised or whether he did not promise — as to that I, of course, have no knowledge, but Comrade Smith told me that Comrade Loud had told him that the Governor has promised to appoint him. Last night I was at a dinner at the University, and I had a seat alongside of the Governor during the dinner and I mentioned this matter to him, and the Governor denied absolutely and flatly that he had ever made any promise. He further said to me, " If you endorse Snyder to-morrow I will appoint him Trustee next week." Now, then, there is the business, there is the argument, and it is not personal to any comrade. We are grateful to Comrade Loud for the good service he has given to the Home, but there are a good many boys in the State who are perfectly willing to give good service, and there isn't enough to pass around. I move the adoption of the resolution.

COMRADE STILLMAN.— During the number of years that I have been a delegate from the Post which I represent I have never stood upon my feet on this floor or the floor of an encampment to debate or discuss any important questions that have come before it for its deliberation. I have always thought and always believed that there were those here who were more experienced and better qualified to discuss and pursue the proper methods for the benefit of this organization and the Grand Army of the Republic, but to-day, without any pre-conceived notions, without any imputations, I feel it a duty and a privilege to say that I am in favor of this resolution. Comrade Snyder will probably be as much surprised as anyone to hear me stand on this floor and say a word in favor of the passage of this resolution. Comrade Snyder's record in the Grand Army of the Republic is known by all of you. They say to know a man you must live with him at home. I want to say I have known Comrade Snyder ever since he first donned the uniform of the United States troops to sustain that flag. I want to say to you I was with him on the 30th day of August, 1862, when we left the city of Troy for the front; I was with him when at Harper's Ferry shortly after our entrance into the Southern States where by the treachery of another we were captured by General Johnston. I want to say to you I was with Comrade Snyder under General Van Cott in the Second Army Corps. I want to say to you, comrades, I was with Comrade Snyder at Appomattox. I was with him when we marched triumphantly through the streets of the city we had left three years previously, he a young man at that time of no financial standing, without the opportunities that other young men had in this country, until now he has risen through his own efforts to a position of affluence.

(Cries of question.)

COMRADE LOUD.— Comrade Tanner has said I served a term. I have not served half a term. I took the unexpired term of Congressman Goulden less than three years ago, and I have never been absent from a meeting of the Trustees of the Home since I was appointed.

COMMANDER KIRCHNER.— The question is on the adoption of the resolution. Are you ready for the question? All those in favor of the adoption of the resolution will say "Aye" and those opposed " No." (After a pause.) It appears to be carried unanimously and is carried unanimously.

COMRADE TANNER.— I have here a resolution relating to the one-half cent a mile extra charge on the Pullman tickets. The Commander-in-Chief said that he was taking hold of that matter and we thought we could consistently and properly leave it in the hands of the Commander-in-Chief, and that is our report.

The report of the committee was adopted.

COMRADE TANNER.— Next is the Volunteer Officers Retirement Bill, favoring that bill, and I will state, as quite a number of comrades are interested in it, that very recently Past Commanders-in-Chief Beard and Comrades Rasseurer and Swords, were working on this bill, and I was told that Judge Dent, Chairman of the House Military Committee, who has always opposed this bill, says now that the bill has passed the Senate, his hands are down and he would not oppose it. Our report is favorable on that.

The report of the Committee was accepted, and the resolution unanimously adopted.

COMRADE TANNER.— This resolution I have in my hand is a combination of thanks to the President, thanks to Secretary McAdoo, thanks to Senator Smoot, thanks to Congress, for the favors we have received, and we unanimously urge its adoption.

The report of the committee was accepted and the resolution unanimously adopted.

COMRADE TANNER.— The next is a message to the boys who are over there. We unanimously recommend its adoption.

The report of the committee was accepted and the resolution unanimously adopted by a rising vote.

COMRADE TANNER.— The next resolution opening the doors of the Grand Army to Sons of Veterans, Spanish War Veterans, and those who may become veterans of this war, when it was offered yesterday Comrade Knobloch said he wanted to be heard, but he explained afterwards he comes from the Post that sent it; they asked him to present it and he refused. The Commander-in-Chief said he would not endorse it, and the report of the Committee is adverse.

The report of the Committee was adopted.

COMRADE TANNER.— Here is a voluminous matter handed to us at the last moment. We have put an endorsement on it " Too late to be considered," and we respectfully refer it to the incoming Council of Administration.

The report of the committee was adopted.

COMRADE TANNER.— Now here is a matter that we felt deserved further consideration, and besides that there isn't real necessity for it. It is a resolution that pronounces in favor when a Grand Army Post surrenders its charter and passes out of existence that certain action be taken concerning its property. The resolution reads:

Whereas, as Sometime, the flags, charters — mementos, relics and other personal and real property —, belonging to the various posts of the Grand Army of the Republic, and to the various Departments as well as to the Commandery-in-chief of the G. A. R. will necessarily pass into other hands from its present ownership, and,

Whereas, the organization of Sons of Veterans is of the lineal blood of their sires of the G. A. R. and therefore are most interested in the preservation of these sacred things as well as the memory of the men of the G. A. R., therefore be it

Resolved by the Department of New York, in Convention assembled at Ithaca, N. Y., in June, 1918, that its representatives of the Commandery-in-chief appointed to be held in the year 1918 be and they hereby are instructed to bring the matter to the attention of that body that the same may be duly considered and such action taken as will result in the legal method of accomplishing the desired purpose; and be is further

Resolved, that the Department of the State of New York, G. A. R. take such action at this present Encampment as will result in the suitable and legal method of transferring its said property and that of the various Posts of this State to the Sons of Veterans' organization, such transfer to take effect at such time as the G. A. R. shall determine.

Our recommendation is that it be referred to the incoming Council of Administration.

The report of the committee was adopted.

COMMANDER KIRCHNER.— Comrade Bush will read a resolution.

COMRADE BUSH.— Commander and Comrades: I was asked to draw up resolutions just a few moments ago respecting our treatment in the city of Ithaca during the encampment, and I will say that when I had finished them the Committee on Resolutions could not be found at the hotel, and that is the reason they were not handed in.

Whereas, many delagates and others who usually attend the annual encampment of the G. A. R. of this Department expressed a fear that from its location and apparent isolation Ithaca would not be a good place in which to meet, that accommodations for housing and feeding the delegates of the G. A. R. and its auxiliaries would be insufficient, and,

Whereas, we have enjoyed the hospitality of the University City now for three or more days and have been well housed and well fed, and entertained most delightfully, that we have been enlightened as to capacity of this great educational center — as a convention city — therefore

Resolved, that the thanks of the encampment are hereby tendered to the Ithaca Board of Commerce, to William Elliott Griffiths, D. D., to Prof. Samuel C. Orth, and to the Mayor, and the people of Ithaca generally for their successful efforts in making this encampment one of the pleasantest, if not the pleasantest, ever held in this Department.

The resolution was unanimously adopted by a rising vote.

COMRADE HUNT.— I would like to respond to this as I, together with Judge Kent, was sent to Albany to get this convention and the only thing we had in view was to make it a success. We thank you for your appreciation of our efforts. When we went before the committee we found them unanimously in favor of coming here, but their fear was that Ithaca was too small. We claimed to be the biggest little city in the country. Well, they decided to come here, and instead of it being a circus to have you come I have been working ever since last February to make it a success. We are glad you came, and we want you to go home knowing there is a little place called Ithaca on the map. (Applause.)

COMRADE BELL.— The committee appointed to consider and recommend candidates for the Council of Administration and for delegates unanimously report the following, and I will say that every member of the committee was present. For Council of Administration for the coming term:

Henry Lily, Post 170; Wm. G. Caw, Post 90; C. A. Weaver, Post 151; Thomas J. McConkey, Post 499; A. H. Stafford, Post 285.

I move, Commander Kirchner, that the report of the committee be adopted and that the entire vote of the encampment be cast for each one of these candidates.

The report of the committee was unanimously adopted and the candidates reported for the Council of Administration declared duly elected.

COMRADE BELL.— The committee further instructs me to report the Delegate ticket as follows:

COMRADE BELL.— I move that the report be adopted and the entire vote of the encampment be cast for each one of these comrades.

The report of the committee was adopted unanimously and the delegates declared elected.

COMRADE BELL.— I am also instructed by the committee to report the list of alternates and to move the adoption of the report of the committee and the election of the alternates whose names are presented. They are as follows:

Delegate at Large

		Post
1. James R. Silliman		600

Delegates

2. John Tregaskis	35
3. Wallace Riley	76
4. George Barden	93
5. William P. Griffith	197
6. Charles L. Wallace	6
7. J. Wetherall	222
8. Phillip M. Wales	338

Delegates — Continued   Post

9. George H. Sears 2
10. E. M. Chamberlain 644
11. Thomas Bergen 466
12. Fred J. Webber 2
13. Richard McCarthy 2
14. Joel Burdick 85
15. Alexander Parsons 51
16. George Wander 2
17. Daniel H. Cole 17
18. Frank M. Fisher 254
19. Ira D. Rowley 523
20. Nelson Simmons 2
21. Henry J. Knapp 667
22. Theodore P. Kellogg 438
23. John K. Chapman 226
24. F. J. Turner 159
25. Louis N. Aarons 29
26. Clinton Beckwith 404
27. E. H. Sentell 109
28. Lewis Hunt 487
29. B. F. Roze 9
30. John H. Nagel.............................. 128
31. Robert H. Longstreet 327
32. William G. Brady 327
33. Jacob Knobloch 112
34. M. V. B. Ives.............................. 214
35. A. E. Dick 103
36. Joseph Benzino 239
37. Newell C. Fulton 391
38. Theo. Cocheu 197
39. George Blair 516
40. James L. Lyons 136
41. John H. Stevens 94
42. Henry A. Kraus 32

Alternate At Large

1. Colvin A. Brainard 9

Alternates	Post
2. C. J. Kellogg	34
3. Caius K. Weaver	151
4. Chauncy Quintard	600
5. Gerome Freeman	...
6. James Flamboy	2
7. Francis A. Brown	76
8. William B. Price	435
9. Bert F. Parsons	327
10. John Treman	40
11. Chas. D. Emery	226
12. C. J. Westcott	119
13. George W. Holsliedge	514
14. H. W. Valentine	...
15. Edward J. Hoffman	435
16. Edward A. Burgoyne	170
17. Andrew Boyd	458
18. Geo. Lowenthal	4
19. James Campbell	458
20. Thomas H. Kiernan	148
21. Fred L. Farley	285
22. Edward P. Burnham	5
23. George Humphreys	349
24. P. J. Sheridan	391
25. William Luff	228
26. John L. Hall	670
27. Rozel Sager	81
28. L. A. Greenleaf	323
29. D. F. McOmber	162
30. Edward M. Griffith	29
31. George S. Parsons	156
32. George B. Herrick	333
33. Miles O'Rielly	327
34. Frank Johnson	354
35. J. W. Nye	379
36. Herman P. Smith	327
37. Henry G. Fritsch	600
38. Chas. Weiley	239

Alternates — Continued   Post

39. John L. Albeling 33
40. C. B. Sturdevant 282
41. W. H. Martin 26
42. Henry C. Draper 148

The report of the committee was unanimously adopted and the candidates whose names were read declared elected.

COMRADE BELL.— I also move that the Adjutant General have authority to make any changes, clerical changes, that may be necessary in the papers as read.

The motion was duly seconded and carried.

COMRADE TANNER.— I move the special order.

COMMANDER KIRCHNER.— We are now ready to carry out the special order that was passed yesterday, that is the order for the election of officers.

The acting Adjutant General read the names of the tellers for the respective comrades to be voted for, as follows:

Teller for Comrade Pilcher—George A. Price, Post 327.
Teller for Comrade Forey — Edward C. Fay.
Teller for Warner — Jas. A. Allis.
Teller for Ostrander — Louis Manner, Post 16.

The comrades named as tellers took their proper positions and the ballots were cast. After the casting of the ballots the tellers retired to count the number cast for each candidate. During the counting the following proceedings were had:

COMMANDER KIRCHNER.—We have at the outpost the Ladies' Auxiliary of the Sons of Veterans, the National President of the Women's Relief Corps, and also the Department President of the Women's Relief Corps. I appoint Comrades Isaacs, Silliman and Parsons as a committee to proceed to the outpost and to escort the ladies to this rostrum, together with whomsoever else may be there.

COMRADE SILLIMAN.— Commander, it gives me great pleasure to introduce the National President of the Women's Relief Corps;

also the President of the Department of New York and the Secretary.

COMMANDER KIRCHNER.— In behalf of the comrades of this department I extend a soldier's welcome. Please be seated. Comrades, I have pleasure in introducing to you the National President of the Women's Relief Corps, Mrs. Lois M. Knaus, the Department President of the Women's Relief Corps, Mrs. Ada T. Gaudineer, and the Department secretary. I would now request Mrs. Knaus, the National President, to address you.

MRS. KNAUS.— Comrades of the Department of New York, while I regret very much not to see more of the comrades here I am glad to see those that are here, and I bring to you the greetings of the National Organization one hundred and sixty 'thousand strong, that are working for you and your comrades, and I want to say this, that we are working for you as we have done for thirty-five years. We have a comrade in Ohio who disputes that. They always say that women are trying to conceal their age and instead of 35 years the Women's Relief Corps is 37 years old, because in Indianapolis in 1881 was the time when the women were first requested to form an organization and not until two years later was it taken care of. Now, comrades, my explanation of this is that in 1881 the Grand Army of the Republic proposed to the women and it took them two years to decide whether they would accept that proposal. (Laughter.) They talked the matter over carefully and in 1883 they decided they would be the auxiliary and go to work with you as your helpmates. We have tried to do our duty ever since and are going to continue to do so.

I want to say to the comrades of New York you have a special interest to me as my husband was a New York soldier. He belonged to the Third New York Cavalry. As I looked at you last night, so many of you, I wondered if I was looking into the faces of any of his comrades because in Ohio we have one in our city that was a comrade of my husband in his regiment, and when in your department that thought was very strong in my mind. Comrades, I wish you success. I hope and pray that we may have you with us for many years to come. I am not going to take any further time. I know you are anxious to get out. I know our Department President is anxious to get off to her work, but I want to say to you that we have taken the boys and we are going to do for them what we tried to do for you. They are your boys and our boys and we are going to stand with them and with you. I want to say one thing that may sound a little hard, but I do not believe this could be won without the women standing back of the boys. We want to stand back of them and encourage them in every way possible. We will knit and we will sew and do everything possible to make them comfortable, and we want them to know we are going to work with them and help them get over the top, and now I am going to say to you that I leave you with an old darkey's blessing that was left with me when he said: " God bless you and keep you. May the Lord always let sunshine on the side of the street which you live on." God bless you and keep you and may we have you for many, many years.

COMMANDER KIRCHNER.— I now take great pleasure in presenting to you Mrs. Ada T. Gaudineer, President of the Relief Corps of the Department of New York.

MRS. GAUDINEER. — Commander Kirchner, and comrades: As President of the Womans' Relief Corps, State of New York, it gives me great pleasure to bring to each comrade the loving greetings of your auxiliary the Woman's Relief Corps, and to render to you the following report of one year's work:

Number of corps in this department............. 207
Number of members in this department.......... 9,659
Cash expended for relief...................... $2,850.45
Estimate value of relief other than money........: 4,302,19
Cash expended from Dept. Relief Fund.......... 160.00
Amount turned over to Posts................... 1,495.25
Total value of Corps property including balance in
   General and Relief Funds.................... 38,496.21
Number of veterans assisted................... 380
Number of veterans' families assisted........... 763

This, Commander Kirchner, is a statement in figures which I hope will meet with your approval, but it does not express the many acts of service for the comrades of the G. A. R. rendered by our organization.

Comrades of the Grand Army of the Republic, the members of your auxiliary, the Woman's Relief Corps, are proud to be identified with you, our country's heroes; as you are the men who have be tried and not found wanting.

The flag that you carried away in the stirring days of '61 and returned to us in '65, without a star missing, and with the assurance that our Nation should be united, under one great flag, stands out to the world to-day as the emblem of a clean, true democracy.

In its high and mighty place the eyes of the whole civilized world are turned to it as the saviour of oppressed humanity. Countless thousands of our lads are following it across the seas, and who can doubt the final outcome? We will win this war, we must win this war. Many of our dear lads have the blood of our Comrades of the Grand Army of the Republic flowing through their veins, and who can doubt when put to the test of fire and shell they will lack courage? You, my comrades, have been their inspiration, as from their youth they have been imbued with patriotism, furnished by the recitation of your glorious achievements in the various battles of the Civil War. So, my comrades, you have twice served your country. First by real service and secondly, by inspiring all who know the history of our land, and love our grand flag, to answer the call of duty and do their part to keep it in its proud place among nations, and prove to all mankind the truth of President Wilson's words on Flag Day, a year ago, " For us there is but one choice — we have made it. We are ready to stand at the bar of history, and our flag shall wear a new lustre. Once more we shall make good with our lives and fortunes the great faith to which we were born, and a new glory shall shine in the faces of our people."

God grant that many of you comrades may be spared to see our boys come marching home, with the flag your sacrifices hallowed held on high proclaiming to all mankind the eternal brotherhood of man.

Respectfully submitted in F. C. & L.

ADA T. GAUDINEER,
Dept. President, 1917–1918.

COMMANDER KIRCHNER.— It gives me great pleasure, comrades, to introduce the Past President of the Department of New York, now the Secretary, Mrs. Regina Demarest.

MRS. DEMAREST.—Commander and comrades of the Department of New York, I know you are busy, and after all this eloquence that has preceded me I do not feel that I could add anything in any way to it. I feel like the country orator who had been in the habit on the Fourth of July of delivering the oration. He spoke a great many years and after a while grew a little tired of his oration and they brought in an orator from somewhere else and of course he carried the crowd in every way, and paralyzed our dear friend, the country orator, so after it was all over, although he had his oration in mind all right he arose and said, " Well, lets fire off the salute and go home." (Laughter and applause.)

COMMANDER KIRCHNER.— I will ask the Judge Advocate, Colonel Joseph E. Ewell, to respond to the Women's Relief Corps.

COLONEL EWELL.— Commander and comrades, National President, State President, and Secretary of the Women's Relief Corps: I desire to congratulate you, ladies, upon your successful and gallant " going over the top " on this occasion. We managed to stand you off at the outpost for a while, and that enabled a large part of the garrison to escape, but now I expect they wish they had not for we surrender unconditionally. We thank you for coming here. We thank you for your kind words. We thank you for your kindly sentiments, and we beg to assure you that to the largest extent and to the fullest degree we are appreciative and responsive, and we reciprocate to the full extent of our capacity to do so all that you have said and done, and we also beg to assure you further that our respect and our regard for the grand and noble organization, the Women's Relief Corps, never reached a higher mark than at the present psychological moment, after listening to the addresses which we have heard at this encampment and which we have just heard. It has been said, I do not know how true, that woman's mission was to civilize and educate man and teach him good manners and make him better and more considerate, more humane, and if such a thing were possible perhaps more beautiful. I do not know whether this is so or not, but we are willing to admit that the Women's Relief Corps has gone a long way in this direction, which we appreciate highly. The Women's Relief Corps is emphatically and distinctly a patriotic organization, and it believes not only in the patriotism of good words but in the patriotism of good works. I do not know of any more patriotic work than to aid the nation in making good its pledges, voiced by President Lincoln in his second inaugural, to care for him who had borne the brunt of battle, and his widow and his orphan. Your noble organization has been engaged for these many years in that splendid work and not only that, but you seem to enjoy it; you seem to have found what Ponce de Leon failed to discover in all his energies — the fountain of enternal youth, and the evidences that we see all around us at his encampment are proof of this fact. It was through the energy and the persistent determination of the Women's Relief Corps that that magnificient institution for the care of veterans and their widows and orphans, which is so magnificently conducted at the present time, was established, and if the Women's Relief Corps in all its existence did nothing beyond that it would be entitled to the lasting gratitude of every comrade, of every soldier and every soldier's friend.

But the activities of the Relief Corps are not limited — the patriotic activities are not limited to the care of old veterans. It goes along on every line where there is a demand and a call for patriotic work, and in these times, during this great war, it is doing its full share along those lines.

Now I will not take up your time further; I will only say that we beg of you to convey to your organization our compliments and our greetings in return for yours, and to assure your organization of our continued respect and high regard, and that we hope you will continue your good work in the future as in the past and with the same reward, honor and approving conscience. (Applause.)

COMMANDER KIRCHNER.— I thank you for coming in. I would now request the comrades to escort the ladies to the door and return with the other delegation that are there.

COMRADE ISAACS.— It gives me great pleasure to introduce Mrs. Harriet Goetz, Past Department President of the Daughters of Veterans, and also Mrs. Howell, Past Department President of the Daughters of Veterans.

COMMANDER KIRCHNER.— Ladies, on behalf of the Grand Army of the Republic, I extend to you a soldier's welcome and we are pleased to hear from you. I present to you, comrades, Mrs. Harriet Goetz, Past Department President of the Daughters of Veterans.

MRS. GOETZ.— Commander and comrades of the Grand Army of the Republic: It is a daughter's greeting I bring to you to-day. We are very proud of being daughters of such men as you are. We do not plead the eloquence of oratory, but we do plead the eloquence that comes from father to daughter. The Commander-in-Chief in our convention yesterday said he never wanted the Grand Army to be forgotten, and at that time I felt like getting to my feet and pledging that as long as a daughter of a veteran lived that the Grand Army of the Republic would never be forgotten. (Applause.) The deeds that you men performed half a century ago will be told to the end of all time. We teach patriotism, we keep green the history of '61–'65 to our utmost, and to-day I bring you the greetings of our Department President and the Daughters of Veterans assembled in convention.

We did not want to intrude on your time, but we felt as though we could not let our duties come to an end without bringing you a greeting to show the love we bear for you and how much we appreciate you and what you have done. (Applause.)

Commander Kirchner.— I now have the pleasure of presenting to you Mrs. Howell.

Mrs. Howell.— Comrades, Sister Goetz was sent here to extend the greetings and I was sent to see that she did it. Having done that my part of the program is finished, but I want to say just one word. I am no gaily feathered nightingale to charm you with my song, or silver tongued orator that can charm you all day long, but the love I bear for you is always fond and true, and you will always find me ready when there is anything to do. (Applause.)

Commander Kirchner.— I want to ask our Quartermaster-General of the Grand Army of the Republic to respond to our daughters.

Quartermaster-General Stowits.— Department Commander and comrades: I would much prefer some comrade who does not know these young ladies as well as I do to respond to their greetings. I do know what they have succeeded in doing in our part of the State. I know what they have done to carry out their share of the great work of the Daughters of Veterans throughout the national organization. I know that they are worthy successors of worthy sires. I know that they demand and must have the support of every man in the Grand Army of the Republic, because the time is coming when it will be necessary for someone to carry on the patriotic work of this great organization, and when you go to the schools and the Sunday schools of this nation there are none so well fitted as they, and they are the natural leaders in this line of work together with the other auxiliaries. All I can say is we thank you, we thank you in behalf of the Grand Army of the Republic of the State of New York, and we wish you God speed. (Applause.)

Commander Kirchner.—We thank you ladies very much for coming.

The tellers having performed their duty are now ready to report the result.

Comrade Price.— The tellers appointed to canvass the vote

COUNCIL OF ADMINISTRATION

HENRY LILLY

ELIAS W. BEACH

AUSTIN H. STAFFORD

WILLIAM H. KILFOILE

SAMUEL IRVINE

of the encampment for Department Commander beg leave to
report as follows:

Total vote 362

Of which Lewis S. Pilcher received............ 203
John H. Forey received...................... 159

362

Majority for Lewis S. Pilcher................. 44

Respectfully submitted,
GEORGE A. PRICE,
EDWARD C. FAY.

COMRADE FOREY.—With malice toward none, with the best of
feeling for every comrade of this department, and with my sincere
thanks to the comrades who have given me their support in this
contest, I move to make the election of Lewis S. Pilcher unanimous. (Applause.)

The motion was duly seconded and carried.

COMMANDER KIRCHNER.— I now declare Comrade Lewis S.
Pilcher elected Commander of this department for the ensuing
year. (Applause.)

COMRADE PRICE.—We beg leave to report that there was cast
for Senior Vice Commander of this department 361 votes, of
which Stuart Warner received 199 and Alson B. Ostrander 161
and George Tait 1, giving Stuart Warner a majority over all
of 37.

Respectfully submitted,
GEORGE A. PRICE,
EDWARD C. FAY.

COMRADE OSTRANDER.— I move, sir, that the election of Comrade Stuart Warner be made unanimous, with thanks to all the
comrades who have expressed their confidence in me.

9

The motion was duly seconded and carried.

COMMANDER KIRCHNER.— I declare Comrade Stuart Warner duly elected Senior Vice Commander for the ensuing year.

I request Comrades Silliman and Little to escort the Commander-elect to the platform. I also request Comrades Stafford and Allis to escort Comrade Stuart Warner, the newly elected Senior Vice Commander, to the platform.

Comrades, Past Department Commander James D. Bell is hereby detailed to install the officers elected for the ensuing year.

The Junior Vice Commander and all other officers elected having been summoned to the platform they were thereupon duly installed, Comrade Isaacs acting as officer of the day.

Commander Pilcher announced the appointment of Comrade William C. Peckham of Post 327, as Assistant Adjutant-General and Quartermaster-General of this department.

COMMANDER PILCHER.— Installing officer, I thank you for the manner in which you have carried the ceremony of the moment. I appreciate all the good services which you are continually performing for your comrades. Please accept not only the thanks of the Department but also those of your humble servant, its present commander.

Perhaps never before has the word " comrade " meant to the members of the Grand Army of the Republic what it does to-day. We were comrades as young men; we have been comrades through all the years of our development as men, as citizens, as we have come up from the boy to the mature man. And now to-day we have not only all the memories of the past to cement this comradeship but we have the additional bond which comes from the conditions of the moment, when we in our old age have that common fellowship which comes from a knowledge of trial and of bereavement which has come to the experience of everyone of us. Now, added to this, at this moment, we have that bond of comradeship which comes from our interest and pride in these sons and grandsons, who have inherited our spirit and are carrying on our work, with the knowledge of those things which inspired us in our youth, and more than that, which inspired us when we strove to preserve the unity of our country and its liberties: we have that bond which comes from the knowledge that in the persons of our sons we are striving to preserve liberty for the whole world. (Applause.) In that spirit I call you to-day my comrades and accept this honor which you confer upon me and renew the pledge which I have already given to do what I can for your advancement as comrades and for the Department of New York, and for the Grand Army of the Republic throughout the whole country. I thank you. (Great applause.)

Comrade Tanner.—We have present with us Mr. Kellogg, Secretary of the Ithaca Board of Commerce, who has an announcement to make. Secretary Kellogg has done a thousand and one things to make our stay pleasant.

Secretary Kellogg extended a cordial invitation to all comrades to visit the Crescent Theatre and view moving pictures of the parade.

The invitation was accepted with thanks.

Comrade Orr.— I move a vote of thanks to Comrade Isaacs for his work as Acting Adjutant-General.

Commander Pilcher.— It gives me great pleasure to put that motion.

Seconded and carried.

Comrade Isaacs.— The work I have performed in this position has been a labor of love — a labor of love for the poor comrade who was not able to be present to perform that duty. I thank you.

Commander Pilcher.— Our duties for this occasion are now ended. I now declare this encampment adjourned without date.

In Memoriam

Solomon W. Russell

It is with sincere regret that we are called upon to announce the death of Past Department Commander Solomon W. Russell, who departed this life at his home in Salem, Washington county, on Thursday, October 18th, aged eighty-one years. Comrade Russell entered the service and was mustered in as Captain of Company A, Seventh New York Cavalry, on September 7, 1861. He resigned therefrom, and subsequently became Adjutant of the 49th Regiment of Infantry of New York, and was promoted to Captain and Major, and was grievously wounded at the Battle of Rappahannock Station, on November 7, 1863 (while on the Staff of his kinsman, General David A. Russell, who was killed at the Battle of Winchester, Va.), and was mustered out of service in June, 1865. He returned home, took up his chosen profession of law and made a distinguished figure in it; not only that, but in all those civic activities of his home town, where he was recognized as its leading citizen. His departure from our midst creates a void that cannot be filled, and his modest, unobtrusive deportment will long be remembered when all that was mortal of him shall have crumbled to decay.

SOLOMON W. RUSSELL, Past Department Commander.

Michael J. Cummings

Past Department Commander Michael J. Cummings died at his home in Brooklyn on January 3, 1918. He enlisted on January 12, 1864, as a private in Company B, 48th Regiment, New York Volunteer Infantry; was wounded at the battle of Olustee, and was honorably discharged as Sergeant September 1, 1865.

After some years spent in private employment he was appointed clerk in the office of the City Clerk of Brooklyn in 1877, and remained there for fifteen or sixteen years, having risen to the office of City Clerk, which he held for some years. Under Greater New York, on January 1, 1898, he became Secretary of the Sewer Department, and when that Department ceased to exist he was transferred to the Sewer Bureau in the Borough President's office in Manhattan, where he remained until his death. In the discharge of his public duties he was careful, prompt and intelligent.

Comrade Cummings was mustered into Thomas C. Devin Post No. 148, Department of New York, on September 12, 1884, and remained an active member until his death. He was Commander of his Post in 1888, and Department Commander of New York in 1909. He was trustee of the Permanent Fund of the Grand Army of the Republic, and Chairman of the board at the time of his death and for a number of years prior thereto. He was for eight years Chairman of the Memorial and Executive Committee, G. A. R., of Kings county.

Comrade Cummings in any body of men was a leader. As a Comrade he was characterized by his readiness and willingness to help a Comrade, regardless of any consideration other than the fraternal tie. Comradeship meant what its name implies to him.

MICHAEL J. CUMMINGS, Past Department Commander.

William A. Boyd

Past Senior Vice Department Commander William A. Boyd died at his home in New York City January 24, 1918. He enlisted April 20, 1861, in the 71st N. Y. S. M., and served ninety days. Re-enlisted in the 62d New York Volunteer Infantry September 13, 1861, and was discharged December 13, by reason of ill health. Mustered into Lafayette Post 140, July, 1905. He was elected Senior Vice Department Commander in 1908, and served as Judge Advocate of the Department, and at the time of his death was Chairman of the Memorial Committee, County of New York, and Trustee of the Woman's Relief Corps Home at Oxford, N. Y.

WILLIAM A. BOYD, Past Senior Vice-Department Commander

ROSTER

OF THE

DEPARTMENT OF NEW YORK

GRAND ARMY OF THE REPUBLIC

ALBANY, NEW YORK

1918

[261]

Department Officers

Department Commander	WILLIAM F. KIRCHNER
Senior Vice-Commander	HENRY S. REDMAN
Junior Vice-Commander	FRANK JOHNSON
Chaplain	REV. REUBEN KLINE
Medical Director	WILLIAM TAYLOR, M. D.

Official Staff

Assistant Adjutant-General .... Assistant Quartermaster-General..	EDWARD J. ATKINSON
Department Inspector	SAMUEL McAULIFFE
Judge Advocate	JOSEPH E. EWELL
Chief Mustering Officer............	JOHN McCLOSKEY
Patriotic Instructor	GEORGE L. HUGHSON
Senior Aide-de-Camp...............	ISIDORE ISAACS

Council of Administration

ELIAS W. BEACH   SAMUEL IRVINE   HENRY LILLY
      WILLIAM H. KILFOILE   AUSTIN H. STAFFORD

Past National Officers

*JOHN C. ROBINSON..............	........Commander-in-Chief, 1877–78
*JOHN PALMER	..........Commander-in-Chief, 1891
*ALBERT D. SHAW...............	..........Commander-in-Chief, 1899
JAMES TANNER	..........Commander-in-Chief, 1905
*JAMES B. McKEAN..............	Senior Vice-Com.-in-Chief, 1866–67
*EDWARD JARDINE	Senior Vice-Commander-in-Chief, 1874
*JOHN PALMER	Senior Vice-Commander-in-Chief, 1879
ALFRED LYTH	Senior Vice-Commander-in-Chief, 1897
*LEWIS E. GRIFFITH.............	Senior Vice-Commander-in-Chief, 1907
*NICHOLAS W. DAY.............	Senior Vice-Commander-in-Chief, 1912
†JOSEPH HADFIELD	Junior Vice-Commander-in-Chief, 1888

Past Department Commanders

*James B. McKean.Saratoga Springs	*Joseph P. Cleary........Rochester
*Daniel E. Sickles...New York City	John C. Shotts............Yonkers
*Edward B. Lansing........Auburn	Edward J. Atkinson.New York City
*John C. Robinson......Binghamton	James S. Graham..... ..Rochester
*Henry A. Barnum...New York City	*Albert D. Shaw.........Watertown
*Stephen P. Corliss..........Albany	*Anson S. Wood............Wolcott
*Edward Jardine ....Albany	Joseph W. Kay...........Brooklyn
*John Palmer ....Albany	N. P. Pond..............Rochester
James Tanner....Washington, D. C.	Chas. A. Orr..............Buffalo
*William F. Rogers.........Buffalo	Allan C. Bakewell...New York City
*James McQuade ....Utica	John S. Koster.......Port Leyden
*L. Coe Young........Binghamton	*Henry N. Burhans.......Syracuse
*Abram Merritt ....Nyack	James M. Snyder.............Troy
*James S. Fraser....New York City	John S. Maxwell........Amsterdam
John A. Reynolds........Fairport	*Harlan J. Swift..............Cuba
*Ira M. Hedges.........Haverstraw	*William H. Daniels....Ogdensburg
*H. Clay Hall..........Little Falls	*M. J. Cummings..........Brooklyn
*Joseph I. Sayles.............Rome	DeWitt C. Hurd ....Utica
*George H. Treadwell........Albany	George B. Loud.....New York City
*N. Martin Curtis.......Ogdensburg	Oscar Smith ....Albany
*Harrison Clark ....Albany	Samuel C. Pierce.......Rochester
*Floyd Clarkson......New York City	James D. Bell........... Brooklyn
Charles H. Freeman........Corning	Zan L. Tidball............Buffalo
*Theodore L. Poole........Syracuse	*Solomon W. Russell.........Salem

DeAlva S. Alexander, Buffalo, transferred from Dept. Potomac.
*W. L. Palmer, Binghamton, transferred from Dept. Dakota.

* Deceased.
† Severed his connection with the Order.

Past Senior Vice Department Commanders

*William F. Rogers.
* James M. Gere.
* Edward B. Lansing.
* John C. Robinson.
John A. Reynolds.
*Samuel Minnes.
*John Palmer.
*Joseph Egolf.
*John G. Copley.
*Constantine Nitzsche.
*Jacob Welsing.
*Henry Osterheld.
*John E. Savery
*Robert Keith.
*H. Clay Hall.
*L. P. Thompson.
C. W. Cowtan.
C. A. Orr.
* J. P. Cleary.
Charles H. Freeman.
*J. K. Hood.
*Homer B. Webb.
*Edward J. Deevey.
*William L. DeLacey.
Edward J. Atkinson.
P. C. Soule.
*C. Hull Grant

*Frederick Cossum.
*George Chappell.
*Rufus Daggett.
John S. Maxwell.
Edward J. Mitchell.
*John H. Swift.
Clark H. Norton.
*M. J. Cummings
*W. Charles Smith.
*E. C. Parkinson.
George E. Dewey.
*Daniel J. O'Brien.
*Jared W. Wickes.
George F. Tait.
*William A. Boyd
James M. Watson.
Samuel C. Pierce.
Daniel H. Cole.
James D. Bell.
Alfred E. Stacey.
A. H. Stafford.
James A. Allis
George Hollands
*Alexander E. Mintee, Buffalo, transferred from Dept., Cal. and Nevada.

Past Junior Vice Department Commanders

*James M. Geer.
*Bradley Winslow.
*V. Krzyanowski.
John A. Reynolds.
*John W. Marshall.
* Willard Bullard.
*Joseph Egolf.
*A. B. Lawrence.
*Edwin J. Loomis.
*Robert H. McCormic.
*George H. Treadwell.
* J. Marshall Guion.
*James F. Fitts.
*Dennis Sullivan.
*Edwin Goodrich.
Frank Z. Jones.
*J. C. Carlyle
*W. B. Stoddard

*G. S. Conger.
*C. Hull Grant.
*Robert Wilson.
*W. L. Scott.
*Gardner C. Hibbard.
Edward A. Dubey.
William F. Kirchner.
Silas Owen.
*Daniel Van Wie.
*John Kohler.
John S. Koster.
N. R. Thompson.
Walter Scott.
Jerre S. Gross.
*Philo H. Conklin.
*Daniel W. Hulse.
*D. C. Bangs.
*David Isaacs.
L. L. Hanchett.

George E. Dewey.
*Edward H. Fassett.
*Daniel J. O'Brien.
*Jared W. Wickes.
James Campbell.
DeWitt C. Hurd.
Robert P. Bush.
*L. O. Morgan.
*Henry E. Turner.
*C. C. Caldwell.
C. J. Westcott.
Nelson Mattice.
David H. Dyer.
Robert Simpson, Jr., M. D.
Isidore Isaacs
* James Loftus
John W. Mullens

* Deceased.

RECAPITULATION OF POSTS BY COUNTIES

ALBANY.

NUMBER.	NAME.	LOCATION.
5	Lew Benedict	Albany.
43	N. G. Lyon	Cohoes.
63	George S. Dawson	Albany.
121	L. O. Morris	Albany.
198	M. H. Barckley	Altamont.
644	William A. Jackson	Albany.
671	General John E. Wool	Watervliet.

ALLEGANY.

86	A. K. Thorp	Belfast.
183	Stephen T. Bartle	Cuba.
195	Revere	Belmont.
237	Burnside	Fillmore.
241	Hatch	Friendship.
247	H. C. Gardner	Bolivar.
296	Seth H. Weed	Canaseraga.
332	Wesley Rolfe	Stanards.
333	Sawyer	Whitesville.
336	Dexter	Wellsville.
427	W. W. Woodworth	Rushford.
428	B. Frank Maxson	Alfred.
481	Edward Seaman	Andover.
502	Wilbur Haver	Angelica.
603	A. & J. Van Nostrand	Short Tract.

BRONX.

96	Oliver Tilden	New York.
136	Vanderbilt	New York.

BROOME.

30	Watrous	Binghamton.
108	Joseph J. Bartlett	Binghamton.
134	Walton Dwight	Johnson City.
150	Henry Williams	Harpursville.
184	Eggleston	Deposit.
199	Eldredge	Whitney Point.
350	Whittlesey	Union.

CANADA.

472	W. W. Cooke	Hamilton, Ontario
532	James S. Knowlton	Toronto.
652	Hannibal Hamlin	London.

CATTARAUGUS.

85	H. W. Wessels	Portville.
222	G. D. Bayard	Olean.
232	Henry Van Arnam	Ellicottville.
246	Fuller	Little Valley
297	D. T. Wiggins	Randolph.
310	Capt. Fancher	Leon.

CATTARAUGUS — *Continued.*

NUMBER.	NAME.	LOCATION.
357	Rust	Great Valley.
359	Darby	Gowanda.
380	Sherwood	Salamanca.
386	C. D. Nash	South Dayton.
508	Alansen Crosby	Franklinville.
655	Wm. T. Wickham	Otto.
666	A. A. Hall	East Randolph.

CAYUGA.

45	Seward-Crocker	Auburn.
155	George C. Stoyell	Moravia.
159	Hudson	Fair Haven.
166	J. E. Whiteside	Weedsport.
175	Lockwood	Port Byron.
201	Capt. G. M. Smith	Kings Ferry.
494	A. A. Hoff	Union Springs.
632	Selah Cornwell	Scipio.

CHAUTAUQUA.

282	H. C. Sturdevant	Kennedy.
285	James M. Brown	Jamestown.
292	James A. Hall	Brocton.
295	Sheldon	Sherman.
317	J. C. Drake	Sinclairville.
324	William Sackett	Westfield.
389	Philander Cook	Panama.
393	William O Stevens	Dunkirk.
403	E. D. Holt	Fredonia.
429	John F. Smith	Stockton.
439	G. L. Pierce	Forestville.
523	R. M. Starring	Silver Creek.
589	Cyrus Adams	Frewsburg.

CHEMUNG.

6	Baldwin	Elmira.
165	L. E. Fitch	Elmira.
416	Wilson Dean:	Millport.
623	General A. S. Diven	Elmira.
672	R. M. McDowell	Elmira.

CHENANGO.

12	Vanderburg	Afton.
40	Admiral Meade	Oxford.
83	E. B. Smith	Norwich.
137	Otis G. Banks	Greene.
196	Edward E. Breed	Oxford.
442	Wm. A. Miles	McDonough.
456	J. E. Parce	South Otselic.
493	Plumb	Sherburne.
576	Weaver	Smyrna.
582	H. H. Beecher	Bainbridge.

CLINTON.

NUMBER.	NAME.	LOCATION.
352	J. S. Stone	Saranac.
366	Walter H. Benedict	Plattsburg.
374	Samuel Cannon	Mooers Forks.
411	Angell	Mooers.
659	Charles H. Bentley	Morrisonville.

COLUMBIA.

118	Byron Lockwood	Philmont.
138	R. D. Lathrop	Hudson.
539	General Logan	Chatham.

CORTLAND.

98	Grover	Cortland.
105	Willoughby Babcock	Homer.
476	William H. Tarbell	McGrawville.

DELAWARE.

132	Frank T. Hine	Franklin.
142	England	Delhi.
177	Bradford	Sidney.
209	Ben Marvin	Walton.
280	Fleming	Downsville.
477	John A. Logan	Stamford.
483	John Plasket	Hancock.

DUTCHESS.

20	Hamilton Sleight	Poughkeepsie.
48	Howland	Beacon.
88	J. H. Ketcham	Wappingers Falls.
104	Armstrong	Rhinebeck.
467	Obed Wheeler	Amenia.
617	Henry Gridley	Millerton.
661	C. N. Campbell	Pawling.

ERIE

2	Chapin	Buffalo.
9	Bidwell-Wilkeson	Buffalo.
87	Crary	Springville.
129	Winfield B. Scott	Tonawanda.
180	George Stoneman	Lancaster.
202	James Ayer	Angola.
220	S. C. Noyes	North Collins.
239	Albert J. Meyer	Buffalo.
254	William Richardson	Buffalo.
398	J. J. Peck	Akron.
432	W. B. Ransom	Clarence.
440	N. J. Swift	Hamburg.
478	Chester Bishop	Colden.
506	Arthur Smith	East Aurora.
542	E. L. Hayward	Buffalo.
553	Robert Orr	Holland.

ESSEX.

NUMBER.	NAME.	LOCATION.
102	Wm. H. Stevenson	Moriah Center.
252	Alfred Weed	Ticonderoga.
379	D'Avignon	Jay.
484	C. D. Beaumont	Keeseville.
533	C. F. Hammond	Crown Point.
594	Robert W. Livingston	Keene Valley.

FRANKLIN.

213	J. W. Pangborn	Malone.
284	W. D. Brennan	Malone.
363	H. L. Aldrich	Brushton.
504	Durkee	St. Regis Falls.
562	A. T. Bailey	Chateaugay.
621	F. M. Bull	Saranac Lake.

FULTON.

17	Ansel Denison	Gloversville.
257	Martin McMartin	Johnstown.
289	McKean	Broadalbin.

GENESEE.

299	Upton	Batavia.
412	Wilbert Fuller	Bergen.

GREENE.

27	Hollister	Coxsackie.
263	A. N. Baldwin	Hunter.
514	John W. Watson	Catskill.

HAMILTON.

531	William Wood	Long Lake.

HERKIMER.

19	Galpin	Little Falls.
110	Chismore	Ilion.
364	S. G. Button	West Winfield.
404	Aaron Helmer	Herkimer.
604	Frank Mann	Frankfort.
664	J. P. Spofford	Dolgeville.

JEFFERSON.

188	Julius Broadbent	Dexter.
269	E. B. Steel	Carthage.
273	Piper	Henderson.
300	H. H. Vebber	Black River.
306	G. W. Flower	Theresa.

JEFFERSON — *Continued*

NUMBER.	NAME.	LOCATION.
323	Joe Spratt	Watertown.
373	Oliver McAllaster	Antwerp.
381	De Alton Cooper	Adams.
410	Albert Dennis	Clayton.
424	James B. Campbell	Alexandria Bay.
441	E. V. Mayhew	Three Mile Bay.
588	Wm. T. Sherman	Natural Bridge.
633	John P. Buckley	Belleville.

KINGS.

10	Rankin	Brooklyn.
11	Barbara Frietchie	Brooklyn.
21	Harry Lee	Brooklyn.
35	Mansfield	Brooklyn.
89	James H. Perry	Brooklyn.
122	Germain Metternich	Brooklyn.
148	Thomas C. Devin	Brooklyn.
152	L. M. Hamilton	Brooklyn.
161	N. S. Ford	Brooklyn.
197	Winchester	Brooklyn.
206	Dakin-Slocum	Brooklyn.
207	William Lloyd Garrison	Brooklyn.
231	Cushing	Brooklyn.
233	Brooklyn City	Brooklyn.
286	Gouverneur K. Warren	Brooklyn.
327	U. S. Grant	Brooklyn.
362	George Ricard	Brooklyn.
399	Clarence D. Mackenzie	Brooklyn.
435	Abel Smith-1st L. I.	Brooklyn.
443	Tefft-Odell	Brooklyn.
499	McPherson-Doane	Brooklyn.
500	B. F. Middleton	Brooklyn.
534	George C. Strong	Brooklyn.

LEWIS.

200	G. D. Bailey	Lowville.
385	H. J. Botchford	Port Leyden.
525	F. M. Leonard	Copenhagen.

LIVINGSTON.

190	J. L. & C. S. Thompson	Dalton.
216	Seth N. Hedges	Dansville.
382	E. S. Gilbert	Livonia.
392	A. A. Curtiss	Geneseo.
417	Craig W. Wadsworth	Nunda.
459	Mark L. Scoville	Mount Morris.
518	William B. Hazen	Springwater.
660	Tilton	Leicester

MADISON.

NUMBER.	NAME.	LOCATION.
49	Reese	Canastota.
160	Knowlton	Cazenovia.
174	John R. Stewart	Oneida.
272	Arthur L. Brooks	Hamilton.
376	W. E. Hunt	De Ruyter.
448	Searle	Brookfield.
624	Carey W. Miner	Georgetown.

MONROE.

	O'Rorke	Rochester.
4	Geo. H. Thomas	Rochester.
84	Myron Adams	Rochester.
106	Peissner	Rochester.
211	E. A. Slocum	Fairport.
236	Cady	Brockport.
270	John H. Martindale	Spencerport.
275	Thomas Farr	West Webster.
288	E. J. Tyler	Pittsford.
369	Lewis Gates	Honeoye Falls.
391	C. J. Powers	Rochester.
397	E. G. Marshall	Rochester.
409	I. F. Quimby	Rochester.
455	Francis E. Pierce	Rochester.

MONTGOMERY.

33	E. S. Young	Amsterdam.
51	Farrell	Canajoharie.
57	Van Derveer	Fonda.
70	Klock	Fort Plain.
356	Alonzo Smith	St. Johnsville.

NASSAU.

365	D. L. Downing	Glen Cove.
527	D. B. P. Mott	Freeport.
544	Moses A. Baldwin	Hempstead.
654	Elijah Ward	Roslyn.

NEW YORK.

8	Phil Kearny	New York.
24	Sumner	New York.
29	James C. Rice	New York.
32	Koltes	New York.
38	Geo. G. Meade	New York.
44	Reno	New York.
62	J. L. Riker	New York.
69	General Shields-Corcoran	New York.
77	General J. S. Wadsworth	New York.
79	Cameron	New York.
80	John A. Rawlins	New York.
100	E. A. Kimball	New York.

New York — *Continued.*

NUMBER.	NAME.	LOCATION.
103	George Washington	New York.
113	Dahlgren-Powell	New York.
128	Joe Hooker	New York.
135	John A. Dix	New York.
140	Lafayette	New York.
146	Alexander S. Webb	New York.
182	Alexander Hamilton	New York.
192	Steinwehr	New York.
234	John A. Andrew	New York.
255	Thaddeus Stevens	New York.
259	Winfield Scott Hancock	New York.
264	Gilsa	New York.
307	Edwin D. Morgan	New York.
313	Peter Cooper	New York.
330	Adam Goss	New York.
394	Robert Anderson	New York.
402	John E. Bendix	New York.
408	Fred Hecker	New York.
436	Veteran	New York.
458	Noah L. Farnham	New York.
516	Farragut—Naval	New York.
557	General James McQuade	New York.
559	William G. Mitchell	New York.
578	Horace B. Claflin	New York.
600	Lloyd Aspinwall	New York.
607	James Monroe	New York.

NIAGARA.

76	Charles P. Sprout	Lockport.
125	Alex. B. Mabon	Sanborn.
126	Peter A. Porter	Wilson.
133	Dudley Donnelly	Niagara Falls.
178	James Compton	Middleport.
228	Melville C. McCollum	Ransomville.
258	Sidney C. Hayes	Barker.
281	Lewis S. Payne	North Tonawanda.
349	C. L. Skeels	Hartland.

ONEIDA.

14	John F. McQuade	Utica.
23	Rowell	Waterville.
31	Ross	New York Mills.
39	Thomas	Prospect.
47	Skillen	Rome.
53	Bacon	Utica.
97	Wheelock	Boonville.
227	N. B. Hinckley	Clinton.
413	G. W. Chadwick	Sauquoit.
482	J. Parson Stone	Camden.
526	James E. Jenkins	Vernon.
551	Ballard	Taberg.
615	Joseph H. Warren	Verona.

ONTARIO.

NUMBER.	NAME.	LOCATION.
7	Gordon Granger	Clifton Springs.
74	Bingham	Naples.
94	Swift	Geneva.
107	Herendeen	Shortsville.
162	Albert M. Murray	Canandaigua.
225	Sheridan Crandall	East Bloomfield.
303	Charles R. Lilly	Cheshire.
597	General John B. Murray	Phelps.

ONONDAGA.

66	Lilly	Syracuse.
151	Root	Syracuse.
164	Benjamin H. Porter	Skaneateles.
278	Moses Summers	Baldwinsville.
358	Joseph Jones	Marcellus.
457	Sanders	Cicero.
608	Geo. H. Bolster	Manlius.
647	Anthony Stacey	Elbridge.
648	Col. Randall	Liverpool.
663	R. D. Pettit	Lysander.
667	R. B. Hayes	Fayetteville.
670	Ben. Higgins	East Syracuse.

ORANGE.

52	Ellis	Newburgh.
58	S. W. Fullerton	Newburgh.
176	F. M. Cummins	Goshen.
266	General Lyon	Middletown.
279	Carroll Van Etten	Port Jervis.
301	Capt. Wm. A. Jackson	Middletown.
546	Emslie	Cornwall-on-Hudson.
564	Fairchild	Walden.
575	John J. Wheeler	Warwick.
598	Ryder	Highland Falls.

ORLEANS.

73	S. & P. Gilbert	Lyndonville.
91	S. J. Hood	Medina.
114	Curtis Bates	Albion.
298	David Jones	Kendall.

OSWEGO.

16	H. L. Farmer	Cleveland.
65	J. D. O'Brian	Oswego.
111	J. B. Butler	Pulaski.
145	Joe Gould	Phoenix.
217	A. J. Barney	Sandy Creek.
262	Sidney C. Gaylord	Redfield.

Oswego — Continued

NUMBER.	NAME.	LOCATION.
271	D. F. Schenck	Fulton.
367	Melzer Richards	Mexico.
387	S. M. Olmstead	Orwell.
418	Isaac Waterbury	Central Square.
434	Hiram Sherman	Vermillion.
599	George Simons	Parish.
609	John Stevenson	S. W. Oswego.

Otsego.

15	Brown	Schenevus.
25	Johnson	Worcester.
26	L. C. Turner	Cooperstown.
119	E. D. Farmer	Oneonta.
124	C. C. Siver	Unadilla.
223	W. A. Musson	Gilbertsville.
256	Weldon	Richfield Springs.

Putnam.

302	Crosby	Brewster.

Queens.

50	George Huntsman	Flushing, L. I.
283	Benjamin Ringold	Long Island City.
368	Alfred M. Wood	Jamaica.
451	Adam Wirth	College Point.
560	Robert J. Marks	Elmhurst.
628	Sheridan	Long Island City.
636	John Corning	Rockaway Beach.

Rensselaer.

18	John McConihe	Troy.
34	George L. Willard	Troy.
141	William B. Tibbits	Troy.
204	Private D. S. Corbin	Rensselaer.
294	Walter A. Wood	Hoosick Falls.
338	John A. Griswold	Troy.
471	Bolton	Troy.
487	Hartshorn	Schaghticoke.

Richmond.

112	Robert G. Shaw	New Brighton.
163	Lenhart	Tottenville.
524	Richmond	Port Richmond, S. I.

Rockland.

82	Waldron	Nyack.
179	Edward Pye	Haverstraw.
521	John P. Jenkins	Suffern.

ST. LAWRENCE.

NUMBER.	NAME.	LOCATION.
156	E. H. Barnes	Gouverneur.
167	Luther Priest	Norwood.
169	W. T. Rice	Hermon.
214	Marsh	Potsdam.
346	H. T. Martyn	Canton.
354	Ransom	Ogdensburg.
415	Alfred I. Hooker	Morristown.
421	Captain Gibson	Winthrop.
425	Col. Hiram Anderson	Massena.
581	Warren B. Waite	Colton.

SARATOGA.

46	Wm. H. McKittrick	Ballston Spa.
92	Luther M. Wheeler	Saratoga Springs.
116	Frank Norton	Schuylerville.
290	Philip Rice	Corinth.
619	Col. Elmer E. Ellsworth	Mechanicville.
630	Gen'l Philip H. Sheridan	Waterford.
665	S. S. Craig	Middle Grove.

SCHENECTADY.

90	Horsfall	Schenectady.

SCHOHARIE.

157	George A. Turnbull	Esperance.

SCHUYLER.

341	Phineas Catlin	Odessa.
423	D. B. Smith	Valois.
515	D. W. Washburn	Watkins.

SENECA.

72	Tyler J. Snyder	Waterloo.
78	Cross	Seneca Falls.
325	Charles T. Harris	Ovid.
438	William E. Avery	Interlaken.
445	A. J. Chestnut	Lodi.

STEUBEN.

81	Custer	Bath.
194	Abram Allen	Canisteo.
226	Doty	Hornell.
240	Rodney E. Harris	Cohocton.
248	General Barry	Bath.
276	William W. Hayt	Corning.
314	Theodore Schlick	Wayland.
372	W. W. Angle	Addison.
470	Monroe Brundage	Hammondsport.
475	John W. Davis	Caton.

Steuben — *Continued.*

NUMBER.	NAME.	LOCATION.
507	Marcy	Avoca.
535	Henry C. Lyon	Pultney.
549	Knox	Savona.
565	J. N. Warner	Woodhull.
583	Moses Dennis	Jasper.
640	C. M. Pierce	N. Cohocton.
649	Gregory	Prattsburg.

Suffolk.

210	Richard J. Clark	Patchogue.
274	Edwin Rose	Sag Harbor.
353	Edward Hunting	Greenport.
426	Samuel Ackerly	Northport.
538	William Gurney	Bay Shore.
627	Lewis O. Conklin	Port Jefferson.
641	J. C. Walters	Huntington.
643	H. B. Knickerbocker	Amityville.
656	Henry A. Barnum	Riverhead.

Sullivan.

205	Ratcliff	Monticello.
293	W. T. Morgan	Rockland.
311	Garrett	Liberty.
431	Teller	Grahamsville.

Tioga.

59	Babcock	Owego.
383	Candor	Candor.
461	Walter C. Hull	Waverly.
464	Dawson	Spencer.
505	Hagadorn	Halsey Valley.
613	Tracey	Apalachin.
646	L. W. Truesdell	Owego.

Tompkins.

41	Sydney	Ithaca.
123	Gregg	Newfield.
250	James E. Mix	Ithaca.
260	L. Dwight Allen	Groton.
572	Treman	Trumansburg.

Ulster.

127	Pratt	Kingston.
168	Johannas LeFevre	Highland.
191	Ward	Ellenville.
212	Eltinge	New Paltz.
215	Tappen	Saugerties.
495	Ketcham	Milton.

Warren.

147	Edgar M. Wing	Glens Falls.
316	B. C. Butler	Luzerne.

WAYNE.

NUMBER.	NAME.	LOCATION.
55	Keeslar	Wolcott.
99	Wm. B. Vosburgh	Newark.
109	Dwight	Sodus Point.
153	A. D. Adams	Lyons.
173	Snedaker	Clyde.
186	A. D. Shaw	Alton.
193	James A. Garfield	Palmyra.
251	D. H. Becker	Red Creek.
291	Sweeting	South Butler.
320	John Hance	Williamson.
406	Myron M. Fish	Ontario.
444	John B. Burrud	Marion.
450	George S. Bradley	Macedon.
501	Remington	Savannah.

WASHINGTON.

267	Horace E. Howard	Granville.
309	John McKee	Cambridge.
326	A. M. Cook	Greenwich.
335	Lou Washburn	Fort Ann.
370	Duncan Lendrum	Argyle.
491	C. E. Mills	Fort Edward.
563	A. H. Tanner	Whitehall.
570	A. L. McDougall	Salem.
587	Wm. M. Collin	Hudson Falls.
642	John C. Lasson	Clemons.

WESTCHESTER.

60	Kitching	Yonkers.
95	Abraham Vosburgh	Peekskill.
120	McKeel	Katonah.
144	Morell	Ossining.
170	Farnsworth	Mount Vernon.
378	Charles Lawrence	Port Chester.
466	Cromwell	White Plains.
496	Ward B. Burnett	Tarrytown.
509	Flandreau	New Rochelle.
590	John C. Fremont	Yonkers.

WYOMING.

101	John P. Robinson	Perry.
130	Gibbs	Warsaw.
218	Tobert	Arcade.
219	Rowley P. Taylor	Attica.
238	Buford	Johnsonburg.
414	Wing	Bliss.
488	George G. Pierce	Castile.

YATES.

93	J. B. Sloan	Penn Yan.
486	Wm. H. Long	Penn Yan.

POST NO.	NAME	MEMBERS IN GOOD STANDING DEC. 31, 1917	DATE OF CHARTER	COMMANDER	ADDRESS
1	O'Rorke	73	Oct. 8, 1866	James N. Splaine	256 Hazelwood ter.
2	Chapin	300	Oct. 9, 1866	Nelson Simmons	149 School st.
4	Geo. H. Thomas	21	Feb. 5, 1875	John A. Reynolds	Fairport
5	Lew Benedict	99	Jan. 30, 1867	John E. Jones	249 Clinton ave.
6	Baldwin	113	June 11, 1868	Sanford D. Haines	205 West Hudson st.
7	Gordon Granger	16	April 6, 1878	Chas. D. Giles	Clifton Springs
8	Phil Kearny	19	Dec. 16, 1866	George H. Stevens	14 W. 40th st.
9	Bidwell Wilkeson	201	April 28, 1880	Calvin A. Brainard	86 16th st.
10	Rankin	57	Feb. 16, 1867	Jacob Callas	491 Columbia st.
11	Barbara Frietchie	19	Oct. —, 1876	Robert H. Davis	136 Smith st.
12	Vanderburg	18	April 19, 1878	R. R. Lord	Afton
14	John F. McQuade	34	April 5, 1879	Robert J. Clark	26 Noyes st.
15	Brown	10	Mar. 11, 1874	W. H. Colegrove	Schenevus
16	H. L. Farmer	10	May —, 1915	Louis Wanner	Cleveland
17	Ansel Denison	57	April 16, 1915	Daniel H. Cole	Gloversville
18	John McConihe	29	Feb. 22, 1886	William H. Kilfoile	334 Congress st.
19	Galpin	54	April 15, 1873	James G. Burney	Little Falls
20	Hamilton Sleight	129	Oct. 31, 1911	Harry E. Murray	64 Garden st.
21	Harry Lee	23	Jan. 28, 1870	T. T. Donovan	484 Greene ave.
23	Rowell	11	May 22, 1868	Rowland J. Roberts	Waterville
24	Sumner	37	Mar. 30, 1867	John M. Fisher	238–240 W. 129th st.
25	Johnson	22	April 8, 1878	Seth M. Flint	Worcester
26	L. C. Turner	21	May 26, 1878	Joel G. White	Cooperstown
27	Hollister	13	Dec. 29, 1874	N. A. Calkins	Coxsackie
29	James C. Rice	73	Dec. 30, 1871	Edward M. Griffiths	556 West 183d st
30	Watrous	132	May 14, 1867	Alfred A. Lord	99 Court st.
31	Ross	24	May 23, 1867	Geo. B. Fairhead	Ilion
32	Koltes	50	June 21, 1867	Jacob Parr	473 East 145th st.
33	E. S. Young	74	April 10, 1875	John L. Abeling	Amsterdam
34	George L. Willard	48	May 9, 1869	David Hilton	393 Tenth st.
35	Mansfield	56	June 11, 1877	Wm. H. Lyons	59 Devoe st.
38	Geo. G. Meade	35	Sept. 21, 1875	Isaac H. Fuhr	41 Fourth place, B'klyn
39	Thomas	14	May 3, 1875	James Hane	Ohio
40	Admiral Meade]	8	April 28, 1903	John Few	W. R. C. Home
41	Sidney	31	Dec. 22, 1876	Edward A. Willson	503 No. Cayuga st.
43	N. G. Lyon	37	Sept. 19, 1867	Charles S. Travis	City Hall
44	Reno	30	April 15, 1875	Jas. C. Montgomery	3610 Broadway
45	Seward Crocker	92	Nov. 10, 1903	Thomas Tallman	12 Evans st.
46	Wm. H. McKittrick	31	Mar. 7, 1875	Andrew J. Freeman	Ballston Spa.
47	Skillen	48	Aug. 29, 1872	L. A. Martin	Rome
48	Howland	18	May 18, 1870	Elijah Mosher	Beacon
49	Reese	29	July 1, 1878	William Taylor, M. D.	Canastota
50	George Huntsman	26	June 24, 1869	R. W. Carman	283 Madison ave.
51	Farrell	19	Mar. 25, 1874	Cornelius Van Alstine	Canajoharie, R. F. D No. 1
52	Ellis	26	Oct. 24, 1867	Curtis Stanton	83 Carter st.
53	Bacon	90	Oct. 24, 1867	Jacob P. Yakey	70 Francis st.
55	Keeslar	27	July 16, 1875	Albert Wamsley	Wolcott

POST NO.	LOCATION	COUNTY	TIME OF MEETING	PLACE OF MEETING
1	Rochester	Monroe	1st, 3d and 5th Thursday	G. A. R. Hall, City Hall Annex
2	Buffalo	Erie	1st and 3d Friday	G. A. R. Hall, Virginia st. an Elmwood ave.
4	Rochester	Monroe	Last Monday	The Osborn House
5	Albany	Albany	Every Thursday, 8 P. M.	31 Green st.
6	Elmira	Chemung	1st and 3d Monday	N. Y. S. N. G. Armory
7	Clifton Springs	Ontario	1st and 3d Tuesday, 2 P. M.	G. A. R. Hall
8	New York	New York	3d Wednesday	168th st. and Broadway
9	Buffalo	Erie	1st and 3d Thursday	Cor. Elmwood ave. and Virginia st.
10	Brooklyn	Kings	2d and 4th Friday	315 Washington st.
11	Brooklyn	Kings	2d Wednesday	Eckford Hall, Greenpoint
12	Afton	Chenango	1st and 3d Saturday	G. A. R. Hall
14	Utica	Oneida	2d and 4th Wednesday afternoon	Oneida County Building
15	Schenevus	Otsego	1st and 3d Thursday, 2 P. M	G. A. R. Hall
16	Cleveland	Oswego	2d Monday	Clay st.
17	Gloversville	Fulton	Alternate Saturday	Foresters Hall, 42 S. Main st.
18	Troy	Rensselaer	1st and 3d Thursday	County Court House, Congress and Second streets
19	Little Falls	Herkimer	1st Friday	G. A. R. Hall, Mary st.
20	Poughkeepsie	Dutchess	Every Wednesday	27 Garden st.
21	Brooklyn	Kings	2d and 4th Thursday	Hart's Hall, 1028 Gates ave.
23	Waterville	Oneida	2d Tuesday Dec., Mar., June and Sept.	Hubbard Block
24	New York	New York	4th Friday	12th Regt. Armory, Columbus and W. 62d sts.
25	Worcester	Otsego	2d and 4th Tuesday	French's Hall
26	Cooperstown	Otsego	1st and 3d Saturday	G. A. R. Hall, 55 Main st.
27	Coxsackie	Greene	1st and 4th Friday afternoon	G. A. R. Hall
29	New York	New York	1st Wednesday	309 West 23d st.
30	Binghamton	Broome	Alternate Friday	State Armory, Washington st.
31	New York Mills	Oneida	2d Friday afternoon	G. A. R. Hall
32	New York	New York	3d Sunday, 3 P. M.	85th st. and Lexington ave.
33	Amsterdam	Montgomery	Every Wednesday, 3 P. M.	East Main st.
34	Troy	Rensselaer	2d and 4th Tuesday	County Court House, Second and Congress sts.
35	Brooklyn	Kings	2d Friday	German Savings Bank Building, Broadway and Boerum st.
38	New York	New York	1st Tuesday	501 Hudson st.
39	Prospect	Oneida	1st and 3d Wednesday	Post-office Hall
40	Oxford	Chenango		W. R. C. Home, Assembly Hall
41	Ithaca	Tompkins	Every Tuesday, 7:30 P. M.	Military Hall
43	Cohoes	Albany	1st and 3d Saturday, 3 P. M.	64 Remsen st.
44	New York	New York	1st Thursday	109 East 116th st.
45	Auburn	Cayuga	Every Tuesday	G. A. R. Hall, 9 Exchang st.
46	Ballston Spa	Saratoga	1st and 3d Tuesday, 7:30 P. M.	K. of P. Hall, Front st.
47	Rome	Oneida	Saturday, 3 P. M.	G. A. R. Hall
48	Beacon	Dutchess	1st Tuesday	541 Main st.
49	Canastota	Madison	2d Monday, 2 P. M.	G. A. R. Hall, De Lano Hall
50	Flushing	Queens	3d Monday	Armory, Broadway
51	Canajoharie	Montgomery	2d Tuesday afternoon	Post rooms, Hammersmith Blk.
52	Newburgh	Orange	3d Tuesday	Cochran's Hall, 117 Brodaway
53	Utica	Oneida	Every Thursday	Oneida County Building
55	Wolcott	Wayne	Wednesday	G. A. R. Hall, Mill st.

POST NO.	NAME	MEMBERS IN GOOD STANDING DEC. 31, 1917	DATE OF CHARTER	COMMANDER	ADDRESS
57	Van Derveer	12	July 29, 1875	John A. Hubbard	Fonda
58	S. W. Fullerton	21	April 14, 1886	Charles Beck	197 City Terrace
59	Babcock	24	Nov. 12, 1867	Geo. R. Resseguie	Owego
60	Kitching	61	Mar. 18, 1868	Augustus Kipp	157 Warburton ave.
62	J. L. Riker	19	May 22, 1873	John Schmidling	Room 1, City Hall
63	George S. Dawson	22	Nov. 26, 1875	A. J. Hinman	349-C Madison ave.
65	J. D. O'Brian	62	Aug. 5, 1878	James K. Prosser	Oswego
66	Lilly	77	June 25, 1870	J. A. Allis	City Hall
69	General Shields-Corcoran	15	Jan. 8, 1898	Patrick H. Doody	156 East 52d st.
70	Klock	17	June 24, 1876	Abraham H. Smith	Starkville
72	Tyler J. Snyder	30	June 25, 1870	Warren E. Lerch	Waterloo
73	S. and P. Gilbert	10	Nov. 26, 1876	Henry H. Vosler	Lyndonville
74	Bingham	23	Dec. 28, 1878	Geo. Rackham	Naples
76	Charles P. Sprout	42	Aug. 30, 1876	Wallace Riley	51 Akron st.
77	Gen. J. S. Wadsworth	27	Dec. 29, 1877	Thomas Hamilton	1993 Amsterdam ave.
78	Cross	24	July 22, 1868	William Durnin	Chapin st.
79	Cameron	11	July 23, 1868	Lucius E. Wilson	67 West 11th st.
80	John A. Rawlins	14	Jan. 22, 1874	Charles Just	52 West 13th st.
81	Custer	48	July 20, 1876	Rozel Seager	Bath
82	Waldron	23	Jan. 30, 1879	Alonzo Jewell	25 Prospect st.
83	E. B. Smith	36	May 9, 1874	Geo. W. Payne	Norwich
84	Myron Adams	53	Jan. 10, 1896	Henry S. Redman	Court House
85	H. W. Wessels	23	Jan. 11, 1879	L. E. Carr	Portville
86	A. K. Thorp	16	May 6, 1879	Elmer Hitchings	Belfast
87	Crary	20	Aug. 15, 1881	Geo. H. Barker	Springville
88	J. H. Ketcham	12	Feb. 13, 1877	George Rush	Wappingers Falls
89	James H. Perry	34	Jan. 23, 1879	Charles H. Lunt	4 Lyossett st., Union Course, Queens Co., L. I.
90	Horsfall	66	May —, 1879	Lewis Cohen	109 Park place
91	S. J. Hood	36	May 19, 1879	Ziba Roberts	Medina, R. F. D. No. 6
92	Luther M. Wheeler	74	June 5, 1877	H. B. Ormsbee	159 Lake ave.
93	J. B. Sloan	68	April 22, 1869	John W. Durham	Branchport
94	Swift	46	May 3, 1869	John H. Stevens	Geneva
95	Abraham Vosburgh	40	July 25, 1879	Geo. L. Hughson	Peekskill
96	Oliver Tilden	21	May 24, 1869	Theodore Weberg	1740 Garfield st
97	Wheelock	30	July 11, 1868	Geo. O. Bridgman	Boonville
98	Grover	34	June 14, 1869	George W. Edgcomb	16 North Church st.
99	Wm. B. Vosburgh	29	July 15, 1879	F. E. Brown	Newark
100	E. A. Kimball	21	April 12, 1871	James T. Walker	375 Bleecker st.
101	John P. Robinson	21	Feb. 9, 1881	W. K. Selden	Perry Center
102	Wm. H. Stevenson	14	Oct. 17, 1874	Charles Acome	Moriah
103	George Washington	62	July 29, 1879	Henry L. Swords	Custom House
104	Armstrong	14	July 14, 1879	A. C. McCurdy	Pine Plains
105	Willoughby Babcock	25	June 15, 1876	Frederick Monk	Homer
106	Elias Peissner	25	June 13, 1871	John J. Augustin	1510 St. Paul st.
107	Herendeen	16	Mar. 9, 1881	Ira M. Dibble	Shortsville
108	Joseph J. Bartlett	56	Feb. 20, 1893	N. E. Rowe	53 Thorpe st.
109	Dwight	10	Aug. 6, 1877	E. H. Sentell	Sodus Point
110	Chismore	55	Sept. 8, 1869	Theodore Harter	Ilion
111	J. B. Butler	40	Aug. 27, 1879	John E. Bentley	Pulaski

ST D.	LOCATION	COUNTY	TIME OF MEETING	PLACE OF MEETING
7	Fonda	Montgomery	1st Saturday, 2 P. M.	Village Hall
8	Newburgh	Orange	2d and 4th Wednesday	Veteran's Hall, 40 Chambers st.
9	Owego	Tioga	1st and 3d Saturday, 2 P. M.	G. A. R. Hall
0	Yonkers	Westchester	1st and 3d Monday	City Hall
2	New York	New York	1st Wednesday	32 Avenue A
3	Albany	Albany	1st Thursday evening, March, June, Sept. and Dec.	G. A. R. Hall, Court House
5	Oswego	Oswego	1st and 3d Friday	State Armory
6	Syracuse	Onondaga	1st and 3d Friday	Oberlander Hall, 628 No. Salina St.
9	New York	New York	2d Tuesday	69th Reg't Armory, 25th st. and Lexington ave.
0	Fort Plain	Montgomery	1st Saturday afternoon	G. A. R. Hall, Canal st.
2	Waterloo	Seneca	Tuesday	G. A. R. rooms
3	Lyndonville	Orleans	1st and 3d Saturday	Masonic Hall
4	Naples	Ontario	2d and 4th Saturday	G. A. R. Hall
6	Lockport	Niagara	Every Saturday afternoon	11 Cottage st.
7	New York	New York	1st Saturday, 8 P. M.	618–620 Ninth ave.
8	Seneca Falls	Seneca	Every Monday	62 Falls st.
9	New York	New York	4th Saturday	301 West 25th st.
0	New York	New York	2d Wednesday	52 West 13th st.
1	Bath	Steuben	2d and 4th Saturday, 2:30 P. M.	G. A. R. Hall
2	Nyack	Rockland	1st Saturday, 2:30 P. M.	G. A. R. Hall, Broadway
3	Norwich	Chenango	Every Tuesday, 1:30 P. M.	North Broad st.
4	Rochester	Monroe	1st Saturday afternoon	City Hall
5	Portville	Cattaraugus	1st and 3d Wednesday afternoon	Worden's Hall, Temple st.
6	Belfast	Allegany	1st and 3d Saturday afternoon	G. A. R. Hall
7	Springville	Erie	1st and 3d Monday	Log Cabin
8	Wappingers Falls	Dutchess	Quarterly	National Bank
9	Brooklyn	Kings	1st and 3d Tuesday	Fidelity Hall, 609 DeKalb ave.
0	Schenectady	Schenectady	Thursday	Armory
1	Medina	Orleans	1st and 3d Tuesday, 2 P. M.	G. A. R. Hall, Center st.
2	Saratoga Springs	Saratoga	1st Wednesday	Pavilion place
3	Penn Yan	Yates	3d Wednesday afternoon	Arcade Hall
4	Geneva	Ontario	1st and 3d Wednesday	Armory, Main st.
5	Peekskill	Westchester	2d Friday	S. O. V. Hall, South st.
6	New York	Bronx	2d Tuesday	2d Battery Armory, Franklin ave. and 166th st.
7	Boonville	Oneida	1st and 3d Saturday	G. A. R. Hall
8	Cortland	Cortland	1st and 3d Wednesday	G. A. R. Hall, 33 Main st.
9	Newark	Wayne	1st Tuesday	Ellicott's Hall
0	New York	New York	3d Saturday 8 P. M.	9th Reg't Armory, 14th st. near 6th ave.
1	Perry	Wyoming	1st and 3d Monday, 2 P. M.	Owens Hall
2	Moriah Center	Essex	2d Saturday, 2 P. M.	G. A. R. Hall
3	New York	New York	1st Thursday	Hotel Astor, Broadway and 44th st.
4	Rhinebeck	Dutchess	2d Saturday	G. A. R. Hall
5	Homer	Cortland	1st and 3d Wednesday	G. A. R. Hall
6	Rochester	Monroe	2d Saturday, 3 P. M.	German Hall, 461 St. Paul st.
7	Shortsville	Ontario	1st and 3d Saturday, 3 P. M.	G. A. R. Hall
8	Binghamton	Broome	2d and 4th Thursday	State Armory
9	Sodus Point	Wayne	1st Wednesday afternoon	G. A. R. Hall
0	Ilion	Herkimer	1st Saturday afternoon	Mechanics Hall
1	Pulaski	Oswego	2d and 4th Saturday afternoon	G. A. R. Hall

POST NO.	NAME	MEMBERS IN GOOD STANDING DEC. 31, 1917	DATE OF CHARTER	COMMANDER	ADDRESS
112	Robert G. Shaw	11	Sept. 23, 1879	Edward Openshaw	New Brighton
113	Dahlgren-Powell	28	Oct. 11, 1869	Matthew B. Brennan	3070 Bainbridge ave.
114	Curtis-Bates	32	Dec. 1, 1893	L. E. Griswold	Albion
116	Frank Norton	6	Aug. 25, 1879	C. H. McNaughton	Schuylerville
118	Byron Lockwood	13	Sept. 17, 1879	J. I. Spoor	Philmont
119	E. D. Farmer	47	June 26, 1871	Wm. H. Brown	Main st.
120	McKeel	21	Sept. 30, 1879	J. A. Tuttle	Katonah
121	L. O. Morris	77	Aug. 20, 1870	Charles Fisher	55 Pine st., Rensselaer
122	Germain Metternich	16	Oct. 11, 1871	Louis Finkelmeier	1038 Madison st.
123	Gregg	17	Sept. 18, 1879	Jonathan Underdown	Newfield
124	C. C. Siver	7	Oct. 4, 1879	W. G. Hotaling	Unadilla
125	Alex. B. Mabon	13	Sept. 12, 1879	Oliver Velzey	Lewiston, R. F. D., 19
126	Peter A. Porter	10	Jan. 1, 1871	John A. Hamblin	Ransomville
127	Pratt	46	Nov. 12, 1879	James H. Everett	Kingston
128	Joe Hooker	19	Nov. 4, 1879	John M. Nagel	301 E. 81st st.
129	Winfield B. Scott	16	Oct. 24, 1879	Charles B. Parker	15 Fremont st.
130	Gibbs	38	June 24, 1871	M. W. Marchant	Rock Glen
132	Frank T. Hine	4	Nov. 22, 1879	Joseph Eveland	Franklin
133	Dudley Donnelly	27	Nov. 13, 1879	Henry W. Gilbert	Niagara Falls
134	Walton Dwight	21	April 12, 1879	I. W. Butler	Johnson City
135	John A. Dix	54	Nov. 15, 1879	John W. Noble	340 W. 57th st.
136	Vanderbilt	21	Nov. 1, 1875	James L. Lyons	951 Whitlock ave.
137	Otis G. Banks	7	Nov. 16, 1879	George Gray	Brisben
138	R. D. Lathrop	37	Dec. 30, 1879	Thos. Berridge	Hudson
140	Lafayette	179	Dec 18, 1830	George W. Case	11 Jay st.
141	William B. Tibbits	21	Jan. 14, 1880	John E. Vandenburgh	558 4th ave., No.
142	England	30	Mar. 11, 1880	William Thompson	Delhi
144	Morell	24	Dec. 15, 1883	Charles Mitchell	Dale ave.
145	Joe Gould	19	Mar. 19, 1880	E. A. Crandell	Phoenix
146	Alexander S. Webb	18	May 11, 1892	John Mulligan	493 Eighth ave.
147	Edgar M. Wing	83	Feb. 17, 1880	George F. Bryant	Glens Falls
148	Thomas C. Devin	64	Feb. 17, 1880	Thomas H. Kiernan	281 Bridge st.
150	Henry Williams	8	Mar. 16, 1880	Geo. E. Hurlburt	Harpursville
151	Root	177	Mar. 31, 1880	Henry C. Ransom	Syracuse
152	L. M. Hamilton	35	April 29, 1880	Wm. Busch	Hansom pl. and Foly ave Jamaica, L. I.
153	A. D. Adams	21	April 15, 1880	Henry Alford	Lyons
155	George C. Stoyell	16	April 26, 1880	Benjamin Wilson	Moravia
156	E. H. Barnes	50	May 5, 1880	Warren B. Pike	Gouverneur
157	George A. Turnbull	11	April 28, 1880	John Hunter	Esperance
159	Hudson	27	May 21, 1880	E. R. Robinson	Fair Haven
160	Knowlton	20	June 18, 1880	Otis H. Jillson	Cazenovia
161	N. S. Ford	21	May 20, 1880	Joseph G. Morrell	1094 E. 95th st.
162	Albert M. Murray	29	May 21, 1880	Orson L. Babbitt	Canandaigua
163	Lenhart	7	May 22, 1880	Hubbard R. Yetman	Tottenville
164	Benjamin H. Porter	11	May 28, 1882	H. H. Loss	Skaneateles
165	L. E. Fitch	27	Dec. 14, 1882	Albert B. Cornell, Sr.	269 W. Cherry place
166	J. E. Whiteside	20	June 29, 1880	T. S. Barker	Weedsport
167	Luther Priest	21	July 4, 1880	H. H. Bailey	Norwood
168	Johannas Le Fever	11	Dec. 14, 1883	Edmund Paltridge	Highland

LOCATION	COUNTY	TIME OF MEETING	PLACE OF MEETING
New Brighton	Richmond	1st Monday of every quarter	Cassiday's coal office, Richmond Terrace
New York	New York	1st Thursday	Florence Hall, Second ave., cor. First st.
Albion	Orleans	Thursday afternoon, P. M. win- ter months	G. A. R. Hall
Schuylerville	Saratoga	1st Thursday, 2 P. M.	Residence H. M. DeLong
Philmont	Columbia	3d Saturday, 2 P. M.	G. A. R. Hall
Oneonta	Otsego	Saturday afternoon, 2 P. M.	G. A. R. Hall, Wescott Block
Katonah	Westchester	2d Saturday afternoon	Homes of Comrades
Albany	Albany	Every Monday	G. A. R. Hall, Court House
Brooklyn	Kings	2d Sunday afternoon	Bushwick and Gates ave.
Newfield	Tompkins	1st and 3d Saturday, 2:30 P. M.	G. A. R. Hall.
Unadilla	Otsego	1st Saturday	Odd Fellows' Hall
Sanborn	Niagara	At call of Commander	I. O. O. F. Hall
Wilson	Niagara	Thursday, 2 P. M.	G. A. R. Hall
Kingston	Ulster	2d and 4th Wednesday	State Armory
New York	New York	2d and 4th Friday	68 Lexington ave.
Tonawanda	Erie	2d and 4th Wednesday	G. A. R. Hall, Adams st.
Warsaw	Wyoming	1st and 3d Saturday, P. M.	G. A. R. Hall
Franklin	Delaware	Saturday evening	Grange Hall
Niagara Falls	Niagara	1st and 3d Tuesday	Armory Hall, Main st.
Johnson City	Broome	Every Friday	G. A. R. Hall, Avenue D
New York	New York	1st Thursday	Tuxedo Hall, 59th st. and Madison ave.
New York	Bronx	2d Monday	2d Field Artillery Armory, Franklin ave. and 166th st.
Greene	Chenango	1st Saturday, 2 P. M.	G. A. R. Hall
Hudson	Columbia	1st Thursday	State Armory
New York	New York	1st and 3d Friday, 1st Friday only June, July and August	69th Reg't. Armory, Lexington ave., and 25th st.
Troy	Rensselaer	1st and 3d Monday	Tibbit's Veteran Hall, 303 River st.
Delhi	Delaware	1st Monday	G. A. R. Hall
Ossining	Westchester	Every Monday	Municipal Building, Croton av.
Phoenix	Oswego	2d and 4th Monday 2:30 P. M.	Meriam Hall, Canal st.
New York	New York	1st Thursday	128 West 17th st.
Glens Falls	Warren	2d and 4th Wednesday	G. A. R. Hall, Crandall Block
Brooklyn	Kings	1st and 3d Friday	12 Nevins st., Johnson Building
Harpursville	Broome	Once a month	Comrade's Homes
Syracuse	Onondaga	2d and 4th Thursday	The Bastable
Brooklyn	Kings	2d and 4th Thursday	Penn Fulton Hall, Pennsylvania ave. and Fulton st.
Lyons	Wayne	1st and 3d Thursday, 2:30 P. M.	Grange Hall, William st.
Moravia	Cayuga	Every Saturday, 7:30 P. M.	Andress Hall
Gouverneur	St. Lawrence	2d and 4th Tuesday	Freeman Block, 1 Clinton st.
Esperance	Schoharie	1st Saturday, 2 P. M.	Red Men's Hall
Fair Haven	Cayuga	Every Saturday evening	G. A. R. Hall
Cazenovia	Madison	1st Monday	Edwin Hall
Brooklyn	Kings	Every other Saturday, 8 P. M.	Abraham's Hall, Conklin ave. and East 95th st.
Canandaigua	Ontario	1st and 3d Saturday, 2 P. M.	G. A. R. Hall, Main st.
Tottenville	Richmond	1st Saturday	Home of Commander
Skaneateles	Onondaga	1st Friday	I. O. O. F. Hall
Elmira	Chemung	2d and 4th Monday	State Armory, East Church st.
Weedsport	Cayuga	1st and 3d Saturday	G. A. R. Hall
Norwood	St. Lawrence	4th Saturday, 2 P. M.	G. A. R. Hall
Highland	Ulster	Last Saturday	G. A. R. Hall, Cor. Main and Grand st.

POST NO.	NAME	MEMBERS IN GOOD STANDING DEC. 31, 1917	DATE OF CHARTER	COMMANDER	ADDRESS
169	W. T. Rice	19	Jan. 28, 1886	F. A. Stalbird	Hermon, R. F. D No
170	Farnsworth	32	July 21, 1880	Abraham Minnerly	145 Washington st.
173	Snedaker	13	July 23, 1880	Chester H. Bowman	Clyde
174	John R. Stewart	23	July 23, 1880	Orange F. Smith	8 Wilbur st.
175	Lockwood	23	July 20, 1880	Wm. H. Root	Port Byron
176	F. M. Cummins	15	May 21, 1883	Robert B. Hock	Goshen
177	Bra lford	13	July 26, 1880	Chas. Wood	Sidney
178	James Compton	14	April 30, 1894	Squire Wiser	Medina
179	Edward Pye	19	Aug. 18, 1880	Alonzo Bedell	Haverstraw
180	George Stoneman	12	Nov. 12, 1896	John Grobe	Forks •
182	Alexander Hamilton	54	Mar. 22, 1884	Duncan J. McMillan	226 West 129th st
183	Stephen T. Bartle	10	Sept. 16, 1880	G. W. Baldwin	Cuba
184	Eggleston	24	Sept. 16, 1885	Milton D. Whitaker	Deposit
186	A. D. Shaw	4	Sept. 15, 1902	Benjamin Seager	Alton
188	Julius Broadbent	29	July 5, 1883	Charles M. Blair	Brownville
190	J. L. & C. S. Thompson	12	Dec. 23, 1884	C. S. Lynde	Dalton
191	Ward	19	Dec. 29, 1880	John Powers	Ellenville
192	Steinwehr	16	Jan. 10, 1883	Henry Fera	206 West 129th st.
193	James A. Garfield	19	Jan. 15, 1881	Robert M. Smith	Palmyra
194	Abram Allen	27	Jan. 22, 1881	W. W. Howell	Canisteo
195	Revere	16	Jan. 20, 1881	James Johnson	Belmont
196	Edward E. Breed	14	Jan. 21, 1881	A. B. Bennett	Oxford
197	Winchester	84	Feb. 2, 1881	John E. Norcross	371 Gates ave.
198	W. H. Barckley	11	Jan. 24, 1881	John T. Stafford	Altamont
199	Eldredge	7	Mar. 9, 1881	W. E. Greenman	Chenango Forks
200	G. D. Bailey	50	Sept. 6, 1882	Wm. W. Stevens	Lowville
201	Capt. G. M. Smith	6	April 23, 1884	S. C. Bradley	Kings Ferry R. D.
202	James Ayer	12	Mar. 17, 1881	Charles Harper	Angola R. D. No. 1
204	Private D. S. Corbin	8	Nov. 19, 1888	James E. Johnson	1484 Broadway
205	Ratcliff	21	Mar. 30, 1881	Wm. B. McMillen	Monticello
206	Dakin-Slocum	34	Feb. 27, 1914	Jacob Rastetter	225 Rutledge st.
207	William Lloyd Garrison	26	April 18, 1881	Theo. Whiting	1865 Dean st.
209	Ben Marvin	47	April 20, 1881	Albert Smith	Walton
210	Richard J. Clark	14	April 22, 1881	Charles Satterley	111 Conklin ave.
211	E. A. Slocum	15	April 25, 1881	J. S. Kelsey	Fairport
212	Eltinge	15	Dec. 14, 1883	Wm. H. D. Blake	New Paltz
213	J. W. Pangborn	10	Jan. 28, 1895	Robert McC. Miller	Malone
214	Marsh	21	May 2, 1881	M. M. Corbin	Potsdam
215	Tappen	10	April 27, 1881	Delaware Y. Smith	Saugerties
216	Seth N. Hedges	49	May 16, 1881	Oscar Woodruff	Dansville
217	A. J. Barney	10	May 5, 1881	John J. Hollis	Laconia
218	Torbert	10	Aug. 19, 1881	Wm. A. Howard	Arcade
219	Rowley P. Taylor	20	Aug. 20, 1881	Elon P. Spink	Attica
220	S. C. Noyes	12	June 20, 1881	E. G. Fenton	North Collins
222	G. D. Bayard	59	June 23, 1881	S. J. Daniels	Olean
223	W. A. Musson	9	June 30, 1881	Perry Springer	Gilbertsville
225	Sheridan Crandall	9	July 3, 1881	C. E. Taylor	East Bloomfield
226	Doty	59	Aug. 11, 1881	Charles D. Emery	Hornell
227	N. B. Hinckley	18	Aug. 17, 1881	W. E. Bowen	Clinton
228	Melville C. McCollum	13	Sept. 17, 1880	William Luff	Lockport, R. F. D. No
231	Cushing	17	Oct. 8, 1881	Wm. J. Courtney	346 Bay Ridge ave.
232	Henry Van Arnam	17	June 4, 1881	John Vaughan	Ellicottville
233	Brooklyn City	19	Aug. 30, 1898	Charles Montgomery	677 Jefferson ave.
234	John A. Andrews	53	Oct. 19, 1881	Frank R. Battles	93 E. 116th st.

T Ɔ.	LOCATION	COUNTY	TIME OF MEETING	PLACE OF MEETING
9	Hermon	St. Lawrence	2d and 4th Friday, 2 p. m.	Grange Hall
0	Mt. Vernon	Westchester	1st and 3d Friday	G. A. R. Hall, 38 So. 4th ave.
3	Clyde	Wayne	Friday afternoon	G. A. R. Hall, Columbia st.
4	Oneida	Madison	2d Friday, 2 p. m.	City Hall, Washington ave.
5	Port Byron	Cayuga	1st and 4th Monday	Odd Fellow's Hall
6	Goshen	Orange	Call of Commander	Corporation Hall
7	Sidney	Delaware	1st and 3d Saturday	I. O. O. F. Hall, Main st.
8	Middleport	Niagara	2d and 4th Thursday	I. O. O. F. Hall.
9	Haverstraw	Rockland	1st Saturday	G. A. R. Hall, Fourth st.
0	Lancaster	Erie	1st Sunday afternoon	Town Hall
2	New York	New York	1st and 3d Tuesday	310 Lenox ave.
3	Cuba	Allegany	2d and 4th Saturday afternoon	G. A. R. Hall
4	Deposit	Broome	1st and 3d Tuesday	Village Hall
6	Alton	Wayne	2d Tuesday	Private Homes
8	Dexter	Jefferson	1st Saturday	Bloom's Hall
0	Dalton	Livingston	2d and 4th Saturday	G. A. R. Hall
1	Ellenville	Ulster	1st Saturday, 2 p. m.	Savings Bank Building
2	New York	New York	2d Thursday	205 E. 56th st., Maennerchor Hall
3	Palmyra	Wayne	2d Tuesday afternoon	G. A. R. Hall
4	Canisteo	Steuben	4th Friday, 2:30 p. m.	G. A. R. Hall
5	Belmont	Allegany	1st and 3d Saturday afternoon	Grange Hall
6	Oxford	Chenango	2d Friday	G. A. R. Rooms
7	Brooklyn	Kings	1st, 3d and 5th Saturday	Masonic Temple
8	Altamont	Albany	1st Saturday	Commercial Hall
9	Whitney Point	Broome	1st Saturday, p. m.	Denning's Hall
0	Lowville	Lewis	1st Saturday, 2 p. m.	G. A. R. Hall
1	Kings Ferry	Cayuga	3d Saturday	G. A. R. Hall, Main st
2	Angola	Erie	1st and 3d Thursday, 2 p. m.	Village Hall
4	Rensselaer	Rensselaer	1st Wednesday	Miller Hall, Forbes ave.
5	Monticello	Sullivan	1st and 3d Saturday	G. A. R. Hall, Prince st.
6	Brooklyn	Kings	2d and 4th Tuesday	547 Ocean ave., home of Orin B. Smith
7	Brooklyn	Kings	1st Monday	1865 Dean st.
9	Walton	Delaware	Saturday, 1:30 p. m.	State Armory
0	Patchogue	Suffolk	1st Wednesday	Lincoln Club Rooms
1	Fairport	Monroe	1st and 3d Saturday, 3 p. m.	Town Hall
2	New Paltz	Ulster	Last Saturday p. m. of March, June, Sept. and Dec.	G. A. R. Hall
3	Malone	Franklin	2d and 4th Wednesday	G. A. R. Hall
4	Potsdam	St. Lawrence	1st Saturday, 2 p. m.	Fireman's Hall
5	Saugerties	Ulster	1st Monday, 2 p. m.	G. A. R. Hall, Main st.
6	Dansville	Livingston	2d Tuesday afternoon	Town Hall
7	Sandy Creek	Oswego	2d and 4th Saturday, 1 p. m.	G. A. R. Hall
8	Arcade	Wyoming	1st Saturday	I. O. O. F. Hall
9	Attica	Wyoming	2d and 4th Monday, 2 p. m.	G. A. R. Hall
0	North Collins	Erie	2d and 4th Monday, 2 p. m.	Log Cabin
2	Olean	Cattaraugus	Thursday, 2 p. m.	L. Y. Miller & Son's Hall
3	Gilbertsville	Otsego	2d and 4th Saturday afternoon	G. A. R. Hall
5	East Bloomfield	Ontario	3d Thursday, 2 p. m.	Methodist Church Parlors
6	Hornell	Steuben	1st and 3d Friday	G. A. R. Hall, 86 Main st.
7	Clinton	Oneida	2d Saturday	Post-office Hall
8	Ransomville	Niagara	2d Saturday afternoon	Town Hall
1	Brooklyn	Kings	Every 2d Monday	Prospect Hall
2	Ellicottville	Cattaraugus	1st and 4th Thursday	G. A. R. Hall
3	Brooklyn	Kings	2d and 4th Saturday	Ceres Hall, Cor. Fulton st. and Troy ave.
4	New York	New York	2d Friday, 8:30 p. m.	301 West 29th st.

POST NO.	NAME	MEMBERS IN GOOD STANDING DEC. 31, 1917	DATE OF CHARTER	COMMANDER	ADDRESS
236	Cady	28	Oct. 13, 1881	George Williams	Brockport
237	Burnside	3	Dec. 4, 1881	P. C. Soule, M. D.	Rossburg
238	Buford	12	Nov. 10, 1881	J. W. Jones	Johnsonburg
239	Albert J. Meyer	40	Dec. —, 1883	Chas. McDowell	307 Cherry st.
240	Rodney E. Harris	14	Oct. 27, 1881	Nicholas J. Wagner	Cohocton
241	Hatch	14	Oct. 28, 1881	Alvia Jordan	Friendship
246	Fuller	13	Nov. 4, 1881	C. P. Rice	Little Valley
247	H. C. Gardner	35	Dec. 19, 1881	Joshua Dunning	Bolivar
248	General Barry	78	Dec. 22, 1881	Henry J. Redfield	Soldiers' Home
250	James E. Mix	24	Oct. 9, 1888	George W. Hunt	705 N. Aurora st.
251	D. H. Becker	10	Feb. 13, 1897	D. N. Hunter	Red Creek
252	Alfred Weed	15	April 1, 1902	James Fergeson	Ticonderoga
254	William Richardson	31	Sept. 10, 1883	John Hoppes	428 Normal ave.
255	Thaddeus Stevens	17	Mar. 23, 1883	Peter W. Mulford	206 West 62d st.
256	Weldon	12	Jan. 14, 1882	H. W. Cadwell	Richfield Springs
257	Martin McMartin	19	Mar. 6, 1882	James H. Parks	307 W. Clinton st.
258	Sidney C. Hayes	14	Mar. 17, 1882	William S. Thompson	Barker
259	Winfield Scott Hancock	44	Jan. 16, 1886	Theo. H. Ernst	314 E. 84th st.
260	L. Dwight Allen	16	Mar. 15, 1882	T. B. Hopkins	Groton
262	Sidney C. Gaylord	5	Mar. 16, 1882	S. J. Griffith	Osceola
263	A. N. Baldwin	11	April 22, 1882	F. A. Barber	Lanesville
264	Gilsa	15	April 26, 1882	John P. Heintz	1007 Sixth ave.
266	General Lyon	68	April 12, 1882	A. B. Wheeler	Middletown
267	Horace E. Howard	15	May 12, 1882	Wm. Cooper	Wells, Vt.
269	E. B. Steel	32	May 12, 1882	William Ohors	Carthage
270	John H. Martindale	20	May 17, 1882	Jacob Shaffer	Adams Basin
271	D. F. Schenck	34	June 16, 1882	J. H. Stewart	Fulton
272	Arthur L. Brooks	19	July 15, 1882	David Williams	Bouckville
273	Piper	6	July 29, 1882	Frank Hadcock	Henderson
274	Edwin Rose	17	Aug. 15, 1882	G. C. Morris	Sag Harbor
275	Thomas Farr	15	July 12, 1882	I. N. Stuart	West Webster
276	William W. Hoyt	48	June 21, 1882	A. P. Hollister	Corning
278	Moses Summers	39	June 24, 1882	A. C. Taylor	Baldwinsville
279	Carroll Van Etten	22	Nov. 2, 1910	F. S. Goble	82 Orange st.
280	Fleming	10	July 3, 1882	S. E. Hunter	Downsville
281	Lewis S. Payne	17	Feb. 22, 1899	J. P. Christgau	North Tonawanda
282	H. C. Sturdevant	19	Aug. 2, 1882	Sumner A. Smith	Kennedy
283	Benjamin Ringold	9	Aug. 5, 1882	Robt. F. MacFarlane	329 Broadway
284	Wm. D. Brennan	33	Aug. 12, 1882	Thomas Denio	Malone
285	James M. Brown	153	Aug. 17, 1882	William Cole	110 Forest ave.
286	Gouverneur K. Warren	50	Sept. 7, 1882	Alonzo D. Mohr	147 Patchen ave.
288	E. J. Tyler	13	June 19, 1884	John B. Bacon	Pittsford
289	McKean	19	Sept. 19, 1882	I. O. Best	Broadalbin
290	Philip Rice	10	Sept. 26, 1882	Thomas Peak	Corinth
291	Sweeting	10	Jan. 30, 1899	Casper Lampman	South Butler
292	James A. Hall	11	Sept. 21, 1882	Alva Mathews	Brocton
293	W. T. Morgan	15	Aug. 3, 1882	Joseph Cammer	Roscoe
294	Walter A. Wood	22	Oct. 2, 1882	John Gibson	Hoosick Falls
295	Sheldon	11	Oct. 1882	Henry Mina	Sherman
296	Seth H. Weed	10	Feb. 25, 1896	Byron Bennett	Canaseraga
297	D. T. Wiggins	25	Oct. 6, 1882	Gilbert F. Gould	Randolph
298	David Jones	7	Oct. 10, 1882	M. W. Kidder	Kendall

ST O.	LOCATION	COUNTY	TIME OF MEETING	PLACE OF MEETING
6	Brockport	Monroe	Thursday	Village Hall
7	Fillmore	Allegany	2d Saturday, 1:30 P. M.	Post Rooms
8	Johnsonburg	Wyoming	Saturday	G. A. R. Hall, No. Main st.
9	Buffalo	Erie	1st and 3d Tuesday	G. A. R. Hall, Elmwood ave. and Virginia st.
0	Cohocton	Steuben	Last Saturday afternoon	G. A. R. Hall
1	Friendship	Allegany	2d and 4th Thursday	G. A. R. Hall
6	Little Valley	Cattaraugus	1st Saturday, 2 P. M.	Town Hall
7	Bolivar	Allegany	1st and 2d Saturday	W. C. T. U. Hall
8	Bath	Steuben	3d Tuesday	G. A. R. Hall
0	Ithaca	Tompkins	2d and 4th Tuesday	Odd Fellows, Temple
1	Red Creek	Wayne	2d and 4th Saturday 7:30 P. M.	G. A. R. Hall
2	Ticonderoga	Essex	1st Thursday, 2 P. M.	I. O. O. F. Hall
4	Buffalo	Erie	2d and 4th Friday, 8 P. M.	G. A. R. Hall, Elmwood ave. and Virginia st.
5	New York	New York	4th Friday, 8:30 P. M.	343 West 35th st.
6	Richfield Springs	Otsego	2d Saturday	G. A. R. Hall
7	Johnstown	Fulton	1st Friday	L. O. O. M. Hall, East Main st.
8	Barker	Niagara	4th Saturday, 2 P. M.	S. of V. Armory
9	New York	New York	2d Thursday	Horton Hall, 110 E. 125 st.
0	Groton	Tompkins	1st and 3d Saturday, P. M.	Opera House Hall
2	Redfield	Oswego	1st and 3d Saturday P. M.	Wilson Hall
3	Hunter	Greene	2d Saturday, noon	Village Hall
4	New York	New York	2d Sunday afternoon	Lexington ave. cor. 85th st., Turn Hall
6	Middletown	Orange	2d Friday	Granger's Hall, 6 E. Main st.
7	Granville	Washington	1st and 3d Tuesday, 2 P. M.	G A. R. Rooms, Pember Opera House
9	Carthage	Jefferson	1st and 3d Monday	Town Hall
0	Spencerport	Monroe	1st Friday, 2 P. M.	Masonic Temple
1	Fulton	Oswego	Every Saturday afternoon	G. A. R. Hall
2	Hamilton	Madison	1st Tuesday, 2 P. M.	G. A. R. Hall, Main st.
3	Henderson	Jefferson		Comrades' homes
4	Sag Harbor	Suffolk	2d and 4th Tuesday	House of Mrs. Wm. L. Polley, Main st.
5	West Webster	Monroe	2d Saturday, 2 P. M.	G. A. R. Hall, Main st.
6	Corning	Steuben	1st and 3d Saturday, 2 P. M.	City Hall, Council Chamber
8	Baldwinsville	Onondaga	1st Saturday, 2 P. M.	City Hall
9	Port Jervis	Orange	2d and 4th Friday afternoon	Odd Fellows Hall
0	Downsville	Delaware	1st Saturday afternoon	Commander's Office
1	North Tonawanda	Niagara	1st and 3d Wednesday	Wattenger Hall
2	Kennedy	Chautauqua	2d Saturday 2 P. M.	I. O. O. F. Hall
3	Long Island City	Queens	1st Wednesday	Queens Co. Court House
4	Malone	Franklin	1st Saturday, 2 P. M.	Foresters' Hall, E. Main st.
5	Jamestown	Chautauqua	1st and 3d Thursday	G. A. R. Hall, 5 E. Third st
6	Brooklyn	Kings	2d and 4th Saturday	879 Gates ave.
8	Pittsford	Monroe	1st Monday	Bacon's residence, Main st.
9	Broadalbin	Fulton	1st Saturday, 2 P. M	G. A. R. Hall
0	Corinth	Saratoga	1st and 3d Friday P. M.	I. O. O. F. Hall
1	South Butler	Wayne	1st and 3d Friday P. M.	I. O. O. F. Hall, Main st.
2	Brocton	Chautauqua	2d and 4th Saturday, 2 P. M.	G. A. R. Hall
3	Rockland	Sullivan	1st and 3d Saturday, 2 P. M.	Dodge's Hall
4	Hoosick Falls	Rensselaer	1st and 3d Wednesday	G. A. R. Hall
5	Sherman	Chautauqua	Second Friday afternoon	W. R. C. Hall
6	Canaseraga	Allegany	4th Wednesday	Windsor Hall
7	Randolph	Cattaraugus	2d Tuesday	Osgood, Main st.
8	Kendall	Orleans	2d and 4th Saturday	Kidder's Hall

POST NO.	NAME	MEMBERS IN GOOD STANDING DEC. 31, 1917	DATE OF CHARTER	COMMANDER	ADDRESS
299	Upton	42	Oct. 25, 1882	W. J. Gilboy	Batavia
300	H. H. Webber	27	April —, 1902	W. J. Horton	Black River
301	Capt. Wm. A. Jackson	45	Jan. 20, 1894	Louis Wientz	55 Monhazen ave.
302	Crosby	14	Oct. 19, 1884	Frank Wells	Brewster
303	Charles R. Lilly	6	Oct. 20, 1882	T. C. Townsend	Cheshire
306	G. W. Flower	20	Nov. 8, 1882	W. F. Swann	Theresa
307	Edwin D. Morgan	62	Jan. 1, 1884	John K. Darragh	35 Morningside ave
309	John McKee	5	Nov. —, 1883	Willard Lawton	Cambridge
310	Capt. Fancher	11	Nov. 2, 1882	Orin W. Bump	Conewango Valley, R. D. No. 2
311	Garrett	18	Nov. 11, 1884	Joel C. Fisk	Liberty
313	Peter Cooper	63	Mar. 3, 1886	Christopher A. Farrell	560 West 180th st.
314	Theodore Schlick	6	Dec. 21, 1882	David Brown	Wayland
316	B. C. Butler	9	Oct. 22, 1888	E. George Dunklee	Hadley
317	J. C. Drake	10	Nov. 25, 1882	John C. Stowell	Dewittville, R. F. D.
320	John Hance	7	Jan. 19, 1886	H. N. Burr	Williamson
323	Joe Spratt	81	Dec. 29, 1882	O. J. Van Wormer	214 No. Massey st.
324	William Sackett	11	July 15, 1882	James Bond	Westfield
325	Charles T. Harris	9	Dec. 30, 1882	Henry Covert	Ovid
326	A. M. Cook	17	Jan. 2, 1883	George L. Tucker	Greenwich
327	U. S. Grant	200	Jan. 30, 1883	Donald A. Manson	114 Milton st.
330	Adam Goss	19	Jan. 17, 1873	Thos. H. Stritch	224 Tillary st., Bklyn.
332	Wesley Rolfe	12	Jan. 18, 1882	Seth Graves	Wellsville, R. F. D. No.
333	Sawyer	11	Feb. 18, 1883	Albertus Burr	Whitesville
335	Lou Washburn	14	Jan. 18, 1883	H. B. Coleman	Fort Ann
336	Dexter	27	Feb. 9, 1883	George H. Blackman	Wellsville
338	John A. Griswold	29	Feb. 27, 1883	George M. Lemon	1202 6th ave., W'vliet
341	Phineas Catlin	9	Mar. 12, 1883	John L. Halpin	Odessa
346	H. T. Martyn	37	Mar. 8, 1883	R. W. Barrows, Sr.	Canton
349	C. L. Skeels	7	Mar. 12, 1883	George Humphrey	Gasport
350	Whittlesey	33	Mar. 12, 1883	P. H. Pierson	42 Ackley ave , Johnsc City
352	J. S. Stone	12	Mar. 19, 1883	J. H. Brissette	Saranac, R. F. D.
353	Edward Hunting	36	Mar. 24, 1883	James Henry Young	Greenport
354	Ransom	49	Mar. 26, 1883	James C. Birge	Ogdensburg
356	Alonzo Smith	11	Mar. 29, 1883	Charles W. Scudder	St. Johnsville
357	Rust	6	May 5, 1883	Israel S. Rickard	Great Valley
358	Joseph Jones	10	Mar. 30, 1883	Elijah H. Baker	Marietta
359	Darby	14	Mar. 30, 1883	L. W. Henry	Gowanda
362	George Ricard	17	Feb. 17, 1887	John S. Hayes	394 Classon ave.
363	H. L. Aldrich	25	April 19, 1883	H. P. Steenberge	Brushton
364	S. G. Button	5	July 21, 1891	Dennis A. Dewey	West Winfield
365	D. L. Downing	13	April 21, 1883	John W. Campbell	Glen Cove
366	Walter H. Benedict	29	May 7, 1883	John H. Moffitt	Plattsburg
367	Melzar Richards	19	April 23, 1883	W. S. Sweetland	Mexico
368	Alfred M. Wood	30	Sept. 21, 1889	William H. Beers	1288 Dean st., Bklyn
369	Lewis Gates	23	April 30, 1883	Edwin Warren	Honeoye Falls
370	Duncan Lendrum	5	May 14, 1883	James A. Harsha	Argyle
372	W. W. Angle	33	May 2, 1883	M. E. Crane	Addison
373	Oliver McAllister	14	May 3, 1883	J. S. Dwyer	Antwerp
374	Samuel Cannon	16	Aug. 26, 1899	William LaPort	Mooers Forks
376	W. E. Hunt	14	May 15, 1883	D. C. Clark	De Ruyter
378	Charles Lawrence	13	May 28, 1883	William Croft	Port Chester
379	D'Avignon	12	May 21, 1883	J. W. Nye	Wilmington

LOCATION	COUNTY	TIME OF MEETING	PLACE OF MEETING
Batavia	Genesee	2d and 4th Saturday	Ellicott Hall
Black River	Jefferson	1st and 3d Wednesday, 1:30 P. M.	I. O. O. F. Hall
Middletown	Orange	1st and 3d Tuesday	I. O. O. F. Hall, North st.
Brewster	Putnam	Irregularly	Masonic Hall
Cheshire	Ontario	1st and 3d Friday	Fire Department Hall
Theresa	Jefferson	1st and 3d Monday	G. A. R. Hall
New York	New York	2d and 4th Wednesday	Masonic Temple, 126th st. and Lenox ave.
Cambridge	Washington	1st and 3d Saturday	Pierce's Hall, Main st.
Leon	Cattaraugus	2d and 4th Saturday, 2 P. M	G. A. R. Hall
Liberty	Sullivan	1st Saturday, 2 P. M.	N. Main st., G. A. R. Hall
New York	New York	1st and 3d Tuesday	The Park & Tilford Building, 310 Lenox ave.
Wayland	Steuben	At Call of Commander	Bank Building, Main st.
Luzerne	Warren	2d and 4th Thursday, 2 P. M.	Odd Fellows Hall
Sinclairville	Chautauqua	2d Friday	Town Hall, Main st.
Williamson	Wayne	2d Monday	G. A. R. Hall
Watertown	Jefferson	1st and 3d Tuesday, 8 P. M.	G. A. R. Hall, Court st.
Westfield	Chautauqua	1st Friday, 2 P. M.	City Hall
Ovid	Seneca	2d and 4th Sunday, 3 P. M.	County Building
Greenwich	Washington	1st and 3d Saturday, 2 P. M.	I. O. O. F. Temple, Academy st.
Brooklyn	Kings	2d and 4th Tuesday	U. S. Grant Hall, 489 Washington ave.
New York	New York	1st Wednesday	69th Regt. Armory, Lexington ave. and 26th st.
Stanards	Allegany	1st and 3d Wednesday, 2:30 P. M.	Home of Comrade W. H. Donihi
Whitesville	Allegany	1st Saturday, 2 P. M.	Lincoln Hall
Fort Ann	Washington	1st Saturday, 1 P. M.	G. A. R. Hall
Wellsville	Allegany	2d and 4th Saturday, 2 P. M.	City Hall
Troy	Rensselaer	3d Wednesday, each month	Court House
Odessa	Schuyler	3d Saturday	Town Hall
Canton	St. Lawrence	1st Saturday, 2 P. M.	Town Hall, Main st.
Hartland	Niagara	Call of Commander	Comrade's homes
Union	Broome	1st and 3d Saturday, 2 P. M.	Red Men's Hall
Saranac	Clinton	2d and 4th Saturday, 2 P. M.	Grange Hall
Greenport	Suffolk	1st and 3d Thursday	Post Hall
Ogdensburg	St. Lawrence	1st Tuesday	G. A. R. Hall, 53 Ford st
St. Johnsville	Montgomery	3d Tuesday	Engine house, Center st.
Great Valley	Cattaraugus	2d Saturday	Town Hall
Marcellus	Onondaga	4th Wednesday	Masonic Club House
Gowanda	Cattaraugus	2d and 4th Saturday, P. M.	Potter Hall
Brooklyn	Kings	1st Friday	574 Broadway
Brushton	Franklin	2d and 4th Tuesday, P. M.	G. A. R. Hall
West Winfield	Herkimer	2d Wednesday	Residence of D. A. Dewey
Glen Cove	Nassau	1st Tuesday	Town Hall
Plattsburg	Clinton	4th Tuesday, 4 P. M.	McBee Hall
Mexico	Oswego	1st and 3d Saturday, 2 P. M.	The Snell Block
Jamaica	Queens	1st Thursday	Fraternity Hall, Herriman ave
Honeoye Falls	Monroe	1st Thursday	Masonic Hall, Main st.
Argyle	Washington	1st Thursday	I. O. O. F. Hall
Addison	Steuben	Last Saturday, 7:30 P. M.	First National Bank Bldg
Antwerp	Jefferson	1st Friday	Farrell's Hall
Mooers Forks	Clinton	1st and 3d Saturday, 2 P. M.	Town Hall
De Ruyter	Madison	1st and 3d Tuesday P. M.	Home of some Comrade
Port Chester	Westchester	2d and 4th Tuesday	G. A. R. Hall, Willet ave.
Jay	Essex	May and December	G. A. R. Hall

POST NO.	NAME	MEMBERS IN GOOD STANDING DEC. 31, 1917	DATE OF CHARTER	COMMANDER	ADDRESS
380	Sherwood	27	July 24, 1891	L. A. Clemons	Salamanca
381	De Alton Cooper	41	June 6, 1883	Daniel D. Bassett	Adams
382	E. S. Gilbert	15	June 15, 1883	J. L. Wallace	Livonia
383	Candor	15	June 15, 1883	John H. Wheeler	Candor
385	H. J. Botchford	16	May 19, 1883	C. M. Thomas	Port Leyden
386	C. D. Nash	8	July 13, 1883	Charles Shults	South Dayton
387	S. M. Olmstead	5	July 20, 1883	Albert J. Potter	Orwell
389	Philander Cook	8	Aug. 13, 1883	J. R. Casselman	Panama .
391	C. J. Powers	64	Aug. 8, 1883	Albert R. Fowler	869 West Cottage st.
392	A. A. Curtiss	15	Aug. 9, 1883	George S. Williams	Geneseo
393	William O. Stevens	20	Aug. 14, 1883	Thomas J. Averill	721 Washington ave.
394	Robert Anderson	52	Feb. 29, 1876	Michael B. Wood	134 West 91st st.
397	E. G. Marshall	77	Sept. 7, 1883	Henry Elson	29 Warner st.
398	J. J. Peck	12	Sept. 10, 1883	James Taylor	Akron
399	Clarence D. Mackenzie	18	Sept. 20, 1883	Uleric P. Eshleman	846 Flatbush ave.
402	John E. Bendix	6	Sept. 28, 1883	S. H. Mildenberg	136 West 77th st.
403	E. D. Holt	26	Oct. 5, 1883	Jesse Putnam	Fredonia
404	Aaron Helmer	40	Sept. 20, 1883	S. C. Clobridge	Herkimer
406	Myron M. Fish	9	Oct. 11, 1883	J. W. Speller	Ontario
408	Friedrich Heeker	9	Oct. 19, 1883	John Muller	410 W. 41st st.
409	I. F. Quinby	27	Mar. 13, 1897	William McVeen	293 Reynolds st.
410	Albert Dennis	10	Oct. 13, 1883	John B. Bezna	Clayton
411	Angell	11	Oct. 13, 1883	A. J. Steinbarge	Mooers
412	Wilbert Fuller	8	Oct. 13, 1883	A. F. Bennett	Bergen
413	G. W. Chadwick	15	April 7, 1888	Wm. E. Kimball	Sanquoit
414	Wing	5	Oct. 15, 1883	J. D. Eager	Bliss
415	Alfred I. Hooker	6	Nov. 15, 1883	Simon Plumsted	Morristown R. F. No. 2
416	Wilson Dean	15	Nov. 9, 1883	R. B. Davidson	Horseheads, R. F. No. 1
417	Craig W. Wadsworth	13	Nov. 7, 1883	Edw. L. Cook	Oakland
418	Isaac Waterbury	17	Nov. 9, 1883	Lyman Morgan	Central Square
421	Captain Gibson	12	Mar. 4, 1892	Milo H. Felton	Brasher Falls
423	D. B. Smith	13	Nov. 17, 1883	George W. Stone	Valois
424	James B. Campbell	18	Nov. 17, 1883	David H. Taylor	Alexandria Bay
425	Col. Hiram Anderson	24	Nov. 17, 1883	Edwin W. Kinney	Massena
426	Samuel Ackerly	9	Nov. 17, 1883	N. S. Ackerly	Northport
427	W. W. Woodworth	11	Mar. 19, 1898	Byron Van Name	Rushford
428	B. Frank Maxson	8	Nov. 24, 1883	T. T. Burdick	Alfred
429	John F. Smith	8	Nov. 26, 1883	J. D. Wilder	Sinclairville
431	Teller	24	Dec. 14, 1883	C. D. Hall	Neversink
432	W. B. Ransom	17	Dec. 14, 1883	Irving U. Miller	Clarence
434	Hiram Sherman	15	Dec. 20, 1883	W. H. Belchamber	New Haven R. F. No. 1
435	Abel Smith-1st L. I	118	June 30, 1870	James D. Bell	91 Rugby Road
436	Veteran	26	Feb. 24, 1883	Henry Montague	912 Main st., New Dham, N. J.
438	William E. Avery	10	Dec. 29, 1883	Theodore P. Kellogg	Interlaken
439	G. L. Pierce	11	Mar. 3, 1884	David T. Smith	Forestville
440	N. J. Swift	22	Jan. 2, 1884	Samuel R. Saunders	Hamburg
441	E. V. Mayhew	21	Jan. 4, 1884	John M. Wilcox	Three Mile Bay
442	Wm. A. Miles	6	Jan. 19, 1884	H. L. Bentley	Cincinnatus
443	Tefft-Odell	44	Jan. 1, 1915	John H. Bock	2345 Foster ave.
444	John B. Burrud	12	Jan. 24, 1884	F. E. Peck	Marion
445	A. J. Chestnut	10	Jan. 29, 1884	Wm. B. Clawson	Lodi
448	Searle	15	Mar. 1, 1884	Elmer Langworthy	Brookfield

POST NO.	LOCATION	COUNTY	TIME OF MEETING	PLACE OF MEETING
380	Salamanca	Cattaraugus	2d and 4th Friday, 2 P. M.	City Hall
381	Adams	Jefferson	1st and 3d Thursday, 2 P. M.	G. A. R. Hall
382	Livonia	Livingston	1st Saturday afternoon	S. O. V. Rooms
383	Candor	Tioga	Alternate Saturday afternoon	Home, J. K. Holly, Main st.
385	Port Leyden	Lewis	No regular meetings	
386	South Dayton	Cattaraugus	2d Saturday, 2 P. M.	Rowe's Hall
387	Orwell	Oswego	1st Saturday, 1:30 P. M.	I. O. O. F. Hall
389	Panama	Chautauqua	1st and 4th Friday	Office of Ambrose Cross
391	Rochester	Monroe	1st and 3d Monday	City Hall Annex, Exchange pl.
392	Geneseo	Livingston	2d Tuesday	S. of V. Hall
393	Dunkirk	Chautauqua	3d Thursday	City Hall
394	New York	New York	1st Saturday	300 8th ave.
397	Rochester	Monroe	1st and 3d Tuesday	City Hall Annex, 37 Exchange st.
398	Akron	Erie	2d Monday, 2 P. M.	Grange Hall
399	Brooklyn	Kings	1st and 3d Tuesday	Room 9, Borough Hall
402	New York	New York	4th Friday	Armory, 62d st. and Columbus ave.
403	Fredonia	Chautauqua	2d and 4th Friday evening	I. O. O. F. Hall, Main st.
404	Herkimer	Herkimer	1st Tuesday afternoon	Municipal Hall
406	Ontario	Wayne	1st Wednesday, 2 P. M.	Grange Hall
408	New York	New York	1st Friday	424 West 49th st.
409	Rochester	Monroe	2d and 4th Thursday evening	City Hall Annex, Exchange st.
410	Clayton	Jefferson	1st and 3d Friday, 2 P. M.	Barker Block
411	Mooers	Clinton	2d Monday	G. A. R. Hall, Mill st.
412	Bergen	Genesee	1st Friday, 2 P. M.	Town Hall
413	Sauquoit	Oneida	2d and 4th Saturday, 2 P. M.	G. A. R. Hall
414	Bliss	Wyoming	1st Tuesday, 2 P. M.	Eager Hall
415	Morristown	St. Lawrence	2d and 4th Tuesday	Woodmen Hall
416	Millport	Chemung	Last Saturday afternoon	White's Hall
417	Nunda	Livingston	1st and 3d Thursday, 2:30 P. M.	Memorial Hall
418	Central Square	Oswego	2d and 4th Saturday, 2 P. M.	Grange Hall
421	Winthrop	St. Lawrence	2d and 4th Saturday, 2 P. M.	Grange Hall
423	Valois	Schuyler	2d Wednesday	K. of P. Hall
424	Alexandria Bay	Jefferson	1st Saturday	Firemen's Hall
425	Massena	St. Lawrence	2d and 4th Saturday, 2 P. M.	Maccabee Hall
426	Northport	Suffolk	1st and 3d Tuesday	G. A. R. Hall
427	Rushford	Allegany	3d Saturday, 2 P. M.	Town Hall
428	Alfred	Allegany	At Call of Commander	Grange Hall
429	Stockton	Chautauqua	Last Saturday	Grange Hall
431	Grahamsville	Sullivan	1st Saturday, 2 P. M.	Odd Fellows Hall
432	Clarence	Erie	1st Tuesday in quarter, 2 P. M.	I. O. O. F. Temple
434	Vermillion	Oswego	2d and last Saturday, 2 P. M.	G. A. R. Hall
435	Brooklyn	Kings	2d and 4th Monday	879–881 Gates ave.
436	New York	New York	2d and 4th Thursday	301 Eighth ave.
438	Interlaken	Seneca	Call of Commander	Masonic Building
439	Forestville	Chautauqua	4th Jan., April, July and Oct.	Adjutant's Office
440	Hamburg	Erie	1st Monday	Library Building, Center st.
441	Three Mile Bay	Jefferson	Call of Commander	Grange Hall
442	McDonough	Chenango	2d Wednesday	Comrades' Homes
443	Brooklyn	Kings	1st and 3d Saturday	Johnston Hall, 8–12 Nevins st.
444	Marion	Wayne	1st Saturday afternoon	Homes of Comrades
445	Lodi	Seneca	1st and 3d Wednesday	G. A. R. Hall
464	Brookfield	Madison	2d and 4th Saturday	G. A. R. Hall

10

POST NO.	NAME	MEMBERS IN GOOD STANDING DEC. 31, 1917	DATE OF CHARTER	COMMANDER	ADDRESS
450	George S. Bradley	13	Mar. 12, 1883	E. A. Oatman, S. V.	Macedon
451	Adam Wirth	11	Fed. 21, 1883	Charles Buser	226 17th st.
455	Francis E. Pierce	52	Mar. 14, 1902	I. H. Chatfield	555 Tremont st.
456	J. E. Parce	11	Mar. 4, 1884	D. M. Webster	So. Otselic
457	Sanders	15	Mar. 4, 1784	W. B. West	Clay R. F. D. No. 1
458	Noah L. Farnham	27	Mar. 22, 1894	Andrew Boyd	65 West 92d st.
459	Mark L. Scoville	22	Nov. 30, 1898	Charles D. Chilson	Mount Morris
461	Walter C. Hull	41	Mar. 10, 1884	J. W. Emblem	Chemung
464	Dawson	6	Mar. 17, 1884	William Tucker	Spencer
466	Cromwell	23	Mar. 19, 1884	E. B. Long	White Plains
467	Obed Wheeler	11	Dec. —, 1898	James Newman	Amenia
470	Monroe Brundage	18	Mar. 22, 1884	Hiram Morrison	Hammondsport
471	Bolton	17	Mar. 25, 1884	Wm. Rochester	599 Second ave.
472	W. W. Cooke	4	Feb. 2, 1891	Thomas Gaston	22 Inchbury st.
475	John W. Davis	6	April 21, 1884	L. A. Wolcott	Caton
476	William H. Tarbell	7	April 26, 1884	John W. Adams	McGraw
477	John A. Logan	53	April 28, 1888	M. S. Keator	Hobart
478	Chester Bishop	8	May 12, 1884	C. H. Ostrander	Glenwood
481	Edward Seaman	10	May 7, 1884	John Deming	Andover
482	J. Parson Stone	40	May 12, 1884	W. W. Elden	Camden
483	John Plasket	34	May 15, 1884	W. H. Smith	Hancock
484	C. D. Beaumont	12	June 12, 1884	C. W. Rowe	Keeseville
486	Wm. H. Long	10	Aug. 17, 1895	Frank Danes	Penn Yan
487	Hartshorn	10	June 3, 1884	Lewis Hunt	Schaghticoke
488	George G. Pierce	4	Jan. 4, 1884	E. D. H. Laird	Castile
491	C. E. Mills	10	June 19, 1884	George Scott	Fort Edward
493	Plumb	11	June 18, 1884	R. H. Griffin	Sherburne
494	A. A. Hoff	17	July 1, 1884	Chas. L. Shergur	Union Springs
495	Ketcham	7	July 1, 1880	C. M. Woolsey	Milton
496	Ward B. Burnett	23	July 1, 1884	Arthur Humphreys	61 Main st.
499	McPherson-Doane	35	Dec. 4, 1896	Thos. J. McConekey	748 Marcy ave.
500	B. F. Middleton	25	Aug. 3, 1884	Wm. Knappmann	348 Stuyvesant ave.
501	Remington	6	July 22, 1884	O. M. Helmer	Savannah
502	Wilbur Haver	14	Aug. 30, 1884	S. D. Travis	Angelica
504	Durkee	11	Aug. 6, 1884	Adnor Somers	St. Regis Falls
505	Hagadorn	9	Aug. 25, 1884	Francis A. Cooper	Halsey Valley
506	Arthur Smith	31	Aug. 21, 1884	Arthur B. Avery	East Aurora
507	Marcy	13	Aug. 15, 1884	Marcus B. Walker	Avoca
508	Alansen Crosby	29	April 6, 1891	James Dempsey	Franklinville
509	Flandreau	14	Dec. 2, 1887	Eben Adams	New Rochelle
514	John W. Watson	36	Sept. 24, 1884	John W. Van Leuven	Catskill
515	D. W. Washburn	31	Sept. 26, 1884	E. M. Morse	Watkins
516	Farragut-Naval	25	Sept. 26, 1884	George Blair	128 West 13th st.
518	William B. Hazen	24	Jan. —, 1887	Harrison E. Allen	Springwater
521	John P. Jenkins	11	Jan. 29, 1889	Thomas W. Hilyer	Suffern
523	R. M. Starring	12	Oct. 23, 1884	W. H. Bartlett	86 Main st.
524	Richmond	35	Nov. 22, 1884	Bernard Mullin	Port Richmond
525	F. M. Leonard	12	Nov. 20, 1884	A. C. Bickford	Copenhagen
526	James E. Jenkins	13	Jan. 14, 1889	George G. Clark	Vernon Center
527	D. P. B. Mott	35	Dec. 2, 1884	W. H. Patterson	Freeport.
531	William Wood	9	Jan. 3, 1885	W. D. Jennings	Long Lake
532	James S. Knowlton	20	May 18, 1891	Thomas Hughes	169 Margueretta st

POST NO.	LOCATION	COUNTY	TIME OF MEETING	PLACE OF MEETING
450	Macedon	Wayne	1st Saturday	Smith's Hall, Main st.
451	College Point	Queens	2d Wednesday, 3 P. M., Mar., June, Sept. and Dec.	Exempt Firemen's Hall, 140th st., near High st.
455	Rochester	Monroe	2d and 4th Monday	City Hall Annex, 37 Exchange st.
456	South Otselic	Chenango	Last Saturday, 2 P. M.	Office of D. M. Webster
457	Cicero	Onondaga	1st Saturday afternoon	G. A. R. Hall
458	New York	New York	1st Friday	307 West 54th st., New Amsterdam Hall
459	Mount Morris	Livingston	2d Tuesday, Mar., June, Sept., and Dec.	G. A. R. Hall
461	Waverly	Tioga	1st and 3d Saturday, 2 P. M.	Town Hall
464	Spencer	Tioga	1st Sunday	Town Hall
466	White Plains	Westchester	1st and 3d Thursday	G. A. R. Hall, 2 Spring st.
467	Amenia	Dutchess	1st Wednesday, 2:30 P. M.	Grange Hall
470	Hammondsport	Steuben	2d and 4th Friday	Red Men's Hall, Sheather st.
471	Troy	Rensselaer	1st and 3d Wednesday	G. A. R. Hall, 634 Second ave
472	Hamilton	Canada		7 Hughson st., South
475	Caton	Steuben	Call of Commander	Private residences
476	McGrawville	Cortland	1st and 3d Monday	I. O. O. F. Hall
477	Stamford	Delaware	1st Monday, 11 A. M.	Masonic Hall
478	Colden	Erie	2d Saturday afternoon	G. A. R. Hall
481	Andover	Allegany	1st and 3d Saturday	G. A. R. Hall
482	Camden	Oneida	Every Saturday afternoon	G. A. R. Hall
483	Hancock	Delaware	1st and 3d Friday, 7 P. M.	G. A. R. Hall
484	Keeseville	Essex		Barber shop of M. Savage
486	Penn Yan	Yates	1st and 3d Tuesday	S. O. V. Hall
487	Schaghticoke	Rensselaer	2d Saturday, 4 P. M.	G. A. R. Hall, Main st.
488	Castile	Wyoming	Call of Commander	G. A. R. Hall
491	Fort Edward	Washington	4th Thursday afternoon	Town Clerks office, 177 B'way
493	Sherburne	Chenango	2d Wednesday	Fuller & Trusdale's office
494	Union Springs	Cayuga	1st and 3d Tuesday	Everett Hall
495	Milton	Ulster	2d and 4th Sunday afternoon	Woolsey's Hall
496	Tarrytown	Westchester	1st and 3d Tuesday	Corporation Hall, 54 Main st.
499	Brooklyn	Kings	1st and 3d Saturday	Johnston Bldg., 12 Nevins st.
500	Brooklyn	Kings	1st and 3d Saturday	879 Gates ave.
501	Savannah	Wayne	Last Thursday	Flag Salt Hall
502	Angelica	Allegany	2d and 4th Friday, 2 P. M.	I. O. O. F. Hall
504	St. Regis Falls	Franklin	2d and 4th Saturday, 10 A. M.	I. O. O. F. Hall
505	Halsey Valley	Tioga	2d and 4th Saturday	G. A. R. Hall
506	East Aurora	Erie	1st Monday, 2 P. M.	East End Firemen's Hall
507	Avoca	Steuben	Call of Commander	Commander's home
508	Franklinville	Cattaraugus	1st and 3d Tuesday afternoon	G. A. R. Hall
509	New Rochelle	Westchester	2d Friday, 8 P. M	City Hall
514	Catskill	Greene	2d and 4th Saturday afternoon	G. A. R. Hall, 347 Main st
515	Watkins	Schuyler	2d and 4th Friday	G. A. R. Hall
516	New York	New York	1st Monday	69th Reg't Armory, Lexington ave , 25th and 26th sts.
518	Springwater	Livingston	1st Saturday afternoon	Odd Fellows Hall
521	Suffern	Rockland	1st and 3d Saturday afternoon	Odd Fellows Hall
523	Silver Creek	Chautauqua	Last Friday	Stebbins Hall
524	Port Richmond	Richmond	1st and 3d Saturday	Masonic Hall
525	Copenhagen	Lewis	Every Tuesday, 10 A. M.	G. A. R. Hall
526	Vernon	Oneida	2d Saturday afternoon	Fireman's Hall
527	Freeport	Nassau	2d and 4th Saturday	I. O. O. F. Hall
531	Long Lake	Hamilton	Call of Commander	Residence C. B. Hanmer
532	Toronto	Canada	3d Saturday, 3 P. M.	Sons of England Hall, cor. Berti and Richmond sts.

POST NO.	NAME	MEMBERS IN GOOD STANDING DEC. 31, 1917	DATE OF CHARTER	COMMANDER	ADDRESS
533	C. F. Hammond	18	Jan. 9, 1885	E. J. Barker	Crown Point
534	George C. Strong	40	Jan. 10, 1885	Samuel Irvine	918 Lafayette ave.
535	Henry C. Lyon	10	Jan. 13, 1881	J. C. Albright	Pulteney
538	William Gurney	6	Jan. 24, 1884	William W. Hulse	Bay Shore
539	General Logan	15	Jan. 27, 1885	P. H. Garrity	Chatham
542	E. L. Hayward	32	Feb. 26, 1885	Gregory J. Langmeyer	80 Langmeyer ave.
544	Moses A. Baldwin	15	Mar. 11, 1885	Thomas V. Smith	Hempstead
546	Emslie	11	Mar. 23, 1885	Thomas Taft	Cornwall-on-Hudson
549	Knox	23	Mar. 13, 1884	Adam Vose	Savona
551	Ballard	11	April 7, 1885	Frank Bassett	Taberg
553	Robert Orr	7	April 6, 1885	B. M. Stanton	Holland
557	Gen. Jas. McQuade	18	May 18, 1885	Isidore Isaacs	1342 Franklin ave
559	William G. Mitchell	18	June 20, 1885	J. H. Lounsberry	249 West 135th st.
560	Robert J. Marks	23	June 20, 1885	John McCloskey	125 Briggs ave., Richmond Hill
562	A. T. Bailey	15	Oct. —, 1885	A. H. Rushford	Chateaugay
563	A. H. Tanner	16	July 15, 1885	Thomas Covil	Whitehall
564	Fairchild	15	Aug. 15, 1885	C. G. Hunt	Walden
565	J. N. Warner	11	Aug. 18, 1885	J. B. Brown	Woodhull
570	A. L. McDougall	18	Aug. 22, 1886	Wm. J. Cruikshank	Salem
572	Treman	11	Sept. 23, 1885	F. B. Fish	Trumansburg
575	John J. Wheeler	17	Oct. 26, 1885	W. J. Rounsavell	Warwick
576	Weaver	12	Oct. 30, 1885	Geo. W. Crumb	Smyrna
578	Horace B. Claflin	40	April 10, 1888	T. H. Robertson	2853 Bainbridge ave.
581	Warren B. Waite	12	Feb. 27, 1886	Henry Selleck, S. V.	South Colton
582	H. H. Beecher	5	May 18, 1893	Daniel T. Banner	Bainbridge
583	Moses Dennis	6	Mar. 5, 1868	A. Murphy	Jasper
587	Wm. M. Collin	16	April 14, 1886	Hiram Hyde	Hudson Falls
588	Wm. T. Sherman	12	April 13, 1891	Fred. A. Simser	Natural Bridge
589	Cyrus Adams	10	Oct. 22, 1895	W. H. Sears	Frewsburg, R. F. D.
590	John C. Fremont	12	May 28, 1886	William Riley	Philipsburg Building
594	Robert W. Livingston	9	June 15, 1888	J. E. Henry, Sen. Vice	Keene
597	Gen. John B. Murray	10	July 8, 1886	Alonzo Spears	Phelps
598	Ryder	13	July 20, 1886	George A. Harris	Highland Falls
599	George Simons	8	July 12, 1886	Sidney Henderson	Parish
600	Lloyd Aspinwall	28	July 17, 1876	James R. Silliman	510 West 112th st
603	A. & I. Van Nostrand	10	Dec. 30, 1886	John S. Pitt	Fillmore, R. F. D. No. 1
604	Frank Mann	13	Nov. 13, 1886	M. K. Ellsworth	Frankfort, R. F. D.
607	James Monroe	22	Mar. 5, 1887	William Leggett	2862 Briggs ave.
608	George H. Bolster	13	Feb. 19, 1887	M. B. Snook	Fayetteville
609	John Stevenson	11	Mar. 10, 1887	George Farnham	Sterling Valley
613	Tracey	6	April 4, 1887	Charles Barto	Apalachin
615	Joseph H. Warren	5	July 2, 1887	F. T. Sleight	Verona
617	Henry Gridley	6	Sept. 17, 1887	Silas Wilkinson	Millerton
619	Col. Elmer E. Ellsworth	20	Aug. 12, 1887	John J. Ashman	Mechanicville
621	F. M. Bull	12	July 23, 1897	Warren C Flanders	Saranac Lake
623	Gen. A. S. Diven	17	Aug. 11, 1897	James N. McAllister	221 Sullivan st.
624	Carey W. Miner	8	May 18, 1888	Jas. Van Hovenburgh	Georgetown
627	Lewis O. Conklin	10	June 18, 1888	Abram Bentley	Port Jefferson
628	Sheridan	14	June 20, 1888	Charles Schonberg	64 Railroad ave., Corona

POST NO.	LOCATION	COUNTY	TIME OF MEETING	PLACE OF MEETING
533	Crown Point	Essex	4th Friday, 2 P. M.	G. A. R. Hall
534	Brooklyn	Kings	2d and 4th Saturday, except July and August	23d Inf. Armory, 1322 Bedford avenue
535	Pulteney	Steuben	2d Tuesday	Goodrich Block
538	Bay Shore	Suffolk	Wednesday	Residence, Wm. W. Hulse
539	Chatham	Columbia	2d and 4th Saturday, 2 P. M.	Tracy Memorial Hall
542	Buffalo	Erie	2d and 4th Tuesday	Herner's Hall, 246 Sycamore st.
544	Hempstead	Nassau	2d Wednesday	Hempstead Bank Building
546	Cornwall-on-Hudson	Orange	4th Tuesday	Corporation Rooms
549	Savona	Steuben	1st Saturday, 2 P. M.	Stinson's Hall
551	Taberg	Oneida	1st and 3d Saturday, 2 P. M.	G. A. R. Hall
553	Holland	Erie	2d Saturday	Office of B. M. Stanton, Main st
557	New York	New York	2d Sunday afternoon	"Tuxedo," cor. Madison ave. and 59th st.
559	New York	New York	2d Wednesday	168th st. and Broadway
560	Elmhurst	Queens	1st and 3d Monday	Exempt Firemen's Hall, B'way
562	Chateaugay	Franklin	2d Tuesday, 1:30 P. M.	Beman Hall
563	Whitehall	Washington	1st Wednesday, 7:30 P. M.	Griswold Hall
564	Walden	Orange	2d Saturday	Laughern Hall, Oak st.
565	Woodhull	Steuben	4th Friday, 1 P. M.	G. A. R. Hall
570	Salem	Washington	1st Friday	Rooms of Union Engine and Hose Co. No. 1
572	Trumansburg	Tompkins	1st and 3d Friday	G. A. R. Hall, Main st.
575	Warwick	Orange	2d Sunday, 2 P. M.	G. A. R. Hall
576	Smyrna	Chenango	2d Saturday	At homes of Comrades
578	New York	New York	2d and 4th Friday	Phoenix Bank Building, 125th st. and Lexington ave.
581	Colton	St. Lawrence	2d Friday, 1:30 P. M.	A. B. Hepburn Library
582	Bainbridge	Chenango	2d and 4th Friday afternoon	Room in Mammoth Block
583	Jasper	Steuben	1st Saturday	Wallace Hall, Main st.
587	Hudson Falls	Washington	2d Friday	Clement's Hall, Main st.
588	Natural Bridge	Jefferson	Alternate Saturday, 2:30 P. M.	G. A. R. Rooms
589	Frewsburg	Chautauqua	Last Friday afternoon	Home of P. E. Miller
590	Yonkers	Westchester	4th Thursday	Philipsburg Building
594	Keene Valley	Essex	1st Saturday	Town Hall
597	Phelps	Ontario	2d and 4th Wednesday, 2 P. M.	G. A. R. Rooms, Gibson Block
598	Highland Falls	Orange	Call of Commander	Goodsell Hall, Main st.
599	Parish	Oswego	2d Tuesday	Firemen's Hall
600	New York	New York	2d and 4th Thursday	Ft. Washington ave. and 168th st., 22d Regt Armory
603	Short tract	Allegany	2d and 4th Saturday	Pitts Hall
604	Frankfort	Herkimer	2d Saturday	K. of P. Hall, Pleasant ave.
607	New York	New York	1st Thursday	Armory, 168th st. near Broadway
608	Manlius	Onondaga	2d and 4th Wednesday after-noon	Smith Hall, Seneca st.
609	S. W. Oswego	Oswego	1st and 3d Tuesday, 1 P. M.	Grange Hall
613	Apalachin	Tioga	1st Saturday	G. A. R. Hall
615	Verona	Oneida	2d and 4th Tuesday	G. A. R. Hall
617	Millerton	Dutchess	2d Saturday, 2 P. M.	Odd Fellows Hall, Main st.
619	Mechanicville	Saratoga	1st and 3d Wednesday	K. of P. Hall
621	Saranac Lake	Franklin	1st and 3d Tuesday	Ledger's Hall
623	Elmira	Chemung	1st and 3d Thursday, 8 P. M.	State Armory, Church st.
624	Georgetown	Madison	1st and 3d Saturday	At home of Commander
627	Port Jefferson	Suffolk	1st Monday	Home of G. W. Kinner
628	Long Island City	Queens	2d Saturday	Court House, Jackson ave.

POST NO.	NAME	MEMBERS IN GOOD STANDING DEC. 31, 1917	DATE OF CHARTER	COMMANDER	ADDRESS
630	Gen. Philip H. Sheridan	15	July 11, 1888	Edward Lafay	Waterford
632	Selah Cornwell	5	July 16, 1888	Francis Flynn	Merrifield
633	John P. Buckley	6	Aug. 12, 1897	H. B. Pierson	Belleville
636	John Corning	8	Mar. 26, 1892	B. L. Dunbar	Howard Beach, L. I.
640	C. M. Pierce	10	April 14, 1902	D. H. Robbins	North Cohocton
641	J. C. Walters	13	Oct. 24, 1889	James Wright	Cold Spring Harbor
642	John C. Lasson	9	Oct. 15, 1889	F. M. Bartholomew	Clemons
643	H B. Knickerbocker	11	Nov. 25, 1889	Geo. W. Lyon	Amityville
644	William A. Jackson	31	Dec. 31, 1889	Frank E. Cooley	144 Washington ave., Rensselaer
646	L. W. Truesdall	17	Feb. 17, 1890	Eli Hutchins	Owego
647	Anthony Stacey	17	Feb. 17, 1890	A. E. Stacey	Elbridge
648	Col. Randall	9	June 16, 1891	Oscar Forger	Liverpool
649	Gregory	13	June 18, 1891	J. H. Potts	Branchport
652	Hannibal Hamlin	5	Nov. 27, 1891	W. T. Peel	538 Waterloo st.
654	Elijah Ward	9	Nov. 11, 1891	Wm. H. Wood	Roslyn
655	Wm. T. Wickham	7	Mar. 31, 1892	Edward Smallman	Cattaraugus
656	Henry A. Barnum	18	May 2, 1892	Albert H. Terry	Riverhead
659	Charles H. Bentley	9	June 6, 1892	Nicholas Lawliss	Cadyville
660	Tilton	6	June 23, 1892	Michael McMahon	Leicester
661	C. N. Campbell	7	Nov. 10, 1894	John E. Banks	Pawling
663	R. D. Pettit	10	Sept. —, 1890	Reuben Terpening	Ira
664	J. P. Spofford	10	Sept. 8, 1892	Levi Helmer	Dolgeville
665	S. S. Craig	11	Sept. 12, 1892	Geo. H. Dingman	Porter Corners
666	A. A. Hall	7	Feb. 15, 1893	L. L. Morton	East Randolph
667	R. B. Hayes	26	Feb. 16, 1893	Duane P. Babcock	Fayetteville
670	Ben Higgins	18	June 7, 1893	Daniel Stryker	East Syracuse
671	Gen, John E. Wool	17	April 25, 1905	G. W. Moore	5 Ball pl.
672	R. M. McDowell	10	May —, 1915	W. H. Hathaway	370½ Fulton st.

POST NO.	LOCATION	COUNTY	TIME OF MEETING	PLACE OF MEETING
630	Waterford	Saratoga	2d and 4th Tuesday	Town Hall
632	Scipio	Cayuga	4th Saturday	Snyder's Hall
633	Belleville	Jefferson	4th Friday	I. O. O. F. Hall
636	Rockaway Beach	Queens	2d Wednesday, 8 p. m.	Gerrey's Hall
640	North Cohocton	Steuben	1st and 3d Saturday, 2 p. m.	G. A. R. Hall
641	Huntington	Suffolk	1st Saturday afternoon	Sammis Hall, Main st.
642	Clemons	Washington	4th Feb. May, Aug. and Nov.	Commander's home
643	Amityville	Suffolk	2d Tuesday afternoon	Post Rooms
644	Albany	Albany	2d and 4th Tuesday	G. A. R. Hall, Court House
646	Owego	Tioga	2d and 4th Saturday, p. m.	G. A. R. Rooms, Lake st.
647	Elbridge	Onondaga	2d and 4th Saturday	G. A. R. Rooms
648	Liverpool	Onondaga	1st Saturday, 7:30 p. m	Comrades Homes
649	Prattsburg	Steuben	2d and 4th Thursday	Masonic Hall
652	London	Canada	Call of Commander	Home of Commander
654	Roslyn	Nassau	Call of Commander	Quartermaster's house, Garden st.
655	Otto	Cattaraugus	2d Wednesday	Town Hall
656	Riverhead	Suffolk	1st and 3d Saturday, 3 p. m.	G. A. R.Hall
659	Morrisonville	Clinton	2d Wednesday of every third month	J. H. Goods office
660	Leicester	Livingston	2d Tuesday	G. A. R. Hall, Main st.
661	Pawling	Dutchess	1st Saturday	Pawling Savings Bank
663	Lysander	Onondaga	1st Saturday	G. A. R. Rooms
664	Dolgeville	Herkimer	2d and 4th Wednesday, 7:30 p. m.	Exempt Fireman's Hall
665	Middle Grove	Saratoga	2d and 4th Saturday, 1:30 p. m.	I. O. O. F. Hall
666	East Randolph	Cattaraugus	Call of Commander	I. O. O. F. Hall
667	Fayetteville	Onondaga	2d Saturday, 3 p. m.	G. A. R. Hall
670	East Syracuse	Onondaga	1st and 3d Wednesday	Municipal Hall
671	Watervliet	Albany	2d and 4th Thursday	Broadway and 16th st.
672	Elmira	Chemung	1st and 3d Sunday afternoon	Schaffer Hall, Hudson st.

INDEX

A

APPENDIX

TOPICAL GUIDE

TO THE

Laws Now in Force Relating to the Grand
Army of the Republic and Veterans
of the War of the Rebellion

NINTH EDITION — 1918

REVISED AND ANNOTATED

BY

JAMES D. BELL

Judge-Advocate, 1909, 1910, 1916
Department Commander, 1914

EXPLANATORY NOTE

For many years, the proceedings of the Department contained numbers of statutes relating to our Order and the right of veterans, printed apparently from the slips as issued by the Secretary of State. For the proceedings of last year, my distinguished predecessor in the office of Judge-Advocate, Judge Lewis E. Griffith, availing himself of the enactment of the Consolidated Laws, arranged the compilation which appeared in the last report. I have used all the laws which he had collected and have added a considerable number to them. No attempt has been made to compile all the laws relating to the Grand Army of the Republic and veterans of the War of the Rebellion, but an attempt has been made to compile all which would ordinarily be required to obtain a comprehensive view of the subject. This Guide is arranged by subjects in alphabetical order and a separate index is, therefore, omitted. All citations are omitted. On a future occasion, the writer may find the time to compile a short digest of useful authorities in regard to veterans' rights.

I have been greatly aided by Mr. W. Burt Cook, Jr., Assistant Librarian, Law Library in Brooklyn, in obtaining the materials used in this Guide:

In addition to the usual abbreviations, the following are employed in this Guide:

a. Amended by or thus amended.

c. Chapter.

C. Consolidated Laws.

C. C. P. Code of Civil Procedure.

Charter. Greater New York Charter, e. L. 1897, c. 378; revised, L. 1901, c. 466.

const. Constituting.

e. Enacted by.

L. Laws.

The Consolidated Laws are thus indicated:

Benev. Orders for Benevolent Orders Law, const. c. 3 C., e. L. 1909, c. 11.

Civil Serv. for Civil Service Law, const. c. 7 C., e. L. 1909, c. 15.

County for County Law, const. c. 11 C., e. L. 1909, c. 16.

Educ. for Education Law, const. c. 16 C., e. L. 1909, c. 21; a. Generally L. 1910, c. 140.

El. for Election Law, const. c. 17 C., e. L. 1909, c. 22.

Executive for Executive Law, const. c. 18 C., e. L. 1909, c. 23.

Gen. Bus. for General Business Law, const. c. 20 C., e. L. 1909, c. 25.

Gen. City for General City Law, const. c. 21 C., e. L. 1909, c. 26.

Gen. Cons. for General Construction Law, const. c. 22 C., e. L. 1909, c. 27.

Gen. Munic. for General Municipal Law, const. c. 24 C., e. L. 1909, c. 29.

Highway for Highway Law, const. c. 25 C., e. L. 1909, c. 30.

Jud. for Judiciary Law, const. c. 30 C., e. L. 1909, c. 35.

Memb. Corp. for Membership Corporation Law, const. c. 35 C., e. L. 1909, c. 40.

Mil. for Military Law, const. c. 36 C., e. L. 1909, c. 41.

Penal for Penal Law, const. c. 40 C., e. L. 1909, c. 88.

Poor for Poor Law, const. c. 44 C., e. L. 1909, c. 46.

Pub. Bldgs. for Public Buildings Law, const. c. 44 C., e. L. 1909, c. 48.

Pub. Off. for Public Officers Law, const. c. 47 C., e. L. 1909, c. 51.

St. Char. for State Charities Law, const. c. 55 C., e. L. 1909, c. 57; a. L. 1909, c. 258.

St. Fin. for State Finance Law, const. c. 56 C., e. L. 1909, c. 58.

State for State Law, const. c. 57 C., e. L. 1909, c. 59.

State Printing Law, const. c. 58 C., e. L. 1909, c. 60.

Tax for Tax Law, const. c. 60 C., e. L. 1909, c. 62.

Town for Town Law, const. c. 62 C., e. L. 1909, c. 63.

Vill. for Village Law, const. c. 64 C., e. L. 1909, c. 64.

J. D. BELL.

Dated, Brooklyn, N. Y., *June* 14, 1910.

NOTE TO SECOND EDITION.

The foregoing introduced the Topical Guide as it appeared in the Proceedings of the Forty-fourth Annual Encampment of 1910.

The Guide seems to have commended itself to the Comrades of the Department, and I have therefore prepared a second, and I trust an improved, edition of it, for the Proceedings of the Forty-fifth Annual Encampment. The amendments made by the Legislature of 1911 have been incorporated in the text, and according to a promise heretofore made, a few useful authorities on veterans' rights and privileges have been added. It was at first intended to keep the citations separate from the Guide, but more mature reflection has convinced me that they will be of greater service when printed in connection with the statutory provisions to which they relate. No attempt has been made to make the annotations exhaustive, the design has been, rather, to select only those of practical use, and references to decisions construing a different state of the law have been excluded. In making these citations, the ordinary abbreviations have been employed, and it has therefore not been deemed necessary to explain them, except to point out that A. G. R. and A. G. O. refer respectively to the annual reports of the Attorney-General of the State and to Sickles' compilation of the opinions of the Attorneys-General. In all other respects the Guide remains unchanged.

I cannot close without expressing my deep obligations to my friend, Mr. Cook, for invaluable assistance in the preparation of this edition.

Dated, Brooklyn, June 6, 1911.   J. D. BELL.

NOTE TO THIRD EDITION.

The amendments made by the Laws of 1912 have been incorporated in the text and a few minor errors corrected.

Dated, Brooklyn, October 16, 1912.   J. D. BELL.

NOTE TO FOURTH EDITION.

The amendments made by the Laws of 1913 have been incorporated in the text.

There is a very considerable body of legislation in the Laws of 1913 which does not fall within the scope of this manual, but is otherwise of interest to veterans of the Civil War, among which may be mentioned chapter 413, providing for Andersonville Monument Commission; chapter 532, providing for the Fiftieth Anniversary of the Emancipation Proclamation; chapter 550, providing for New York Battle Fields Commission for the battle fields of Gettysburg, Chattanooga and Antietam; chapter 717, providing for a Monument to the Twenty-fifth New York Cavalry in the District of Columbia; chapter 725, providing for the appropriation of $150,000 for the celebration of the Fiftieth Anniversary of the Battle of Gettysburg; chapter 734, in relation to the monument to Gen. N. M. Curtis, formerly Department Commander, at Ogdensburg, N. Y.; and chapter 761, providing for a monument to Meagher's Irish Brigade and Corcoran's Irish Legion, in New York City. J. D. BELL.

Dated, Brooklyn, October 20, 1913.

NOTE TO FIFTH EDITION.

The amendments made by the Laws of 1914 have been incorporated in the text and some changes made in the annotations.

Dated, Brooklyn, September 24, 1914. J. D. BELL.

NOTE TO SIXTH EDITION.

The amendments made by the laws of 1915 have been incorporated in the text and some errors have been corrected.

Dated, Brooklyn, August 13, 1915. J. D. BELL.

NOTE TO SEVENTH EDITION.

The amendments made by the Laws of 1916 have been incorporated in the text, a few corrections made in the annotations and a new topic " Retirements and Pensions " added.

Dated, Brooklyn, August 24, 1916. J. D. BELL.

NOTE TO EIGHTH EDITION.

The amendments made by the Laws of 1917 have been incorporated in the text. There is pending a concurrent resolution to amend the Constitution of the State in regard to preference. It has passed the present Legislature by the necessary two-thirds vote and has been referred by it to the Legislature to be chosen in 1918. It extends the preference for military or naval service, but seems to leave the preference to the Civil War veterans untouched.

The resolution reads as follows:

"Section 1. *Resolved* (if the Assembly concur), That section nine of article five of the constitution be amended to read as follows:

"§ 9. Appointments and promotions in the civil service of the state, and of all the civil divisions thereof, including cities and villages, shall be made according to merit and fitness to be ascertained, so far as practicable, by examinations, which, so far as practicable, shall be competitive; provided, however, that honorably discharged soldiers, sailors and marines who have served as such in the army, navy or marine corps of the United States in the time of war, and who are citizens and residents of this state, shall be entitled to preference in appointment and promotion over all others, without regard to their standing on any list from which such appointment or promotion may be made, in the following order:

"1. All honorably discharged soldiers, sailors or marines who served as such in the army, navy or marine corps of the United States during the civil war;

"2. All honorably discharged soldiers, sailors or marines who served as such in the army, navy or marine corps of the United States during the war with Spain or the insurrection in the Philippine Islands prior to July fourth, nineteen hundred and two, who were residents of this state at the time of enlistment.

"Laws shall be made to provide for the enforcement of this section."

Dated, *November* 1, 1917.   J. D. BELL.

NOTE TO NINTH EDITION.

I have inserted the amendments made by the Laws of 1918 in their proper places. It is worthy of remark that by chapter 345 of the Laws of 1918 three thousand dollars was appropriated for the transportation and maintenance of survivors of the Seventy-ninth Regiment of New York Veteran Volunteers (Highlanders) and certain other persons and for the dedication of a monument to said veterans erected on the battlefield of Knoxville, Tennessee.

I have inserted, as being of interest to our patriotic order, section 674 of the Education Law, added by chapter 246 of the Laws of 1918, which provides for the exclusion of any text-book from the public schools of this State containing disloyal matters or statements. That section reads as follows:

" § 674. **Text-books containing seditious or disloyal matter.** No text-book in any subject used in the public schools in this state shall contain any matter or statements of any kind which are seditious in character, disloyal to the United States or favorable to the cause of any foreign country with which the United States is now at war. A commission is hereby created, consisting of the commissioner of education and of two persons to be designated by the regents of the University of the state of New York, whose duty it shall be on complaint to examine text-books used in the public schools of the state, in the subjects of civics, economics, English, history, language and literature, for the purpose of determining whether such text-books contain any matter or statements of any kind which are seditious in character, disloyal to the United States or favorable to the cause of any foreign country with which the United States is now at war. Any person may present a written complaint to such commission that a text-book in any of the aforesaid subjects for use in the public schools of this state or offered for sale for use in the public schools of this state contains matter or statements in violation of this section, specifying such matter or statements in detail. If the commission determine that the text-book against which complaint is made contains any such matter or statements, it shall issue a certificate disapproving the use of such text-book in the public schools of this state, together with a statement of the reasons for its disapproval, specifying the matter found unlawful. Such certificate of disapproval of a text-book, with a detailed statement of the reasons for its disapproval, shall be duly forwarded to the boards of education or other boards or authorities having jurisdiction of the public schools of the cities, towns or school districts of this state, and after the receipt of such certificate the use of a text-book so disapproved shall be discontinued in such city, town or school district.

"Any contract hereafter made by any such board of education or other school authorities for the purchase of a text-book in any of such subjects, which has been so disapproved, shall be void. Any school officer or teacher who permits a text-book in any of such subjects, which has been so disapproved, to be used in the public schools of the state, shall be guilty of a misdemeanor."

J. D. BELL.

Dated, BROOKLYN, *September* 23, 1918.

TOPICAL GUIDE

BURIAL AND BURIAL PLOTS

1. BURIAL AND HEADSTONE (Poor)

§ 84. *Burial of soldiers, sailors and marines* — The board of supervisors in each of the counties shall designate some proper person or commission, other than that designated for the care of poor persons, or the custody of criminals, who shall cause to be interred the body of any honorably discharged soldier, sailor or marine, who has served in the military or naval service of the United States, or the body of the wife or widow of any soldier, sailor or marine, married to him previous to nineteen hundred and ten, who shall die such widow, and who shall hereafter die without leaving sufficient means to defray his or her funeral expenses, but such expenses shall in no case exceed fifty dollars. If the deceased has relatives or friends who desire to conduct the burial, but are unable or unwilling to pay the charge therefor, such sum shall be paid by the county treasurer to the person so conducting such burial upon due proof of the claim, made to such person, or commission of the death and burial of the soldier, sailor or marine, or the wife or widow of such soldier, sailor or marine, and audit thereof. Such interment shall not be made in a cemetery or cemetery plot used exclusively for the burial of poor persons deceased, and the board of supervisors of each county is hereby authorized and empowered to purchase and acquire lands, or to appropriate money for the purchase and acquisition of lands, for a cemetery or cemetery plot for the burial of any such honorably discharged soldiers, sailors or marines and their wives and widows and also to provide for the care, maintenance, or improvement of any cemetery or plot where such honorably discharged

[x]

soldiers, sailors or marines and their wives and widows are buried or may hereafter be buried.   (a. L. 1915 c. 445.)

§ 85. *Headstones to be provided* — The grave of any honorably discharged soldier, sailor or marine who served in the army or navy of the United States or of the wife or widow of such an honorably discharged soldier, sailor or marine, whose body has been heretofore or shall hereafter be interred pursuant to the last preceding section, the grave of any honorably discharged soldier, sailor or marine who served in the army or navy of the United States who shall have been heretofore buried in any of the counties of this state, but whose grave is not marked by a suitable headstone, and who died without leaving means to defray the expense of such headstone, or whose grave shall have remained unmarked for twenty-five years by a suitable headstone, shall be marked by a headstone containing the name of the deceased, the war in which he served, and, if possible, the organization to which he belonged or in which he served. The headstone at the grave of the wife or widow of such an honorably discharged soldier, sailor or marine shall contain the name of the deceased, the war in which her husband served, and, if possible, the organization to which he belonged or in which he served. Such headstone shall not cost more than twenty-five dollars, and shall be of such design and material as shall be approved by the board of supervisors, and the expenses of such burial and headstone as above provided for, and a reasonable sum for the services of the person or commission designated in section eighty-four and the necessary expenses of said person or commission, shall be a charge upon and shall be paid by the county in which the said soldier, sailor or marine, or the wife or widow of such soldier, sailor or marine, shall have died; and the board of supervisors or other board or officer vested with like powers, of the county of which such deceased soldier, sailor or marine, or the wife or widow of such soldier, sailor or marine, was a resident at the time of his or her death, is hereby authorized and directed to audit the account and pay the expenses of such burial and headstone, and a reasonable sum for the services of the person or commission designated in section eighty-four and the necessary expenses of said person or commission; provided, however, that in case such deceased soldier, sailor or marine, or the wife or widow of such soldier, sailor or marine, shall be at the time of his or her death an inmate of any state institution, including state hospitals and soldiers' homes, or any institution, supported by the state and supported by public expense therein, the expense of such burial and headstone shall be a charge upon the county of his or her legal residence. It shall be the duty of the person or commission in this article provided prior to the annual meeting of the board of supervisors to make an annual report to such board of supervisors of all applications since the last annual report for burial and the erection of tombstones as provided herein together with the amounts allowed; all applications herein referred to shall accompany said annual report and be placed and kept on file with the board of supervisors. (a. L. 1915, c. 147.)

includes: ANNOTATIONS

Mexican war veterans. A. G. R., 1896:242–43.
veterans even though not honorably discharged. A. G. R., 1911 (Feb. 25).
expense chargeable to county of residence, though death occur in another
    county. A. G. R., 1889:182–83; A. G. R., 1910:590–92.
"without leaving means," construed. People ex rel. Brown v. Prendergast,
    146 A. D. 713 [1911].

2. BURIAL PLOT AND REMOVAL OF REMAINS (Town)

§ 336. *Soldiers' burial plot* — The town board in each of the towns of this state may upon the application in writing of any veteran soldiers' association in the town, or upon a petition in writing of five or more veteran soldiers in towns where no veteran soldiers' organization exists, purchase or provide a soldiers' plot in one or more cemeteries where no burial plots are now owned by soldiers' organizations, in which burial plots deceased soldiers may be interred, and except in the county of Broome, may also provide for the annual care of soldiers' burial plots in cemeteries, at the rate of not to exceed fifty cents for each soldiers' grave in such burial plot or plots and the expense shall be included in the town expenses, assessed, levied and collected in the same manner as other town expenses are levied and collected.

In the county of Broome, the board of supervisors shall provide for the annual care of soldiers' burial plots, either heretofore or hereafter established, in all cemeteries in such county, at the rate aforesaid, and the expense thereof shall be a county charge audited, assessed, levied and collected in the same manner as are other county charges.   (a. L. 1914, c. 235.)

§ 337. *Removal of remains of deceased soldiers* — Upon a verified petition presented to a judge of a court of record by any soldiers' organization in any town or city in this state by a majority of its officers, or a majority of any memorial committee in any town or city where there are two or more veteran soldiers' organizations, upon the petition of five or more veteran soldiers, the judge to whom said verified petition is presented shall make an order to show cause returnable before him at a time and place within the county in not less than fourteen nor more than twenty days from the date of presentation of said petition, why the remains of any deceased soldiers buried in potter's field, or in any neglected or abandoned cemeteries, should not be removed to and reinterred in a properly kept incorporated cemetery in the same town or city or in a town adjoining the town or city in which the remains of a deceased soldier are buried, and to fix the amount of the expenses for such removal and reinterment, and the order to show cause shall provide for its publication in a newspaper, to be designated in the order, which is published nearest to the cemetery from which the removal is sought to be made, once in each week for two successive weeks. The verified petition presented to the judge shall show that the petitioners are a majority of the officers of a veteran soldier organization, or a majority of a memorial committee in towns or cities where two or more veteran soldier organizations exist, or that the petitioners are honorably discharged veteran soldiers in towns or cities where no veteran soldier organization exists, and (1) the name of the deceased soldier or soldiers whose remains are sought to be removed, and if known the company and regiment in which he or they served; (2) the name and location of the cemetery in which he is interred and from which removal is asked to be made; (3) the name and location of the incorporated cemetery to which the remains are desired to be removed and reinterred; (4) the facts showing the reasons for such removal. Upon the return day of the order to show cause and at the time and place fixed in said order, upon filing proof of publication of the order to show cause with the judge, if no reason or objection is made thereto, he shall make an order directing the removal of the remains of said deceased soldier or soldiers to the cemetery designated in the petition within the town or city or within a town adjoining the town or city in which the remains are then buried and shall specify in the order the amount of the expenses of such removal, which expenses of removal and reinterment, including the expense of the proceeding under this section, shall be a charge upon the county in which the town or city is situated from which the removal is made and such expenses shall be a county charge and audited by the board of supervisors of the county and paid in the same manner as other county charges. On and after the removal and reinterment of the remains of the deceased soldier or soldiers in the soldiers' plot, the expenses for annual care of the grave in the soldiers' burial plot to which the removal is made shall be annually provided by the town or city in which the remains were originally buried, at the rate of not to exceed fifty cents per grave and shall be paid annually to the incorporated cemetery association to which the remains of each deceased soldier may be removed and reinterred. The petition and order shall be filed in the county clerk's office of the county in which the remains of the deceased soldier were originally interred, and the service of a certified copy of the final order upon the cemetery association shall be made prior to any removal. Any relative of the deceased soldier or soldiers, or the officer of any cemetery association in which the remains of the deceased soldier or soldiers were originally interred, or the authorities of the county in which the soldier or soldiers were originally buried, may oppose the granting of said order and the judge shall summarily hear the statement of the parties and make such order as the justice and equity of the application shall require. Any headstone or monument which marks the grave of the deceased soldier shall be removed and reset at the grave in the cemetery in which the removal is permitted to be made and in each case the final order shall provide the amount of the expenses of such removals and reinterment and resetting of the headstone or monument, including the expenses of the proceedings under this section; except that where provision is otherwise made for the purchase or erection of a new headstone, monument or marker at the grave in the cemetery to which such removal is permitted, such old headstone or monument need not be so removed and reset, in which case such final order shall not provide for the expense of resetting. The order shall designate the person or persons having charge of the removals and reinterments. Upon completion of the removal, reinterment and resetting of the headstones or monuments, the person or persons having charge of the same shall make a verified report of the removal, reinterment and resetting of the headstone or monument and file the report in the clerk's office of the proper county. The word " soldier " shall be construed to mean an honorably discharged soldier, sailor or marine who served in the army or navy of the United States, and the words " soldiers' plot," shall be construed to mean a plot of land in any incorporated cemetery set apart to be exclusively used as a place for interring the remains of deceased veteran soldiers of the United States.

ANNOTATIONS

applies only to soldiers' graves within such town plots, not to private burial plots. A. G. R., 1910:589-90.

CHILDREN OF VETERANS

1. No Fees on Appointing Certain Guardians   (C. C. P.)

§ 2499. *Fees for copying or recording papers* — * * * On the appointment of a guardian, if it appears that the application is made for the purpose of enabling the minor to receive bounty, arrears of pay or prize money, or pension due, or other dues or gratuity from the federal or state government, for the services of the parent or brother of such minor in the military or naval service of the United States, no fees shall be charged or received. (a. L. 1914, C. 443 — part of former § 2501 without change.)

2. Preference, Cornell University   (Educ.)

§ 1037. *State scholarships in Cornell University* — The several departments of study in Cornell university shall be open to applicants for admission thereto at the lowest rates of expense consistent with its welfare and efficiency, and without distinction as to rank, class, previous occupation or locality. But, with a view to equalize its advantages to all parts of the state, the institution shall receive students to the number of one each year from each assembly district in this state, to be selected as hereinafter provided, and shall give them instruction in any or in all the prescribed branches of study in any department of said institution, free of any tuition fee or of any incidental charges to be paid to said university, unless such incidental charges shall have been made to compensate for materials consumed by said students or for damages needlessly or purposely done by them to the property of said university. The said free instruction shall, moreover, be accorded to said students in consideration of their superior ability, and as a reward for superior scholarship in the academies and public schools of this state. Said students shall be selected as the legislature may from time to time direct, and until otherwise ordered as follows:

1. A competitive examination, under the direction of the education department, shall be held at the county court-house in each county of the state, upon the first Saturday in June, in each year, by the city superintendents and the school commissioners of the county.

2. None but pupils of at least sixteen years of age and of six months' standing in the common schools or academies of the state, during the year immediately preceding the examination, shall be eligible.

3. Such examination shall be upon subjects designated by the president of the university and upon question papers prepared under the direction of the commissioner of education.

4. The city superintendents and school commissioners of each county shall immediately after the close of the examination forward to the commissioner of education all answer papers submitted by candidates in such examination, all statements of candidates and a report of the names of candidates in such form as the commissioner of education shall require.

*   *   *   *   *   *   *

7. In certifying the qualifications of the candidates, preference shall be given, where other qualifications are equal, to the children of those who have died in the military or naval service of the United States.

8. Notices of the time and place of the examinations shall be

given in all the schools having pupils eligible thereto, prior to the first day of January in each year, and shall be published once a week, for three weeks, in at least two newspapers in each county immediately prior to the holding of such examinations.   *   *   *

9.   *   *   *   Students enjoying the privileges of free scholarships shall, in common with the other students of said university, be subject to all the examinations, rules and requirements of the board of trustees or faculty of said university, except as herein provided.

2. PREFERENCE IN STATE SCHOOL FOR BLIND   (Educ.)

§ 991. *Requisites for admission* — All blind persons of suitable age and capacity for instruction, who are legal residents of the state, shall be entitled to the privileges of the New York state school for the blind, without charge, and for such a period of time in each individual case as may be deemed expedient by the board of trustees of said school; provided, that whenever more persons apply for admission at one time than can be properly accommodated in the school, the trustees shall so apportion the number received, but each county may be represented in the ratio of its blind population to the total blind population of the state; and provided further, that the children of citizens who died in the United States service, or from wounds received therein during the late rebellion, shall take precedence over all others.

CIVIL SERVICE — *See* Preference and Removal
CONSTITUTION, RIGHTS OF VETERANS UNDER — *See* Preference

DEPARTMENT OF NEW YORK, G. A. R.

1. INCORPORATED   (L. 1885, c. 11)

Section 1. Ira M. Hedges, of Haverstraw, department commander; Lester P. Thompson, of Phelps, senior vice-department commander; James C. Carlyle, of New York, junior vice-department commander; George B. Squires, of Brooklyn, assistant adjutant-general; Horatio N. Wood, of Haverstraw, assistant quartermaster-general; John H. Dye, M. D., of Buffalo, medical director; S. S. Ballou, of Dalton, chaplain; William C. Reddy, of New York, judge-advocate; James S. Graham, of Rochester, inspector, and Robert Keith, of Troy, chief mustering officer, being the officers of, and Theodore L. Poole, of Syracuse, John Beattie, of New York, Herman W. Thum, of New York, William H. Bright, of Utica, and I. Samuel Johnson, of Warsaw, being the elected members of the council of administration of, and their associates, the delegates from subordinate posts, to the department encampment of the voluntary association, known as the Grand Army of the Republic, within the limits of the state of New York, and their successors as such officers and delegates, are hereby created a body politic and corporate, in fact and in name, by the name of "The Department of New York Grand Army of the Republic," and as such shall have the right to sue and be sued, to purchase and hold, and to take by gift, devise and bequest, real and personal estate, not to exceed in the aggregate, in value, the sum of one hundred thousand dollars, and to sell and dispose of the same as occasion may require, to have a corporate seal and at pleasure to alter and change the same, and to have succession, that is, this charter shall not determine nor said corporate existence cease except by act of legislature, so long as there shall be one hundred or more members of said Grand Army of the Republic in good standing under its rules, residing within the limits of the state of New York, who shall desire the continuance of the same.

§ 2. The objects of said corporation shall be:

1. To preserve and strengthen those kind and fraternal feelings which bind together the soldiers, sailors and marines who united to suppress the late rebellion, and to perpetuate the memory and history of those who died that the nation might live.

2. To assist such former comrades in arms who may need help and protection, and to extend needful aid to the widows and orphans of our deceased comrades.

3. To maintain true allegiance to the United States of America, based upon a paramount respect for, and fidelity to, the national constitution and laws, to discountenance whatever tends to weaken loyalty, incites to insurrection, treason or rebellion, or in any manner impairs the efficiency and permanency of our free institutions, and to encourage the spread of universal liberty, equal rights and justice to all men.

§ 3. The management and disposition of the property of said corporation shall be vested in a board of fifteen trustees, to be composed of the fifteen persons first named in section one of this act, and their successors in office, who shall be annually selected in the manner provided for by the rules and regulations of the Grand Army of the Republic. Said trustees shall severally hold office till their respective successors shall have duly qualified in accordance with said rules and regulations. They shall constitute, and be known, also, as the "department council of administration," and shall have all the powers vested in department councils of administration by said rules and regulations. Except for the defrayment of the necessary and current expenses of said corporation, and for salaries, the appropriation of funds by said trustees shall be by and with the consent of a majority of the members of said corporation, who shall be present at regularly called meetings or department encampments. Vacancies in the board of trustees shall be filled in the manner provided in rules and regulations aforesaid for filling vacancies in department councils of administration.

§ 4. The corporation hereby created shall have the powers of and be subject to the restrictions prescribed in title three, chapter eighteen, part one of the Revised Statutes of the state of New York.

§ 5. When said corporation shall be finally dissolved, its property remaining after payment of all its debts, shall become the property of the state of New York and be preserved in a museum to be provided therefor. (a. L. 1889, c. 92)

2. Room in Capitol, Etc. (Pub. Bldgs.)

§ 5. *Room for the Grand Army of the Republic* — There shall continue to be set apart and suitably furnished by the superintendent of public buildings, the rooms in the capitol now under the charge of the commander of the Grand Army of the Republic for the department of New York, and such rooms so furnished shall remain under the charge of such commander and such officers who are members of such department as he or his successors may appoint, and be used by him and them for the purpose of storing the supplies and property of such Grand Army and its relics and mementoes of the war and arranging and preserving the history of individuals belonging to organizations of the state who served in the army, navy or marine corps, during the late war of the rebellion, or of citizens of this state who served in the regular army, navy or marine corps of the United States, which such Grand Army of the Republic may collect and desire to preserve as a part of the history of the state. Such records shall be accessible at all times under suitable rules and regulations to members of the Grand Army of the Republic and others engaged in collecting historical information. The commander of the Grand Army of the Republic for the department of New York shall annually report to the legislature, on or before April first, such portions of the transactions of the Grand Army of the Republic as he deems to be of interest to that organization and to the people of the state.

By State Printing Law, § 11, one thousand copies of the report are to be printed for the use of the Grand Army.

EXEMPTION

1. From Military Duty (Mil.)

Section 1. *Persons subject to military duty; exemptions —* All able-bodied male citizens, between the ages of eighteen and forty-five years, who are residents of this state, shall constitute the militia, subject to the following exemptions:

   *   *   *   *   *   *

3. All persons in the army, navy or volunteer forces of the United States, or who have been honorably discharged therefrom.

  *   *   *   *   *   *   *

Annotation

by reason of honorable discharge. A. G. O., 342–44 [1865].

2. From Poll Tax (Vill.)

§ 103. *Poll tax —* Unless a village decides not to impose a poll tax, all men, between the ages of twenty-one and seventy years, residing in the village, are liable to an annual poll tax of one dollar, except exempt firemen, active members of the fire de-

partment of the village, honorably discharged soldiers and sailors
who lost an arm or leg in the service of the United States during
the late war, or who are unable to perform manual labor by reason
of injuries received or disabilities incurred in such service, clergymen and priests of every denomination, paupers, idiots and
lunatics.   *   *

ANNOTATIONS

receipt of pension not sufficient proof of disability.   A. G. R., 1903:337–38;
A. G. R., 1904:208–09.

probably applicable to village incorporated under special act.   A. G. R.,
1904:302–04.

3. FROM LABOR FOR REMOVAL OF SNOW (Highway.)

§ 79. *Assessment of labor for the removal of snow* — The town
superintendent of a town in which the obstructions in the highways caused by snow shall be removed by the labor of persons
and corporations liable to assessment in each town for highway
taxes, pursuant to the last preceding section shall annually on or
before November fifteenth divide the town into a convenient number of highway districts and file a description thereof in the office
of the town clerk, and before such date shall make an estimate
giving the probable number of days' labor needed during the
following year for the removal of obstructions caused by snow in
the highways and for the prevention of such obstructions and shall
assess one day's labor upon each male inhabitant of the town
above the age of twenty-one years, excepting honorably discharged
soldiers and sailors who lost an arm or a leg in the military or
naval service of the United States, or who are unable to perform
manual labor, by reason of injuries received or disabilities incurred in such service, members of any fire company formed or
created pursuant to any statute, and situated within such town,
persons seventy years of age or over, clergymen and priests of
every denomination, paupers, idiots and lunatics. The balance
of such estimated number of days shall be apportioned and assessed upon the estate, real and personal, of every inhabitant of
the town, including corporations liable to taxation therein, as the
same shall appear by the last assessment-roll of the town, and
upon each parcel or tract of land owned by the nonresidents, excepting such as are occupied by an inhabitant of the town, which

shall be assessed to the occupant. The assessment of labor for personal property must be in the district in which the owner resides, and real property in the district where it is situated, except that the assessment of labor upon the property of corporations may be in any district or districts of the town, and such labor may be worked out or commuted for as if the corporation were an inhabitant of the district; but the real property within an incorporated city or village exempted from the jurisdiction of the town superintendent, and personal property of an inhabitant thereof, shall not be assessed for such labor by the town superintendent. Whenever the assessors of any town shall have omitted to assess any inhabitant, corporation or property therein, the town superintendent shall assess the same, and apportion the labor as above provided. (Added by L. 1909, c. 488; a. L. 1910, c. 136.)

ANNOTATION

proper evidence of disability. A. G. R., 1889:73-74.

4. From Execution; Pensions, Etc. (C. C. P.)

§ 1393. *Military pay, rewards, etc., exempt from execution and other legal proceedings* — The pay and bounty of a non-commissioned officer, musician or private in the military or naval service of the United States or the state of New York; a land warrant, pension or other reward heretofore or hereafter granted by the United States, or by a state, for military or naval services; a sword, horse, medal, emblem or device of any kind presented as a testimonial for services rendered in the military or naval service of the United States or a state; and the uniform, arms and equipments which were used by a person in that service, are also exempt from levy and sale, by virtue of an execution, and from seizure for non-payment of taxes, or in any other legal proceeding; except that real property purchased with the proceeds of a pension granted by the United States for military or naval services, and owned by the pensioner, or by his wife or widow, is subject to seizure and sale for the collection of taxes or assessments lawfully levied thereon.

ANNOTATIONS

Bounty and pay.

a. Exempted.

while in hands of person to whom paid. A. G. R., 1895:229.

given by pensioner to wife and used by her in purchasing real estate. Whiting v. Barrett, 7 Lans. 106 [1872].

received by deserter enlisting under assumed name. Youmans v. Boomhower, 3 T. & C. 21 [1874].

being exempt, gift by recipient of it to his wife not in fraud of creditors. Youmans v. Boomhower, 3 T. & C. 21 [1874]; Spaulding v. Keyes, 125 N. Y. 113 [1889].

property purchased with money received as retired pay. A. G. R., 1910 [Dec. 23].

b. Not exempted.

property purchased with bounty money or pay. A. G. R., 1902:286; A. G. R., 1911 [Mar. 27]: People ex rel. Kenny v. Reilly, 41 A. D. 378 [1899].

Pension. Wildrick v. DeVinney, 18 W. D. 355 [1884].

exemption, if attacked, must be enforced by action. King, in re, 24 A. D 605 [1897].

waiver of provisions of act estops from relying on it thereafter. Omans v. Beeman, 66 Misc. 625 [1906].

" seizure " defined. Strohm, in re, 51 Misc. 481 [1910].

exemption personal to pensioner. A. G. R., 1894:215–18.

a. Exempted.

deposited in bank by pensioner in his own name. Burgett v. Fancher, 35 Hun 647 [1885]; Stockwell v. Bank of Malone, 36 Hun 583 [1885]; A. G. R., 1889:307–08.

loaned on bond and mortgage. A. G. R., 1890:135.

in whatever form found during pensioner's lifetime. A. G. R., 1895:225–26.

so long as it can be distinguished from other money. A. G. R., 1893:211.

not assets in executor's hands and not liable for payment of debts of deceased veteran. Hodge v. Leaning, 2 Dem. Surr. 553 [1884].

contra; if loaned on note, amount collected thereon is assets. Beecher v. Barber, 6 Dem. Surr. 129 [1888].

cannot be taken from father for support of his pauper child. St. Lawrence State Hospital v. Fowler, 15 Misc. 159 [1895]; aff'd 13 A. D. 436 [1897].

b. Not exempted.

used in business and losing its identity. A. G. R., 1891:208; Wygant v. Smith, 2 Lans. 185 [1869].

mother's pension, after her death, in favor of decedents not constituting her immediate family. Winans, in re, 5 Dem. Surr. 138 [1887].

deposited in bank and certificate of deposit taken in return. Kennedy, in re, 1 Con. Surr. 181 [1888]; Beecher v. Barber, 6 Dem. Surr. 129 [1888].

paid as interest does not exempt principal to its amount; nor when expended in improvements to real estate when assessed valuation of property is not thereby exempted. A. G. R., 1892:249.

Pension bought property.
a. Exempt.
   to amount put into property, not surplus. Countryman v. Countryman, 28
      Supp. 258 [1893].
   occupied as home by pensioner and family. Buffum v. Forster, 77 Hun 27
      [1894]; Yates County National Bank v. Carpenter, 119 N. Y. 550 [1890].
   where purchased by soldier's widow with pension money due her late
      husband. Tyler v. Ballard, 31 Misc. 540 [1900].
b. Not exempted.
   conveyed by grantee to his wife upon her oral agreement to reconvey;
      not exempt as against wife's creditors. Fritz v. Worden, 20 A. D. 241
      [1897].
   exemption waived by mortgaging property. Monroe v. Button, 20 Misc. 494
      [1897].
c. Loss of exemption.
   surety on bail bond may claim exemption by reason of purchase of property
      with pension money, although stating in the justification that it was
      not exempt. King v. Warren, 42 Misc. 317 [1903].
   contra; exemption may be renounced. McMahon v. Cook, 107 A. D. 150
      [1905].

5. FROM TAXATION; REAL PROPERTY BOUGHT WITH PENSION
(Tax.)

§ 4. *Exemption from taxation* — The following property shall
be exempt from taxation:

    *   *   *   *   *   *   *

5. All property exempt by law from execution, other than an
exempt homestead. But real property purchased with the proceeds of a pension granted by the United States for military or
naval services, and owned by the pensioner, or by his wife
or widow, is subject to taxation as herein provided. Such
property shall be assessed in the same manner as other real property in the tax districts. At the meeting of the assessors to hear
the complaints concerning assessments, a verified application for
the exemption of such real property from taxation may be presented to them by or on behalf of the owner thereof, which application must show the facts on which the exemption is claimed, including the amount of pension money used in or toward the purchase of such property. No such exemption on account of pension money shall be allowed in excess of five thousand dollars. If
the assessors are satisfied that the applicant is entitled to the exemption, and that the amount of pension money exempt to the extent authorized by this subdivision used in the purchase of such
property equals or exceeds the assessed valuation thereof, they

shall enter the word " exempt " upon the assessment-roll opposite the description of such property. If the amount of such pension money exempt to the extent authorized by this subdivision used in the purchase of the property is less than the assessed valuation, they shall enter upon the assessment-roll the words " exempt to the extent of .... dollars " (naming the amount), and thereupon such real property, to the extent of the exemption entered by the assessors, shall be exempt from state, county and general municipal taxation, but shall be taxable for local school purposes, and for the construction and maintenance of streets and highways. If no application for exemption be granted, the property shall be subject to taxation for all purposes. The entries above required shall be made and continued in each assessment of the property so long as it is exempt from taxation for any purpose. The provisions herein, relating to the assessment and exemption of property purchased with a pension, apply and shall be enforced in each municipal corporation authorized to levy taxes.   (a. L. 1914, c. 278.)

exempt.   ANNOTATIONS
a. Purchase.
    with widow's pension. People ex rel. Scott v. Williams, 6 Misc. 185 [1893].
    with proceeds of pension certificate. A. G. R., 1892:171–72.
    by committee of lunatic in his own name, with lunatic's pension money.
        People ex rel. Canaday v. Williams, 90 Hun 501 [1895].
    with pension money so far as it can be traced or distinguished. A. G. R.,
        1894:215 18; A. G. R., 1895:343–44.
    with retired pay. A. G. R., 1910:682–84.
    by pensioner with pension money, conveyed by him to his wife and re-
        conveyed by her to pensioner. A. G. R., 1896:206–08.
    must be purchased during pensioner's life. A. G. R., 1896:78–81.
    by pensioner and conveyed by him to his wife before his death. A. G. R.,
        1902:280–81.
b. Tenancy.
    must be occupied by pensioner, his wife or widow. A. G. R., 1902:280–81.
    but part may be rented. A. G. R., 1910:673–75.
c. Extent of exemption.
    assessment on exempt property void. Lapolt v. Maltby, 10 Misc. 330 [1894].
    where pensioner's wife is tenant with him by the entirety, assessment in
        his name set aside. Toole v. Oneida County Supervisors, 13 A. D. 471
        [1897].
    to extent of amount invested, when assessed as one item; not intent of
        statute to make pro rata basis, depending upon extent of occupancy.
        A. G. R., 1911 [Jan. 31].

from tax to meet bonds for purpose of installing village water system. A. G. R., 1911 [May 15].

d. Personal property.
coal purchased with pension money and delivered at pensioner's house, exempt from levy for collection of school tax. Strong v. Walton, 47 A. D. 114 [1900].

e. Claim, by verified application to assessors. People ex rel. McGrane v. Rilley, 21 Misc. 363 [1897]; Baumgarten, in re, 39 A. D. 174 [1899]; Toal v. New York, City of, 175 N. Y. 69 [1901].
(personalty.) Clark v. Smith, 31 Misc. 490 [1900].

f. Exempt real property taxable for schools and highways. A. G. R., 1908: 494-95; A. G. R., 1909:631-33; People ex rel. Kenny v. Reilly, 41 A. D. 378 [1899]; Strong v. Walter, 47 A. D. 114 [1900].

g. Disabilities of owner.
may vote on incorporation or reincorporation of village. A. G. R., 1898: may not vote on proposition at village election. A. G. R., 1908:539-41. 108-09.

not exempt.

a. Purchase.
by widow with proceeds of widow's pension. A. G. R., 1909:572-73.
by child with proceeds of minor's pension. A. G. R., 1907:437-39; A. G. R., 1909:554-55.
with bounty money or pay. A. G. R., 1911 [Mar. 27]; People ex rel. Kenny v. Reilly, 41 A. D. 378 [1898].

b. Residue above part purchased with pension money. Peek, in re, 80 Hun 122 [1894]; Murphy, in re, 9 Misc. 647 [1894].
(bounty.) People ex rel. Breed v. Wells, 10 Misc. 195 [1894].
if tax voluntarily paid upon whole property, owner estopped from recovering it from county. McKibben v. Oneida County, 25 A. D. 361 [1898].

6. FROM CERTAIN TAXABLE TRANSFERS   (Tax.)

§ 221. *Exceptions and limitations.*— Any property devised or bequeathed * * * to any person who is a bishop or to any religious, educational, charitable, missionary, benevolent, hospital or infirmary corporation, wherever incorporated, including corporations organized exclusively for bible or tract purposes and corporations organized for the enforcement of laws relating to children or animals or real property to a municipal corporation in trust for a specific public purpose shall be exempted from and not subject to the provisions of this article. There shall also be exempted from and not subject to the provisions of this article personal property other than money or securities bequeathed to a corporation or associations wherever incorporated or located, organized exclusively for the moral or mental improvement of men or women or for scientific, literary, library, patriotic, cemetery or historical purposes or for two or more of such purposes and used exclusively for carrying out one or more of such purposes. But no such corporation or association shall be entitled to such exemption if any officer, member or employee thereof shall receive or may be lawfully entitled to receive any pecuniary profit from the operations thereof except reasonable compensation for services in effecting one or more of such purposes or as proper beneficiaries of its strictly charitable purposes; or if the organization thereof for any such avowed purpose be a guise or pretense for directly or indirectly making any other pecuniary profit for such corporation or association or for any of its members or employees or if it be not in good faith organized or conducted exclusively for one or more of such purposes * * * (a. L. 1910, c. 600, c. 706; L. 1911, c. 732; L. 1916, c. 548; L. 1917, c. 53.)

THE FLAG

1. On Schools, Salute, Etc.   (Educ.)

§ 710. *Purchase and display of flag* — It shall be the duty of the school authorities of every public school in the several cities and school districts of the state to purchase a United States flag, flag-staff and the necessary appliances therefor, and to display such flag upon or near the public school building during school hours, and at such other times as such school authorities may direct.

§ 711. *Rules and regulations* — The said school authorities shall establish rules and regulations for the proper custody, care and display of the flag, and when the weather will not permit it to be otherwise displayed, it shall be placed conspicuously in the principal room in the school-house.

§ 712. *Commissioner of education shall prepare program* — 1. It shall be the duty of the commissioner of education to prepare, for the use of the public schools of the state, a program providing for a salute to the flag and such other patriotic exercises as may be deemed by him to be expedient, under such regulations and instructions as may best meet the varied requirements of the different grades in such schools.

2. It shall also be his duty to make special provision for the observance in the public schools of Lincoln's birthday, Washington's birthday, Memorial day and Flag day, and such other legal holidays of like character as may be hereafter designated by law when the legislature makes an appropriation therefor.

2. On the Capitol   (Pub. Bldgs.)

§ 4. *Powers and duties of superintendent* — The superintendent shall:

*   *   *   *   *   *   *

5. Cause the flag of the United States and the state flag bearing the arms of the state, to be displayed upon the capitol building during the daily sessions of the legislature and on public occasions, and cause the necessary flagstaffs to be erected therefor. Cause the flag of the United States to be appropriately displayed at all times in the Senate chamber and in the Assembly chamber The necessary expenses incurred thereby shall be paid out of the treasury on the warrant of the comptroller.

*   *   *   *   *   *   *

3. No Foreign Flag to be Displayed   (Pub. Bldgs.)

§ 81. *Display of foreign flags on public buildings* — It shall not be lawful to display the flag or emblem of any foreign country upon any state, county or municipal building; provided, however, that whenever any foreigner shall become the guest of the United States, the state or any city, upon public proclamation by the governor or mayor of such city, the flag of the country of which such public guest shall be a citizen may be displayed upon such public buildings.

4. American Flag at Polling Places   (El.)

§ 300-a. *Display of American flag* — The American flag shall be displayed in each polling place in this state by the board of inspectors during the hours when such boards are in session. The board, body or officer now charged with the duty of defraying the expenses of conducting primaries and elections shall furnish said

flag, which shall be approximately three feet by five feet in size.
(Added L. 1913, c. 783.)

5. IN COURT ROOMS OF INFERIOR CRIMINAL COURTS IN CITY
OF NEW YORK   (L. 1910, c. 659)

§ 116. *American flag to be displayed in court rooms* — It shall
be the duty of the officers, employee or person having the care of
any court room used for any magistrate or court under this act
to display the American flag supplied under the preceding section
in each such room during all hours that any court provided for in
this act is in session. Any officer, employee or person neglecting
to comply with the requirements of this section shall thereby incur
a penalty of ten dollars for each day that such neglect continues.
(Added L. 1917, c. 399.)

FLAG, IMPROPER USE OF — *See* Protection
HEADSTONES — *See* Burial

HOME AT BATH

ARTICLE 5   (Pub. Bldgs.)

§ 60. *Trustees* — The property heretofore conveyed to the state
by the corporation known as the Grand Army of the Republic
soldiers' home of New York, and all property heretofore or hereafter acquired by the state for the same purpose, shall continue to
be known as the New York State soldiers and sailors' home, and
shall continue to be under the management and control of a board
of trustees consisting of twelve members, of which the governor,
attorney-general and the commander of the department of New
York, Grand Army of the Republic, shall be *ex officio* members;
and the remaining nine members shall be reputable citizens of the
state appointed by the governor, by and with the advice and consent of the senate, and each shall hold office for three years. No
trustee shall receive any compensation for his services as such
trustee or otherwise, except the trustee elected to act as secretary
who may receive a reasonable annual compensation for his services, to be fixed by the board, with the approval of the comptroller,
not exceeding the sum of two hundred and fifty dollars. The

board shall annually elect by ballot a president, secretary, treasurer and executive committee, but the offices of secretary and treasurer may be held by one trustee or separately as the board may determine. The board shall be known as the board of trustees of the New York state soldiers and sailors' home.

§ 61. *Powers of trustees* — The board of trustees shall have possession of all property belonging to or constituting such home and may complete the buildings therein already commenced or hereafter to be erected, and keep them in readiness for occupation with any funds appropriated therefor or that may come into their hands for such purpose, and may pay any existing indebtedness of such corporation which shall be or might become a lien upon such property or any part thereof. The board may make contracts in its name, subject to the approval of the comptroller, for work and materials for the completion of the buildings on such property, the furnishing thereof and of supplies for use and consumption therein, but shall spend no money and incur no indebtedness for such purpose beyond the appropriation previously made therefor by the legislature. It may adopt rules and regulations, subject to like approval, specifying the duties of the officers of the home, the government of its inmates, fixing the terms and conditions of admission thereto and the cause and manner of expulsion therefrom. The board may require and take in its name any security by way of bond or otherwise from any person appointed or elected by it, for the faithful performance of his duties, and for truly accounting for all moneys or property received by him for or on account of the board of trustees or in the performance of such duties. And the said board shall have power to organize and maintain a band, the same to be paid for out of the maintenance funds of the home, not exceeding six thousand dollars per annum.

§ 62. *Sale of liquor at home* — The board of trustees, upon complying with the provisions of the liquor tax law, are hereby authorized to sell ale and beer to the members of said home, upon the premises of said home, under such rules and regulations as said trustees shall prescribe, and the provisions of clause one, section twenty-three and clause six of section twenty-nine of said liquor tax law, shall not apply to the New York state soldiers and sailors' home.

§ 63. *Disposition of proceeds of sale* — The board of trustees shall expend the net proceeds of such sales for the support of the library and reading room of said home and for such other purposes as they shall deem best for the comfort and amusement of the inmates of said home.

§ 64. *Admission to home* — Every honorably discharged soldier or sailor who served in the army or navy of the United States during the late rebellion, the Spanish-American war or the insurrection in the Philippines, who enlisted from the state of New York, or who shall have been a resident of this state for one year preceding his application for admission, and who shall need the aid or benefit of such home in consequence of physical disability or other cause within the scope of the regulations of the board, shall be entitled to admission thereto, subject to the conditions, limitations and penalties prescribed by the rules and regulations of the board, provided preference of admission be given to veterans of the civil war in case of lack of accommodations. The board of trustees shall require an applicant for admission to such home to file with the application for admission his own affidavit of residence and such affidavit shall be received as prima facie evidence of the residence of such applicant in any action or proceeding against the county of his residence, in which the residence of such applicant shall be material. (a. L. 1912, c. 190.)

§ 65. *Transfer of inmates to State hospital* —Any soldier or sailor regularly admitted into the home found to be insane, may be transferred by an order of the president and secretary of the board of trustees and the superintendent of the home to any state hospital for the insane, there to remain at the expense of the home until legally discharged, and such expense shall be paid out of the maintenance fund of the home, at the same rate as is charged for the support of the county insane.

§ 66. *Annual report* — Such board shall, annually, on or before January fifteenth, make to the legislature a detailed report of all its receipts and expenditures and of all its proceedings for the previous year, with full estimates for the coming year verified by the president and treasurer.

§ 11. *Soldiers and sailors' home exempted* — The New York state soldiers and sailors' home is hereby exempted from the man-

agement and control of the state board of charities, and in respect
to said institution said board is hereafter only to exercise its constitutional right to visit and inspect.

ANNOTATIONS.

ex-officio trustees abolished and home placed under supervision of fiscal
supervisor by L. 1909, c. 149. A. G. R., 1910 [May 7].
contra; J. A., Opinion No. 2, 1911.
may not exchange tallow with private concern for soap; state finance law
requires sales and purchases to be for cash. A. G. R., 1910 [May 3].
residents neither gain nor lose a voting residence. A. G. R., 1892:237;
A. G. R., 1895:297–98; A. G. R., 1898:278–83; Silvey v. Lindsay, 107
N. Y. 55 [1887]; Smith, in re, 44 Misc. 384 [1904].

HOME AT OXFORD
ARTICLE 13 (St. Char.)

§ 250. *Establishment of home* — The home for the aged dependent veteran and his wife, veterans' mothers and widows and
army nurses, known as "New York state woman's relief corps
home," is hereby continued.

§ 251. *Board of managers* — The home shall be under the control of a board of seven managers, appointed in accordance with
the provisions of section fifty-one of this chapter, a majority of
whom shall be appointed from the members of the grand army
of the republic of the department of New York and the woman's
relief corps, auxiliary to the grand army of the republic, department of New York. Appointments shall be so made that there
will be at all times four women and three men members of said
board. (a. L. 1910, c. 449.)

§ 252. *Official oath* — Before entering on their duties the said
managers shall respectively take and subscribe to the usual oath
of office, which oath may be taken and subscribed before the judge
of any court of record of this state, or any notary public having
a seal, and shall be filed in the office of the secretary of state.

§ 253. *Organization of board* — It shall be the duty of said
board of managers to elect a president, secretary and an executive
committee from their number. (Renumbered L. 1910, c. 449.)

§ 254. *Report to legislature* — Said board of managers shall annually on or before January fifteenth, make to the legislature a detailed report of its proceedings for the preceding fiscal year, together with a complete statement of its receipts and expenditures, the condition of the institution, and full estimates of the appropriation required for its maintenance, including therein ordinary repairs. It shall also include in its report a statement of any special appropriations required and the reasons therefor. (Renumbered L. 1910, c. 449.)

§ 255. *Admission to home* — Every honorably discharged soldier or sailor or marine who served in the army or navy of the United States, for a period not less than ninety days, during the war of the rebellion, and who shall have been a resident of this state for one year next preceding the application for admission, and the wife, widow and mother of any such honorably discharged soldier or sailor or marine, and army nurses who served in said army or navy and whose residence was at the time of the commencement of such service, or whose residence shall have been for one year next preceding his or her application for admission to said home within the state of New York, and who shall need the aid or benefit of said home in consequence of physical disability or other cause within the scope of the regulations of the board, shall be entitled to admission to said home after the approval of the application by the board of managers and subject to the conditions, limitations and penalties prescribed by the rules and regulations adopted by said board. Provided, however, said soldier or sailor or marine shall be a married man and shall be accompanied or attended by his wife during the time he may be an inmate of said home, and in case of the death of the wife, while an inmate of said home, the veteran may remain an inmate of said home with the consent of the superintendent, approved by the board of managers, but no wife or widow of a soldier or sailor or marine shall be admitted as an inmate of said home unless due and sufficient proof is presented of her marriage to such soldier or sailor or marine at least fifteen years prior to the date of such application. The board of managers shall require an applicant for admission to such home to file with the application for admission his own affidavit of residence and in addition thereto the affidavit of at least two householders in and residents of the county of which he claims at the time of such application to be a resident; and such affidavits shall on presentation be accepted and received as sufficient proof, unless contradicted, of the residence of such applicant in any actions or proceedings against such county in which such residence of such applicant is material. If, after having been an inmate of such home, an honorably discharged soldier, sailor or marine, or the wife or widow of an honorably discharged soldier, sailor or marine, or an army nurse, shall reassume his or her former residence in any county, or shall acquire a new residence in any other county, and shall become entitled to relief as provided by article six of the poor law, the poor authorities within whose jurisdiction such honorably discharged soldier, sailor or marine, or the wife or widow of an honorably discharged soldier, sailor or marine, or an army nurse, resides, may, instead of providing relief as required by the poor law, return him or her to such home, to be maintained therein. (a. L. 1912, c. 310.)

§ 256. *Powers of board of managers* — The board of managers shall have charge of all the affairs of the institution, with power to make all necessary by-laws, rules and regulations for its government and proper management, and for the admission and discharge of inmates. It shall have power to select a treasurer, to appoint and remove a superintendent of the institution, who shall be its chief executive officer. It shall also have power to appoint such other subordinate officers as may be necessary, and for just cause remove any or all of them from office. Under proper rules and regulations and in accordance with the provisions of the civil service law they may delegate the power to hire and discharge subordinate employees to the superintendent. (Renumbered L. 1910, c. 449.)

§ 257. *Record* — The board of managers shall keep in a book provided for that purpose and kept in the institution, a fair and full record of the doings of the board, which shall be open at all times to the inspection of its members and such other persons and officers of the state as are by law vested with the powers of visitation and inspection, or appointed by the governor, the legislature or other competent authority to make an inspection or investigation of the institution. (Renumbered L. 1910, c. 449.)

§ 258. *Gifts and bequests.* The board of managers may receive, retain and expend any money or other personal property given or bequeathed to the home for the purposes for which it is given or, if unaccompanied by conditions or limitations, for any of the purposes of the home or of the inmates thereof that the board shall deem advisable. (Added L. 1918, c. 86.)

ANNOTATIONS.

board of managers.

may not appoint one of their own number superintendent. A. G. R., 1897: 105–06.

may remove any employee, unprotected by civil service law, at regular or properly called special meeting. A. G. R., 1906:261–64.

pension money belonging to inmates may not be used for extra compensation or employment of extra help. A. G. R., 1905:391.

pension fund or donations made by individuals need not be turned into state treasury. A. G. R., 1911 [Apr. 5].

admission of soldier's widow

denied, where remarried to another soldier after 1880. A. G. R., 1899: 301–02.

thirty years' absence of husband entitles wife to be regarded presumptively as widow. A. G. R., 1909:868–70.

INCORPORATION

1. OF POSTS   (Benev. Orders.)

§ 2. *Organization* — Either of the following orders:

*   *   *   *   *   *

9. A post of the Grand Army of the Republic, chartered and installed according to the regulations of that organization;

*   *   *   *   *   *

May elect at any regular communication, convocation, encampment or other regular meeting thereof, by whatever name known, held in accordance with the constitution and general rules and regulations of such grand lodge, chapter, commandery or council, or other governing body to which it belongs, or with which it is connected, and in conformity to its own by-laws, if it has any, three trustees for such lodge, chapter, commandery, consistory, council, temple, post, court, tribe, grotto, aerie or camp, who shall be members thereof in full membership and in good and regular

standing therein; and may file in the office of the secretary of state
a certificate of such election, signed and acknowledged by the first
three elective officers of such lodge, chapter, commandery, consistory, council, temple, post, court, tribe, grotto or aerie, stating
the time and place of such election and that the same was regular,
the names of such trustees, and the term, severally, for which
they are elected to serve, and the name of the lodge, chapter, commandery, consistory, council, temple, post, court, tribe, grotto,
aerie or camp, for which they are elected. (a. L. 1909, c. 240,
§ 4; L. 1910, c. 420.)

§ 3. *Powers* — Such trustees may take, hold and convey by
and under the direction of such lodge, chapter, commandery, consistory, council, temple, post, aerie or camp, all the temporalities
and property belonging thereto, whether real or personal, and
whether given, granted or devised directly to it or to any person
or persons for it, or in trust for its use and benefit, and may sue
for and recover, hold and enjoy all the debts, demands, rights and
privileges, and all buildings and places of assemblage, with the
appurtenances, and all other estate and property belonging to it
in whatsoever manner the same may have been acquired, or in
whose name soever the same may be held, as fully as if the right
and title thereto had been originally vested in them; and may purchase and hold for the purpose of the lodge, chapter, commandery,
consistory, council, temple, aerie, post or camp, other real and
personal property, and demise, lease and improve the same. They
may also issue their bonds or other evidences of indebtedness in
such amounts and for such time and in such form as they shall
determine for the exclusive purpose of raising money to pay for
any real estate purchased and held by them, and for the improvement of the same, as hereinabove provided, and may mortgage
such real estate for the purpose of securing the bonds or other evidences of indebtedness so issued by them. The proceeds of such
bonds or other evidences of indebtedness shall be applied exclusively to pay for such real estate and the improvement thereof.
Every such lodge, chapter, commandery, consistory, council,
temple, post, aerie or camp may make rules and regulations, not
inconsistent with the laws of this state, or with the constitution
or general rules or laws of the grand lodge or other governing

body to which it is subordinate, for managing the temporal affairs thereof, and for the disposition of its property and other temporal concerns and revenue belonging to it, and the secretary and treasurer thereof, duly elected and installed according to its constitution and general regulations and law, shall, for the time being, be *ex officio* its secretary and treasurer. No board of trustees for any lodge, chapter, commandery, consistory, council, temple, aerie, post or camp filing the certificate aforesaid, shall be deemed to be dissolved for any neglect or omission to elect a trustee annually, or fill any vacancy or vacancies that may occur or exist at any time in said board, but it shall and may be lawful for said lodge, chapter, commandery, consistory, council, temple, aerie, post or camp to fill such vacancy or vacancies at any regular communication thereafter to be held, and till a vacancy arising from the expiration of the term of office of a trustee is filled, as aforesaid, he shall continue to hold the said office and perform the duties thereof.   (a. L. 1910, c. 420.)

§ 4. *Terms of trustees* — * * *   If other than a lodge or chapter of Free and Accepted Masons, the trustees first elected shall be divided by lot by the officers making the certificate of election, so that the term of one will expire in one year, one in two years, and one in three years thereafter.   One trustee shall annually thereafter be elected by such lodge, chapter, commandery, consistory, council, temple or post, by ballot, in the same manner and at the same time as the first three officers thereof severally are or shall be elected according to its constitution, by-laws and regulations; and a certificate of such election under the hands of such officers and the seal of the lodge, chapter, commandery, consistory, council, temple or post, if it has any, shall be made, and shall be evidence of such election and entitle the person so elected to act as trustee.   If any trustee dies, resigns, demits, is suspended or expelled, removes from the state, or becomes incapacitated for performing the duties of his office, his office shall be deemed vacant.   Such lodge, chapter, commandery, consistory, council, temple or post may, at any regular communication, convocation, encampment or other regular meeting, by whatever name known, fill any vacancy in the office of trustee, by ballot, which election shall be certified in like manner and with like effect as an annual election, and the person so elected shall hold his office during the unexpired term of the trustee, whose place he was elected to fill.

§ 5. *Powers of trustees* — Such trustees shall have the care, management and control of all the temporalities and property of the lodge, chapter, commandery, consistory, council, temple or post, and they shall not sell, convey, mortgage or dispose of any property except by and under its direction, duly had or given at a regular or stated communication, convocation, encampment or meeting thereof, according to its constitution and general regulations. They shall at all times obey and abide by the directions, orders and resolutions of such lodge, chapter, commandery, consistory, council, temple or post, duly passed at any regular or stated communication, convocation, encampment or meeting thereof not in conflict with the constitution and laws of this state or of the grand body to which it shall be subordinate, or of such lodge, chapter, commandery, consistory, council, temple or post.

*   *   *   *   *   *   *

§ 6. *Reorganization* — Any such lodge, chapter, commandery, consistory, council, temple or post heretofore incorporated by the laws of this state, or thereby heretofore enabled to take and hold real or personal property, or both, may surrender its act of incorporation, charter or privilege so conferred upon it, and may become enabled to take and hold real or personal property, or both, under the provisions of this chapter, on making and filing a certificate in the manner specified in this chapter, and stating therein, in addition to what is required in such a certificate, the surrender of such act of incorporation, charter or privilege, specifying the same. The property theretofore held and possessed by it shall be fully vested in its trustees, who shall have all the rights, powers and privileges, and be subject to all the provisions of this chapter.

§ 7. *Joint corporations* — Any * * * post of the Grand Army of the Republic chartered and installed according to the regulations of that organization; * * * may unite in forming a corporation for the purpose of acquiring, constructing, maintaining and managing a hall, temple or other building, or a home for the aged and indigent members of such order and their dependent widows and orphans, and of creating, collecting, and maintaining a library for the use of the bodies uniting to form such corporation. Each body hereafter uniting to form such corporation shall at a regular meeting thereof, held in accordance with its constitution and general rules and regulations or by-laws, elect a member thereof for a term of one, two or three years, as the rules, regulations and by-laws of the body may prescribe, to represent it in such corporation.

If the bodies uniting to form such corporation do not exceed thirty in number, then each representative so elected shall be a trustee of said corporation, and shall make and file in the office of the clerk of the county where such building is, or is to be located, a certificate of such election signed and acknowledged by the highest two officers of the body electing him, stating the time and place of the election, its regularity, the name of the trustee, and the name of the body from which he was elected. If the bodies uniting to form such corporation shall exceed thirty in number then the representatives elected as hereinbefore provided, shall assemble annually at a time and place fixed by the constitution, by-laws, rules and regulations of the corporation, and shall elect from amongst themselves a president, vice-president, secretary and treasurer, each of whom shall be *ex officio* trustees of the corporation, and not less than nine or more than twenty-four other trustees. In case only two bodies unite to form such corporation, the number of trustees to be elected from each body shall not be less than one or more than three, who shall be elected in the manner above prescribed and whose certificate of election shall be made and filed in the manner above prescribed.

The trustees so elected shall make, acknowledge and file with the secretary of state a certificate stating the name of the corporation to be formed, its purposes and objects, the names and places of residence of the trustees, the names of the bodies which they respectively represent, the names of the bodies uniting to form the corporation and their location, and the name of the town, village or city and the county where such building is, or is to be located; and thereupon the several bodies so uniting shall be a corporation for the purposes specified in such certificate. (a. L. 1915, c. 492.)

§ 8. *Trustees* — The persons executing such certificate and named therein, shall be the board of trustees of such corporation. If but two bodies unite to form such corporation, its by-laws may prescribe the terms of office of the trustees. If more than two bodies so unite, the trustees shall divide themselves by lot into three classes, not including, however, the president, vice-president, secretary and treasurer, if such officers shall have been elected as provided in section seven hereof, who shall be one year trustees, so that the term of office of the first class shall expire in one year; the term of office of the second class, in two years; and the term of office of the third class, in three years, provided, however, that no trustee shall continue as such after he has ceased to be a representative.

On a vacancy occurring in the office of a trustee of such corporation, the body which he represented shall fill such vacancy, provided the bodies uniting to form such corporation do not exceed thirty in number, and the person so chosen shall hold office for three years, if chosen on the expiration of the term of his predecessor, and otherwise, until the expiration of the original term.

But if the bodies uniting to form such corporation exceed thirty in number, then any vacancy occurring by reason of the expiration of a term or by failure of any trustee to be re-elected as a representative, shall be filled for three years or for the balance of the unexpired term as the case may be, by the representatives in annual session; and any vacancy occurring otherwise than as above specified, shall be filled until the next annual meeting of the representatives by the body that has lost representation by reason of the vacancy, when it shall be filled by said representatives for the remainder of the unexpired term. If the bodies uniting to form such corporation exceed thirty in number, then the representatives, but if less than thirty in number then the board of trustees, may admit or prescribe rules and regulations for the admission as members of such corporation of other bodies chartered or instituted by the same general governing body as any of the bodies named in such certificate, or by any superior or higher jurisdiction or governing body of the order to which any of such bodies belong, and may prescribe rules and regulations for the withdrawal, expulsion or suspension of any body or bodies having membership in such corporation when the representatives of such corporation exceed thirty in number.

Where the bodies uniting to form such corporation do not exceed thirty in number, the board of trustees shall fix the term of office of such trustees elected to represent new members of such corporation at one, two or three years, and shall so apportion such new trustees that as nearly as possible the terms of office of one-third of the trustees of such corporation shall expire annually. * * *.

Every corporation formed under this chapter must file annually immediately after its annual meeting, in the clerk's office of the county where such building is or is to be located, a certificate giving the names and addresses of the principal officers of the corporation and the names and addresses of the members of the board of trustees, and the names and location of all bodies admitted to or withdrawn or expelled from membership since the filing of the last preceding certificate.

§ 9. *Powers of joint corporations* — Such corporation may acquire real property in the town, village or city in which such hall, home, temple or building is or is to be located, and erect such building or buildings thereupon for the uses and purposes of the corporation, as the trustees may deem necessary, or repair, rebuild or reconstruct any building or buildings that may be thereupon and furnish and complete such rooms therein as may appear necessary for the use of such bodies or for any other purpose for which the corporation is formed; and may rent to other persons any portion of such building or real property for business or other purposes. Until such real property shall be acquired or such building erected or made ready for use, the corporation may rent and sublet such rooms or apartments in such town, village or city as may be suitable or convenient for the use of the bodies mentioned in such certificate, or of such other bodies as may desire to use them, and the board of trustees may determine the terms and conditions on which rooms and apartments in such building or buildings, when erected, or which may be leased, shall be used and occupied. Before such corporation composed of not more than thirty bodies shall purchase or sell any real property, or erect or repair any building or buildings thereupon, and before it shall purchase any building or part of a building for the use of a corporation, it shall submit to the bodies constituting the corporation, the proposition to make such

sale or purchase, or to erect or repair any such building or buildings, or to rent any building or part thereof, for the use of the
corporation; and unless such proposition receives the approval of
two-thirds of the bodies constituting the corporation, such proposition shall not be carried into effect. The evidence of the approval of such proposition by any such body shall be a certificate
to that effect signed by the presiding officer and secretary of the
body, or the officers discharging duties corresponding to those of
the presiding officer and secretary, under the seal of such body.
But where land is purchased for the purpose of erecting a hall,
home or temple thereon, the buildings upon such land at the time
of such purchase may be sold by the trustees without such consent.
The powers of the board of trustees of every corporation created
hereunder and composed of more than thirty bodies, respecting
sales, purchases and repairs, shall be fixed by the by-laws adopted
by the representatives of the various bodies composing such corporation, or shall be determined by such representatives when
assembled in annual session. Every corporation created hereunder
shall have power to enforce, at law or in equity, any legal contract
which it may make with any of the bodies composing it respecting
the care and maintenance of members or other dependents of such
body, the same as if such body or bodies were not members of the
corporation. Any corporation created hereunder shall have power
to take and hold real and personal estate by purchase, gift, devise
or bequest subject to the provisions of law relating to devises and
bequests by last will and testament or otherwise. (a. L. 1913,
c. 11.)

§ 10. *Mortgaging property* — If the funds of the corporation
shall not be sufficient to pay for any real property purchased by
the board of trustees in pursuance of law, or for the construction,
repair or rebuilding of a suitable building or buildings, and the
finishing or furnishing of apartments therefor, the corporation
may issue its bonds bearing interest, semi-annually, for such
additional sum as may be required therefor, and may execute to
any such trustee or trustees, as the board may select, a mortgage
upon its real property as security for the payment of such bonds.
The proceeds of such bonds shall be applied to the payment of
debts of the corporation incurred by the purchase of such real

property, or the construction and repair of a building or buildings thereupon or the finishing or furnishing of apartments therein. Any of the bodies specified in section seven may invest its funds in the bonds authorized by this section to be issued. Such corporation shall have authority also to borrow of any person or corporation such sum as in the judgment of its board of trustees may be required to pay the cost of the construction, repair, rebuilding or reconstruction of any such building or buildings, and the finishing or furnishing of apartments therein, and to secure the payment of any moneys so borrowed, and to execute and deliver its bond for the sum so borrowed, and to secure the payment of the same by mortgage upon its real property as collateral thereto. (a. L. 1911, c. 307.)

§ 11. *Reincorporation of joint corporations* — A corporation heretofore organized, the members whereof represent lodges or bodies in any of the benevolent or fraternal orders mentioned or described in section seven hereof, may by a two-thirds vote of all its members present and voting at a regular or regularly called meeting thereof, proceed to reincorporate under this chapter with the same name and for the same purposes for which it was originally organized. In thus proceeding to reincorporate, the board of trustees or directors may be increased or diminished within the limits prescribed by section seven hereof, but any decrease in such membership shall not take effect so as to affect the term of office of any trustee or director of the old corporation. Such trustees or directors and the other officers of the old corporation shall continue to serve as such under the reorganized corporation for the term for which they were originally elected or appointed. Such reorganization shall not effect a dissolution of the corporation, but shall be deemed a continuation of its corporate existence without affecting its property rights, or its liabilities, or the liabilities of its members or officers as such; but thereafter it shall have only such other rights, powers and privileges and be subject only to such other duties and liabilities as a corporation created for the same purpose under this chapter.

2. OF ORGANIZATIONS OF VETERANS (Memb. Corp.)

ARTICLE 5

VETERAN SOLDIERS' AND SAILORS' ASSOCIATIONS

§ 160. *Certificate of incorporation* — Twenty-five or more honorably discharged soldiers or sailors of the Union army or navy, or the male descendants of such soldiers or sailors, may become a corporation for social, literary, patriotic, charitable and historical purposes, by making, acknowledging and filing a certificate stating the particular object for which the corporation is to be created; the name of the proposed corporation; the town, village or city in which its principal office is to be located; the names of fifteen persons to be its directors until the first annual meeting, and the times for holding its annual meetings.

Such certificate shall not be filed without the approval, indorsed thereupon or annexed thereto, of a justice of the supreme court.

On filing such certificate, in pursuance of law, the signers thereof, their associates and successors shall be a corporation in accordance with the provisions of such certificate; but no person shall be eligible to membership of such corporation unless he have the same qualifications as the persons authorized to sign the certificate of incorporation thereof.

§ 161. *Shares* — The by-laws of such a corporation may provide that the property of the corporation shall be divided into transferable shares of one hundred dollars each, entitling the holder thereof to one vote for each share, at all meetings of the corporation. Each shareholder shall be liable to the amount unpaid on the shares held by him, for the debts and liabilities of the corporation; but shall not be entitled to receive any interest or dividends thereon. Such a corporation shall be a membership corporation and not a stock corporation.

§ 162. *Property* — All sums over the necessary expenses of such corporation and over and above the amount necessary to discharge the principal and interest on any mortgage or bond issued by it shall be held by the directors as a fund for the purchase of memorials, preservation of relics and historical evidences and trophies, and for charity to Union veterans, their families or descendants.

3. Of Soldiers' Monument Corporations (Memb. Corp.)

ARTICLE 11

Soldiers' Monument Corporations

§ 170. *Certificate of incorporation* — Three or more persons may become a corporation for the purpose of erecting a monument, monuments or memorial, including a memorial hall or building, to perpetuate the memory of the soldiers and sailors who served in the defense of the Union in the war of the rebellion, or in the army or navy of the United States in the late war with Spain, or of the army or navy of the United States in any war in which the government of the United States has been engaged, including the American revolution on the side of the Colonies; such monument or memorial alike to perpetuate the memory of those soldiers and sailors, who, since rendering such military or naval service have become resident of and die in the town, city or county in which such monument or memorial is erected; by making, acknowledging and filing a certificate, stating the particular object for which the corporation is to be created; the name of the proposed corporation; the number of its directors, not less than six nor more than twelve; the names and places of residence of the persons to be directors until the first annual meeting, and the time for holding its annual meetings. Such certificate shall not be filed without the approval, indorsed thereupon or annexed thereto, of a justice of the supreme court. On filing such certificate, in pursuance of law, the signers thereof, their associates and successors shall be a corporation in accordance with the provisions of such certificate.

§ 171. *Property; erection of monuments* — Such a corporation may acquire and hold, within the county in which its certificate of incorporation is recorded, not more than five acres of land to be used exclusively for the erection of a suitable monument or monuments or other memorial to perpetuate the memory of the soldiers and sailors who served in defense of the Union in the war of the rebellion, or who served in the army or navy of the United States in the late war with Spain, or in the army or navy of the United

States in any war in which the government of the United States has been engaged, including the American revolution on the side of the Colonies; such monument or memorial alike to perpetuate the memory of those soldiers and sailors who, since rendering such military or naval service, have become resident of and die in the town, city or county in which such monument or memorial is erected. Such a corporation may erect any such monument, monuments or memorial upon any public street, square or ground of any town, city or village, with the consent of the proper officers thereof, or may purchase or accept the donation of land suitable for that purpose; and may take and hold the·property given, devised or bequeathed to it in trust, to apply the same or the income or proceeds thereof for the erection, improvement, embellishment, preservation, repair or renewal of such monument, monuments or memorial, or of any structure, fences or walks upon its lands, or for planting or cultivating trees, shrubs, flowers and plants, in and around or upon its lands, or for improving or embellishing the same in any manner consistent with the design and purposes of the association, according to the terms of such grant, devise or bequest. It may take by gift or purchase any lots or lands in any cemetery within such county to be used and occupied exclusively for the burial of honorably discharged soldiers and sailors who served in either of such wars, and for the erection of suitable monuments or memorials therein. A town clerk or the board of trustees of a village shall, upon the petition of twenty-five resident taxpayers, submit to a biennial town meeting or village election, as the case may be, a proposition to raise by taxation a sum stated therein, not exceeding five hundred dollars in any one year, for the purpose of erecting such a monument, or contributing to the expense of such a monument, erected by a corporation under this section, or for repairing or improving the same and the grounds thereof; and such tax shall be levied in the manner prescribed by law for levying general taxes in such town or village, and when raised shall be applied to the purposes specified in such proposition.

The property of any corporation formed pursuant to laws of eighteen hundred and sixty-six, chapter two hundred and seventy-three, as amended by laws of eighteen hundred and eighty-eight, chapter two hundred and ninety-nine, shall be exempt from levy and sale on execution, and from all public taxes, rates and assessments, and no street, road, avenue or thoroughfare shall be laid through the lands of such association held for the purposes aforesaid without the consent of the trustees of such corporation, except by special permission of the legislature of the state.

§ 172. *Improvement taxes* — A tax may be levied and collected on the taxable property in a town, village or city in which such monument, monuments or other memorial may be erected, for the purpose of repairing or improving the same and the grounds thereof; and such tax shall be levied in the manner prescribed by law for levying general taxes in such town, village or city.

§ 173. *Transfers of moneys from unincorporated association to incorporated association in same place* — Any unincorporated association which shall have been organized solely for the purpose of raising funds to be devoted to the erection of a monument or memorial to perpetuate the memory of the soldiers and sailors who served in the defense of the Union in the late war may, by a majority vote of all its members who shall be present and voting at a meeting thereof, called as in this section provided, transfer to and vest in any incorporated association which shall have been organized under a general statute, or under the foregoing sections of this article for the sole purpose of erecting a like monument or memorial in the same town or village where such unincorporated association is located, any or all money which it shall have accumulated for such object, except as hereinafter provided, provided that such transfer does not conflict with any provision of the constitution or by-laws of such association, and that it shall be made and the money so transferred shall be accepted by such incorporated association in trust to apply the same, or the income thereof, exclusively for the purposes mentioned in section one hundred and seventy-one of this article. Any member of such unincorporated association who shall have contributed individually to the fund so raised, and paid such contribution into the treasury of such association, the same appearing upon the books of the treasurer, shall be entitled to demand and receive the amount of such contribution from the treasurer of such association, in case such transfer shall be made and before the same shall be consummated, upon filing with the president or secretary of such unincorporated association his or her affidavit to the effect that he or she has not approved of such transfer by vote or otherwise. No vote upon the question of transferring the funds of such unincorporated association as hereinbefore provided for shall be had or taken except at a meeting of such asociation especially called for that purpose by the president or secretary or other managing officer thereof, upon notice given at least ten days before the time fixed for such meeting, personally or by mail to each member of such association whose residence or post-office address is known, which notice shall state the subject of the meeting to be the consideration of making such transfer pursuant to this section.

ANNOTATION

Wyoming county soldiers' monument trustees; sheriff not eligible for membership. A. G. R., 1903:289.

Leave of Absence — *See* Memorial Day.
License (free) to Peddle — *See* Privileges.

MEMORIAL DAY

1. Holiday (Gen. Cons.)

§ 24. *Holiday and half-holiday* — The term holiday includes the following days in each year: The first day of January known as New Year's day; the twelfth day of February, known as Lincoln's birthday; the twenty-second of February, known as Washington's birthday; the thirtieth day of May, known as Memorial day; the fourth day of July, known as Independence day; the first Monday of September, known as Labor day; the twelfth day of October, known as Columbus day, and the twenty-fifth day of December, known as Christmas day; and if either of such days is Sunday, the next day thereafter; each general election day and each day appointed by the president of the United States or by the governor of this state as a day of general thanksgiving, general fasting and prayer or other general religious observances. The term half-holiday includes the period from noon to midnight of each Saturday which is not a holiday. (a. L. 1909, c. 112.)

" Holidays and half-holidays shall be considered as Sundays for all purposes relating to the transaction of business in the public offices of the state and of each county." (Pub. Off. § 62.)

ANNOTATION

Memorial day a legal holiday but not a *dies non*; any business may be transacted except such acts as are expressly excepted by statute. Morel v. Stearns, 37 Misc. 486 [1902].

2. LEAVES OF ABSENCE ON (Pub. Off.)

§ 63. *Leave of absence for veterans on Memorial day* — It shall be the duty of the head of every public department and of every court of the state of New York, of every superintendent or foreman on the public works of said state, of the county officers of the several counties of said state, and of the head of every department, bureau and office in the government of the various cities and villages in this state, to give leave of absence with pay for the twenty-four hours of the thirtieth day of May, or such other day as may, according to law, be observed as Memorial day, to every person in the service of the state, the county, the city or village, as the case may be, who served in the army or the navy of the United States in the war of the rebellion, or who served in the regular or volunteer army or the navy or the marine corps of the United States during the war with Spain or during the insurrection in the Philippine islands, or who has served in the regular army or navy or marine corps of the United States, and who was honorably discharged from such service. A refusal to give such leave of absence to one entitled thereto shall be neglect of duty. (a. L. 1910, c. 335.)

3. NEW YORK CITY APPROPRIATION (Charter)

§ 245. The board of estimate and apportionment shall have power in its discretion to annually include in its final estimate such sum as it may deem proper for the due observance of Memorial day to be expended by the memorial committee of the Grand Army of the Republic and by the United Spanish War Veterans and Army and Navy Union and Army and Navy Veterans in the various boroughs of said city, or in such other manner as to the said board of estimate and apportionment shall seem proper. (a. L. 1916, c. 115; L. 1917, c. 221.)

4. THIRD CLASS CITIES, APPROPRIATION (Gen. City)

§ 12. *Money for Memorial day in cities of the third class* — The common council of any city of the third class is hereby authorized to appropriate and set aside each year a sum not exceeding three hundred dollars for the purpose of providing for the due and proper observance of Memorial day in such city. (a. L. 1909, c. 288.)

§ 13. *Moneys; how expended* — The moneys thus appropriated shall be expended under the direction of a board composed of the mayor and the commanders and quartermasters of the Grand Army posts and United Spanish War Veteran camps and the commanders and treasurers of Sons of Veterans camps of such city. The whole amount of such money appropriated or any part thereof may be spent by such board in observance of Memorial day. Bills properly verified for all claims and expenditures arising under this or the preceding section, shall be presented to and audited by such board and shall be paid by the common council of any such city. The moneys appropriated shall be raised by tax on the real and personal property liable to taxation in any such city in the same manner as the ordinary expenses of maintaining the city government. (a. L. 1915, c. 85.)

5. TOWN BOARD, APPROPRIATION (Town)

§ 136. *Appropriation by town board for Memorial day* — It shall be lawful for the town boards of any town in this state at any regular or special meeting to vote any sum of money not exceeding fifty dollars in any year, or in towns of over five thousand inhabitants according to the last preceding state enumeration, in which are maintained two or more posts of the Grand Army of the Republic, a sum not exceeding one hundred dollars in any year, for the purpose of defraying the expenses of the proper observance of Memorial or Decoration day, which amount shall be assessed, levied and collected in the same manner as other expenses of said town are assessed, levied and collected and shall be paid to the supervisor of such town and be disbursed by him in such manner as the town board of such town may direct upon vouchers properly receipted and audited by the town board of such town; except that in any town in which there may be a post of the Grand Army of the Republic, such post may direct the manner and extent of such observance and the supervisor shall pay the expense thereof upon the order or orders of the commander or quartermaster of such post, which orders shall be his vouchers for such payment, and in case there may be two or more posts of the Grand Army of the Republic in any such town, the commanders and quartermasters of such posts, by concurrent action, shall direct the supervisor of such town what proportion of such money so raised shall be expended by each of such posts, which proportion shall be paid by such supervisor upon the order or orders of the commander and quartermaster of each of such posts. In case there is a post in a town adjoining a town in which no post is located, whose membership includes at least three residents of such town having no post, the post shall appoint a committee of not less than three of its members who are residents of the said adjoining town in which the post is not located, and the supervisor of said town shall pay the expenses of observance of Memorial or Decoration day upon the order or orders of said committee or a majority thereof, which orders shall be his vouchers for such payment.

§ 136-a. *Additional appropriations for Memorial day upon the adoption of a proposition therefor* — Upon the adoption of a proposition therefor, by the qualified electors of the town entitled to vote thereon, as hereinafter provided, the town board of any town may appropriate from town funds a sum not exceeding the amount which it is authorized by the provisions of this section to raise by tax for the purpose of defraying the expenses of the proper observance of Memorial or Decoration day, in addition to any moneys which such town board is authorized to provide for by section one hundred and thirty-six of this chapter. A proposition directing the appropriation of town moneys for the additional expenses of the proper observance of Memorial or Decoration day, under the provisions of this section may be submitted to the electors of the town qualified to vote thereon at a biennial or special town meeting in the manner provided in this chapter for the submission of propositions for raising or appropriating money, except that no such proposition shall be submitted unless at least ten percentum of the qualified voters of the town unite in a written application therefor addressed to the town clerk. Such proposition shall be deemed adopted if it receive the affirmative vote of a majority of the qualified electors voting thereon. Moneys appropriated for the purposes of this section shall be raised by taxation in the same manner as other town expenses, but shall not exceed in any one year a sum equal to twenty-five hundredths of a mill on each dollar of the assessed valuation of property in the town according to the assessment-roll last preceding the date of submission of the proposition. A proposition adopted as aforesaid shall continue in force until rescinded by a proposition submitted and adopted in like manner, but not more than one such proposition either directing the appropriation or rescinding a former proposition shall be adopted in any one year. Moneys appropriated under the provisions of this section shall be kept separate and apart from those provided for in section one hundred and thirty-six of this chapter and shall be expended under the direction of the town board. (Added L. 1912, c. 185, a. L. 1915, c. 412.)

6. SARATOGA SPRINGS, APPROPRIATION (L. 1866, c. 220)

§ 54. For the purpose of providing the means of sustaining the several departments and defraying the expenses of the corporation the board of trustees are authorized to levy and collect an annual tax in amounts and for the purposes, as follows:

* * * * * * * * * *

9. Such sum as the board of trustees deem advisable to appropriate for Luther M. Wheeler Post No. 92, G. A. R., for the proper observance of Memorial Day, which said sum the board of trustees of the village of Saratoga Springs is hereby authorized to appropriate. (Added L. 1913, c. 169.)

7. RENSSELAER CITY CHARTER (L. 1913, c. 481)

§ 69. *Money for Memorial Day observance* — The common council is hereby authorized to appropriate and set aside each year a sum not exceeding two hundred dollars for the purpose of providing for the due and proper observance of Memorial Day. The moneys thus appropriated shall be expended under the direction of a board composed of the mayor and the commanders and quartermasters of the Grand Army posts and United Spanish War Veteran camps of such city. The whole amount of such money appropriated or any part thereof may be spent by such board in observance of Memorial Day. Bills properly verified for all claims and expenditures arising under this section, shall be presented to and audited by such board and shall be paid by the common council. The moneys so appropriated shall be included in the budget raised by tax as one of the ordinary expenses of the city government.

ANNOTATIONS

town board to appropriate. A. G. R., 1898:199–200.
posts in towns adjoining town with no post have equal rights in control and management of Memorial day services there. A. G. R., 1903:340–42.

MONUMENTS AND MEMORIALS

1. COUNTIES MAY ERECT (County)

§ 40. *Soldiers' monument*—Any such board (of supervisors) may also, by vote of two-thirds of its members, raise and appropriate such moneys as it may deem necessary, for the erection within the county of public monuments, in commemoration of the federal soldiers and sailors in the late war of the rebellion, or of any other public person or event, and for repairing and remodeling such monuments; all moneys so raised shall be expended by direction of the board of supervisors; but no county officer shall receive any compensation for services rendered pursuant to this section.

2. TOWNS MAY ERECT (Town)

§ 45. *Power of town meeting to make appropriation for public monuments* — It shall be competent for electors of any town, at any regular town meeting at any regular election to vote any sum of money, to be designated by a majority of all the electors voting at such town meeting or election, for the purpose of erecting a

public monument within such town in memory of the soldiers of
such town or in commemoration of any public person or event;
but no debt shall be created nor shall any tax be imposed on any
town for such purpose unless the same shall have been voted for
by a majority of the legal voters of the town affected, voting at
such election. The board of supervisors may legalize the vote of
any town for such purpose, and after such vote they may raise or
authorize the specified sum or sums of money to be raised for
such purpose in any of the modes provided for by law for raising
money for towns. All moneys expended by any town for the
purposes authorized by this section shall be expended under the
direction of the supervisor, town clerk and justices of the peace
of such town or a majority of them or by a commissioner or commissioners for that purpose appointed by such town officers or by
a majority of them. But nothing in this section shall affect the
right of the electors to vote on a proposition heretofore directed
to be submitted by a board of supervisors, or the power of a board
of supervisors to carry into effect the vote upon such proposition.

ANNOTATION

law discussed. A. G. R., 1903:408–10.

3. VILLAGES MAY ACQUIRE LANDS (Gen. Munic.)

§ 72. *Acquisition of lands for erection of monuments* — The
governing board of a village or town, or the trustees of a monument association, may acquire not to exceed three acres of land,
for the erection of a soldiers' monument, or a monument or other
structure as a memorial of some distinguishing or important event
in the history of the state or nation, and for laying out such
lands as a public park or square, if such lands are vacant or have
buildings thereon not exceeding two thousand five hundred dollars in value, and if a judge of the county, or a justice of the
supreme court of the district, in which such memorial is to be
erected, shall give his written approval of the acquisition of such
lands for such purpose.

4. TRUSTEES MAY ACCEPT (Pub. Bldgs.)

§ 3. *Powers and duties of trustees* — The trustees of public
buildings shall: * * *

6. Have power to accept and receive for erection or location in any of the public buildings or grounds such statues, monuments, memorials or tablets having reference to historical events in the history or acts of the citizens or soldiers of the state of New York as shall meet their approval, provided that such gifts are erected or located without expenditure from the state treasury.

MONUMENT CORPORATIONS — *See* Incorporation.
MT. McGREGOR ceded to United States. State, § 25, par. 6.
POLL TAX — *See* Exemption.

POST MEETING ROOMS

1. IN ARMORIES (Mil.)

§ 186. *Control of armories* — * * * On the application of one or more posts of the Grand Army of the Republic, or other veteran organizations of honorably discharged union soldiers, sailors or marines of any war of the United States, or sons of such veterans, approved by the commanding officers of the brigade of the national guard in whose jurisdiction armories, the property of the state are located, and the officer in charge of such armory, subject also to the approval of the adjutant-general of the state and under such restrictions as he may prescribe, the officer in charge of any state armory designated by the adjutant-general of the state shall provide a proper and convenient meeting room or rooms in such armory where such posts or other veteran organizations may hold regular and special meetings, without the payment of any expense therefor. (a. L. 1913, c. 558.)

§ 192. *Use of armories* — Armories shall only be used as follows:

* * * * * * * * * *

(b) By posts of the Grand Army of the Republic or other veteran organizations of honorably discharged union soldiers, sailors or marines of any war of the United States or of sons of such veterans as provided in section one hundred and eighty-six of this chapter. (a. L. 1909, c. 240, § 56.)

2. IN ORLEANS, WAYNE AND GREENE COUNTIES (Town)

§ 137. *Appropriation by town board in Orleans and Greene counties for rooms for posts* — It shall be lawful for the town board of any town in the counties of Orleans and Greene at any regular or special meeting to vote a sum of money not exceeding one hundred dollars in any year, and for the town board of any town in Wayne county at a regular or special meeting to vote a sum of money not exceeding two hundred dollars in any year, for the purpose of assisting in defraying the rental of rooms for the holding of meetings of any post of the Grand Army of the Republic, located in such town. In case there is a post in a town adjoining a town in which no post is located, whose membership includes at least ten residents of such town having no post, it shall be lawful for the town board of such town having no post, at any regular or special meeting, to vote any sum of money, not exceeding fifty dollars in any year, for the purpose of assisting in defraying the rental of rooms in such adjoining town, for the holding of meetings of a post of the Grand Army of the Republic. All moneys hereby authorized shall be assessed, levied and collected the same as other town expenses and shall be paid to the quartermaster of such post by the supervisor, on proof to such supervisor that the post is not receiving under the provisions of this article from a town or towns more than the actual rental of such rooms. (a. L. 1914, c. 150.)

CAYUGA COUNTY, *see* L. 1906, c. 323; ONTARIO COUNTY, *see* L. 1907, c. 173; SENECA COUNTY, *see* L. 1907, c. 358; WYOMING COUNTY, *see* L. 1906, c. 175.

3. LEASE OF PUBLIC BUILDINGS FOR (Gen. Munic.)

§ 77. *Leases of public buildings to Grand Army posts* — A municipal corporation may lease, for not exceeding five years, to a post or posts of the Grand Army of the Republic, or other veteran organization of honorably discharged union soldiers, sailors or marines, a public building or part thereof, belonging to such municipal corporation, except school-houses in actual use as such, without expense, or at a nominal rent, fixed by the board or council having charge of such buildings, and provide furniture and furnishings, and heat, light and janitor service therefor, in like manner. (a. L. 1917, c. 583.)

4. MEMORIAL HALL IN WATERTOWN (L. 1913, c. 364)

Section 1. The board of supervisors of Jefferson county shall submit to the electors thereof at the general election to be held in such county on the fourth day of November, nineteen hundred and thirteen, a proposition to authorize the board of supervisors of such county to expend not more than one hundred thousand dollars in acquiring a site in the city of Watertown, and erecting thereon a soldiers and sailors' memorial hall. If for any reason such submission shall not be made at the general election to be held on the fourth day of November, nineteen hundred and thirteen, it shall be made at the next general election thereof, to be held in said county. Such proposition shall be in the following form: Shall the board of supervisors be authorized to expend not more than one hundred thousand dollars in acquiring a site and erecting a soldiers and sailors' memorial hall? The provisions of the election law in relation to the submission of propositions and the form of ballots therefor shall apply to the submission of such proposition. If a majority of the votes upon such proposition shall be in the affirmative, the board of supervisors of such county may acquire a site for such memorial hall in the city of Watertown and may cause to be erected thereon a soldiers and sailors' memorial hall at an expense not exceeding in the aggregate for the acquisition of the site and the construction and equipment of the building one hundred thousand dollars.

§ 2. Such building when completed shall be deemed a memorial to the soldiers and sailors who enlisted from the county of Jefferson and served in any war in which the United States as a nation has ever been engaged, including so much of the revolutionary war as was carried on previous to the signing and promulgation of the Declaration of Independence by the continental congress, and such purposes shall be properly indicated by tablet or otherwise. The soldiers and sailors' memorial hall and historical association of Jefferson county shall have the management of such memorial hall, and shall authorize the use thereof for military drills by a camp or camps of the Sons of Veterans of such county; and as a headquarters and place of meeting of such Sons of Veterans and any auxiliary society of such Sons of

Veterans; and as a place of meeting by the Historical Society of Jefferson county; and as a place for the proper displaying and storing of such property in the way of relics as belongs to the said Historical Society and such as may hereafter be donated to it for preservation and for safekeeping. Conveniences for such purposes will be provided for in said building. It shall also be used as a place of meeting for the LeRay de Chaumont Chapter of the Daughters of the American Revolution; as a place of meeting for the Julia Dent Grant Circle of the G. A. R., for a place of meeting of the Northern Frontier Chapter of the Daughters of the War of 1812; as a place of meeting for Joe Spratt Post, No. 323, G. A. R.; for a place of meeting for the Relief Corps Auxiliary to said post; and for the storage and preservation of such personal property owned by these organizations as they may have in their possession, respectively. The said hall when completed and so erected to be used so far as may be for meetings for the assemblage of the people at different times to promote patriotic objects, but not to be used to the exclusion of the proper use of the societies whose names are given herein. Rules and regulations for the occupancy of said building not inconsistent with the purposes of this act may be made from time to time by the board of supervisors of Jefferson county.

5. IN CERTAIN COUNTIES (TOWN)

§ 137. *Appropriation by town boards in Livingston, Oneida, Orleans, Wayne and Greene counties for rooms for posts* — It shall be lawful for the town board of any town in the counties of Livingston, Orleans or Greene at any regular or special meeting to vote a sum of money not exceeding one hundred dollars in any year, and for the town board of any town in the counties of Oneida or Wayne at a regular or special meeting to vote a sum of money not exceeding two hundred dollars in any year, for the purpose of assisting in defraying the rental of rooms for the holding of meetings of any post of the Grand Army of the Republic, located in such town. In case there is a post in a town adjoining a town in which no post is located, whose membership includes at least ten residents of such town having no post, it shall be lawful for the town board of such town having no post, at any regular or special meeting, to vote any sum of money, not exceeding fifty dollars in any year, for the purpose of assisting in defraying the rental of rooms in such adjoining town, for the holding of meetings of a post of the Grand Army of the Republic. All moneys hereby authorized shall be assessed, levied and collected, the same as other town expenses and shall be paid to the quartermaster of such post by the supervisor, on proof to such supervisor that the post is not receiving under the provisions of this article from a town or towns more than the actual rental of such rooms. (a. L. 1917, c. 339.)

6. In Norwich (L. 1914, § 313)

14. The sum of seventy-five dollars shall be raised and paid each year for the rent of the Norwich Post of the Grand Army of the Republic, and such sum, when paid towards the rent of said Grand Army of the Republic rooms, shall be in addition to any amount paid for the relief of the Grand Army of the Republic as provided by subdivision ten of this section and by general law, and also in lieu of a compliance with any provision of section seventy-seven of chapter twenty-nine of the laws of nineteen hundred and nine. (a. L. 1917, c. 421.)

PREFERENCE IN APPOINTMENT

1. Conferred. (Constitution, Art. V.)

§ 9. *Civil service appointments and promotions*—Appointments and promotions in the civil service of the state, and of all the civil divisions thereof, including cities and villages, shall be made according to merit and fitness, to be ascertained, so far as practicable, by examinations, which, so far as practicable, shall be competitive; provided, however, that honorably discharged soldiers and sailors from the army and navy of the United States in the late civil war, who are citizens and residents of this state, shall be entitled to preference in appointment and promotion without regard to their standing on any list from which such appointment or promotion may be made. Laws shall be made to provide for the enforcement of this section.

2. REGULATED. (Civil Serv.)

§ 21. *Preferences allowed honorably discharged soldiers, sailors and marines* — In every public department and upon all public works of the state of New York and of the cities, counties, towns and villages thereof, honorably discharged soldiers, sailors and marines from the army and navy of the United States in the late civil war who are citizens and residents of this state, shall be entitled to preference in appointment and promotion without regard to their standing on any list from which such appointment or promotion may be made to all competitive and non-competitive positions, provided their qualifications and fitness shall have been ascertained as provided in this chapter and the rules and regulations in pursuance thereof; and a person thus preferred shall not be disqualified from holding any position in the civil service on account of his age or by reason of any physical disability, provided such age or disability does not render him incompetent to perform the duties of the position applied for. Whenever any list of eligible persons, prepared under authority of this chapter, shall contain the names of honorably discharged soldiers, sailors and marines entitled to preference as aforesaid, any reference in this chapter or in the rules and regulations in pursuance thereof to the persons standing highest on such list shall be deemed to indicate those standing highest of those entitled to preference by the provisions of this section and such persons shall be given preference on any list of registered applicants for employment in the labor service, in accordance with the dates of their several applications as though such applications had been filed prior to those of any persons on such lists not entitled to the preference provided by this section. A refusal to allow the preference provided for in this and the next succeeding section to any honorably discharged soldier, sailor or marine, or a reduction of his compensation intended to bring about his resignation shall be deemed a misdemeanor, and such honorably discharged soldier, sailor or marine shall have a right of action therefor in any court of competent jurisdiction for damages, and also a remedy by mandamus for righting the wrong.

ANNOTATIONS

Preference

upheld.

deputy sheriffs and turnkeys at jails. A. G. R., 1889:228–29.

court crier, Montgomery county. A. G. R., 1889:241.

police court clerk, Syracuse. A. G. R., 1896:316–22.

id., Brooklyn. A. G. R., 1896:324–25.

superintendent of charities, Auburn; applies to every public department and to all public works of state, cities and villages. A. G. R., 1892:136.

laws reviewed. A. G. R., 1897:291–93.

laws affecting New York city discussed. A. G. R., 1898:159–63.

longer term of military service does not give one veteran preference over another. A. G. R., 1894:270.

Burke v. Holtzmann, 110 A. D. 564 [1906].

laborer class; when placed on eligible list by civil service commission, appointing officer may not challenge right to be there because no examination was had.

People ex rel. Weintz v. Burch, 79 A. D. 156 [1903].

People ex rel. Qua v. Gaffney, 69 Misc. 36 [1910]; affd. 201 N. Y. 535.

street superintendent, Saratoga Springs.

People ex rel. Carroll v. New York City Civil Service Board, 5 A. D. 164 [1896].

bridgetender; position transferred to new schedule; appointments must be made from list under new, not old, schedule.

People ex rel. Hamilton v. Stratton, 174 N. Y. 531 [1903].

appointing officer may not raise question of competency of veteran on eligible list.

People ex rel. Sears v. Tobey, 153 N. Y. 381 [1897].

police court clerk, Syracuse; *see also, supra,* A. G. R., 1896; 316–22.

Sullivan v. Gilroy, 55 Hun 285 [1890].

laborer class; L. 1887, c. 464 held constitutional.

Wortman, in re, 2 Supp. 324 [1888].

holds L. 1884, c. 410, constitutional.

a. Age does not limit.

People ex rel. Kittenger v. Buffalo Civil Service Commissioners, 20 Misc. 217 [1897].

no age limit may be fixed by rules.

People ex rel. Van Petten v. Cobb, 13 A. D. 56 [1897].

special agent, excise department; civil service commission may not strike name from list on ground of age and physical disability.

People ex rel. Washburn v. French, 52 Hun 464 [1889].

New York city police.

People ex rel. Hall v. Little Falls, 8 Supp. 512 [1889].

decision of appointing authorities as to physical capacity, made in good faith, not disturbed.

Sullivan v. Gilroy, 55 Hun 285 [1890].

laborer class.

b. Dependent upon passing examination and attaining eligible list.

capitol orderlies, watchmen, etc. A. G. R., 1899:344–50.

Allaire v. Knox, 168 N. Y. 642, affirming 62 A. D. 29 [1901].

Keymer, in re, 148 N. Y. 219 [1899].

People ex rel. Huber v. Adam, 116 A. D. 613 [1906].

change of position from laborer to competitive class.

People ex rel. Hoyt v. Ballston Spa, Trustees of Village, 19 A. D. 567 [1897].

appointing officer not compelled to appoint veteran, unless competent.

People ex rel. Sweeley v. Wilson, 146 N. Y. 401, affirming 12 Misc. 174 [1895].

c. Eligible list may be subdivided only by existing localities; eligibility to appointment may not be denied resident by arbitrarily dividing lists.

People ex rel. Melledy v. Shea, 73 A. D. 232 [1902]; People ex rel. Coyne v. Shea, 73 A. D. 239 [1902].

d. Must be seasonably claimed.
People ex rel. McCullough v. Snyder, 106 A. D. 28 [1905].
four years' delay held laches.
denied.
school district collector. A. G. R., 1902:306.
locktenders and patrolmen on canals. A. G. R., 1911 [Feb. 20].
McGuire, in re, 50 Hun 203 [1888].
promotion, New York city police.
People ex rel. Warschauer v. Dalton, 159 N. Y. 235 [1899].
inspector of water supply to shipping, New York city.
People ex rel. McNeile v. Glynn, 128 A. D. 257 [1908].
transfer tax appraiser.
People ex rel. Burlingame v. Hayward, 19 A. D. 46 [1897].
school district official.
People ex rel. Collins v. Kraft, 50 A. D. 621, case 3 [1900].
teamster on canal.
People ex rel. Balcom v. Mosher, 163 N. Y. 32 [1900].
L. 1899, c. 370, § 13 held unconstitutional as interfering with constitutional right
of appointment by local authorities.
People ex rel. Hall v. Saratoga Springs, Trustees of Village, 159 N. Y. 568
[1898], affirming 35 A. D. 141.
head of public department in village.
People ex rel. Ballou v. Wendell, 57 Hun 362 [1890].
county court crier.
People ex rel. Balch v. Yonkers, Mayor of, 14 Supp. 455 [1891].
health officer; position independent of every department of city government.
Schuyler v. New York, City of, 95 A. D. 305 [1904].

Sweet v. Partridge, 66 A. D. 309 [1901].
laborer on public works of state.
a. Confidential positions.

defined; performance of official duties does not establish confidential relations. People ex rel. Drake v. Sutton, 88 Hun 173 [1895].

who are deputies; deputy superintendent of public buildings. Ostrander,
in re, 146 N. Y. 404 [1895].

collector of taxes. People ex rel. Stephens v. Barden, 8 Supp. 960 [1890].
b. Appointing officer as judge of competency, where no examination has been
held.

decision final, as to lack of capacity, when made in good faith. People
ex rel. Lockwood v. Saratoga Springs, Trustees of Village, 54 Hun 16
[1889]; People ex rel. Milliken v. Newburg, Commissioners of Almshouse,
65 Hun 169 [1892]; People ex rel. Mesick v. Scannell, 63 A. D. 243
[1901].

qualifications must be shown by affidavit. People ex rel. Waterman v.
Knapp, 4 Supp. 825 [1889].

satisfactory proof of preferential standing must be furnished. A. G. R.,
1889:87–88; People v. Wallace, 55 Hun 149 [1889].

common council cannot be compelled to confirm an appointment. People
ex rel. Hall v. Little Falls, 8 Supp. 512, case 3 [1889]; People ex rel.
Snyder v. Summers, 9 Supp. 700 [1890].
c. Equality of preference.

veteran has no preference over veteran volunteer fireman. People ex rel.
Conlin v. Dobbs Ferry, Village of, 63 A. D. 276 [1901].
d. Vacancy.

courts cannot compel appointing officer to fill vacancy. People ex rel. Tre-
gaskis v. Palmer, 9 A. D. 252 [1896].
e. Penalty.

liability of appointing officer, criminally.   People v. Wallace, 55 Hun 149 [1889].

action for damages for failure to accord preferences on action for injury to property rights and survives, on death of veteran.   Burke v. Holtzmann, 117 A. D. 292 [1907]; affd. 196 N. Y. 576.

f. Transfer.

employee of state engineer's office.   A. G. R., 1909:13–15.

of person already in service, when not a promotion, takes precedence of veteran's preference.   A. G. R., 1905:404–05.

g. Dividing list.

The Civil Service Law applies to the City of New York, except as limited or repealed by the provisions of the city charter.   The Civil Service Commission of the City of New York has no authority to divide, after an examination, those thereby qualified to promotion in clerical positions into separate eligible lists according to their residences in the different boroughs, and to prefer those from one of such residential lists to the exclusion of others not upon such list who are entitled to preference by the result of such examination.   People v. Fetherston, 168 A. D., 416 [1915].

PRIVILEGES

1. FREEDOM OF VENDING AND SELLING   (Gen. Bus.)

§ 32. *Licenses to soldiers and sailors* — Every honorably discharged soldier, sailor or marine of the military or naval service of the United States, who is a resident of this state and a veteran of the late rebellion, or of the Spanish-American war, or who shall have served beyond sea, shall have the right to hawk, peddle, vend and sell by auction his own goods, wares or merchandise or solicit trade within this state, by procuring a license for that purpose to be issued as herein provided.

On the presentation to the clerk of any county in which any soldier, sailor or marine may reside of a certificate of honorable discharge from the army or navy of the United States, which discharge shall show that the person presenting it is a veteran of the late rebellion or of the Spanish-American war, or that he has served beyond sea, such county clerk shall issue without cost to such soldier, sailor or marine a license certifying him to be entitled to the benefits of this article.   A license issued without cost under the provisions of this section, shall be personal to the licensee, and any assignment or transfer thereof shall be absolutely void.   A person assigning or tranferring, or attempting to assign or transfer any such license contrary to the provisions of this section shall be guilty of a misdemeanor.   (a. L. 1915, c. 175.)

(The foregoing provision is controlling over all ordinances and by-laws of towns or other municipal corporations. Gen. Bus. §35; Town §210.)

ANNOTATIONS.

no fee required. A. G. R., 1897:192–93.
municipal ordinances regulating licenses.
  Buffalo, City of v. Linsman, 113 A. D. 584 [1906].
licensee under this act held to comply therewith.
  Eggleston v. Scheibel, 60 Misc. 250 [1908].
licensee must observe those designed to prevent obstruction of streets.
conformity required to those closing auction sales at 6 p. m. A. G. R., 1904:427–28.
Niagara reservation; licensee may be excluded by rules of board of managers. A. G. R., 1899:291–92.
excepted trades; bill posting. A. G. R., 1907:564–65.
id., junk dealing; license must be taken out in municipality where principal place of business is. A. G. R., 1903:389–92.

2. Brevet Commissions for War Service   (Mil.)

§ 79. *Brevet commissions* — The governor may, * * * also confer upon officers in active service in the active militia, who have previously served therein in a higher grade, or who have previously served in the forces of the United States in time of war, brevet commissions of a grade equal to the highest grade in which they previously served. * * * (a. L. 1909, c. 371.)

3. Service in U. S. Army or Navy   (Id.)

Section 58 makes such service a qualification for commission in the naval militia, and section 71, as amended, L. 1909, c. 371, makes it a qualification for commission in the National Guard.

4. War Service Gives Higher Rank   (Id.)

§ 57. *Retirement of commissioned officers* — * * * Any commissioned officer of the naval militia who shall be retired under section eighty-two, upon his own request, shall have rank on the retired list of the grade next higher to that held by him in active service, provided he shall have been an officer in the United States navy in time of war. (a. L. 1909, c. 233.)

5. War Service and Police Retirement   (Charter)

§ 355. * * * Any member of the police force who has, or shall have performed duty on any such force aforesaid, for a period of twenty-five years or upwards, being of the age of fifty-five years, or any member of any such police force who is an honorably discharged soldier or sailor from the army and navy of the United States in the late civil war, who shall have reached the age of sixty years, or any such soldier or sailor who has performed duty on any such force for a period of twenty years, upon his own application in writing, provided there are no charges against him pending, must be relieved and dismissed from said force and service by the department and placed on the roll of the police pension fund and awarded and granted, to be paid from said pension fund, an annual pension during his lifetime of the sum not less than one-half of the full salary or compensation of such member so retired. * * *

6. WHEN UNIFORM MAY BE WORN (Mil.)

§ 239. * * * *Unlawful wearing of uniforms and devices indicating rank* —Any person who shall * * * wear any uniform or any device, strap, knot or insignia of any design or character used as a designation of grade, rank or office, such as are by law or by general regulation, duly promulgated, prescribed for the use of the active militia or similar thereto; except members of the army and navy of the United States and the national guard and naval militia of this or any other state, officers of the independent military organizations so designated in section two hundred and forty-one of this chapter, members of associations wholly composed of soldiers honorably discharged from the service of the United States and members of the order of Sons of Veterans, shall be guilty of a misdemeanor and in addition thereto shall forfeit to the people of this state one hundred dollars for each offense, to be sued for in the name of the people by a judge-advocate. * * *

PROCESSIONS AND PARADES

1. IN CITIES (Gen. City)

§ 5. *Certain parades and processions forbidden; penalty* —All processions or parades occupying or marching on any street of any city to the exclusion or interruption of other citizens in their

iii

individual right and use thereof, excepting the National Guard and the police and fire departments, and the associations of veteran soldiers, are forbidden, unless written notice of the object, time and route of such procession or parade be given by the chief officer thereof, not less than six hours previous to its forming or marching, to the police authorities of such city; and such police authorities may designate to such procession or parade how much of the street in width it can occupy with especial reference to crowded thoroughfares through which such procession may move; and, when so designated, the chief officer of such procession or parade shall be responsible that the designation is obeyed; and it shall be the duty of the police authorities to furnish such escort as may be necessary to protect persons and property and maintain the public peace and order. A person wilfully violating any provision of this section shall be guilty of a misdemeanor, punishable by a fine not exceeding twenty dollars or imprisonment not exceeding ten days, or both.

2. PERMISSION OF CERTAIN (Mil.)

§ 241. *Military parades and organizations by unauthorized bodies prohibited* — No body of men, other than the active militia and the troops of the United States except such independent military organizations as were on the twenty-third day of April, eighteen hundred and eighty-three, and now are, in existence, and such other organizations as may be formed under the provisions of this chapter, shall associate themselves together as a military company or organization, or parade in public with firearms in any city or town of this state. No body of men shall be granted a certificate of incorporation under any corporate name which shall mislead, or tend to mislead, any person into believing that such corporation is connected with or attached to the National Guard or Naval Militia of this state in any capacity or way whatsoever. In case any such certificate has been heretofore or may hereafter be granted, which in the judgment of the adjutant-general of the state, misleads or tends to mislead anyone into believing that such corporation is connected with or attached to the National Guard or Naval Militia in any capacity or way whatsoever, the adjutant-general of the state shall notify such corporation, in writing, to forthwith discontinue the use of its said corporate name and forthwith take the necessary steps to change its name pursuant to the statute in such case made and provided, to some name not so calculated to mislead. In the event such proceedings are not forthwith taken and completed within six months from the service of said notice, the attorney-general is authorized and directed to bring an action to procure a judgment vacating or annulling the act of incorporation of such corporation, or any act renewing the corporation or continuing its corporate existence or annulling the existence of such corporation. No city or town shall raise or appropriate any money toward arming or equipping, uniforming or in any other way supporting, sustaining or providing drill rooms or armories for any such body of men; but associations wholly composed of soldiers honorably discharged from the service of the United States, or members of the order of Sons of Veterans may parade in public with firearms on Decoration day, or on May first, known as Dewey day, or upon the reception of any regiments or companies of soldiers returning from such service, and for the purpose of escort duty at the burial of deceased soldiers, and students in educational institutions where military science is a prescribed part of the course of instruction and cadet organizations composed of youths under eighteen years of age, under responsible instructors, may, with the consent of the governor, drill and parade with firearms in public under the superintendence of their instructors. This section shall not be construed to prevent any organization authorized to do so by law from parading with firearms, nor to prevent parades by the national guard or naval militia of any other state. The independent military organizations mentioned in this section, not regularly organized as organizations of the national guard or naval militia, are hereby made subject to the orders of the governor in case of emergency or necessity, to aid the national guard or naval militia in quelling invasion, insurrection, riot or breach of the peace provided the officers and members of such organization shall, when so called upon, first sign and execute and deliver through their commanding officer to the officer to whom it is ordered to report, a form of enlistment in form to be prescribed by the governor in regulations or orders for a term not less than thirty days nor more than ninety days at one time; and if the service of such organization shall not be required for the full term of their enlistment they shall be discharged by the order of the governor. All members of such independent organizations when called into service of the state, as herein provided for, shall be equipped and paid by the state, and shall be protected in the discharge of their duties, and in obeying the orders of the governor, as though a part of the national guard or naval militia of the state. Any person violating any provision of this section shall be deemed guilty of a misdemeanor. (a. L. 1913, c. 41; L. 1916, c. 564.)

3. Regulation of, on Sunday (Penal)

§ 2151. *Processions and parades on Sunday* — All processions and parades on Sunday in any city, excepting only funeral processions for the actual burial of the dead, and processions to and from a place of worship in connection with a religious service there celebrated, are forbidden; and in such excepted cases there shall be no music, fireworks, discharge of cannon or firearms, or other disturbing noise. At a military funeral or at the funeral of a United States soldier, sailor or marine, or of a national guardsman, or of a deceased member of an association of veteran soldiers, sailors or marines, or of a disbanded militia regiment, or of a secret fraternal society, or of an association of employees of the national, state or municipal government, music may be played while escorting the body; also in patriotic military processions on Sunday previous to Decoration day, known as Memorial Sunday, to cemeteries or other places where memorial services are held, and also by organizations of the national guard or naval militia, or of an association of employees of the national, state or municipal governments, attending religious service on Sunday; but in no case within one block of a place of worship where service is then being celebrated. A person wilfully violating any provision of this section is punishable by a fine not exceeding twenty dollars or imprisonment not exceeding ten days, or both. (a. L. 1914, c. 328.)

4. When Arms May be Carried in (Penal)

§ 1897. *Carrying and use of dangerous weapons* — * * * Any person not a citizen of the United States, unless authorized by license issued as hereinafter prescribed, who shall have or carry firearms, or any dangerous or deadly weapons in any place, at any time, shall be guilty of a misdemeanor, and if he has been previously convicted of any crime he shall be guilty of a felony. * * * This section shall not apply to the regular and ordinary transportation of firearms as merchandise, nor to sheriffs, policemen, or to other duly appointed peace officers, nor to duly authorized military or civil organizations, when parading, nor to the members thereof when going to and from the places of meeting of their respective organizations. (a. L. 1911, c. 195; L. 1917, c. 580.)

PROTECTION BY PENAL PROVISIONS

1. Badge and Button (Penal)

§ 2240. *Unauthorized wearing or use of badge, name, title of officers, insignia, ritual or ceremony of certain orders and societies.* 1. Any person who wilfully wears the badge or the button of the Grand Army of the Republic, the insignia, badge or rosette of the Military Order of the Loyal Legion of the United States, or the Military Order of Foreign Wars of the United States, or the badge or button of the Spanish war veterans, or the Order of the Patrons of Husbandry, or the Benevolent and Protective Order of Elks of the United States of America, or of any society, order or organization, of ten years' standing in the state of New York, or uses the same to obtain aid or assistance within this state, or wilfully uses the name of such society, order or organization, the titles of its officers, or its insignia, ritual ceremonies, unless entitled to use or wear the same under the constitution and by-laws, rules and regulations of such order or of such society, order or organization, is guilty of a misdemeanor. (a. L. 1915, c. 320.)

2. Any person who shall wilfully wear the shield of the Union Veteran Legion, or who shall use or wear the same to obtain aid or assistance thereby within this state, unless he shall be entitled to use or wear the same, under the rules and regulations of the Union Veteran Legion, shall be deemed guilty of a misdemeanor, and upon conviction, shall be punished by imprisonment for a term not

to exceed thirty days in the county jail, or a fine not to exceed twenty dollars, or by both such fine and imprisonment.

2. THE FLAG PROTECTED (Penal)

§ 1425. * * *

16. Any person, who in any manner, for exhibition or display, shall place or cause to be placed, any word, figure, mark, picture, design, drawing, or any advertisement, of any nature upon any flag, standard, color, shield or ensign of the United States of America or state of New York, or shall expose or cause to be exposed to public view any such flag, standard, color, shield or ensign, upon which after the first day of September, nineteen hundred and five, shall have been printed, painted or otherwise placed or to which shall be attached, appended, affixed, or annexed, any word, figure, mark, picture, design, or drawing, or any advertisement of any nature, or who shall expose to public view, manufacture, sell, expose for sale, give away, or have in possession for sale, or to give away or for use for any purpose, any article, or substance, being an article of merchandise, or a receptacle of merchandise or article or thing for carrying or transporting merchandise, upon which after the first day of September, nineteen hundred and five, shall have been printed, painted, attached, or otherwise placed, a representation of any such flag standard, color, shield or ensign, to advertise, call attention to, decorate, mark, or distinguish, the article or substance, on which so placed, or who shall publicly mutilate, deface, defile, or defy, trample upon, or cast contempt, either by words or act, upon any such flag, standard, color, shield or ensign, shall be deemed guilty of a misdemeanor, and shall also forfeit a penalty of fifty dollars for each such offense, to be recovered with costs in a civil action, or suit, in any court having jurisdiction, and such action or suit may be brought by or in the name of any citizen of this state, and such penalty when collected less the reasonable cost and expense of action or suit and recovery to be certified by the district attorney of the county in which the offense is committed, shall be paid into the treasury of this state; and two or more penalties may be sued for and recovered in the same action or suit. The words flag, standard, color, shield or ensign, as used in this

subdivision or section, shall include any flag, standard, color, shield, ensign, or any picture or representation, of either thereof, made of any substance, or represented on any substance, and of any size, evidently purporting to be, either of, said flag, standard, color, shield or ensign, of the United States of America, or of the state of New York, or a picture or a representation, of either thereof, upon which shall be shown the colors, the stars, and the stripes, in any number of either thereof, or by which the person seeing the same, without deliberation may believe the same to represent the flag, colors, standards, shield or ensign of the United States of America or of the state of New York.

This subdivision shall not apply to any act expressly permitted by the statutes of the United States of America, or by the United States Army and Navy regulations, nor shall it be construed to apply to a certificate, diploma, warrant, or commission of appointment to office, ornamental picture, article of jewelry, stationery for use in private correspondence, or newspaper or periodical, on any of which shall be printed, painted or placed, said flag, standard, color, shield or ensign disconnected and apart from any advertisement.

The possession by any person, other than a public officer, as such, of any such flag, standard, color, shield or ensign, on which shall be anything made unlawful at any time by this section, or of any article or substance or thing on which shall be anything made unlawful at any time by this section shall be presumptive evidence that the same is in violation of this section, and was made, done or created after the first day of September, nineteen hundred and five, and that such flag, standard, color, shield, ensign, or article, substance, or thing, did not exist on the first day of September, nineteen hundred and five. (a. L. 1917, c. 779.)

ANNOTATIONS

G. A. R. post flag with name and designation of post for parades not a violation. A. G. R., 1905:535-36.

unconstitutional so far as it attempts to destroy existing property rights. People ex rel. McPike v. Van De Carr, 178 N. Y. 425 [1904].

PUBLIC BUILDINGS — See Post Meeting Rooms.

Civil Service Law, section 21, makes it a misdemeanor to refuse to give the preferences and privileges accorded to veterans by that and the succeeding section. See PREFERENCE.

Penal Law, sections 935, 936 and 936a, declare to be crimes certain fraudulent practices on secret fraternities.

RELIEF OF INDIGENT VETERANS

AT HOME BY G. A. R. POSTS (Poor)

§ 80. *Relief of soldiers, sailors and marines, and their families.* No poor or indigent soldier, sailor or marine who has served in the military or naval service of the United States and who has been honorably discharged from such service nor his family nor the families of any who may be deceased, shall be sent to any almshouse, but shall be relieved and provided for at their homes in the city or town where they may reside, so far as practicable, provided such soldier, sailor or marine or the families of those deceased, are, and have been, residents of the state for one year; and the proper auditing board of such city or town or in those counties where the poor are a county charge, the superintendent, if but one, or superintendents of the poor, as such auditing board in those counties, shall provide such sum or sums of money as may be necessary to be drawn upon by the commander and quartermaster of any post of the Grand Army of the Republic, or of any camp of the United Spanish War Veterans of the city or town, made upon the written recommendation of the relief committee of such post or camp; or if there be no post or camp in a town or city in which it is necessary that such relief should be granted, upon the like request of the commander and quartermaster and recommendation of the relief committee of a Grand Army post, or a camp of the United Spanish War Veterans, located in the nearest town or city, to the town or city requested to so furnish relief, and such written request and recommendation shall be a sufficient authority for the expenditures so made; and such auditing board of such city or town or in those counties where the poor are a county charge, the superintendent, if but one, or superintendents of the poor, as such auditing board in those counties may also pay to the chairman of the relief committee of such Grand Army post or camp of the United Spanish War Veterans, a reasonable sum for his services in connection therewith. (a. L. 1915; L. 1917, c. 129.)

§ 81. *Post or camp to give notice that it assumes charge.* The commander of any such post or camp which shall undertake to supervise the relief of poor veterans or their families, as herein provided, before his acts shall become operative in any town, city or county, shall file with the clerk of such town, city or county, a notice that such post or camp intends to undertake such supervision of relief, which notice shall contain the names of the relief committee, commander and other officers of the post or camp; and also an undertaking to such city, town or county, with sufficient and satisfactory sureties for the faithful and honest discharge of his duties under this article; such undertaking to be approved by the treasurer of the city or county, or the supervisor of the town, from which such relief is to be received.   Such commander shall annually thereafter, during the month of October, file a similar notice with said city or town clerk, with a detailed statement of the amount of relief requested by him during the preceding year, with the names of all persons for whom such relief shall have been requested, together with a brief statement in each case, from the relief committee, upon whose recommendation the relief was requested, provided, however, that in cities of the first class said notice and said detailed statement shall be filed with the comptroller of such city, and said undertaking shall be approved by him, and provided further that in any city of the first class which is now or may hereafter be divided into boroughs, such notice, and such detailed statement each in duplicate shall be filed with the comptroller, and he shall forward one of said duplicates to the commissioner or deputy commissioner of charities for the borough in which the headquarters of such post or camp is situated, except that in the boroughs of the city of New York, no undertaking shall be filed by the commander or the committee of the post or camp nor shall any annual statement of the amounts of relief granted be required.   And it shall be the duty of the commissioner of charities to annually include in his estimate, of the amount necessary for the support of his department, such sum or sums of money as may be necessary to carry into effect the provisions of sections eighty, eighty-one, eighty-three, and except in the city of New York, eighty-four and eighty-five of this chapter, and the proper officers charged with the duty of making the budget of any such city shall annually include therein such sum or sums of money as may be necessary for that purpose.   Provided, further, that in the city of New York the relief shall be paid direct to the beneficiaries by the commissioner of public charities on a written recommendation signed by the relief committee, the commander and the quartermaster of such post or camp. The comptroller of the city of New York shall, out of the amount appropriated for such relief, provide a cash fund to be placed under the control of the commissioner of public charities from which to pay such relief, and he shall replenish said fund upon presentation of properly receipted recommendations for the amounts paid out of said fund. Moneys actually laid out and expended except in the boroughs of the city of New York by any such post or camp for the relief specified in section eighty of this chapter shall be reimbursed monthly to such post or camp by the comptroller on vouchers duly verified by the commander and quartermaster of said post or camp, showing the date and amount of each payment, the certificate of the post or camp relief committee, signed by at least three members, none of whom shall have received any of the relief granted by the post for which reimbursement is asked, showing that the person relieved was an actual resident of such city, and that they recommend each payment, and the receipt of the recipient for each payment, or in case such receipt could not be obtained, a statement of such fact, with the reason why such receipt could not be obtained. Such vouchers shall be made in duplicate on blanks to be supplied by the comptroller and shall be presented to the commissioner of public charities for the borough in which the headquarters of the post or camp is situated, and if such commissioner is satisfied that such moneys have been actually expended as in said voucher stated, he shall approve the same, and file one of said duplicates in his office and forward the other to the comptroller, who shall pay the same by a warrant drawn to the order of the said commander. And provided further that in the city of New York if the comptroller is satisfied that a poor or indigent soldier, sailor or marine, who has served in the military or naval service of the United States, or his family, and has been honorably discharged therefrom, or the families of any who may be deceased, are in actual want, and that immediate relief is needed by either, provided he or they shall have been residents of the state for the year last past, and is or are actual residents of said city, he may, in his discretion authorize and empower the commander of the post or camp to furnish relief to him or them in a reasonable amount, and pay the amount by warrant to the commander of the post or camp, taking the receipt in duplicate of the commander of the post or camp therefor, and file one of said receipts in his office, and forward the other to the commissioner or deputy-commissioner of charities for the borough in which the headquarters of the post or camp is situated; and said duplicate receipts shall be the vouchers for the payment of the same. And provided further, that in any city, county or borough in which Grand Army posts or camps have organized or may organize a memorial and executive committee, the latter shall be regarded as a post of the Grand Army of the Republic or a camp of the United Spanish War Veterans. And the chairman, treasurer or almoner and bureau of relief or relief committee referred to, shall exercise the same privileges and powers as the commander, quartermaster and relief committee of a post or camp, on complying with the requirements of this and the preceding section. Wilful and false swearing to such voucher shall be deemed perjury and shall be punishable as such. (a. L. 1916, c. 532.)

§ 82. *Posts or camps to appoint joint relief committees in certain cities* — In all cities of this state containing less than one hundred thousand inhabitants, where there are more than one post of the Grand Army of the Republic or camp of the United Spanish War Veterans, there shall be appointed and constituted a joint relief committee, consisting of one member from each post of the Grand Army of the Republic and from each camp of the United Spanish War Veterans in said city, which shall have complied with the provisions of law as hereinafter provided, to be chosen in such manner as such post or camp shall direct, and one member appointed by the auditing board of said city, to which all orders for relief drawn by the commander or quartermaster of any post of the Grand Army of the Republic or camp of the United Spanish War Veterans in said city shall be referred; and no relief shall be furnished under the provisions of sections eighty or eighty-one of this chapter, except upon the approval and recommendation of said committee or a majority of the members thereof. No posts of the Grand Army of the Republic or camp of the United Spanish War Veterans shall be entitled to membership in said committee unless such post or camp shall have complied with the provisions of the preceding section, and in case such post or camp shall fail to so comply with the provisions of said section and to select a member of said committee, the commander or quartermaster shall not be entitled to draw upon the fund provided by the auditing board of said city as provided in section eighty of this chapter.   (a. L. 1910, c. 102.)

§ 83. *Poor or indigent soldiers, sailors or marines without families* — Poor or indigent soldiers, sailors or marines provided for in this article, who are not insane, and who have no families or friends with whom they may be domiciled, may be sent to a soldiers' home.   Any poor or indigent soldier, sailor or marine provided for in this chapter, or any member of the family of any living or deceased soldier, sailor or marine, who may be insane, shall, upon recommendation of the commander and relief committee of such post of the Grand Army of the Republic or camp of the United Spanish War Veterans, within the jurisdiction of which the case may occur, be sent to the proper state hospital for the insane.   (a. L. 1910, c. 102.)

§ 86. *Persons entitled to relief* — No poor or indigent woman who served not less than ninety days as a nurse in hospital, field or camp with the military or naval service of the United States, in the war of the rebellion, the Spanish-American war or the war of the Philippine insurrection, shall be sent to any almshouse, but shall be relieved and provided for at her home in the city or town where she may reside, so far as practicable, provided such woman nurse is, and has been a resident of the state for one year. (Added L. 1913, c. 595.)

§ 87. *Application for relief; by whom made* — Upon application being made by such woman nurse poor person to the superintendent of the poor of the county where such woman nurse poor person resides, or to any other officer charged with the support and relief of the poor, and on satisfactory proof being made that such woman nurse is a poor person as defined in this section, such superintendent or other officer or such proper auditing board of such city or town, or in those counties where the poor are a county charge, the superintendent, if but one, or superintendents of the poor, as such auditing boards in those counties, shall provide such sum or sums of money as may be necessary to be drawn upon by the president and treasurer of the New York State Department of the National Association of Civil War Army Nurses made upon the written recommendation of such relief committee of such New York State Department of the National Association of Civil War Army Nurses, and such written request shall be sufficient authority for the expenditures to be made. Immediately upon such relief and aid being provided for, the written recommendation of the relief committee of the New York State Department of the National Association of Civil War Army Nurses, and all other testimony and all facts relating thereto, together with a verified statement of the sum or sums of money expended shall be transmitted to the state board of charities. Such board shall examine all matters relating thereto and if satisfied that such expenditure was proper, and that the expenses thereof were actually and necessarily incurred in such care and support, shall audit and allow the amount of such expense, which when so audited and allowed shall be paid by the state treasurer, on the warrant of the comptroller, to the person incurring the same out of any money appropriated therefor. The amount of such aid and its duration shall be determined by the state board of charities. The New York State Department of the National Association of Civil War Army Nurses shall on the first day of January and the first day of July of each year furnish to the state board of charities a verified statement of the names and addresses of its officers, and the names and addresses of its relief committee. No person shall be aided under the provisions of this act who is receiving or may hereafter receive an annuity from this state. (Added L. 1913, c. 595.)

2. RELIEF MAY BE MADE A COUNTY CHARGE   (County)

§ 12. *General Powers* — The Board of Supervisors shall:

*   *   *   *   *   *   *   *   *   *   *   *

32. The board of supervisors in any county in which the poor are a town charge may by resolution provide that a soldier, sailor or marine who has served in the military or naval service of the United States and who has received an honorable discharge from service, or his family or the family of any who may be deceased

shall be relieved and provided for as a county charge. Application for such relief and the granting thereof shall be governed by sections eighty, eighty-one and eighty-two of the poor law. (Added L. 1915, c. 243.)

ANNOTATIONS

Statutory provisions examined. A. G. R., 1897:83; A. G. R., 1904:321–23.

Residence of applicant; rules for determining. A. G. R., 1889:44–45.

Where residence not gained in any town, is a county charge. A. G. R., 1889: 387–88.

Town taking care of its own poor included in scope of act. A. G. R., 1899: 246–47.

Indigent veteran entitled to medical attendance. A. G. R., 1904:212–13.

Legislative intent to secure relief for veterans even though not honorably discharged. A. G. R., 1911 [Feb. 25].

Applies to children or other relatives of soldiers, sailors or marines who live in one home, under one head or manager, at time relief is furnished, whether they be under or over 21 years of age, but not to a man or woman living separate from the home and having formed other relations. A. G. R., 1910:578–80.

Relief through post:

time of filing notice by post. A. G. R., 1889:230–33; A. G. R., 1891:201–02.

bond, when to be given; no prescribed form. A. G. R., 1891:201–02.

town authorities may require bond. A. G. R., 1890:278.

amount of relief, who to recommend. A. G. R., 1889:230–33.

common council may exercise discretion as to amount of appropriation for relief; further appropriation cannot be compelled. People ex rel. Crammond v. Rome Common Council, 136 N. Y. 489 [1893].

money to be retained by poor authorities to be drawn as needed. A. G. R., 1891:201–02; A. G. R., 1889:52–53; A. G. R., 1890:212.

necessity of relief a question to be decided by officers and relief committee of post; their requests and recommendations binding on town authorities. A. G. R., 1899:244–46.

Attorney-General overruled and the recommendation of post officers held not binding on local authorities. People ex rel. Conde v. Meyers, 161 A. D. 315.

Town auditors justified in disallowing bill for relief where expenditures were made before order, no detailed statement of items furnished and circumstances showed other substantial sources of relief. Sums paid must be certified. People ex rel. Hovey v. Leavenworth, 90 Hun 48 [1895].

Voucher; indorsement of beneficiary. A. G. R., 1889:52–53.

Post cannot take possession of pension received by veteran receiving relief. A. G. R., 1889:223–24.

Where post has organized committee in adjoining town, such committee shall have charge of expenditure of relief money. A. G. R., 1903:340–42.

Overseer of poor may act only in case of failure by post. A. G. R., 1889: 230–33.

Public officer who wilfully disobeys provisions of poor law relative to care of indigent veterans and their families guilty of misdemeanor; may be prosecuted therefor within two years of commission of offense. A. G. R., 1911 [Mar. 20].

REMOVAL AND TENURE

1. No Probation (Civ. Serv.)

§ 9. *Unclassified service; classified service* — * * * All appointments or employments in the classified service, except those of veterans of the civil war, honorably discharged from the military or naval service of the United States, shall be for a probationary term not exceeding the time fixed in the rules.

2. Removal, Review, Reinstatement (Id.)

§ 22. *Power of removal limited* — Every person whose rights may be in any way prejudiced contrary to any of the provisions of this section shall be entitled to a writ of mandamus to remedy the wrong. No person holding a position by appointment or employment in the state of New York or in the several cities, counties, towns or villages thereof who is an honorably discharged soldier, sailor or marine, having served as such in the Union army or navy during the war of the rebellion, or who is an honorably discharged soldier, sailor or marine, having served as such in the army or navy of the United States during the late war with Spain or the incidental insurrection in the Philippines prior to July fourth, nineteen hundred and two, or who shall have served the term required by law in the volunteer fire department of any city, town or village in the state, or who shall have been a member thereof at the time of the disbandment of such volunteer fire department shall be removed from such position except for incompetency or misconduct shown after a hearing upon due notice upon stated charges, and with the right to such employee or appointee to a review by a writ of certiorari. If the position so held by any such honorably discharged soldier, sailor or marine or volunteer fireman shall become unnecessary or be abolished for reasons of economy or otherwise, the said honorably discharged soldier, sailor or marine or volunteer fireman holding the same shall not be discharged from the public service, but shall be transferred to any branch of the said service for duty in such position as he may be fitted to fill, receiving the same compensation therefor, and it is hereby made the duty of all persons clothed with power of appointment to make such transfer effective. The burden of proving incompetency or misconduct shall be upon the person alleging the same. In every county of the state wholly included within the limits of a city but not comprising the whole of such city, no regular clerk or head of a bureau or person holding a position in the classified state civil service, subject to competitive examination, shall be removed until he has been allowed an opportunity of making an explanation; and in every case of removal the true grounds thereof shall be forthwith entered upon the records of the department of the office in which he has been employed, and a copy filed with the state civil service commission. In case of a removal, a statement showing the reasons therefor shall be filed in the department or office where such clerk, head of a bureau or person had been employed. Whenever such offices, positions or employments in every county of the state hereinbefore specified are abolished or made unnecessary, it shall be the duty of the head of the department or office in which such persons had been employed, to furnish the names of the person or persons affected to the state civil service commission, with a statement in the case of each of the date of his original appointment in the service. It shall be the duty of the state civil service commission forthwith to place the names of said persons upon a list of suspended employees for the office or position or for the class of work in which they have been employed, or for any corresponding or similar office, position or class of work, and to certify the said persons for reinstatement or re-employment in the order of their original appointment before making certification from any other list. The failure of any person on any such list for reinstatement or re-employment to accept after reasonable notice, an office or position in the same county and at the same salary or wages as the position formerly held by him, shall be held to be a relinquishment of his right to reinstatement as herein stated. Nothing in this section shall be construed to apply to the position of private secretary, cashier or deputy of any official or department. (a. L. 1910, c. 264.)

§ 23. *Compensation of veterans reinstated by order of the courts* — Any honorably discharged soldier, sailor or marine, who having served as such in the Union army or navy during the war of the rebellion, shall have been, or may hereafter be removed from any position held by him by appointment or employment in the state of New York or in the several cities, counties, towns or villages thereof in contravention or violation of any provision of section twenty-two of this article and who shall have been restored to such position or employment either by a peremptory writ of mandamus of the supreme court or by final order on a writ of certiorari, as authorized by said section twenty-two, shall be entitled to receive and shall receive from said state or the city, county, town or village thereof under which said position or employment was held by him, the same compensation therefor from the date of such unlawful removal to the date of his said restoration to said position or employment which he would have been entitled by law to have received in such position or employment but for such unlawful removal, and such veteran shall be entitled to a writ of mandamus to enforce the payment thereof, but such compensation or salary or wages, due in such position or employment, shall be subject to the provisions of sections four hundred seventy-four and four hundred seventy-five of the judiciary law for services rendered in either or both said special proceedings but otherwise shall be paid only directly to such veteran.

3. RETENTION IN NEW YORK CITY (Charter)

§ 127. All veterans either of the army or navy or the volunteer fire departments, now in the service of either of the municipal and public corporations hereby consolidated, who are now entitled by law to serve during good behavior, or who can not under existing law be removed except for cause, shall be retained in like positions and under the same conditions by the corporation constituted by this act, to serve under such titles and in such way as the head of the appropriate department or the mayor may direct.

§ 355. [Provides for retirements from the police force of the city of New York and contains this limitation on the power of the police commissioner to compulsorily retire.] * * * The said commissioner may in like manner relieve and dismiss from the service and place on the roll of the police pension fund, and grant and award a pension to any member of said force other than an honorably discharged soldier or sailor of the Mexican or late civil war who shall have reached the age of sixty years. * * *

what is removal.   Annotations

Beach v. New York, City of, 10 Supp. 793 [1890].

departmental action reducing number of clerks and suspending incumbent from further service.

Waters v. New York, City of, 43 Misc. 154 [1904].

assignment to lower position with lower rate of compensation.
what is reduction.

People ex rel. Strahan v. Feitner, 29 Misc. 702 [1899]; affd. 49 A. D. 101.

what is not removal.

Black v. New York, City of, Education Board, 92 Supp. 118 [1904].

reasonable reduction of salary not amounting to removal or forced resignation.

Leach v. Woodbury, 75 A. D. 503 [1902].

revocation of detail of street sweeper as assistant to section foreman.

People ex rel. Schurmann v. Coler, 38 A. D. 615 [1899].

transfer, on consolidation, of Brooklyn street inspector with reduced salary.

People ex rel. Goetchious v. Follett, 24 Misc. 510 [1898]; Tiffany, in re, 179 N. Y. 455 [1904]; Williams v. Darling, 67 Misc. 205 [1910].

failure to reappoint.

People ex rel. O'Brien v. Scannell, 164 N. Y. 572, affirming 53 A. D. 161 [1900].

retirement of fireman for disability on pension.

Walters v. New York, City of, 190 N. Y. 375 [1907].

reducing salary of clerk, on consolidation, to conform to general plan.

a. Discharge in good faith because services are no longer needed.

Kenny, in re, 52 A. D. 385 [1900].

sewer inspector, New York city.

People ex rel. Nason v. Feitner, 58 A. D. 594 [1901].

position abolished on economic grounds.

People ex rel. Hartough v. Scannell, 48 A. D. 445 [1900]; affd. 163 N. Y. 599.

fire hydrant inspector; abolished for reasons of economy.

People ex rel. Nutall v. Simis, 18 A. D. 199 [1897].

tinsmith, city department.

People ex rel. Reynolds v. Squier, 10 A. D. 415 [1896].

lack of work.

People ex rel. Patten v. Waring, 62 Supp. 966 [1895].

ground of economy in public service.

Vincent v. Cram, 27 Misc. 158 [1899].

recreation pier attendants.
upheld.

People ex rel. Percival v. Cram, 164 N. Y. 166 [1900].

People ex rel. Russell v. Fire Commissioners, 76 Hun 146 [1894].

one never entitled to office originally.

People ex rel. Wren v. Goetting, 133 N. Y. 569, affirming 8 Supp. 742 [1890].

clerk, Brooklyn police court.

People ex rel. McKnight v. Glynn, 56 Misc. 35 [1907].

transfer tax appraiser.

People ex rel. Ellithrope v. Judges, Superior Court of Buffalo, 9 Supp. 691 [1890].

court crier.

People ex rel. Griffin v. Lathrop, 142 N. Y. 113 [1894].

keeper, state prison.

People ex rel. Pine v. Martin, 53 A. D. 19 [1900].
armorer, state arsenal.
People ex rel. Baird v. Nixon, 158 N. Y. 221 [1899].
commissioner. East river bridge, New York city.
People ex rel. McAvoy v. School Board, Richmond, 43 A. D. 613 [1899].
janitor union free school.
People ex rel. Foley v. Long Island City, Education Board, 84 Hun 417 [1895].
positive refusal to obey reasonable order.
People ex rel. Hannan v. Troy, Health Board, 153 N. Y. 513 [1897].
officer appointed without examination.
People ex rel. Joyce v. VanWart, 36 A. D. 518 [1899]; affd. 158 N. Y. 720.
abolition of position by legislature.
People ex rel. Sullivan v. Waring, 36 Supp. 1119 [1895].
acceptance of another city position held acquiescence in discharge.
Porter v. Howland, 24 Misc. 434 [1898].
public school teacher not a city employee.
Shaughnessy v. Fornes, 172 N. Y. 323 [1902].
board of aldermen a legislative body and not subject to civil service restrictions.
b. Upon hearing; charges.
People ex rel. Brady v. Brookfield, 6 A. D. 445 [1896]; affd. 151 N. Y. 674.
though informal, veteran is estopped from objecting if he appear and take part.
People ex rel. Gilon v. Coler, 78 A. D. 248 [1903]; affd. 175 N. Y. 510.
charges justified.
People ex rel. Brennan v. Scannell, 62 A. D. 249 [1901].
when court will not review the facts.
c. Failure to reappoint incumbent, holding for fixed term, also performing duties of another office.
People ex rel. Curran v. Albion, Trustees of Village, 61 A. D. 71 [1901].
poundmaster.
denied.
fire marshal, Rochester. A. G. R., 1897:322–23.
Murray, in re, 17 Misc. 185 [1896].
county employee.
People ex rel. Haverty v. Barker, 1 A. D. 532 [1896]; affd. 149 N. Y. 607.
tax assessor; feeble health not sufficient proof of incompetency.
People ex rel. O'Connor v. Brady, 49 A. D. 238 [1900].
building inspector; protected by L. 1896, c. 821.
People ex rel. Speight v. Coler, 157 N. Y. 676, affirming 31 A. D. 523 [1898].
collector of fees, Wallabout market, Brooklyn; retention under consolidation.
People ex rel. Stutzbach v. Coler, 168 N. Y. 416 [1901].
alleged lack of funds.
People ex rel. Thain v. Constable, 65 A. D. 176 [1901].
inspector, New York city building department.
People ex rel. Cunliffe v. Cram, 34 A. D. 313 [1898].
painter and inspector of painting, New York city dock department.
People ex rel. Herrick v. Feitner, 27 Misc. 153 [1899]; affd. 42 A. D. 622.
law applies to all departments in all cities.
People ex rel. Miller v. Feitner, 27 Misc. 153 [1899]; affd. 42 A. D. 622.
deputy tax commissioners, New York city.
People ex rel. Strahan v. Feitner, 29 Misc. 702 [1899]; affd. 49 A. D. 101.
reduction of salary, lowering of grade, less important duties.

People ex rel. Washburn v. French, 52 Hun 464 [1889].
compulsory retirement of New York city policeman at age of 60.

People ex rel. Brymer v. Gray, 32 A. D. 458 [1898].
fire marshal of Brooklyn ; consolidation.

People ex rel. Murphy v. Howell, 13 Supp. 217 [1891].
Brooklyn bridge employee.

People ex rel. Schumann v. McCartney, 34 A. D. 19 [1898].
street cleaning force.

People ex rel. Broderick v. Morton, 156 N. Y. 130, reversing on other grounds
24 A. D. 563 [1897].
laborer, state department of public buildings.

People ex rel. Williamson v. Scannell, 34 Misc. 709 [1901].
order of commissioner retiring fireman signed beforehand in blank and delivered
during absence of commissioner from city.

People ex rel. Williams v. Ward, 72 Misc. 446 [1911].
signing release for injuries received, not a resignation. No legal removal.

People ex rel. Denholm v. Welde, 27 Misc. 697 [1899].
clerk, commissioner of jurors, New York county.

People ex rel. Fallon v. Wright, 150 N. Y. 444 [1896].
warden, city prison, New York city.

Seeley v. Stevens, 190 N. Y. 158 [1907].

Stutzbach v. Coler, 168 N. Y. 416 [1901].
clerk in finance department, New York city.

a. Abolishment of office in bad faith.

McDonald, in re, 34 A. D. 512 [1898].
superintendent.

People ex rel. Bean v. Clausen, 50 A. D. 324 [1900].
demand not necessary for reinstatement.

People ex rel. Hart v. LaGrange, 7 A. D. 311 [1896].
firemen.

People ex rel. Vanderhoof v. Palmer, 3 A. D. 389 [1896].

People ex rel. Shields v. Scannell, 48 A. D. 69 [1900].
assistant secretary, fire department, New York city.

b. Incapacity.

People ex rel. Metcalf v. McAdoo, 109 A. D. 892 [1905]; affd. 184 N. Y. 268.
veteran police sergeant; not required to be fit for " full police duty."

c. Removal on charges.

People ex rel. Fleming v. Dalton, 158 N. Y. 175 [1899].
opportunity to make explanation.

People ex rel. Miller v. Elmendorf, 42 A. D. 306 [1899].
charges must be definite and certain.

People ex rel. Shuster v. Humphrey, 156 N. Y. 231 [1898].
removal must be on charges as made.

People ex rel. Brady v. O'Brien, 9 A. D. 428 [1896].
refusal to permit accused to have counsel.

People ex rel. Long v. Whitney, 143 A. D. 17 [1911].
charges must be substantial.
confidential positions; deputies.

Gilfillan, in re, 127 A. D. 846 [1908]; affd. 193 N. Y. 655.
mortgage tax deputy not in exemption class.

McDonald v. Mayor of New York, 32 Supp. 280 [1895].
appointee of New York city court clerk.

People ex rel. Rossney v. Armbruster, 59 Hun 597 [1891].
superintendent of streets, Rochester, a confidential office; *see also* A. G. R., 1890:
145–48
People ex rel. Conway v. Barker, 14 Misc. 360 [1895].
deputy tax commissioner, N. Y. city, not a deputy.
People ex rel. Webb v. Clarke, 54 A. D. 588 [1900].
county detective in district attorney's office confidential.
People ex rel. Tate v. Dalton, 158 N. Y. 204 [1899].
water registrar, Brooklyn borough not confidential *see also* A. G. R., 1898 : 396.
People ex rel. Kenny v. Folks, 89 A. D. 171 [1903].
superintendent of outdoor poor, Richmond borough, not a deputy.
People ex rel. Flood v. Gardiner, 157 N. Y. 520 [1899].
subpœna server, New York county district attorney's office, is confidential.
People ex rel. Fitzpatrick v. Greene, 181 N. Y. 308 [1905], reversing 97
    A. D. 502.
veteran policeman N. Y. city, has absolute right to retirement, effective on making
    application therefor ; charges filed subsequently, and prior to commissioner's
    order granting retirement, do not affect right.
People ex rel. Sweet v. Lyman, 157 N. Y. 368 [1898].
special agent, excise department, confidential; *contra;* Weaver, in re, 72 Misc. 438
    [1911] ; affd. 147 A. D. 420 ; 204 N. Y. 676.
People ex rel. O'Keeffe v. McFadden, 75 A. D. 264 [1902].
deputy collector of assessments and arrears, borough of Brooklyn, a confidential
    position.
    People ex rel. Brady v. O'Brien, 9 A. D. 128 [1896].
dockmaster not a confidential position.
People ex rel. Crummey v. Palmer, 152 N. Y. 217 [1897].
assistant warrant clerk, comptroller's office, city of Brooklyn, a confidential position.
People ex rel. Thompson v. Ransom, 13 Supp. 370 [1891].
court messenger a confidential position.
People ex rel. Breckenridge v. Scannell, 160 N. Y. 103 [1899].
examiner, fire marshal's office, New York city, not a confidential position.
People ex rel. Jussen v. Scannell, 51 A. D. 360 [1900].
secretary, fire department, New York city, a confidential position.
People ex rel. Jacobus v. Van Wyck, 157 N. Y. 495 [1899].
assessor, New York city, confidential position.
People ex rel. Rodenbough v. Voorhis, 63 A. D. 249 [1901].
superintendent, bureau of elections, New York city, not a confidential position.
People ex rel. Ryan v. Wells, 176 N. Y. 462 [1903].
deputy tax commissioner, New York state, a deputy.
Sargent v. Gorman, 131 N. Y. 191 [1892].
chief clerk of sheriff a confidential position.
Shaughnessy v. Fornes, 172 N. Y. 323 [1902].
assistant sergeant-at-arms, New York city common council, a confidential position.
transfer.
Gilfillan, in re, 127 A. D. 846 [1908]; affd. 193 N. Y. 655.
mortgage tax deputy, county clerk's office; cannot claim transfer to dissimilar post.
Jones v. Wilcox, 80 A. D. 167 [1903].
burden on veteran to show qualification to fill position to which he seeks transfer.
People ex rel. Wardrop v. Adams, 51 Hun, 583 [1889].
may not replace another officer, to whose duties those of abolished office have been
added.

People ex rel. Croft v. Keating, 49 A. D. 123 [1900].

must be a vacancy before assignment to it can occur.

People ex rel. Breckenridge v. Scannell, 160 N. Y. 103 [1899].

faithful non-veterans not to be discharged to create vacancy to which transfer may be made.

Pratt v. Phelan, 67 A. D. 349 [1901].

engineer, Troy pumping station, entitled to transfer.
temporary service.

Eckerson v. New York, City of, 176 N. Y. 609, affirming 80 A. D. 12 [1903].

People ex rel. O'Connor v. Adams, 133 N. Y. 203 [1892].

People ex rel. Haggerty v. Clausen, 29 Misc. 701 [1899].

People ex rel. Uhrie v. Gilroy, 60 Hun 507 [1891].

retention of non-veteran to exclusion of veteran.

Barton, in re, 69 Misc. 38 [1910].

McCloskey v. Willis, 15 A. D. 594 [1897].

People ex rel. Thornton v. Board of Public Parks, 17 Supp. 589 [1892].

People ex rel. Stutzbach v. Coler, 168 N. Y. 416 [1902].

People ex rel. Baldwin v. McAdoo, 110 A. D. 432 [1905]; appeal dismsd. 190 N. Y. 530.

veteran must seasonably claim rights.

Beal v. Bingham, 112 Supp. 465 [1908].

New York city policeman retired compulsorily for disability; may not claim subsequently full pension.

Gaffney, in re, 84 Hun 503 [1895].

two years' delay held laches.

McDonald, in re, 34 A. D. 512 [1898].

four months' delay excusable.

People ex rel. Harper v. Adams, 18 Supp. 896 [1892].

People ex rel. O'Connor v. Brady, 49 A. D. 238 [1900].

two months' delay excusable.

People ex rel. Shea v. Bryant, 28 A. D. 480.

two years' delay held laches.

People ex rel. McDonald v. Clausen, 50 A. D. 286 [1900]; affd. 163 N. Y. 523.

People ex rel. Young v. Collis, 6 A. D. 467 [1896].

four months' delay held laches.

People ex rel. McCullough v. Cram, 15 Misc. 12 [1895].

People ex rel. O'Brien v. Cruger, 12 A. D. 536 [1896].

People ex rel. Ross v. Dooling, 61 Misc. 428 [1908].

must state facts which superior may verify.

People ex rel. Strahan v. Feitner, 29 Misc. 702 [1899]; affd. 49 A. D. 101.

four months' delay excusable.

People ex rel. Goetchious v. Follett, 24 Misc. 510 [1898].

formal application for reappointment necessary, where incumbent holds for a fixed term.

People ex rel. Miller v. Justices of Sessions, 78 Hun 334 [1894].

eight months' delay held laches.

People ex rel. Croft v. Keating, 49 A. D. 123 [1900].
nine months' delay held laches.
People ex rel. McDonald v. Lantry, 48 A. D. 131 [1900].
People ex rel. Tierney v. Scannell, 27 Misc. 662 [1899].
delay caused by uncertainty as to rights, owing to conflict of judicial decisions,
      excusable.
People ex rel. Vanderhoof v. Palmer, 3 A. D. 389 [1896].
four months' delay held laches.
People ex rel. Dixon v. Simonson, 64 A. D. 312 [1901].
Shay, in re, 15 Supp. 488 [1891].
Stutzbach v. Coler, 168 N. Y. 416 [1901].
damages.
Bean v. Clausen, 113 A. D. 129 [1906].
where proceedings for reinstatement have become impossible, from transfer of
      jurisdiction, action for damages lies against officer who removed him.
Fallon v. Wright, 82 A. D. 193 [1903].
counsel fees cannot be recovered in judgment.
Hilton v. Cram, 190 N. Y. 535, affirming 112 A. D. 35 [1906].
mandamus proceedings a prerequisite.
criminal liability.
Hilton v. Cram, 112 A. D. 35 [1906]; affd. 190 N. Y. 535.
Vanderhoof, in re, 3 A. D. 389 [1896].
recovering of salary during period of exclusion.
Caldwell v. New York, City of, 148 A. D. 304 [1911]; appeal dismd. 210
N. Y. 576.
one not discharged to give employment to another, not entitled to compensation
      after reëmployment, for period during which city did not need his services.
Douglas v. Brooklyn, Board of Education, 21 A. D. 209 [1897].
discharged and later reëmployed; no recovery.
O'Hara v. New York, City of, 167 N. Y. 567, affirming 46 A. D. 518 [1900].
People ex rel. Blair v. Grout, 44 Misc. 526 [1904].
rule that payment of salary to de facto officer prior to notice to city of irregularity
      in removal is complete defense to action to recover such salary by officer
      removed does not apply in case of reinstated veteran.
Sullivan v. New York, City of, 33 Misc. 314 [1900].
one taking no steps to reinstatement and performing no duties cannot recover salary,
      where another has performed the services and been paid therefor.
REMOVAL OF REMAINS — See Burial.

RETIREMENTS AND PENSIONS

1. RETIREMENT FROM STATE SERVICE   (Civil Serv.)

§ 21-a. *Retiring veterans of the late civil war and granting them pensions.* Every soldier, sailor, or marine of the army or navy of the United States in the late civil war, honorably discharged from service, who shall have been employed for a continuous period of ten years or more in the civil service of the state of New York and the several cities and counties thereof, and who shall have reached the age of seventy years, upon his own request, or if employed in manual labor, shall be retired from his employment by the State of New York and the several cities and counties thereof, and thereafter and during his life, the state department or institution which employed him at the time of his retirement, shall pay to him, in the same manner that the salary or wages of his former position were customarily paid by him, an annual sum equal in amount to one-half the salary or wages paid to him in the last year of his employment; provided, however, that the amount so to be paid to such retired veteran shall not exceed the sum of one thousand dollars per annum. (Added L. 1916, c. 438; L. 1917, c. 768.)

2. RETIREMENT IN PUBLIC BUILDINGS DEPARTMENT
(Pub. Bldgs.)

§ 3. *Powers and duties of trustees* — The trustees of public buildings shall: * * *

8. Have power, in their discretion, to retire any employee in the department of public buildings who is an honorably discharged soldier, sailor or marine of the army or navy of the United States in the late civil war, and who shall have been employed for a continuous period of five years or more in such department and who shall have reached the age of seventy years. Such retirement may be upon the application of such veteran, or the trustees may take such action on their own motion. Upon being retired pursuant to this act such person shall be paid in the same manner that the salary or wages of his former position were customarily paid to him an annual sum equal in amount to one-half the salary or wage paid to him in the last year of his employment, provided, however, that the amount so paid to such retired veteran shall not exceed the sum of one thousand dollars per annum. (Added L. 1918, c. 142.)

3. RETIREMENT IN ADJUTANT-GENERAL'S OFFICE (Mil.)

§ 19-a. *Retiring veterans of the late civil war and granting them pensions* — Every soldier, sailor or marine of the army or navy of the United States in the late civil war honorably discharged from service who shall have been employed for a continuous period of ten years or more in the office of the adjutant-general of the state of New York and who shall have reached the age of seventy years may, upon his own request and the approval of the adjutant-general, or upon being incapacitated for performing the duties of his position, shall be retired from such employment, and thereafter during his life the adjutant-general shall pay to him in the same manner that the salary or wages of his former position were customarily paid to him an annual sum equal in amount to one-half the salary or wages paid to him in the last year of his employment; provided, however, that the amount so to be paid to such retired veteran shall not exceed the sum of one thousand dollars per annum. (Added L. 1918, c. 557.)

4. RETIREMENT FROM NEW YORK CITY SERVICE (Charter)

§ 165. Any member of the board of estimate and apportionment is hereby authorized, whenever in his judgment it shall be to the interest of the public service, to recommend to said board the retirement from active service of any officer, clerk or employee who shall have been in the employ of the city of New York or of any of the municipalities, counties or parts thereof which have been incorporated into the city of New York for a period of twenty years if an honorably discharged soldier, sailor or marine, who served as such in the union army or navy during the war of the rebellion and otherwise for a period of thirty years and upward and who shall have become physically or mentally incapacitated for the further performances of the duties of his position. The term of service, however, shall not be affected by any change in title, duty or salary or by any promotion or by any vacation or leave of absence or by any temporary disability by reason of sickness or accident or by any transfer from one department or office to another department or office during the period of service, or by any change of any of the boards, bureaus or departments in which service shall have been performed from an office paid by fees to a salaried office. But this section shall not apply to any person who is, or may be, entitled to share in the police pension fund, or in

TOPICAL GUIDE TO THE

the fire department relief fund, or in the public school teachers' retirement fund, or in the health department pension fund, or in the retirement fund of the 'College of the City of New York. (a. L. 1912, c. 497.)

5. Retirement by Appellate Division (Jud.)

§ 117. *Retirement of employees by the appellate division of the second department.* The appellate division of the supreme court of the second department is hereby authorized in its discretion to retire any clerk, assistant clerk, stenographer, interpreter, librarian, attendant or typewriter operator who shall have served as such in the supreme court in and for the second or ninth judicial districts or in any court which has been consolidated with the said supreme court and who shall have become physically or mentally incapacitated for the further performance of the duties of his position, provided such service in one or more of such positions has continued for a period of twenty-five years or more; or any honorably discharged soldier or sailor of the civil war serving as such clerk, assistant clerk, stenographer, interpreter, librarian, attendant or typewriter operator who at the time of such retirement shall have served continuously for a period of ten years and who shall have reached the age of seventy years. Any person retired from service pursuant to this section shall be paid an annual sum or annuity to be determined by the appellate division of the second department not exceeding one-half of the average amount of his annual salary or compensation for a period of two years preceding the time of such retirement. Such annuity shall be paid in equal monthly installments during the lifetime of the person so retired, and the amount thereof shall otherwise be collected and paid in the same manner as the salary or compensation of such person was required to be collected and paid at the time of such retirement. (Added L. 1915, c. 557; a. L. 1918, c. 508.)

SOLDIERS' MONUMENTS — *See* Incorporation and Monuments.
TAX — *See* Exemptions.
TAXABLE TRANSFERS — *See* Exemptions.
VETERANS' RIGHT TO PEDDLE — *See* Privileges.

WAR RECORDS

1. BUREAU OF RECORDS   (Mil.)

§ 19. *Bureau of records of the war of the rebellion; completion and preservation of the records and relics; free inspection of the same and quarters in the capitol* — 1. The adjutant-general of the state shall establish and maintain as part of his office, a bureau of records of the war of the rebellion, in which all records in his office relating to such war, and relics shall be kept. He shall be the custodian of all such records, relics, colors, standards and battle flags of New York volunteers now the property of the state or in its possession, or which the state may hereafter acquire or become possessed of, and he shall appoint a chief of this bureau who shall hold office under his direction for six years.

2. The adjutant-general of the state by all reasonable ways and means, shall complete such records and gather from every available source such colors, standards and battle flags as were borne by New York state troops in the war of the rebellion, and such statistics and historical information and relics as may serve to perpetuate the memory and heroic deeds of the soldiers of the state, and keep and carefully preserve the same in such bureau.

3. He is authorized to request and accept from incorporated associations of veterans of the different regiments, statements and information duly authenticated by them, descriptive of their colors, standards and battle flags, together with the number and class of arms of the regiment, the date and place of muster into the service of the state and also into the service of the United States, the period of service, and the date and place of muster out, the date of departure for the seat of war, the various battles and engagements and places of service, including garrison duty, the time of joining brigades, corps and armies, with the time and nature of the service, and the names of colonels of such regiments, the names of those killed in action, including those who died of wounds, and the names of those who died of disease during their period of service. He is further authorized to ask the co-operation and assistance of the adjutant-general of the United States, and of the city, county and town authorities and officials, and of the Grand Army of the Republic, the Military Order of the Loyal Legion, and of organizations and persons in the state of New York

and elsewhere in the collection of such other information, relics, memorials and battle flags as is contemplated by this article, in order to make as complete as possible the records, history and statistics of the patriotic service of the volunteer soldiers of the state during the war of the rebellion.

4. The adjutant-general of the state is directed to cause to be transcribed and kept in books of record in such bureau the historical facts, information and statistics as provided above; and is authorized to determine a convenient size for the volumes in which such statistics and historical data may be bound, and to request veteran associations and others proposing to supply such historical data and information to furnish the same on printed or manuscript sheets of a uniform size to correspond with the size of such volumes.

5. He is further authorized to provide locked and sealed cases with glass fronts, as nearly air-tight as practicable, in which shall be kept and displayed the colors, standards and battle flags above mentioned, and receive placards in duplicate, which incorporated regimental veteran associations are privileged and empowered to furnish and upon which shall be inscribed synopses of the historical information and statistics herein provided to be furnished to such bureau by regimental veteran associations, or failing to receive such data and information from such veteran associations, for the preparation of such placards, he may utilize the authentic information which he may obtain from other sources, as herein provided, which placards shall be uniform in size and color and shall be attached to or conspicuously placed in proximity to the colors, standards and battle flags to which they refer. If any placard or inscription shall be lost, destroyed or removed, the adjutant-general of the state shall at once replace it by duplicate of the original on file.

The legislature shall annually make suitable appropriations to enable the adjutant-general of the state to carry out the provisions of this section.

6. The books, records and other property and relics deposited in such bureau shall be open to inspection and use, except the use of the colors, standards and battle flags, at such reasonable hours and under such regulations as the adjutant-general of the state may

determine. No battle flag, book or any property placed in such
bureau for the purpose of this article, shall be removed therefrom,
or from the immediate custody and control of the adjutant-general
of the state without an act of the legislature.

7. The trustees of the capitol are authorized and directed to
provide suitable and convenient quarters for the bureau of records
whenever the adjutant-general of the state shall require and make
demand therefor, and to properly fit up and prepare the same for
the safe-keeping of such records, books and property, and for the
display of such colors, standards, battle flags and relics which shall
be known and maintained as the hall of military records. The
several municipalities of the state may deposit their record books
and papers relating to the war in the archives of the hall for safe-
keeping, and transcripts therefrom shall be furnished on application by the chief officer of the municipality without cost to it.
Officers or soldiers may deposit therein their discharge papers,
descriptive lists, muster rolls or company or regimental books and
papers for safe-keeping.

The interest arising from the investment of the funds contributed by towns, cities and individuals for the erection of a
hall of military records shall be devoted to the maintenance of
the hall of military records provided in this section.

Annotation

positions therein are in military, not civil, service. A. G. R., 1910: 692–96.
For Military Record Fund, see St. Fin. § 100.

2. State Historian to Edit War Records   (Executive)

§ 90. *Appointment of state historian* —The governor shall appoint, by and with the advice and consent of the senate, a state
historian, whose duty it shall be to collect, collate, compile, edit
and prepare for publication all official records, memoranda and
data relative to the colonial wars, war of the revolution, war of
eighteen hundred and twelve, Mexican war and war of the rebellion, together with all official records, memoranda and statistics
affecting the relations between this commonwealth and foreign
powers, between this state and other states and between this state
and the United States.

See L. 1913, c. 424, amending the Education Law.

DISCARD